SAP PRESS e-books

Print or e-book, Kindle or iPad, workplace or airplane: Choose where and how to read your SAP PRESS books! You can now get all our titles as e-books, too:

▸ By download and online access
▸ For all popular devices
▸ And, of course, DRM-free

Convinced? Then go to **www.sap-press.com** and get your e-book today.

SAP® HANA

SAP PRESS

SAP PRESS is a joint initiative of SAP and Rheinwerk Publishing. The know-how offered by SAP specialists combined with the expertise of Rheinwerk Publishing offers the reader expert books in the field. SAP PRESS features first-hand information and expert advice, and provides useful skills for professional decision-making.

SAP PRESS offers a variety of books on technical and business-related topics for the SAP user. For further information, please visit our website: *www.sap-press.com*.

Penny Silvia, Rob Frye, Bjarne Berg

SAP® HANA

An Introduction

Rheinwerk®
Publishing

Bonn • Boston

Editor Meagan White
Acquisitions Editor Kelly Grace Weaver
Copyeditor Yvette Chin
Cover Design Graham Geary
Photo Credit iStockphoto.com/3451372/mevans; /18132624/Jeja
Layout Design Vera Brauner
Production Marissa Fritz
Typesetting III-satz, Husby (Germany)
Printed and bound in the United States of America, on paper from sustainable sources

ISBN 978-1-4932-1407-5

© 2017 by Rheinwerk Publishing, Inc., Boston (MA)
4th edition 2017

Library of Congress Cataloging-in-Publication Data
Names: Berg, Dr., author. | Silvia, Penny, author. | Frye, Rob, author.
Title: SAP HANA : an introduction / Bjarne Berg, Penny Silvia, Rob Frye.
Description: 4th edition. | Bonn ; Boston : Rheinwerk Publishing, 2016.
Identifiers: LCCN 2016040317 | ISBN 9781493214075 (alk. paper)
Subjects: LCSH: Database management. | Business enterprises--Data processing.
 | SAP HANA (Electronic resource)
Classification: LCC QA76.9.D3 B473 2016 | DDC 005.74--dc23 LC record available at https://lccn.loc.gov/2016040317

Contents at a Glance

Dear Reader,

In this day and age, things move quickly—news first comes from people on the ground with smartphones, we can order most anything from Amazon and get it the same day, and new releases come every 6 months, rather than every few years. Patience, at least in business, no longer seems a virtue!

SAP HANA means many things for many different people, but there's one thing most can agree on: its speed. Whether it's serving as your database, your application platform, or helping you make the jump to SAP S/4HANA, SAP HANA helps you react more quickly to the changing world. With one new expert author (welcome, Rob!) added to our all-star team of Penny and Dr. Berg, three all-new chapters (not to mention those so heavily updated they barely resemble their former selves), this new edition is keeping up the pace.

As always, your comments and suggestions are the most useful tools to help us make our books the best they can be. Let us know what you thought about the fourth edition of *SAP HANA: An Introduction*! Please feel free to contact me and share any praise or criticism you may have.

Thank you for purchasing a book from SAP PRESS!

Meagan White
Editor, SAP PRESS

Rheinwerk Publishing
Boston, MA

meaganw@rheinwerk-publishing.com
www.sap-press.com

Contents

13

Acknowledgments

We would like to thank Brandon Harwood, Nick Le, Michael Barker, Michael Vavlitis, Fernando Ibarra-Avila, Arman Avetisyan, Riley Harrington, Nicole Cortazzo, and Lilisee Thao at ComeritLabs in North Carolina for their diligence and flexibility in support of this writing effort, including setting up and maintaining hardware used in developing the fourth edition of SAP HANA: An Introduction. We'd also like to thank Phil Vondras, Dale Young, Gagan Reen, and Chris Dinkel. Finally, we'd like to thank Marc Becker, Thomas Jung, and Sergey Kuperman for supporting our exploration of SAP HANA XS Advanced.

Finally, we're forever indebted to our friends, colleagues, and families for their infinite patience during a long spring and summer spent writing. We couldn't do any of this without their support.

Introduction

SAP HANA continues to evolve with each release—and we're happy to have this book evolve right along with it. Welcome to the fourth edition of *SAP HANA: An Introduction*, with new information about SAP HANA in the cloud, SAP S/4HANA, the SAP Web IDE, and the SAP HANA Web-Based Development Workbench.

If you're new to this book, here's a roadmap for your journey:

▸ In **Chapter 1**, we offer an introduction to the topic with general explanations of in-memory computing, row and column storage, and how they come together in SAP HANA.

▸ In **Chapter 2**, we get a little more specific about the solution, with information on what SAP HANA can (and can't!) do, big data solutions, and specific implementation options.

▸ **Chapter 3** is brand new, and contains information on SAP as an application platform, with coverage of SAP HANA XS Classic, SAP HANA XSA, and the SAP Web IDE.

▸ **Chapter 4** is also all new, and provides an introduction to SAP's PaaS offering, SAP HANA Cloud Platform.

▸ **Chapter 5**, the final all-new chapter, provides information on SAP S/4HANA, with a focus on SAP S/4HANA Finance and SAP S/4HANA Materials Management and Operations.

▸ In **Chapter 6**, we introduce you to the first steps in planning an SAP HANA implementation, now expanded with information for all four types of on-premise versions.

▸ In **Chapter 7**, we offer an introduction to reporting with SAP HANA with coverage of SAP's business intelligence tools, including SAP BuinessObjects Lumira, connecting these tools to SAP HANA, and SAP HANA Live.

▸ **Chapter 8** explains the options for data modeling with SAP HANA, with coverage of calculation views (both dimensional and cube) and the SAP HANA Web-Based Development Workbnech

- **Chapter 9** contains information about data provisioning with SAP Data Services, SAP Landscape Transformation, the SAP (Sybase) Replication Server, and SAP HANA smart data access (SDA).

- Finally, in **Chapter 10**, we round out the book with a discussion of SAP HANA administration, with all-new information on the SAP HANA Cockpit, multitier data management, and more.

Through four editions, it has always been our goal to give you the information you need to hit the ground running and prepare you for the next steps in your SAP HANA journey. We trust you'll find that our latest work continues in this tradition.

Penny Silvia
Rob Frye
Dr. Berg

Learn what in-memory computing and big data have to do with SAP HANA and take your first steps to understanding what SAP HANA can and can't do.

1 In-Memory Computing, Big Data, and SAP HANA

SAP HANA was introduced to the business world as an in-memory database (IMDB), particularly as a database for SAP BusinessObjects Business Intelligence (SAP BusinessObjects BI). Positioned and sold as a database with the power to make existing (and new) SAP systems run at a blinding pace, SAP HANA is—at its core—a database. However, it is no longer "just" a database. As SAP's development platform and technology landscape, SAP HANA enables business and organizational transformation.

SAP HANA truly has evolved dramatically since its introduction and is now the cornerstone of SAP's technology platform and development platform for the future. SAP is acquiring new tools and developing existing ones with the expectation that SAP HANA will be the underlying platform—and thus is also building new tools and capabilities that are optimized for working with SAP HANA. Much like SAP Solution Manager, SAP HANA is becoming a more and more integrated part of the overall suite of SAP capabilities and the question of *if* you will be utilizing SAP HANA as part of your technology landscape is now a question of *when* and *to what extent* you will be using SAP HANA.

With this in mind, SAP continues to position SAP HANA as an enabling technology to support highly optimized business processes and analytics and as the foundation for capabilities that never before have been possible in an SAP-based environment. Organizations that leverage an SAP HANA-based platform have the potential—the power—to build applications and solutions that can be used to address challenges that were previously thought to be impossible. Airlines and freight forwarders are using SAP HANA-enabled solutions for route optimization and profitability, retailers are using SAP HANA-enabled solutions for identifying fraud and price-fixing with their suppliers, and they're doing it all in real time. Stock levels are being valued and assessed in real time. You can also assess the impact of decisions, financial postings, and pricing alterations in real time. When you start removing the technology barriers that were assumed to be immovable, that is when you can truly implement business process change and optimization.

In this chapter, we'll get you started with SAP HANA basics by offering a conceptual explanation of in-memory computing and big data, two major concepts that play a part in SAP HANA, and explaining why they are key to the technical changes enabled by SAP HANA. We will also introduce, and hopefully explain, one of the key differences between SAP HANA and your traditional databases—column-based data storage and retrieval versus row-based data storage and retrieval. You will see how this seemingly small change dramatically changes how you interact with your data and at what speed.

Throughout this chapter, we'll put information into a nontechnical context that will hopefully remove some of the uncertainty associated with in-memory computing and big data in general as well as with SAP HANA specifically. Subsequent chapters will get into much deeper levels of technical discussion, but these early chapters are meant to help all levels of your organization—from management to technical support staff—understand what SAP HANA is, what it isn't, what your options are, and what this all means for you.

1.1   Introduction to In-Memory Computing and Big Data

To understand how much SAP HANA can do, you first have to conceptually understand SAP HANA as a technology—as an in-memory database. "In-memory computing" and "big data" are trendy terms these days, especially with regard to SAP HANA. Because it's important to understand both concepts before getting into the specifics of SAP HANA as a solution, this section will introduce these terms.

1.1.1   In-Memory Computing and Analytics

In-memory computing, at its core, is the ability to keep large amounts of data in the main memory (RAM) of a server so that it is available for faster processing by business applications. Think of it as the amount of information you can keep on your desk versus what you have in your filing cabinets or storage units. Having this information at your fingertips is particularly important when you need to get answers quickly—for analytics, for instance, or for any application that relies on vast amounts of data. The use of in-memory processing has become more and more prevalent as the price of computer memory drops and with the exponential growth of data in organizations.

When looking at SAP HANA and other IMDBs and their options, benefits, and capabilities, it is important, however, to understand that there is a difference between an in-memory database and a database with caching. True IMDBs use memory as the main persistence (storage) of the data and just rely on the disk to guarantee durability of the data (by storing the transaction logs on disks).

Databases with caching, however, still have the disk as the main store for your data and create "memory snapshots" of the data to accelerate processing. However, any changes and updates on the data are still processed at the disk level, and the cache needs to be reprocessed. Therefore, you will see improved performance over traditional databases but not the same high-powered acceleration of true in-memory databases.

An easy way to differentiate IMDBs from databases with caching is to think how databases will operate when NVRAM (nonvolatile RAM) is commercially available. NVRAM is random-access memory that retains its information when power is turned off—so IMDBs will be able to get rid of the disks, while databases with caching won't.

Because organizations need to access information contained both within and external to their systems, solutions have had to be developed to meet those needs. Business leaders are increasingly being asked to make real-time decisions in today's highly dynamic and challenging business environments. This expectation is putting more and more pressure on IT departments and business leadership to find and provide new and faster ways to get information and insight into the hands of decision makers. Waiting for data to work its way through a complex data model and data warehouse, and then finally to your reports, is no longer good enough. Even if your report runs in 10 *seconds*, the data itself could well have taken 8 to 10 *days* to get into the system! Your business users demand full visibility about what is happening *now* and need the ability to react in near real time. They need to be able to respond as situations are happening and as markets shift—not 2 weeks later.

Consider this scenario: A retailer monitors a customer's real-time behavior in a store or on a website. This monitoring draws on historical data from its loyalty system about that customer's behavior, combines that with the customer's "likes" on Facebook or other social media sites, and then sends coupons or promotions directly to the customer's cell phone—for items they are standing in front of (or viewing onscreen). This long dreamed-of vision can be made a reality today in part due to in-memory computing technology and the ability to immediately access and sift through large amounts of information in real time. By moving data off disk and into main memory, the retrieval time for the data is next to nothing—significantly boosting performance and allowing for this possible scenario.

At its heart, in-memory computing is a technology that allows the processing of massive quantities of data in the main memory, which provides immediate results from analysis and transactions. From a hardware-based point of view, a *process* requires three components to perform the necessary actions once you hit the execute or run button: a processor to perform the calculations, storage to store the data, and a system that transfers data between the two. As you might expect, the slowest of the actions performed with these components—the actual accessing and selecting of the stored information—is the bottleneck for the performance for anything that requires significant data analysis.

> **Example**
>
> Let's say you get a notice from the Internal Revenue Service (or your particular governing tax authority) about information you put on your tax returns 3 years ago. You likely have easy access to the current year's receipts in your desk drawers and could pretty quickly get to anything for this year. However, your old tax information could be in a box in your basement or in a storage locker somewhere.
>
> In order to respond to the IRS letter, you must do the following:
>
> 1. Understand what information you need to answer the question(s).
> 2. Remember the location of the information.
> 3. Go to that information location.
> 4. Sort through everything to find the specific pieces of information required to answer the question.
> 5. Use that information to recalculate taxes due.
> 6. Prepare the response (report) for the IRS.
>
> All of these steps are required to respond to a query, whether to the IRS or to your boss. In most cases, *getting to* that information is going to take the longest amount of time.

Now, let's put a spin on this scenario. You still get contacted by the IRS and have to figure out what information you need to respond, but all of your receipts and information are loaded into a computer system. In this scenario, you simply have to define and execute a query, and the system immediately pulls the information it needs, performs the calculations, and presents you with the information you need to be able to respond. *This* is an in-memory solution.

When looking at in-memory systems, you are looking for the data to be processed in real time or as close to real time as technically possible. To achieve that level of performance, in-memory computing follows a simple tenet: speed up data access and minimize data movements. The main memory (RAM) is the fastest storage type that can hold a significant amount of data. (Although CPU registers and CPU caches are faster to access, their usage is limited to the actual processing of data.) Data in main memory (RAM) can be accessed 100,000 times faster than data on a hard disk. Clearly, compared with keeping data on hard disk, leveraging this in-memory capability can improve performance just by dramatically decreasing access time to retrieve the data and make it available to your reporting and analytic solutions or other applications.

In-memory computing also allows for significant levels of data compression, reduces the needs for data redundancy (you don't have to create a multilevel data model with prepopulated data or rolled-up data at six different levels to try to mitigate performance), and allows for built-in calculation engines. Combining these things allow you to dramatically reduce the time the whole process needs—from data identification and data retrieval to calculation and presentation—to be dramatically faster. A report that used to take an hour to run can now run in seconds.

We could say much more about in-memory computing, and entire books on the subject are available, but our goal here is to keep things simple. Before we end our explanation, though, we do want to address one question that seems to keep surrounding in-memory computing for those who are considering an in-memory solution for the first time: If my data is all in RAM, like my active documents or in process work, what happens if I lose power?

Let's compare this situation to a Microsoft Word document in which you haven't clicked the SAVE button yet. If your computer crashes before you click SAVE and write that document to your hard drive, have you lost all of your work? After all, your document is in the *memory* of the computer until you click SAVE—not the hard drive. If you haven't clicked SAVE, and your computer crashes, you *might* get a version in recovery mode, but it's also possible that you'll find yourself rewriting your document. The good news is that you won't run into this same problem with SAP HANA and solutions built on and for SAP HANA because it is considered *ACID (atomicity, consistency, isolation, and durability) compliant*.

In database technology, ACID refers to the set of requirements that are assessed for reliability:

- A transaction has to be *atomic*; that is, if part of a transaction fails, the entire transaction has to fail and therefore leave the database state unchanged.

- The *consistency* of a database must be preserved, meaning that only valid data will be written to the database. If, for some reason, a transaction is executed that violates the database's consistency rules, the entire transaction will be rolled back, and the database will be restored to a state consistent with those rules. On the other hand, if a transaction successfully executes, the database will be taken from one state that is consistent with the rules to another state that is also consistent with the rules.

- A transaction must be *isolated* so that no one transaction interferes with any other transaction.

- Finally, a transaction has to be *durable*; that is, after a transaction has been committed to the database, it will remain there.

Although the first three requirements are not affected by in-memory technologies, the durability requirement cannot be met by storing data in main memory alone. Main memory is volatile storage, which means it loses its content if it loses power. To make data persistent, it has to reside on nonvolatile storage, such as hard drives.

The medium used by a database to store data (in this case, main memory) is divided into pages. When a transaction changes data, the corresponding pages are marked and written to nonvolatile storage (a hard drive not at risk of power failures) in regular intervals. In addition, a database log captures all changes made by transactions. Each committed transaction generates a log entry that is written to nonvolatile storage. These steps ensure that all transactions are permanent.

In-memory databases can save changed pages in savepoints (Figure 1.1), which are asynchronously written to persistent storage at regular intervals (the default is every 5 minutes for SAP HANA). This log is written synchronously. In other words, a transaction is not committed before the corresponding log entry has been written to persistent storage—in order to meet the durability requirement that was described earlier—thus ensuring that SAP HANA meets (and passes) the ACID test.

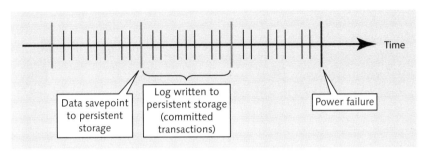

Figure 1.1 Savepoints and Logs

After a power failure, the database can be restarted, and the database pages are restored from the savepoints. The database logs are applied to restore the changes that were not captured in the savepoints. This ensures that the database can be restored in memory to exactly the same state as before the power failure.

In other words, if you forget to pay your electric bill and the power gets shut off to your in-memory database hardware, you don't have to panic. Instead, you should take comfort that you will have a key operational requirement satisfied with your SAP HANA implementation: disaster recovery, the ability of the system to restore itself after a catastrophic event such as a power outage or corruption that required a system shutdown.

If you are considering a pilot program for your SAP HANA solution, disaster recovery is a key area that you will want to validate and that will help you gain the confidence of your operational team. In fact, disaster recovery is the single most important proof point that customers will want to confirm before fully embracing and transitioning over to SAP HANA. Organizations want to be able to literally pull the plug on their SAP HANA-powered test boxes to see what happens and to determine what failover systems will kick in, how long the system will be down, and what the operational impact will be overall. Understanding the impact of system crashes (which happen to every system, to some degree, at some point) and disaster recovery will help organizations assess where to begin their SAP HANA journey and what system(s) they are prepared to shift to an SAP HANA platform.

Disaster recovery becomes absolutely vital when you consider SAP HANA for your transactional systems, such as SAP S/4HANA or SAP S/4HANA Finance (formerly SAP Simple Finance). Confirming the capability for disaster recovery is the single most important validation point discussed by customers who are considering adopting SAP Business Suite powered by SAP HANA or SAP S/4HANA. If you have SAP Business Warehouse powered by SAP HANA, for instance, and that system goes down, you can reload it, and your report may be a bit late, but it's not the end of the world. However, if your sales order processing on SAP HANA goes down, and you can't book, bill, or ship orders, you have a much bigger problem.

> **Note**
>
> If you're not yet familiar with all of the different options for SAP HANA—SAP Business Suite on SAP HANA, SAP S/4HANA, SAP BW on SAP HANA, and so on—don't worry. We'll introduce you to your options and get into greater detail in later chapters.

The best way to mitigate this problem is to prevent it. You do this by building in strong test and success criteria into your pilot programs and validation projects, in concert with your technical and operational support teams. Doing so will give everyone comfort and confidence in putting your mission-critical transaction systems on an SAP HANA platform.

1.1.2 Big Data

One of the reasons that in-memory computing is such a big deal is because of changing information consumption trends. The need and demand for immediate and insightful access to data are becoming more and more vital for the future. The importance of historical or trend reporting is decreasing, while data visualization and the ability to react as something is happening continue to increase in importance. Additionally, predicting and, ultimately, impacting or influencing future outcomes (based on historical performance and on influences both inside and outside the organization) are the highest goals of an organization and rely on data—both structured and unstructured.

Times are clearly changing, and as a result, organizations are seeking alternatives for their data, information, and analytic needs. What do your users demand that is not being met with the current tools and technologies that are available and deployed for their use? You would get a certain answer to that question if you asked the IT department, of course, but if you ask the users of the systems—from the business perspective—you'll probably hear something like: "We heard about massive volumes of data sitting ready for use in the our transaction systems, but it isn't accessed or can't be accessed." If asked why this is the case, your users will likely respond with one or more of the following reasons:

▸ It's too hard to retrieve.

▸ It takes too long to load it into a data warehouse.

▸ I've always been told a data warehouse is for aggregated data.

▸ We don't have enough space in the data warehouse to hold everything.

▸ The reports can't handle that much data.

▸ I don't really know what to ask for, and they won't give me "everything."

You'll find that, as your users and your organization mature in their perspective on technology and information, their demands for information and how that information is available to them will increase (see Figure 1.2).

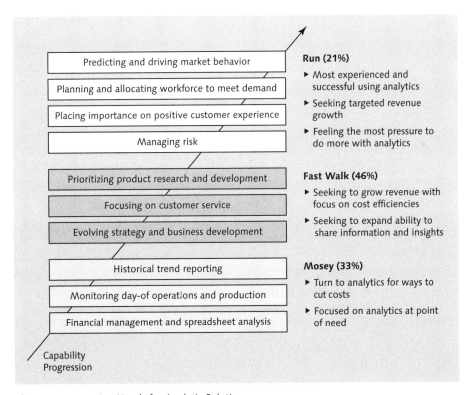

Figure 1.2 Increasing Needs for Analytic Solutions

As you progress through these levels of capabilities and needs, you'll start requiring massive amounts of data (both structured and unstructured) to address these solutions—this is what is known as *big data*. The phrase "big data" has been thrown around in the analytics industry to mean many things. In essence, big data refers, not only to the massive—nearly inconceivable—amount of data that is available to us today, but also to the fact that this data is rapidly changing. People create trillions of bytes of data per day. More than 90% of the world's data was created between 2009–2012 and is expected to double every 18 months. Web pages, social media, text messages, Instagram images, and memes make up an endless stream of information available at our fingertips—but how to harness it, make sense of it, and monetize it are major challenges.

The types of problems that organizations are trying to solve today, and the level of information they desire, require more than simply bringing in more sales orders and financial postings; organizations are trying to gain insight into how and why consumers do what they do and get ahead of the curve. You don't want to have to sort through thousands of lines of a report to find the key pieces of information—you want something to jump right out at you and tell you what is important. Organizations want insight into how customers really feel about their products: What are they saying on social media sites? Which stores do they *look* in versus *shop* in?

Organizations are seeking a single tool for advanced analytics that can uncover new meaningful correlations, patterns, relationships, and trends by sifting through large amounts of data (big data) stored in repositories using pattern-recognition technologies as well as statistical and mathematical techniques with hundreds of possible variables and millions of observations.

Big data isn't necessarily about using more resources (as you might think would be required when dealing with massive amounts of information). Organizations aren't just looking to sift through massive volumes of data but to find and leverage tools that will use the resources at hand more efficiently and more effectively. The goal is to drastically reduce the cost and time necessary for gaining valuable market research information on the desired products. This information can now be acquired in a matter of minutes, as compared to a few days, or even weeks, in traditional, semimanual processes. You can use that data to support decision making and compete based on a different (read: more informed) understanding of the market around you. A good analogy is from Christopher Frank of Forbes who likened big data to the movie *Moneyball*:

> *If you have read Moneyball, or seen the movie, you witnessed the power of big data—it is the story about the ability to compete and win with few resources and limited dollars.*

In addition, organizations also want to have the ability to intuitively design complex models to predict what is likely to happen in the future based on what has happened in the past and what is happening now (via sales, social media, etc.), along with other desired variables that may influence future conditions.

So, while big data might seem like some other department's problem—or a problem of managing size and scope of information—it is really the foundation of an organization's ability to reach that ultimate goal: predicting and driving behavior to desired outcomes.

Gathering information and the analysis of that information are at the core of the new demand for insight. However, organizations are either not getting what they need or are not trusting what they get. Consider the following:

▶ Business leaders frequently make decisions based on information they don't trust, don't have at all, or don't have at the right time.

▶ Business leaders say they don't have access to the information they need to do their jobs.

▶ A vast majority of CIOs consider business intelligence and analytics part of their visionary plans to enhance competitiveness.

▶ CEOs say they need to do a better job capturing and understanding information rapidly to make swift business decisions.

If you are a business user, you'll want to incorporate all of this data into your repositories so you can bring it into your analyses. Now that data storage and processing are so inexpensive, you can have all of your data available for analysis and no longer only have to work with aggregated data. If you are an IT person, you have to find strategies for, not only bringing in and storing massive amounts of data, but also making data available to your user community on an as-needed basis. Your paradigm has to shift because the old way of capturing, staging, and storing data is no longer sufficient. Both structured and unstructured data will continue to grow at astronomical rates, and you must address both of these types of data. Addressing these data challenges presents an excellent opportunity to create and deliver reporting and analytic solutions that can bring together these massive amounts of data in a trusted and secure environment that is accessible to the organization.

Big data presents five main challenges:

▶ **Volume**
How do you deal with massive volumes of rapidly changing data coming from multiple source systems in a heterogeneous environment?

▶ **Scope**
How do you determine the breadth, depth, and span of data to be included in cleansing, conversion, and migration efforts?

▶ **360-degree view**
With all of the information that is now available, how do you achieve 360-degree views of your customers and harness the kind of detailed information that's available, such as who they are, what they are interested in, what is the best way to target them, and what they are going to buy?

▶ **Data integrity**
How do you establish the desired data integrity levels across multiple functional teams and business processes? What does data integrity mean across your organization? Is it merely complete data (something in every required field)? Or does it include accurate data, that is, that the information contained within those fields is both correct and logical?

▶ **Governance process**
How do you establish procedures across people, processes, and technology to maintain a desired state of governance? Who sets the rules? Are you adding a level of administration? Are there "Gold" clients in your data?

Each of these is difficult because you are trying to bring together massive amounts of rapidly changing data from a multitude of sources with tremendous variety in real time and then manage, maintain, and make this data available to your organization for whatever its various definitions of insight might be—without necessarily knowing beforehand what the insight needs to be.

> **Example**
>
> What are specific some examples of where this might come into play in your organization?
>
> ► How about customer engagement? Gaining a single view of the "value" of your customer (perhaps in real time while you are negotiating with the customer) so you can make the most impactful decisions on where and how to invest in this customer or how to price to this customer? Run predictive analytics factoring in unstructured social media sentiment to determine how to drive large market target campaigns.
>
> ► How about fraud management? Use big data tools to unlock hidden patterns and trends that would otherwise have slipped through the cracks of your system.
>
> These two simple examples show how big data can be a very real and tangible asset to your organization—*if* you can harness it in a meaningful way.

As we hope we've shown, the potential of in-memory computing and the necessity of a powerful computing engine for big data make the two an ideal match. *This* is where SAP HANA comes in.

1.2   Column-Based versus Row-Based Storage

One of the other main differences between traditional databases and the newer databases like SAP HANA is that they are organized differently; newer databases are organized to optimize the access and processing of information. For SAP HANA, this optimization means that data is primarily organized in columns versus in rows. To illustrate why this is important and how this affects how you access and work with your data, consider the following.

Over the past thirty years, many algorithms have been developed to build indexes. For example, *B-tree indexes* are a way to structure data that keeps data sorted and allows searches, sequential access, insertions, and deletions. B-tree indexes were originally based on physical tables with up to seven nodes, something that made them very large and often caused them to become unbalanced. An unbalanced B-tree index means that there are more members in one node than in the others. Think of this as a phone book. Initially, there may be similar numbers of people in each section, for example, 500 with a last name starting with "J" and 500 with a last name starting with "K." In a single-node index, you open the first page of the phone book and simply see that the "Js" start on page

89. After you open that page, you scan and look for "Jensen." If you have a static phone book, finding people surnamed "Jensen" would as easy as finding people surnamed "Koswalski." But what happens if another 1,500 Koswalskis moved into your town? Now you have 500 entries in "J" and 2,000 entries in "K," so searching for Jensen is faster than searching for Koswalski. In other words, the index has become unbalanced.

Naturally, you can solve this by adding a second node to the index so that the Koswalskis with a first name starting with "A" are on certain pages and those with "B" are on others. This way, you can keep adding index pages to the phone book. The first generation of indexes worked in this way (actually they are somewhat more mathematically based, but for our purposes, this is good enough to understand the concepts).

In the 1990s, relational database management systems (RDBMS) became more advanced, and new indexing methods were added. The first new method created pointers instead of physical tables for indexes. These indexes were easier to modify and balance. Some vendors such as Oracle actually made indexes that balanced themselves automatically. About twenty years ago, academics invented newer bitmap indexes, which were truly different from those based on the B-tree idea— and were smaller and also much faster. Then, during the past decade, index methods proliferated, including star-joins, hash, ngram, inverted, opt-eval, and many more. Differences also emerged in how new records were inserted, how indexes could be merged, compression options, fault tolerance (when errors occur), and the overall speed of data retrieval. This research and development has in large part been fueled by the growing size of the Internet and the millions of users seeking electronic information.

What does this all have to do with SAP HANA? As mentioned, one of the key differentiators of SAP HANA is how it indexes your data: column-based organization as opposed to row-based organization. Relational databases organize data in tables that contain data records, and the difference between row-based and column-based storage is the way in which the table is stored (Figure 1.3). As the descriptions suggest, *row-based storage* stores a table in a sequence of rows, and *column-based storage* stores a table in a sequence of columns.

Both storage models have advantages and disadvantages, as discussed in Table 1.1.

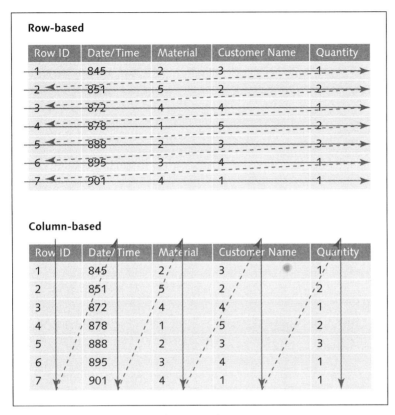

Figure 1.3 Row-Based versus Column-Based Storage

	Row-Based Storage	**Column-Based Storage**
Advantages	Data is stored together and is easy to insert or update.	Only relevant columns are read during the selection process, and any column can serve as an index or key for data retrieval.
Disadvantages	During selection, all data must be read.	Updates of data are not as efficient in column-based storage as in row-based storage.

Table 1.1 Advantages and Disadvantages of Row-Based versus Column-Based Storage

One of the disadvantages of row-based storage is that, regardless of which rows are actually involved, all data must be read. Even if your query is not asking for a customer name, for example, that field is still read by the system when executing the query request. When applied to an SAP BW database, the row data that you think is a single row is spread across multiple tables; master data is separate (generally) from the fact table, so the data has to be constructed in response to a query, making the entire process slower. By using column-based storage, SAP HANA addresses this problem because only relevant columns are read during the selection process.

However, column-based storage also has a disadvantage. In a row-based format, to update a field (e.g., when a customer changes his order from a blue car to a silver car), the system finds the row and updates the information. In a column-based format, however, the system has to find the right column and *then* the right row for the update, so the write process is not as efficient.

Although this inefficiency is fairly minor, let's explain how SAP has addressed the issue: SAP HANA does not update during updates. (Sounds perfectly logical, doesn't it?) Instead, SAP HANA inserts the new line of information. SAP HANA, specifically, has a row-based delta buffer, which processes write operations as efficiently as the row store; the delta buffer is then merged to the main data column store, from time to time. Write (insert, update, and delete) operations are always done against the delta buffer first, and read (select) operations always read both the delta buffer and the main column store. Because most of the data is in the column store, reading operation only negligibly degrade performance, due to a small amount of data held in the row-based delta buffer. In this way, SAP HANA's column store can be very efficient to both transactional and analytical scenarios.

In addition, not all of the columns of a row are usually needed for processing, especially in analytic queries. You generally don't ask for every possible piece of information for every report requirement (although some people may want all of the possible information and will filter it down from there). Using this column structure for the data and the database itself reduces or eliminates scanning unnecessary data when executing a query, thus making it that much faster and more efficient than traditional row-based access.

> **Example**
>
> When executing an analytical scenario, the system often processes and calculates data in one column across multiple rows; for example, a sales report sums all the values for "sales revenue" column across all rows or some rows that match a given filter (e.g., year = 2015). That sum operation, in a column-based database, can be realized with much fewer computational cycles (since the values to be summed are sequentially stored) than a row-based store.

The basic idea behind column-based indexes is that there are repeated patterns, or occurrences, in the data that you can reduce in the index creation and compression process. To illustrate this point, let's look at a simplified example.

In Figure 1.4, the table contains only one record for Jane Hansen, who is a Gold customer, lives in North Carolina, was born in 1959, and has an income of $71,927. Although you can use data compression, if you index this by rows, reducing the data set further is not possible. However, if you look at the data from a column perspective, you'll see quite a bit of data redundancy (Figure 1.5).

Row ID	Name	State	Class	Birth date	Income
1	Jane Hansen	NC	Gold	8/7/1959	$ 71,927
2	Olav Petersen	TX	Silver	2/24/1963	$ 35,633
3	Peter Johnsen	FL	Platinum	1/1/1959	$ 144,077
4	Thomas Berg	TX	Gold	2/13/1981	$ 85,087
5	John Beatty	FL	Platinum	12/26/1958	$ 123,456
6	Jim O'Brian	NC	Silver	6/11/1977	$ 76,506
7	Jeff Pinolli	NY	Platinum	5/9/1971	$ 73,503
8	Carol VanZyck	NY	Platinum	3/13/1969	$ 68,987
9	Fredrick Davidson	FL	Gold	9/8/1980	$ 100,600
10	Tone Leffler	CA	Platinum	2/10/1955	$ 105,943
11	Carol Hansen	CA	Silver	9/9/1980	$ 112,096
12	Jim Petersen	NY	Gold	2/23/1974	$ 41,080
13	Jeff Johnsen	CA	Platinum	3/10/1978	$ 118,481
14	Peter Berg	FL	Platinum	12/14/1981	$ 50,900
15	Thomas Beatty	IN	Silver	10/25/1954	$ 78,304
16	John O'Brian	IN	Gold	11/27/1970	$ 38,809
17	Olav Pinolli	CA	Gold	10/1/1955	$ 157,105
18	Jane VanZyck	FL	Platinum	6/27/1960	$ 151,067
19	Tone Davidson	NC	Silver	11/19/1958	$ 63,169
20	Fredrick Leffler	SC	Gold	12/21/1973	$ 65,628

Figure 1.4 Data Set by Rows

In addition to the standard compression, you can now remove data redundancy in the columns. For example, there are only three values of customer class in the data (SILVER, GOLD, and PLATINUM), and only seven states are represented by these twenty records. Removing data redundancy lends itself to better data reduction in the indexes as well as significant performance benefits when accessing data. In short, column-based stores have the benefit of high compression rates (reduction of the overall size of your database and therefore the amount of hardware required to support the system), scan operations (easier to search), and in-cache client processing of aggregation (easier to group and aggregate). By also including the Row

35

ID in the column-based index, SAP HANA maintains the "ownership" of the values in the index that can still be "mapped" back to the other fields on the record.

Row ID	Name	State	Class	Birth date	Income
1	Jane Hansen	NC	Gold	8/7/1959	$ 71,927
2	Olav Petersen	TX	Silver	2/24/1963	$ 35,633
3	Peter Johnsen	FL	Platinum	1/1/1959	$ 144,077
4	Thomas Berg	TX	Gold	2/13/1981	$ 85,087
5	John Beatty	FL	Platinum	12/26/1958	$ 123,456
6	Jim O'Brian	NC	Silver	6/11/1977	$ 76,506
7	Jeff Pinolli	NY	Platinum	5/9/1971	$ 73,503
8	Carol VanZyck	NY	Platinum	3/13/1969	$ 68,987
9	Fredrick Davidson	FL	Gold	9/8/1980	$ 100,600
10	Tone Leffler	CA	Platinum	2/10/1955	$ 105,943
11	Carol Hansen	CA	Silver	9/9/1980	$ 112,096
12	Jim Petersen	NY	Gold	2/23/1974	$ 41,080
13	Jeff Johnsen	CA	Platinum	3/10/1978	$ 118,481
14	Peter Berg	FL	Platinum	12/14/1981	$ 50,900
15	Thomas Beatty	IN	Silver	10/25/1954	$ 78,304
16	John O'Brian	IN	Gold	11/27/1970	$ 38,809
17	Olav Pinolli	CA	Gold	10/1/1955	$ 157,105
18	Jane VanZyck	FL	Platinum	6/27/1960	$ 151,067
19	Tone Davidson	NC	Silver	11/19/1958	$ 63,169
20	Fredrick Leffler	SC	Gold	12/21/1973	$ 65,628

Figure 1.5 Data Set by Columns

> **Note**
>
> For ease of understanding, these examples oversimplify SAP HANA's internal algorithms for indexes and compression—they are actually quite complex. For example, for dictionary compression, SAP HANA uses bit-coded log2 (NDICT) bits, and for value ID sequencing, SAP HANA uses prefix coding, run length coding, cluster coding, sparse coding, and indirect coding. However, unless you are a computer scientist, you don't need to worry about how these algorithms work.

You get the basic idea—column-based indexes are often preferred due to the smaller and faster indexes they tend to produce. It's important to note that, in some cases, SAP HANA's scan operations are so fast that indexes aren't needed at all, and column data is simply accessed in memory scans directly. SAP HANA also has fuzzy and phrase search features and a text engine that supports indexing of text.

The fundamental differences between row-based stores and column-based stores are summarized in Table 1.2.

Row Store	Column Store
▸ It is a relational engine to store data in row format.	▸ Read functionality is improved significantly, and write functionality is also improved.
▸ It is a pure in-memory store.	▸ Highly compressed data resides in memory.
▸ It has an in-memory object store (in future) for liveCache functionality.	▸ No real files are used, just virtual files.
▸ Transactional version memory is the heart of the row store.	▸ Optimizer and executer handle queries and execution plans.
▸ Write operations mainly go into transactional version memory.	▸ It supports delta data for fast write.
▸ INSERT also writes to the persisted segment.	▸ It has asynchronous delta merge.
▸ The visible version is moved from memory to the persisted segment.	▸ It enables a consistent view manager.
▸ Outdated record versions are cleared from transactional version memory.	▸ The main store is compressed and read optimized; data is read from the main store.
▸ Row store tables have a primary index.	▸ The delta store is optimized for write operations.
▸ Row ID maps to the primary key.	▸ Asynchronous merge moves the data from the delta store to the main store.
▸ Secondary indexes can be created.	▸ Compression is created by the dictionary compression method and other applied compression methods.
▸ Row ID contains the segment and the page for the record.	▸ Even during the merge operation, the column table will still be available for read and write operations. For this purpose, a second delta and the main store are used internally.
▸ Indexes in the row store only exist in memory.	
▸ The index definition is stored with table metadata.	▸ The merge operation can also be triggered manually with an SQL command.

Table 1.2 Row Store versus Column Store

1.3   Summary

You should now be armed with questions that you didn't know to ask before, along with a stronger baseline understanding of the history and applications for in-memory computing and big data, and you are beginning to understand how SAP HANA can be used to address these issues within your organization.

With this baseline firmly in hand, we will now build upon that foundation and fully explore SAP HANA. We will look at what it is and what it isn't. We will look at how SAP HANA can be used to address the needs of your organization, how SAP HANA addresses big data issues and more.

As we continue, we'll look at all of these topics in more detail so that, by the end of this book, you'll have the information you need to fully assess SAP HANA and understand its implications for your organization.

*Now that you understand the foundational concepts of SAP HANA,
let's apply those and learn about the use cases for SAP HANA and how
it might fit into your business.*

2   SAP HANA as a Database

Welcome to SAP HANA! In this chapter, we'll introduce you to SAP HANA, building on the previous discussions of in-memory computing and big data and applying those concepts to SAP HANA. We will talk about the different use cases for
SAP HANA: as a database for non-SAP applications, as a database for SAP Business
Warehouse (SAP BW), and as the database for SAP S/4HANA. Finally, we cover
some of the other major SAP HANA capabilities, from SAP HANA smart data
streaming to the SAP HANA Graph Engine and beyond.

2.1   The Fundamentals of SAP HANA

SAP HANA is a database, a technology, and a platform. Both evolutionary and
revolutionary in how it enables analysis of very large, nonaggregated data at
unprecedented speeds, SAP HANA allows entirely new types of transactions and
analyses to be performed. Current solution landscapes that are organized as silos
(Figure 2.1) create delays and complexities that hinder agility and innovation in
our organizations.

The SAP HANA database is a fully in-memory solution and is the foundation for
SAP's future development. SAP has optimized the SAP HANA database to take
advantage of technology advances in hardware, software, and processing. SAP
HANA seeks to create a landscape that alleviates the complexities and delays associated with siloed environments by enabling an environment in which there is
"only" a single instance of the data—accessible to all applications. SAP HANA
seeks to be that one platform that allows for simplified IT, accelerated insights,
and innovative modern applications (apps).

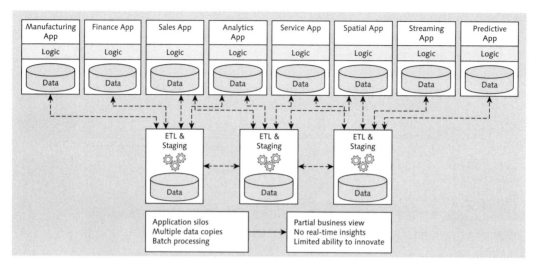

Figure 2.1 Silos in Solution Landscapes

SAP HANA is flexible, data-source-agnostic (meaning it does not care where the data comes from) in-memory database that allows you to hold and work with massive volumes of data in real time, without the need to aggregate or create highly complex physical data models (as you would have had to do to model the same data in SAP BW). The SAP HANA in-memory database solution is a combination of hardware and software that optimizes row-based, column-based, and object-based database technologies to exploit parallel processing capabilities.

Inside the in-memory computing engine (IMCE) of SAP HANA, many different components manage the access and storage of data (Figure 2.2). First, the disk storage is typically a file system that allows for data security and logging of activities, which is managed in the persistence layer. Additionally, a relational engine manages the row or column store. Whether your implementation will use a row or column store depends on the content you're implementing as well as the system you're placing on top of SAP HANA (i.e., SAP BW or SAP Business Suite). All systems will use a combination of row and column stores. However, when you're building your own data set from tools such as SAP Data Services (extract, transform, and load [ETL]-based replication), you'll have an option to implement either method.

Several tools are available for moving data within SAP HANA. For example, using SAP (Sybase) Replication Server (RS) and the SAP HANA Load Controller (LC), you can provide log-based replication, or you can leverage SAP Landscape Transformation (SLT)'s trigger-based data replication or use SAP Data Services for traditional scheduled data movements.

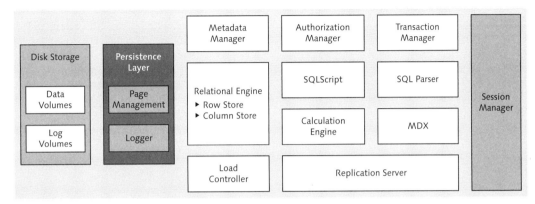

Figure 2.2 The In-Memory Computing Engine of SAP HANA

For access to data in frontend tools, SAP HANA provides support for SQLScript and multidimensional expressions (MDX) as well as an SQL parser. Also, a hyperfast calculation engine can perform in-memory calculations. In Chapter 7, we'll look at all of the options for accessing the SAP HANA system with business intelligence and reporting tools.

Internally, the SAP HANA system also manages security, transactions, and metadata (data about the data) in three IMCE components that are integrated with the session manager, which keeps an eye on who is accessing the system and how the result set and dialogues are managed. Overall, the IMCE is a complex, internal SAP HANA component that is bundled together as an appliance to simplify installation and management.

Before we go into greater detail about how SAP HANA handles big data or how you may want to implement SAP HANA for your organization, let's discuss the important aspects of what SAP HANA can do and what it can't do. Understanding both equally is important so that you can make sure you're starting down a successful implementation path.

2.1.1   What SAP HANA Can Do

For the spectrum of analytic needs that you can address with your SAP HANA-enabled solution, take a look at Figure 2.3.

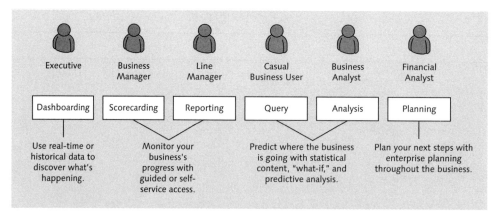

Figure 2.3 SAP HANA Analytic Capabilities

As you can see, your SAP HANA-based solution can address a variety of business needs. Remember that SAP HANA has the power to bring together and analyze billions of rows of information in under a second. The options and capabilities this power enables vary by industry and by user, but your organization's needs can be generally divided in two categories: broad analytic needs and focused analytic needs, as shown in Figure 2.4.

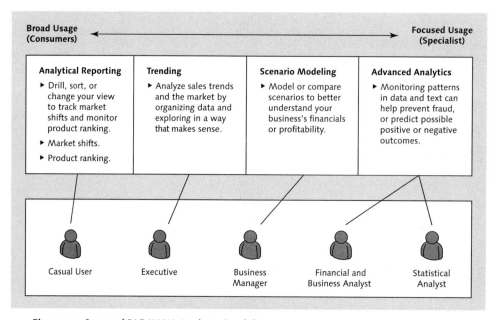

Figure 2.4 Scope of SAP HANA Analytic Capabilities

With all of this in mind, the scope of the types of applications that you need addressed is really only limited by what your organization can define.

SAP HANA's potential for practical application spans industries and use cases, such as the following:

- Trading
- Customer retention
- Telecommunications
- Manufacturing
- Traffic control
- Fraud prevention

These use cases all require massive amounts of data available at any time and are just a few of the endless opportunities being developed. Currently, the most common uses for SAP HANA include the following:

- Call detail record analysis
- Point-of-sale analysis
- Quality and production analysis
- Smart grid/smarter utilities
- RFID tracking and analytics
- Fraud/risk management and modeling
- A complete and full understanding of customers' needs and habits
- Predictive modeling
- "What-if" scenarios
- Pricing optimization
- Advanced transaction processing (for example, using SAP S/4HANA Finance)

2.1.2 What SAP HANA Can't Do

Now that you have a basic idea of what SAP HANA is and what it can do, it's important to understand what SAP HANA isn't:

- SAP HANA is not a reporting solution and does not have a built-in reporting capability. You have to install and attach a business intelligence tool—such as the SAP BusinessObjects Business Intelligence (SAP BusinessObjects BI) plat-form—to generate reports. (For more information on SAP BusinessObjects BI and SAP HANA, see Chapter 7.)

▶ SAP HANA is not an extract, transform, and load (ETL) tool. SAP HANA needs either a standalone ETL tool or SAP Data Services to bring data into it. (For more information on ETL for SAP HANA, see Chapter 9.)

▶ SAP HANA is not a data modeling tool. To create data models, you can use SAP HANA Studio, or if you are using SAP BW on SAP HANA, you can continue to use the SAP BW data modeling tools. (For more information on SAP HANA Studio, see Chapter 8.)

▶ SAP HANA is not a module of SAP ERP and is a completely different tool from SAP ERP. SAP HANA can be the database upon which your SAP ERP solution sits, but it isn't a transaction system in and of itself.

▶ SAP HANA is not SAP BW. SAP BW is a tool for a persistent, highly structured data model based on an extended star-schema concept.

▶ SAP HANA is not a data quality management tool—but you should have one!

2.2   Big Data Solutions

As we discussed earlier, SAP HANA is a platform as much as it is a technology and is, in many ways, driven by the needs of organizations to address big data needs and challenges. We have already considered how this in-memory solution can be used to address data access at much higher speeds and in different ways (column versus row storage). Now let's look at how those baseline capabilities and needs come together with solutions and capabilities specifically built for addressing big data with the SAP HANA platform. We'll also look at how SAP HANA addresses the needs for data accessibility and retention to support "hot, warm, and cold" data needs with dynamic tiering. We'll show how SAP HANA can access data from any source via SAP HANA smart data access (SDA) and how it can integrate and coexist with your existing solutions, including Hadoop.

2.2.1   SAP HANA

Big data isn't going anywhere, and if anything, it's getting bigger. Your organization's need to bring together data from inside and outside sources is even more important as social media and other forces outside the organization increasingly impact how your organization is viewed and how your customers act. The good news is that SAP HANA not only handles big data but also allows you to build or optimize applications and processes to work with this data in ways that have never been possible before.

One of the key big data capabilities that organizations request is a 360-degree view of the customer—the fullest, most complete picture of customers—so that you can understand their buying habits, what will be effective promotions versus what will be wasted effort, and what drives them to buy. Previously, creating this big data view within an SAP system nearly impossible, but with SAP HANA, you have new capabilities for addressing this need with the ability to work in (near) real time with a wide variety of data—both structured and unstructured.

To address this and other big data requirements, SAP HANA must overcome the data challenges that your internal systems (your SAP systems) aren't in control of, such as volume and scope. You'll also have to deliver trustworthy data and have the controls and governance in place to continue to deliver that trustworthy data. So let's look at these key areas of concern and how SAP HANA addresses each of them:

▶ **Data volume**
SAP HANA has the capability to conduct massive parallel processing (MPP). SAP HANA systems (up to 100 TB and beyond) can process enormous amounts of data, as SAP HANA is putting all of this data in memory, not on drives. With the expansion of SAP HANA toolsets to address hot, warm, and cool data (more to follow on this subject very shortly), you can effectively manage all of your data.

▶ **Data scope**
SAP HANA can hold enormous amounts of data, so it can address whatever scope of information you need. However, you must still determine what information, from the nearly limitless array of options, will come into SAP HANA and how to use it. SAP HANA *can* hold massive amounts of data, but it doesn't mean that you *should* put massive amounts of information into the system if it's not relevant or applicable to a business need. You need to evaluate the cost of bringing all of that data into SAP HANA, how it will be stored and staged, and the cost(s) associated with all of this. Although the technical barriers to using massive data scopes are effectively removed, you do not have carte blanche to create a 100+ TB SAP HANA system just because you can.

▶ **Data integrity**
Data integrity speaks directly to the issue of trusting the data. If you are presenting these solutions to the leaders of your organization as ways to gain insight and visibility into vast amounts of data—and you are telling them that they have the ability to make decisions that drive business activities on a real-time basis—then they better trust that data. Data integrity implies that you can depend on the data to know that the results are repeatable and that the data is trackable. Now, with the ability to load these massive volumes of data into a single environment—SAP HANA—you can trust your data more because you have (potentially) eliminated a series of data migrations, transformations, and extracts across multiple environments.

▶ **Data governance**
Making sure that the data and the system *stay* trusted goes hand in hand with having trusted data. Data governance makes sure that the key system points, measures, and metrics that business leaders depend on follow some basic rules. SAP HANA doesn't address governance directly because governance is a process and a business procedure issue. However, thanks to its ability to give you (near) instant visibility of your data and information, SAP HANA can quickly highlight problems for you.

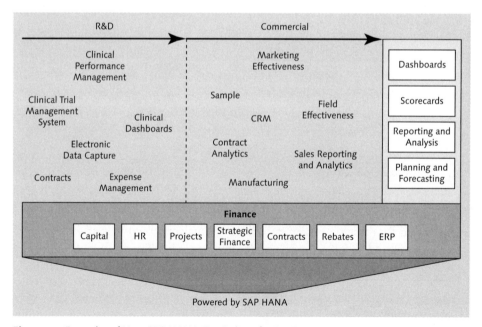

Figure 2.5 Examples of How SAP HANA Can Deliver for Big Data

Big data problems—or, perhaps better put, the analytics that require big data—are excellent use cases for SAP HANA. Figure 2.5 shows some examples of how SAP HANA can deliver analytics that require massive amounts of data. SAP HANA users want point-of-sale information, prescriptions, banking transactions, credit card activity, mobile devices, machine readers, GPS tags, and inputs from tens of thousands of trucks or rail car sensors. The types of potential data requirements—and the inputs of that data—are truly endless.

> **Example**
>
> One practical use case that requires big data from numerous input sources (that would previously not have been possible to address with standard SAP solutions) is assessing sales impact.
>
> For example, a consumer products company wants to assess the impact of in-store demonstrations and coupon handouts to point-of-sale activity on a real-time basis to make sure it can restock as quickly as needed. This requirement needs to bring in point-of-sale data from the grocery store; historical sales information to compare period-over-period sales to see that the sales during demonstrations and couponing are outside of the norm; orders and delivery information to understand the grocer's buying patterns, how much is on order, and when it's due to be delivered; and logistics information to understand how quickly the consumer packaged goods company could restock if required. To complicate this example even further, the company could add in weather information to see if the weather was driving additional sales (e.g., perhaps it is hot outside and the company is giving away samples and coupons on ice cream) and how outside factors are affecting its efforts.

SAP HANA can build analytic applications by using MPP power and in-memory capabilities to push enormous amounts of data from multiple systems into user-defined BI applications that can be used to make (near) real-time business decisions.

2.2.2 Dynamic Tiering

Even though today's hardware and memory capacities allow you to keep enormous amounts of data in memory, you still need to consider how to compress your overall database size (even in memory). This compression is one of the keys of success—along with keeping the price manageable—with SAP HANA.

To help manage your database size and cost, SAP has introduced the ability to tier your data within an SAP HANA database. If you're familiar with SAP BW you are probably familiar with the concept of data tiering—even though you may not realize it. Data tiering is the "art" of identifying and labeling different data sets as hot, warm, or cool and organizing your database (or solution): The hottest data (the data you use the most frequently and that changes the most) is the most readily available to you. The coolest data (the data you use the least frequently and change the least) is still available to you but sits a bit to the side, still accessible and connected to the system but not taking up high-value resources.

In SAP BW solutions, you could have created a multilayered data model that used the SAP BW Accelerator to preaggregate, index, and optimize your hot data so that you can retrieve and report on the data as quickly as possible. You may have older, but still important, data sitting in large Operational Data Store (ODS) objects or DataStore Objects (DSOs) that took longer to sort through but could be read by your queries and were still on the main SAP BW system. You might also have legacy data or considerably older data sitting attached to the system via a nearline storage (NLS) archiving solution. You may have chosen to use NLS storage because it was less expensive than disk storage even though accessing the data on the NLS archiving solution is slower.

With the introduction of SAP HANA, many people thought—and still do—that now, because you *can* store all of your atomic-level information in a single place and make it readily available for analysis, you *should*. What they did not immediately count on was the cost of storing all of that data—not just in terms of hardware but in the licensing cost of SAP HANA itself.

SAP HANA licensing was originally based on the amount of data that would be stored in it. This licensing structure created a need to balance how much data was stored in SAP HANA (regardless of the fact that you *could* store everything) with the cost of the hardware and licenses for SAP HANA itself. As a result, some organizations limited what they moved into the SAP HANA environment(s) and therefore limited the potential benefits and capabilities that they would gain from their SAP HANA implementation.

To help address this issue, SAP has introduced dynamic tiering to the SAP HANA platform. Dynamic tiering is a native big data solution for SAP HANA that adds smart, disk-based extended storage to your SAP HANA database. An actual SAP HANA dynamic tiering service (esserver) is added to your SAP HANA system, and this service creates the extended store and extended tables that will store your warm (or whatever you designate) data.

These new tables will behave like any other SAP HANA tables but reside on the disk-based extended store and therefore will reduce the size of your physical SAP

HANA database (and the associated licensing costs). You set up the controls for what data should go where, and the system will then automatically determine which tier to store the data in. The SAP HANA in-memory store will hold the most frequently accessed "hot" data that is most valuable to you, while the "warm" or "cool" data will be held in the extended storage tier because that data is less frequently accessed and therefore not necessary to be in the higher-cost, in-memory database directly.

The extended table concept is a relatively new one and applies to "warm" data. Since you don't need to access this warm data constantly—and only you can decide what is hot, warm, and cool data for your organization—you don't need this data to be sitting in a high-value, in-memory database. However, you do need to be able to access it on demand. These extended tables will be managed within SAP HANA and, since they are within the SAP HANA system, can be used as though they were regular, persistent tables. These tables are actually located in a disk-based data storage, however, which has been integrated into the SAP HANA system.

Dynamic tiering is invisible to your users, who will use the entire system as a single database. The data in the warm memory is accessed using algorithms, which are optimized for the extended tables on the disk-based storage.

If you have organized your SAP BW data so that your warm data is stored in DSOs and then move your SAP BW database to SAP HANA, you can configure these objects to make SAP HANA create an extended table instead of a native SAP HANA table for that data, and that data will be written directly to the disk-based data storage. Since the extended table is logically located in SAP HANA, the SAP HANA optimizer can access this table as it would any other SAP HANA table, and you will see a significant performance improvement when using analytics against that data even though that data is not in the in-memory portion of the SAP HANA system.

Note that SAP HANA dynamic tiering is not the same as using an NLS archiving solution. An NLS solution takes "cold" or "cool" data that is considered old and infrequently used and moves it out of the SAP HANA environment and onto an accessible NLS archiving solution. The SAP solution offered for NLS is SAP IQ (although other NLS vendors also offer solutions). The difference between the extended table concept of dynamic tiering and an NLS solution is that, with an NLS solution, the data is actually deleted from the SAP HANA environment and stored on separate servers.

Extended tables and NLS servers offer different solutions—even though they sound rather similar. Data can be accessed and categorized in different ways, as summarized in Table 2.1.

Extended Tables	Nearline Storage
SAP HANA main memory is optimized.	Data persistence is optimized in the larger system landscape.
Extended tables are an integral and integrated part of the system.	Storage is on separate server.
Extended tables handle complete tables.	NLS is for selected semantic data slices (old, cold data).
All types of data manipulation are possible (create, read, update, delete).	Data is written once to the NLS and then is read-only.
Business-critical data accessibility service-level agreements are met.	Non-business-critical data accessibility service-level agreements are met.
Costs are managed by optimizing high-value, in-memory tables.	Costs are reduced by removing data from the SAP HANA environment.

Table 2.1 Traditional Extended Tables versus NLS Tables

You should take into account architecture and hardware considerations when determining if and how you will use SAP HANA dynamic tiering as well as the design decisions for what will be in "hot" storage versus warm or cool storage. A considerable amount of detailed information is available for you and your system administrators when you are ready to make this move.

2.2.3 SAP HANA Smart Data Access

Dynamic tiering addresses the ability to stage and structure data "within" the SAP HANA system for maximizing system resources (and minimizing costs) for hot, warm, and cool data. Now, what about the data that isn't in SAP HANA and that you don't want to bring into SAP HANA for whatever reason? Do you have to load data into SAP HANA to work with it? Are there any ways to remotely access data and still integrate it into your analytics?

Welcome to SAP HANA smart data access (SDA). First introduced in 2013 with SAP HANA SPS 6, SDA has been designed to provide access to data outside of your main, connected system. (Those systems are not directly "attached" like source systems that feed SAP BW, for instance.) SDA is a virtualization tool used within SAP BW as the source for Open ODS views and for query access to data in SAP IQ as a nearline storage solution.

With SDA, data can be merged in heterogeneous enterprise data warehouse (EDW) landscapes (data federation) and ultimately be brought together for your analysis. Unlike earlier SAP tools that required you to prestage any and all data by making it reside in the one database, SDA makes it possible to access remote data without having to replicate the data in the SAP HANA database beforehand. SDA can work with Teradata databases, SAP Sybase ASE, SAP IQ, Intel Distribution for Apache Hadoop, and SAP HANA instances, among others. SAP HANA handles the data like local tables on the database. Automatic data type conversion makes it possible to map data types from databases connected via SDA to SAP HANA data types.

With SDA, the data from other sources will remain in virtual tables. Virtual tables created within SAP HANA will point to remote tables in the identified different data sources. These connections will enable real-time access to data regardless of its location and, at same time, will not affect the SAP HANA database. Authorized users can then write SQL queries in SAP HANA, which would operate on virtual tables. SAP HANA's query processor optimizes these queries and executes the relevant part of the query in the target database, returns the results of the query to SAP HANA, and completes the operation. Figure 2.6 shows what this process looks like.

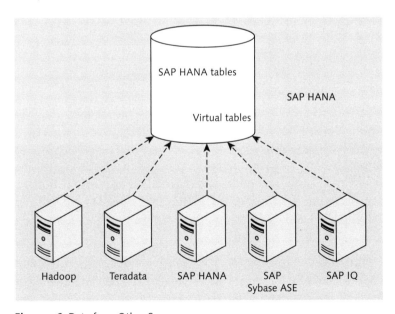

Figure 2.6 Data from Other Sources

Note

As of SAP HANA SPS 10, the following remote data sources are supported: SAP HANA, SAP IQ, SAP ASE, SAP Event Stream Processor, SAP MaxDB, Teradata Database, Microsoft SQL Server 2012, Oracle 12c, IBM DB2, Hadoop Hortonworks HDP 2.3, and IBM Netezza Appliance. With the release of SPS 12 (Q2 2016), SAP is extending this to include additional data sources like Google+, IBM Informix, or *e-mail.pst* files.

SDA optimizes the execution of queries by working with SQL queries on virtual tables within SAP HANA. SAP HANA's query processor optimizes the queries and executes the relevant part in the connected database, returns the result to SAP HANA (directly merging the results with the persistent data in your system), and completes the operation. Some prep work is required to create relationships and links; you connect and define facts and master data from the source via associations in the Open ODS view. Those facts and master data are joined directly at the database level at query runtime, together with operations on the navigation attributes.

For Open ODS views, SDA makes it possible to use data sources that are not managed by the SAP BW system at all. When working with SDA, therefore, you can expand modeling in the SAP BW system with little effort, allowing you to consume persistent data stored in SAP HANA tables and effectively create an open ETL connection between outside systems and your virtual tables.

How might you utilize this capability?

▸ Make other data warehouses transparent for the SAP BW system's SAP HANA database.

▸ Quickly incorporate data from other business entities (acquisitions, mergers) long before your systems are integrated.

▸ Consume SAP HANA data mart scenarios from a connected database.

▸ Begin your SAP HANA journey without replacing any existing databases by using SDA to bring data together for analysis in a standalone SAP HANA environment.

Of course, some things need to be set up to make this functionality possible, and, depending on what version of SDA you are using, you may be limited in what you can do. First, let's take a quick look at the prerequisites for SDA.

To use SDA as the source type for Open ODS views or for query access to nearline storage data, you must first ensure the following steps have been taken:

- You have installed the ODBC (Open Database Connectivity) drivers for the databases that you want to connect with SDA.

- You have connected the other databases to SDA as remote sources, paying particular attention here to which databases are supported in which versions for SDA.

> **Note**
>
> SAP HANA system authorization `CREATE REMOTE SOURCE` is required to create a remote source. If the remote source is not created with the SAP<SID> user but with a different database user instead, then this database user must assign the corresponding object authorizations to the SAP<SID> user (`CREATE VIRTUAL TABLE` and `DROP`).

- The remote data is accessed from the SAP BW system with the database user that connected the SAP BW system to the SAP HANA database. When creating a remote source in SAP HANA, you specified a user for the connection to the source database. SAP HANA passes the SQL statements on to this user. Make sure that this user has sufficient authorizations in the relevant schemas and tables in the source database.

As mentioned, earlier versions of SDA had some limitations, most notably lacking the ability to modify any data in virtual tables. Later versions have made considerable progress with these capabilities, and we recommend that you familiarize yourself with all available documentation on SDA prior to installing and using it.

SAP has stated that they plan future innovations for SDA that will allow for:

- Kerberos-constrained delegation for Hadoop
- Support for mass data movement
- Additional support for conversion of SDA adapters to SAP HANA smart data integration (SDI) adapters
- Metadata sync for schema change for remote tables
- XB support
- Further enhancements in caching capabilities
- Data synchronization from bottom up and top down
- Ability to pull hierarchical data directly into SAP HANA and perform operations on it

- Virtual tenant database in SAP HANA to consolidate applications into a single SAP HANA system without the need to move data

- Capability to virtualize a database object into a cloud extension

- Seamless administration of SDI adapters in SDA

You can see from these planned innovations and future direction that SAP has a long and rich future planned for SDA.

For more information, refer to SAP Notes 1868702 and 1868209. You will also find key pieces of information in the *SAP HANA Administration Guide* and the *SAP HANA Security Guide*, both available and updated from SAP.

2.2.4 SAP HANA Vora and Hadoop

No conversation about big data is complete without discussing *Hadoop*, which is a topic that comes up more and more as clients become more comfortable with the concept (and reality) of SAP HANA. Hadoop performs integration and consolidation of structured and unstructured big data, which can then be seamlessly integrated within SAP HANA via SAP IQ, SAP Data Services, or R queries to build analytic scenarios. Many organizations have existing Hadoop strategies or solutions and want to determine whether SAP HANA complements or competes with those strategies.

If you are not familiar with Hadoop, here is a quick primer. Hadoop was developed to address the need to process enormous amounts of data that was always changing, such as web data. In the simplest terms, Hadoop is an integration technology for big data that spreads data out over clusters. You then push that data into applications so you can work with it. And, although able to store and access significant amounts of data, Hadoop is not ideally suited for the fast, drilldown, slice-and-dice demands of today's business requirements.

SAP has worked to make Hadoop data available in its real-time analytics since 2012, but with the introduction of SAP HANA Vora, they have taken a significant leap forward. Running on-premise or on the cloud, SAP HANA Vora is an in-memory query engine that plugs into the Apache Spark framework and is designed to work with any distributed file system (not just Hadoop).

The key benefits and features of SAP HANA Vora are as follows:

- Drilldowns on Hadoop Distributed File System (HDFS)

- Mashup API enhancements

▸ Compiled queries

▸ SAP HANA-Spark Adapter

▸ Unified landscape

▸ Open programming

SAP HANA Vora can be used to extend your SAP HANA platform, allowing you to keep appropriate data on Hadoop servers. You can also use this extendibility as part of your data tiering with rules that set data temperature management, designating data between SAP HANA in-memory servers, dynamic tiering, and Hadoop. All this data will be available for your analytics. SAP HANA Vora allows social, Internet of Things (IoT), and cloud-based source data to be understood in the context of core enterprise data to reveal business-coherent insights in real time. Figure 2.7 shows a solution diagram of the SAP HANA Vora engine.

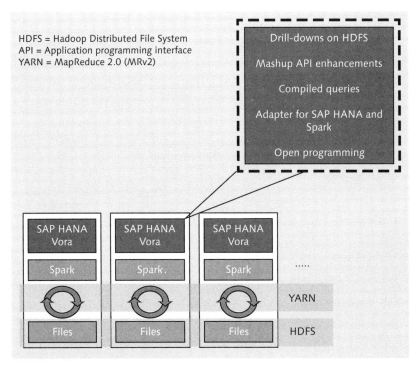

Figure 2.7 SAP HANA Vora Engine

SAP HANA Vora can be used as a standalone application as it is a completely new and different code base than SAP HANA. In other words, you do not have to have

SAP HANA in order to run or use SAP HANA Vora, but you certainly can use it in conjunction with SAP HANA. As a result, your data scientists and analysts who are familiar and comfortable with the Apache Spark framework and its programming tools can continue to use this environment and work with the tools they are used to.

When you think about how SAP HANA Vora might be used in your organization, some good use cases come to mind. Think about being able to being able to work in real time with access to *all* of your data—the data in SAP and the data outside SAP. You can react quickly with newer, more informed insights drawn from all of that data. You can create precision marketing campaigns factoring in lessons from your customers' postings on social media and other forums. Think of fraud detection scenarios or risk mitigation. With SAP HANA Vora, you can imagine virtual plants and facilities with complex simulations.

With SAP HANA Vora now generally available, its use cases will be limited only by the imagination of the SAP community—just as the early SAP HANA adopters created use cases and scenarios that were never imagined by the developers who created the tool.

Big data and in-memory applications are foundational reasons for SAP introducing and continuing to expand SAP HANA's capabilities. With this in mind, let's now look at the ways your organization may implement SAP HANA and how it can add the benefits of big data and in-memory computing to your organizations.

2.3   SAP HANA for Non-SAP Use Cases

Let's now delve into conversations about how you can implement SAP HANA at your organization and the different purposes it can serve. There are two basic use cases for SAP HANA in the non-SAP world. You will either use SAP HANA as a platform for an analytics solution or as the platform for a transaction processing system. Those use cases are similar in that both will be sitting completely outside your existing (or future) SAP environments and will require additional tools. But, in both cases, you will harnessing the speed and power of this in-memory database that engages so well with big data requirements. So let's look at each.

2.3.1   SAP HANA for Non-SAP Analytics

The first use case for SAP HANA implementations we will discuss is as a data warehouse for analytics, which can be implemented either on an organization's enterprise data warehouse or as a *sidecar* to augment existing analytic or reporting requirements. (Alternatively, SAP HANA can be the *only* analytics/reporting environment for the organization, but for our purposes, let's focus on its potential use with other non-SAP systems.) The data warehouse implementation of SAP HANA for analytics does *not* involve SAP BW nor any other SAP products or systems—just SAP HANA.

Earlier, we described SAP HANA as fundamentally a database and an enabler of solutions. In this implementation of the product, though, SAP HANA becomes more. SAP HANA incorporates an entire set of components and tasks: hardware, the SAP HANA database, the specific software components that you'll be required to implement, the modeling studio, your BI tools, and the administration of SAP HANA.

However, SAP HANA is not a fully contained plug-and-play solution. (In fact, SAP HANA is not plug and play in any scenario.) When you purchase this implementation of SAP HANA, you get the following:

▸ SAP HANA Studio

▸ SAP Host Agent 7.2

▸ SAPCAR 7.10

▸ SAP (Sybase) Replication Server (RS) 16

▸ SAP HANA Load Controller (LC) 1.00

▸ SAP Landscape Transformation 1—SHC for ABA

You can't implement this set of technologies as is because you still need hardware, a BI tool (unless you intend to access data via Microsoft Excel), and a data integration tool. Your source systems (the systems where the data comes from) for your SAP HANA databases are not required to be SAP environments, but the implications of your choice of source system will determine which data loading tool you can work with and your options for those tools.

The good news and the bad news about the data warehouse implementation of SAP HANA for analytics is that you build it from scratch. In other words, it offers you more freedom and flexibility but also comes with additional work. You have to design and build how the data gets loaded; the limited data model; the users, security, and authorizations; the interface to the BI solution (that you must install and implement); and the reporting and analytic layer.

Although this might sound daunting, you'll reap the following benefits in the end:

- Reporting solutions that you could never before develop with your SAP tools
- Real-time (or very near real-time) visibility to massive amounts of highly detailed data
- Billions of rows of information at your fingertips
- Billions of rows of operational-level, highly detailed SAP and/or non-SAP transaction data accessible in seconds
- Billions of rows of non-SAP data accessible at your fingertips
- Reporting or analytic solutions that take a massive amount of computing power or manual data aggregation
- Levels of insight available within seconds of an event, so that you can react, predict, and ultimately influence the behaviors of your employees, vendors, and customers by understanding how they act and react

As you can see, even with the limitations of using SAP HANA as a data warehouse, the potential benefits and new capabilities in analytics and reporting alone make it worth the effort!

Remember that the intent of the data warehouse implementation of SAP HANA for analytics is to build new, large-volume in-memory databases and then create a corresponding data model and set of reporting and analytic capabilities. This implementation of SAP HANA is not dependent on the SAP BW constructs that you may or may not already have in place.

Table 2.2 lists some things to consider when estimating the effort for an implementation of SAP HANA as a data warehouse.

Driver	Key Consideration
Use case selection	SAP business process or non-SAP data need
Data acquisition	ETL tool/process selection and configuration using SLT, SAP (Sybase) Replication Server (RS) or SAP Data Services

Table 2.2 Considerations for SAP HANA as a Data Warehouse

Driver	Key Consideration
Enterprise data warehouse (EDW) impacts	Re-engineering of any existing EDW solutions or manual processes
Access/user interaction	SAP BusinessObjects BI (or other BI tool) integration or impacts (universes, dashboards, SAP BusinessObjects Explorer data, reports)
Data modeling	SAP HANA modeling objects (attribute, analytical, and calculation views)
Security	SAP HANA security model design
Landscape	SAP HANA sizing and landscape install
Operations	Disaster recovery, backup, and availability

Table 2.2 Considerations for SAP HANA as a Data Warehouse (Cont.)

As you consider the scope and effort for your SAP HANA implementation, you will be able to build a staffing model and timeline for the implementation. Data warehouse SAP HANA implementations can take from a few weeks to a few months. The setup and installation of the system itself—the empty database—requires a week or less, including knowledge transfer time to your administration resources. The rest of the effort is in defining and building the solution and supporting components.

An organization can build and test a simple SAP HANA solution (not to be confused with the SAP product SAP S/4HANA Finance, which we'll discuss in Section 2.6 and Chapter 5) in a matter of a few weeks if all of the right pieces are in place at the outset to make the data readily available. In other words, the data should be harmonized, and the reports and/or analytics should be well defined and understood.

A "Simple" SAP HANA Solution

A "simple" SAP HANA solution validates and tests system performance and overall concepts, acting more as a pilot program than a proof of concept. The difference is that a pilot is an actual production solution—albeit a small one or one with a single, highly targeted use case or goal. These solutions can be used to "validate" the SAP HANA capabilities to the organization and the user community and can then be leveraged as a foundation to build upon.

Of course, if you need a larger, more complex initial SAP HANA project, you can certainly plan for a longer project. A complex pilot project looking at credit card transactions at a large financial institution, for example, might take three months.

Regardless of whether your project is a small pilot or a large, complex program, you should engage or bring in experienced SAP HANA experts to assist or work with your internal team. Although building an SAP HANA solution in many ways mirrors building a traditional (non-SAP) BI solution, this *is* a new technology with new tools and capabilities for you to work with.

Next, we'll discuss both the technical and skill requirements for a company considering implementing SAP HANA as a data warehouse. We'll conclude the section with a high-level overview of what a project plan involves and some considerations for choosing this SAP HANA implementation option.

Technical Requirements

Implementing SAP HANA as a data warehouse requires building from scratch. The necessary architecture is shown in Figure 2.8.

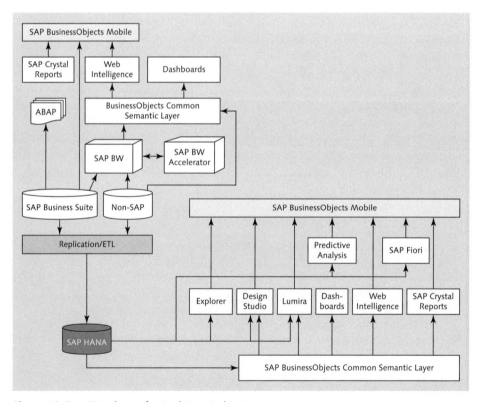

Figure 2.8 Data Warehouse for Analytics: Architecture

This architecture enables you to create new reporting and analytic solutions for your transaction data. However, it also allows you to take an additional data set from those transaction systems that is timelier, more detailed, and with more volume and bring it into the SAP HANA database.

The SAP HANA database requires specific hardware and the operating systems necessary for that hardware, a list of which is available from SAP.

> **Note**
>
> As of April 2016, almost 700 different hardware options, from more than a dozen different vendors, are available. SAP maintains a full list of certified hardware via the SAP HANA Hardware Directory at the following location: *www.sap.com* • PARTNER • SAP PARTNER HARDWARE CERTIFIED FOR SAP HANA.

With the hardware, you also must acquire or develop the necessary operational support to cover things such as disaster recovery, high-availability preparation, SAP HANA system administration support, rack and stack of the SAP HANA box itself, and so on.

You'll also have to get the necessary information into SAP HANA in the first place. Planning an SAP HANA implementation is covered in Chapter 6, but let's start with a brief overview here. You'll primarily use the SAP Landscape Transformation (SLT) tool for loading SAP ERP data, although as of the SP 4 version of the tool, you can also use it for non-SAP data. (You won't get the same real-time data loading that you can get from SAP ERP data, but you can get near real time if you configure it appropriately.) Your other choice for loading non-SAP or non-SAP BW data is to use SAP Data Services, which is the ETL tool that SAP gained through its acquisition of BusinessObjects. SAP Data Services will allow you to access data sets from non-SAP and non-SAP BW environments and bring them into your SAP HANA environment. You will again not get the real-time data movement that you can get from the SAP ERP system, but you can get close to real time by configuring it appropriately.

You'll also need to purchase, install, and implement a BI tool. Remember not to confuse SAP HANA with a BI tool. SAP HANA is a *database* for BI tools. The easiest tool to integrate into your SAP HANA-based solution is the SAP BusinessObjects BI suite of tools because it's part of SAP. An access point for data from Microsoft Excel is also available.

Many businesses have asked whether it's possible to use noncertified BI tools on top of their SAP HANA analytic environments. Opinions vary on this subject. Objectively, access points into SAP HANA for Excel, multidimensional expressions (MDX), or SQL are available, which implies that there are ways to get data out of SAP HANA and into other tools. However, what you need to test is whether you'll get the benefits and capabilities of SAP HANA—the power and the speed—if you are accessing the data via these other connectors and not via the native SAP interface points. For third-party tools on top of an SAP HANA database for analytic or transactional purposes, SAP has committed to working with vendors to enable and certify the use of such products. However, little anecdotal information is available about what really works and to what degree. This information will develop over time as customers demand extensions of SAP HANA's capabilities into their existing toolsets.

Skill Requirements

When implementing SAP HANA as a data warehouse, your BI and SAP BW developers will probably understand the general concepts but may not be familiar with the particular tools that SAP HANA employs or the nuances of the SAP HANA solution. With appropriate training and experience, however, these resources will quickly pick up the SAP HANA skills required. All of your traditional data warehousing and BI skills (SAP and non-SAP) will be useful with SAP HANA. This skill development is not that different from taking your SAP BI developers and shifting them over to building custom data warehouses, for instance. The concepts remain—the tools are what change.

Whether your existing hardware administrators and SAP Basis team can assume SAP HANA activities or whether you need an entire full-time employee (FTE) depends on several factors, but you do have options. Figure 2.9 shows some of the skills you may need depending on the size and scope of your implementation.

> **Note**
>
> See Chapter 6 for additional information on the individual job roles in an SAP HANA implementation.

Let's look at each category listed for the types of skills that you'll need and see how they come into play when using SAP HANA as a data warehouse.

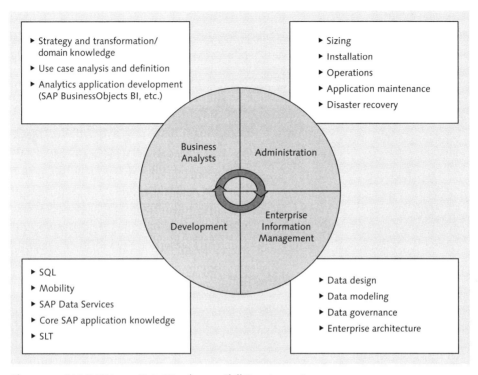

Figure 2.9 SAP HANA as a Data Warehouse: Skill Requirements

Administration

First, you'll need what you traditionally think of as administration skills, which cover your infrastructure and operational needs and the rack and stack of the SAP HANA box itself. You'll need someone to install the SAP HANA software and the operating and file systems on the SAP HANA box. You can probably negotiate these services from the hardware vendor from whom you purchased the SAP HANA box.

You'll also need to arrange and manage the remote function call (RFC) connections to the source system(s) and the BI tool(s). You'll need someone to look at disaster recovery, ensure high availability, and provide overall application maintenance. In this category, you should include someone to set up and manage user access and accounts as well as security and authorizations.

If you're looking at enabling these solutions for mobile applications, you'll also need people who understand mobile applications and architecture. Advanced use cases for SAP HANA leverage its power and data accessibility for mobile-enabled solutions.

Business Analysts

Your business analysts will determine the base use case and business need that drive the SAP HANA implementation. They may identify reporting or analytic needs that are not currently addressed or that take so much time and effort that they are unmanageable in their current state.

Your use cases will likely be driven by your business analysts initially. If IT is trying to drive this solution, then the use cases will have to be verified and fully mapped out with your business analysts and users who will work with the team to determine the following needs and requirements:

- Source systems
- Data needs
- Data transformations
- Data relationships
- Calculations
- Key performance indicators (KPIs)
- Reports
- Presentation layer
- Security and user access

Your business analysts will also uncover transformational opportunities now that you have this in-memory solution in place. *Transformational opportunities* are completely new insights and perspectives into your business; they answer to the kinds of questions that previously you couldn't even think of asking. Your business analysts will also drive the final visualization of the solution, that is, what the user experience (UX) needs to be. Is this a dashboard? What are the measures and metrics to be shown? What is the level of drilldown and supporting detail required?

If they are super users—that is, they traditionally do their own data manipulation—you may also be required to get this community trained on the modeling tools of SAP HANA. If your users chafed at other data modeling tools because they felt limited, they should be trained on SAP HANA. For your nontechnical users, SAP HANA training might be overkill; instead of training them on modeling capabilities, just focus on the reporting aspects.

You'll also want to train this user audience on the BI tools you'll be attaching to the SAP HANA environment. You'll develop an initial set of reports as part of the core implementation, but the true power of this solution will be in enabling the on-demand analytics that this audience will need.

Enterprise Information Management

You'll also need enterprise information management (EIM) skills—traditionally referred to as ETL (extract, transform, and load) skills—for getting data into SAP HANA. You have a few options for how to do this.

The first is using the SAP Landscape Transformation (SLT) Replication Server. SLT is the engine that will move your data from the transaction systems into the SAP HANA database. If you're planning to extract SAP ERP transactional data into SAP HANA, SLT capabilities will give you that real-time or near real-time data visibility. Before SP 4, SLT would only work for SAP ERP transaction system data but now can be used for non-SAP data as well.

If you are using SLT, you'll need people to identify the relevant data tables and fields within the SAP transaction system, which may require the skills of your core SAP ERP developers and configuration experts. They will configure the source system for the RFC connection to SAP HANA and make sure the data has a place to go within the SAP HANA system. If you aren't using the SLT capabilities because you are bringing in non-SAP data, you'll likely be using a traditional ETL approach and a tool such as SAP Data Services.

In any case, you'll need the services and skills of a data architect to make sure that you have a full understanding of all of the data, data sources, data fields, and overall enterprise data structure that you want to bring into SAP HANA. Your data architect will be working closely with an overall SAP HANA architect. This SAP HANA architect will look at the big picture of the entire solution that will be SAP HANA-enabled and developed. Don't forget that SAP HANA is a database, so while you're putting the data in memory, you still need a level of structure that requires modeling. While you need to do some work here, SAP HANA's in-memory database means less work for you than if you used a persistent data model (such as SAP BW). Your SAP HANA architect will account for all aspects of the use case, including potential future uses, and help build out the right solution for you. Your SAP HANA architect should also be involved in any aspects of ETL design and overall data design.

Development

You'll then need a BI developer who is highly skilled in whichever BI tool you have attached to your SAP HANA system. This person will build the user experience and interfaces for your general user community. This person will work closely with the mobile architects to make sure there are appropriate versions and levels of information for your mobile user community. Just because you *can* query a billion rows doesn't mean you should, and you need to look at the user experience and integrate that into the overall solution. You must align what you *can* do with what you *should* do and then finally decide what you *will* do when it comes to SAP HANA-enabled solutions.

All of this may sound intimidating, but it shouldn't be. You would bring all of these skills into the design and development of a traditional data warehouse and BI solution, that is, a non-SAP solution. If you have a traditional, non-SAP enterprise data warehouse in your organization, you likely have many of these core skills within your organization already. However, realize that your traditional EDW people will understand the *concepts* that need to be designed and deployed but will not understand the *technology* that SAP HANA employs and will likely not have practical experience in designing and building an in-memory solution. So, although you'll have some of what you need from within your SAP and EDW teams, they will need training on how to transition those skills into this technology. A paradigm shift will also have to take place concerning what a BI solution should deliver and how to design the data model when the data is not persistent but in memory only.

Project Plan Steps

At a very high level, the steps in implementing SAP HANA as a data warehouse are as follows:

1. Work with your hardware vendor to determine the amount of hardware you need and, of course, work with SAP to secure the appropriate licenses for SAP HANA.

2. Determine which BI tool you will implement and then secure licenses for that solution.

3. Your administration team installs the software and the build and then tests that the necessary RFC connections are in place. The team begins setting up the appropriate operational support processes for disaster recovery, high availability, and so on.

4. Identify the necessary data feeds and their corresponding source systems. Work with the business analysts to identify the necessary data and supporting transformations necessary. Use an SLT connection for each source system—if

you are on a compatible version of SAP HANA—or use SLT for SAP ERP data and SAP Data Services for non-SAP data. (For more technical information about data provisioning for SAP HANA, see Chapter 9.)

5. Work with your data modelers to build the appropriate data model using the SAP HANA tools and work with your ETL developers to match the ETL requirements to the necessary data model and transformation requirements. (For more technical information about data modeling, see Chapter 8.)

6. Work with the business analysts and the overall user community to determine what the user experience and interface should look like. Start working with your report developers to build the required BI interface—making sure that your reports cascade (allow for drilldown) as required.

7. Your support team builds the appropriate user accounts and profiles and assigns security and authorizations.

8. After everything is tested and good to go, release the solution to users.

Of course, these steps have been greatly simplified, and reality is *not* that simple. But these are the high-level, basic steps involved in deploying SAP HANA as a data warehouse. To put the development cycle into a flow that many experienced SAP users are accustomed to, Table 2.3 shows the phases of a typical project and some key activities from lessons learned.

Strategize	Design	Build	Run
▸ Determine how SAP HANA delivers the proposed value. Identify corresponding uses cases, KPIs, and calculations.	▸ Select and understand the SAP ERP tables you need.	▸ Re-create table relationships in SAP HANA.	▸ Design new back-up procedures for in-memory applications and data.
▸ Make sure that the use case and analytics strategy are compatible.	▸ Determine whether you need to address any master data issues.	▸ Model the master data and join conditions.	▸ Understand how much reload time is required for restoring mission-critical data after failure.
▸ Identify what role an SAP HANA adoption will play, including the potential impacts.	▸ Create analysis authorizations to restrict different levels of users.	▸ Load SAP ERP tables into SAP HANA.	▸ Develop business alternative procedures to be run during downtime.
		▸ Use a suitable tool such as Excel or a web tool to decide how to build above the SAP HANA layer.	▸ Develop high-availability and disaster recovery capabilities.

Table 2.3 Project Phases for Implementing SAP HANA as a Data Warehouse

Choosing SAP HANA as a Standalone Analytics Solution

The use case and benefits of working with SAP HANA for your non-SAP analytics applications should be readily apparent by now. You can harness the power of SAP HANA while not being constrained by the structure of an SAP BW data model.

You get to build from scratch—a custom build exactly matching your wants and needs. You design your ETL requirements, your data movements, your data model, your transformations, and your reporting layer. For some, this freedom is a good thing—those who prefer a "best of breed" approach by picking the best of each tool independently. However, many people prefer a "best of integration" approach and want to work with the most cohesive team; these people prefer a package of tools that are already guaranteed to work together well.

If you choose SAP HANA as a standalone analytics solution (with no SAP BW or SAP BI connection), the disadvantage is that you lose some of the capabilities associated with SAP BW, such as business content, which is a library of predelivered SAP BW solutions (data sources, ETL logic, cubes, reports, queries, and more) that are part of the SAP BW licensing scheme. The Business Content repository, available at *http://help.sap.com/bicontent/*, consists of hundreds of predefined solutions from SAP that customers can use in part or in whole. With SAP HANA, you can decide, for example, that you want to use *just* the premapped and translated SAP BW extractors to get data out of your SAP ERP system—and avoid transparent tables to decode the logic—and build your own cubes, queries, and reports. Or you may decide to use the SAP BW extractors and cubes and then modify the cubes to suit your own data requirements to build your own queries and reports. And, as another option, you can also decide to use the Business Content solution—including the reports—for standard, nondifferentiating business processes (such as your accounts receivable analysis, for example) completely as they are delivered. This library can be a tremendous value to organizations who have spent time and money decoding the often confusing logic of SAP core tables and creating clean data mappings. If you are bringing SAP transaction data into this new SAP HANA analytics environment, these data extractors may be valuable to you. However, if you are working with only non-SAP data, then these have little value.

As you can see, there are decisions to be made with this implementation of the SAP HANA database. If you're looking at SAP HANA purely—or primarily—to speed up your SAP BW solution, then this isn't necessarily the right version of SAP HANA for you. If you're looking to address reporting or analytics problems outside of your SAP BW system—involving tons of data or for reporting in real time against your operational SAP transaction data—then it may be just what you need.

2.3.2 SAP HANA for Non-SAP Applications

Another option for SAP HANA is as a standalone (not attached to your core SAP systems) engine for transaction processing or as a transaction system with embedded analytics.

Remember SAP HANA is a database at heart, and as such, you can use it as a foundation for your transaction systems as well as for the analytics systems we discussed earlier. Essentially, new applications can be built on the SAP HANA platform to address business needs that were previously not feasible.

For example, let's say you are in charge of a fan experience for a globally recognized, major sporting event or tournament. You want to expand on the fan experience—for those in attendance as well as those watching on TV or streaming it. You want to be able to capture the emotion of the fans, capture their commentary as they cheer on or bemoan their teams. You want to engage the fans with interactive experiences. You want to help users find the online store where they can purchase goods supporting their teams or where you can quickly put products up for sale involving whatever trend, saying, or meme is personifying this event. Maybe you want to create a trivia game that people can play against anyone else in the world—and earn points that can be redeemed for tickets or merchandise in your store. You would want to make this as real time an experience as possible—for those at the event as well as those watching from elsewhere.

How would you build something like that? What tools would you need? A non-SAP application of SAP HANA might be a great fit in this case. Think about the pieces: real time, structured and unstructured data, inputs from multiple sources, and vast amounts of information to capture and work with.

Building this capability or application with an SAP HANA backbone involves pretty much the same steps as it would to build a non-SAP HANA analytic environment.

You will need to do all of your design work, of course, from the fan experience to the user interface to the ETL and data mapping. You would also have to determine where the many sources of data would be coming from and how you will get them (e.g., Facebook or Instagram). Perhaps you want to create a dedicated app for the event itself. Which tools will you select for each of these components? What algorithms do you need to create? What are you trying to learn with all of these inputs? What behavior do you want to drive?

Nearly every business process today that requires high volumes of data has a degree of analytics either directly built into it or derived from it. Of course, applications that take and process thousands of sales orders in a day are still needed, but the data from those sales orders can then also be analyzed. Are those thousands of sales order placed today the right orders? Were sales targets met? If we didn't meet our targets, where did we fail? If we surpassed the target, why and how can we repeat that? Processing information and activity is only one part of the business equation; analyzing the results of those activities and applying this information to the goals of the business helps make the decisions about if, how, and where the business is moving.

If you are thinking this sounds just like building a BI application with an SAP HANA backbone, you are pretty much right. SAP HANA can certainly be used to be the engine of a high-volume, real-time application that captures disparate information from a multitude of sources, including those that have nothing to do with SAP.

Now, what skills will you need to build our example application? After design, you need to identify where the data inputs will be from and what tool(s) you will use to get that data into your system. You will need data mapping and data modeling to create relationships as well as hardware and security—all the same skills and tools that you would need to build any custom application.

With this all mapped out, then you would build your custom application to suit your needs exactly. With SAP HANA as the database, you'll have an engine to handle the heavy lifting of analysis and the sheer volume of data that you'll be working with.

There is no rulebook on what can and can't be built with SAP HANA, whether inside or outside the core framework of SAP systems. You can create route optimization applications or applications that help manage safety in large cities. Applications to maximize the fan experience at sporting events really have been created. Preventative maintenance applications are being built. Technical barriers limiting what can be done are being lifted, and organizations are limited only by their imaginations and the creativity of their teams.

2.4   SAP BW on SAP HANA

SAP BW on SAP HANA was the first significant step in SAP's goal of being a major player in the database space and of having its transaction systems running on an SAP HANA database in short order. Running SAP BW on SAP HANA allows you to leverage what SAP has dubbed the massive parallel processing (MPP) capabilities of SAP HANA to query and report against those massive SAP BW cubes and get results in seconds (or less). Because SAP HANA is much faster than regular relational databases such as Oracle or Microsoft SQL Server, the data warehouse performs much faster, and your reports will run much faster. SAP BW on SAP HANA is really the beginning of SAP's long-term direction: using SAP HANA as the underlying database for existing solutions.

If you choose an SAP BW on SAP HANA implementation, there are three possible ways to do it:

1. Migrate your entire SAP BW system to SAP HANA.

2. Set up a new SAP BW system (with an SAP HANA database) alongside your existing SAP BW system and use that new SAP BW environment for particularly challenging or new requirements, which is known as a *side-by-side* or *sidecar* installation. A sidecar installation allows you to keep your standard reporting that has been tested and is running fine without needing to change everything over. You can design new solutions in the new SAP BW system and move other things over when you have the time, budget, or need.

3. Implement an SAP BW system for the first time and then run SAP HANA for it. This implementation offers all of the advantages of SAP BW without the less-than-elegant data modeling that has been required in the past to address performance with larger SAP BW solutions.

> **Note**
>
> We provide more technical details about planning an SAP BW on SAP HANA implementation in Chapter 6.

If you already have SAP BW, you can use all of the work you've already built into your solution. You don't need to do any complex data modeling. (However, you'll also inherit all of the designs you built into your SAP BW solution, which may not always be ideal.)

One of the advantages of SAP BW on SAP HANA is faster data loads (Figure 2.10). As of SAP BW 7.4, data activations and data transformations are done in memory, which typically results in data load performance improvements in the 30%–50% range (sometimes even faster). With SAP BW 7.3 on SAP HANA, data load benefits are restricted primarily to data activation. Since the data transformation occurs in memory in SAP BW 7.4, we highly recommend using this version when moving to SAP HANA.

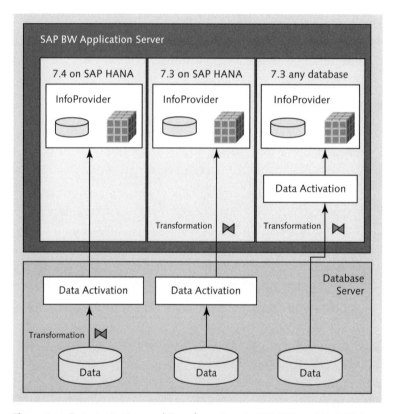

Figure 2.10 Data Activations and Transformations in SAP BW on SAP HANA

SAP BW 7.4 on SAP HANA also gives you the capability of loading data directly using operational data provisioning (ODP) functionality and operational delta queues. Using these functionalities allows you to quickly create data loads that can be executed periodically (e.g., every 20 minutes) or loaded synchronously as records are created in the transaction system. The result is a real-time data warehouse with SAP BW on SAP HANA (Figure 2.11).

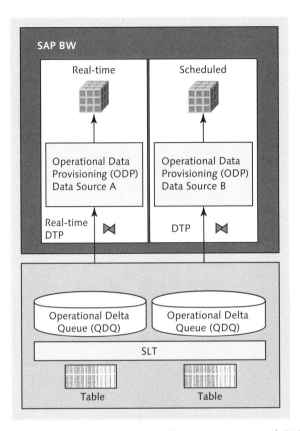

Figure 2.11 Real-Time Operational Data Provisioning with SAP BW 7.4 on SAP HANA

For most companies, dramatically faster query performance is really the key business case to move SAP BW to SAP HANA. Consider a real-life example: After moving a 38 TB SAP BW system to SAP HANA, a large oil and gas company benchmarked their 98 most-used SAP BW queries to see how much faster the new system was relative to their old Oracle 11g database. They found that, while the average performance was 16.6 times faster, some queries were over 300 times faster. This performance improvement was particularly true for queries that did high volumes of subtotals and had complex calculations.

This company also found that SAP HANA was almost three times faster than the older SAP Business Warehouse Accelerator (SAP BW Accelerator) technology. This performance improvement was mainly due to the fact that many online analytical processing (OLAP) functions were done in memory, while SAP BW Accelerator does these calculations in application servers. By pushing as much of the application logic to the database server as possible, SAP HANA reduced data transfers to the application server (Figure 2.12). This trend started in SAP BW 7.3 with RKFs, exception aggregation, and handling of hierarchies. In SAP BW 7.4 SP 6, we see even more OLAP functionalities moving to the database, including exception aggregations of formulas, advanced hierarchy handling, and the treatment of noncumulative key figures at the database server level.

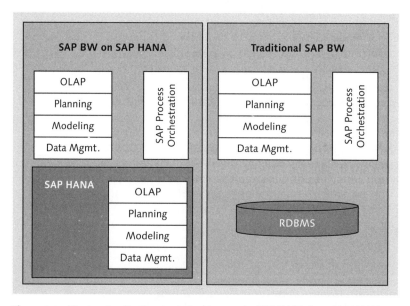

Figure 2.12 *Moving Application Logic to Memory in SAP BW 7.4 on SAP HANA*

To take full advantage of the power of SAP HANA, queries leverage the internal SAP HANA aggregation engine for summarizations and subtotaling. Therefore, executing queries on SAP BW isn't merely a question of faster data read times; the query logic is also executed much more quickly.

In the broadest terms, SAP HANA provides the following improvements:

▶ **Better report performance**
Because you are now running on an in-memory database, your database reads for queries will be much faster than on your existing Oracle or DB2 systems. Anecdotal results from early adopters show results that are 10 to 1,000 times faster for reports. You will, however, still depend on the latency of the data getting into your SAP BW environment from your transaction system(s). If it takes

8–10 days to move data around your environments before it is ready to be loaded into SAP BW, SAP HANA cannot change that.

▶ **Faster data loads**
Some customers show massive improvements (loads that once took 3 hours are now running in 3 minutes). These faster data loads are key to getting your data into your SAP BW system—it still has to work its way through your business processes and be deemed ready to be loaded, which is a process issue, not a technology issue.

▶ **Smaller database**
Databases converted to SAP HANA compress data on average 4 times; however, some customers have seen results up to 10 times. You'll gain benefits, not only from the compression algorithms, but also by being able to reduce the overall database by removing unnecessary objects from your data model.

▶ **Reduced cost of development**
Developers can work much faster in SAP HANA (because there is less to design and build), so they are much more productive, which reduces the cost of development.

▶ **Highly detailed data**
Because SAP HANA can store data at the lowest levels of granularity without the need for aggregation, you can bring over, store, and report on any level of detail or drilldown into as much detail as you want.

▶ **Transformational opportunities**
With the capabilities of SAP HANA and the ability to bring in and report against massive amounts of data, you can take a new view of your SAP BW system as a tool to address large and complex reporting solutions that bring together both SAP and non-SAP data.

▶ **Agility**
With the ability to create leaner, crisper data models and to get rid of the complex physical modeling required to address performance, you can push out new solutions faster.

▶ **Adoption**
Many times, the barrier to SAP BW adoption centers on the (perceived) usability and responsiveness of SAP BW systems. A faster system that has more data will go a long way to bridging those adoption issues because you'll be able to be more responsive to the user requirements, providing users with a faster, more effective system.

If you already have SAP BW, moving to SAP HANA will also give you the opportunity to assess your existing SAP BW data model and identify the (many) opportunities to flatten it out. Think about a traditional SAP BW system and database scenario where you need to bring in 5 years of highly detailed sales data for a complex analysis of pricing and customer buying trends. With SAP BW, you would have started with (a series of) DSOs. You would then aggregate your data into at least one layer of InfoCubes but would probably have decided that, for performance reasons, you were going to break up that one big cube into five smaller cubes—one for each of the 5 years of data you are looking at. And, then, for the current year cube and to accommodate future data, you likely would have partitioned the fact table for additional performance gains. And, of course, you would have had to put a MultiProvider on top of all of those cubes and then build aggregates. You might have even had to build a series of layers of cubes as you aggregated more and more for each level to get to a point where the fact table sizes were reasonable for performance. Stacking layers of data-aggregating cubes is exhausting work and results in overly complicated data structures.

With SAP BW on SAP HANA, you don't have to do all that. You simply bring in all of that detailed data and set up the simple data model that is required. In addition, you have the opportunity to look at your entire SAP BW model and decide what you don't need any more. What did you build only to address the performance needs of your user communities? For years, we've advocated that SAP BW could address your reporting needs, that it wasn't limited by any size constraints, and that it was all in how you modeled the system and what you used for tools (aggregates, precalculations, etc.). Now you have the opportunity to challenge that thought process and create a leaner model.

The implication of this, however, is that you have to deconstruct and rebuild a great deal of your SAP BW system, so you'll need to determine if you have the time, budget, and appetite for that. You don't have to decide to do this all at once or even now. You can make these changes as changes to your requirements demand, or as you feel like it. But you won't gain all of the potential speed and performance advantages until you optimize your model. Many real-world SAP BW installations have been in place for 10 years or more. These systems are mature in terms of the solutions they offer to their user base and also in the level of complexity—or creativity—that has been deployed in their designs. Customers who were the *really* early adopters of SAP BW technology had to get very creative with designing their data models to allow for the amount, volume, and granularity required for their solutions. As these systems have grown and the database has grown along with them, the cubes have, in many cases, reached hundreds of millions of rows each. The standard SAP BW technology struggled with processing a query against hundreds of millions of rows of data in a timely manner. Clients were required to break up the cubes into a series of small(er) cubes that were tied together via MultiProviders. They had to build complex aggregates that added time to data loading and updating. They looked at hardware-based solutions and added SAP BW Accelerator to their landscape. All of these approaches helped make large SAP BW systems more accessible and more responsive. But the overhead—in resources, skills, and hardware—can also be onerous.

Existing SAP BW customers can use SAP HANA to take advantage of all its benefits *and* leverage the significant investments they have already made in their SAP BW solutions. These customers want to take advantage of SAP HANA to run SAP BW faster—run their thousands of SAP BW reports and queries faster—and then start building new and more advanced applications knowing that this new capability will allow them to build faster, leaner solutions.

Now that you've had a crash course in SAP BW on SAP HANA, let's take a look at the technical and skill requirements for this type of implementation. As before, we'll conclude with a high-level overview of what a project plan would look like.

2.4.1 Technical Requirements

The implementation architecture of SAP BW on SAP HANA is shown in Figure 2.13.

This architecture differs from the implementation of SAP HANA as a data warehouse in that SAP HANA is now directly attached to SAP BW. As a result, SAP HANA is your database, not a separate instance. You aren't required to build new ETL layers or design a data model from scratch. You can use your existing SAP BW models and structures.

Those are all good things, but there's one big catch: this level of SAP HANA has version requirements. Because you are using SAP HANA as a database for your SAP BW system, that SAP BW system must be at a certain version and level. You must be on at least SAP BW 7.3 (Unicode) with SAP BusinessObjects BI 4.0 (if you are using the SAP BusinessObjects BI toolset). When assessing how quickly, easily, and at what cost you can implement SAP BW on SAP HANA, the first thing you need to determine is whether you need a system upgrade.

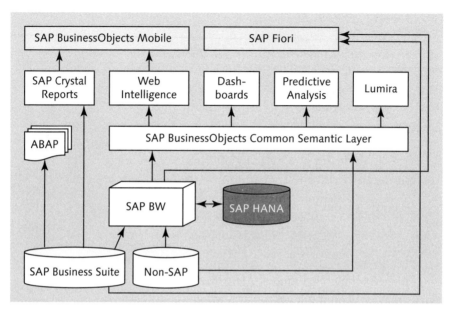

Figure 2.13 SAP BW on SAP HANA: Architecture

The next thing you need to look at whether the hardware for your existing SAP BW system is compatible with your new SAP HANA database. As with the data warehouse implementation of SAP HANA, you'll need hardware that can handle the needs and power of the SAP HANA database. The following components are in play:

▶ **Server**
SAP HANA runs on SUSE Linux Enterprise Server (SLES) as well as Red Hat. These large rack-mount systems can take up to 8 CPUs and 80 cores. You can also basically "stack" these on top of each other for your scale-out options. You can purchase this software on the Internet from the big vendors, but you may also be able to negotiate a deal with your regular hardware partner. Showcase systems that are 100 TB are available.

▶ **RAM**
A great deal of RAM is required and should be matched to the CPUs. Twenty cores allow 256 GB RAM, leading to a maximum of 1 TB of RAM with current CPUs.

▶ **Log storage**
The trick to quickly recovering an SAP HANA system that goes down—due to power loss, for example—is the ability to quickly restore via the logs.

▶ **Data storage**
  The requirement for data storage is 4x RAM. On all of the certified single-node configurations, this is cheap serial-attached SCSI (SAS) direct storage. You need this so you can power down the appliance and do backups, among other things. For multinode configurations, some form of shared storage is required—either a storage area network (SAN) or local storage replicated using, for example, IBM's GPFS (General Parallel File System).

Therefore, when you're looking at the hardware side of implementation costs and planning, you need to determine if your existing hardware will meet the preceding requirements. You'll also have to make sure your hardware is compatible with the server versions that SAP HANA requires, which means that you might have to look at a new series of hardware. If that is the case, the good news is that you'll need much less hardware than your current solution requires because of compression ratios. Your hardware vendor can help you decide how much of your existing hardware can be leveraged for this new solution. You'll also need to plan for racking and stacking the box, just like with the data warehouse implementation of SAP HANA. On average, this will take a couple days when you factor in knowledge transfer to your existing support team.

After you have SAP HANA as your database, you'll likely want to change a few things about your SAP BW system. You should first get rid of all of the aggregates on your cubes. Why? Aggregates on a traditional, non-SAP HANA BW system precalculated certain results so you would not have to spend the time during query and report processing to compile and calculate those results. Aggregates dealt with bad performance—or at least slow performance—particularly when your SAP BW cubes and data sets started to get very large. After you convert your SAP BW to an SAP HANA database, you'll no longer need those aggregates to precalculate to accommodate poor system performance. As far as SAP HANA is concerned, aggregates are a completely unnecessary overhead and add no value whatsoever. Getting rid of aggregates will also improve your data loading because you won't have to roll up your data to aggregates anymore.

Finally, you may wonder what you need to do with your SAP BW cubes after you implement SAP HANA. You don't have to do much, but you do need to convert your SAP BW cubes to SAP HANA cubes. This simple process allows the cubes to be stretched across the SAP HANA database in the new columnar format, which also reduces some of the overall size of the cubes themselves.

2.4.2   Skill Requirements

For the additional skills and components that come into play when looking at SAP BW on SAP HANA, *see* Figure 2.14.

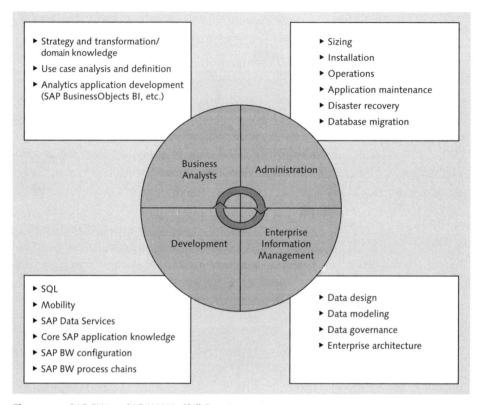

Figure 2.14 SAP BW on SAP HANA: Skill Requirements

The skills required are similar to the ones required for implementing SAP HANA as a data warehouse; however, there are a few new, specific skills worth discussing.

Administration

The first major new or different skill is that your team—or your implementation partner—needs to be skilled in performing database migrations. Your current SAP BW database must be migrated from its existing Oracle or DB2 over to the new SAP HANA database. You'll want to bring experienced resources to the team for this activity, although this may not be something that you need to specifically get your own people trained in because you likely won't need to perform this conversion often.

You'll also need all of the key operations supported for your new SAP BW system as you do for your existing SAP BW system. This time, however, your system administrators need to know how to manage the SAP HANA database. Your SAP Basis team needs to know how to manage SAP BW disaster recovery in an SAP HANA environment, including how to restore the system. The team needs to know their options for scaling the environment up and out as the system grows. The team will need to know how to troubleshoot the different data-loading capabilities and keep those remote function call (RFC) connections up and running.

The good news for your team is that they can use all of their existing skills for general SAP Basis system activities management. User management is still all contained within the SAP BW framework. User security and authorizations are still the same and are done in the SAP BW system itself.

Business Analysts

Your business analysts are likely already involved in the design and usage of your existing SAP BW solution. If they aren't, they should be. As with SAP HANA as a data warehouse, business analysts define and drive the requirements, assess the solution fit to the business needs, and drive innovation and change. They are searching for the transformational opportunities that this new, high-power solution can offer them and the organization as a whole.

If you are considering SAP BW for the first time and will be using it on top of SAP HANA, it's crucially important that you involve your business analysts and super user or power user communities to identify and gather all of the appropriate requirements. If you try to implement SAP BW on SAP HANA simply as an IT toolset, you won't be doing your organization any service—remember, the power of the solution is in satisfying business requirements. Your business analysts know exactly what is really going on within the business when it comes to the necessary steps to gather, transform, and compile the massive amounts of data necessary for their complex reporting and analytic solutions.

Enterprise Information Management

The enterprise information management (EIM) model and data components make up a huge component in an SAP BW on SAP HANA environment, as with any SAP

BW system. You are (potentially) bringing data into your SAP BW system from any number of sources, and the secret to success is ensuring that all these disparate kinds of data make sense to the SAP BW system. Your EIM team needs to consider the following questions and agree on the next steps when it comes to data:

- What data is coming in?
- How clean is that data?
- Is the data harmonized?
- Are the key data structures aligned?
- Will you encounter data inconsistencies with things such as order numbers, customer numbers, and so on?
- What is the governance plan to keep data clean?
- Who is allowed to create new measures, metrics, calculations, and KPIs?

This entire thought process needs to go into your solution, just as it does when designing a traditional SAP BW system. These considerations become all the more important when you are building this for SAP HANA because you are now going to be bringing in *billions* of rows of data—instead of "merely" millions of rows of data. More data means more opportunity for insight, but it also means more opportunity for error, confusion, and contradiction.

Development

For SAP BW on SAP HANA, you'll conceptually need the same skills that you always needed with SAP BW. You need people who understand the data sources, including how to get the data into SAP BW; how to manage it after it's in SAP BW; how to model the data; and how to organize it effectively. You need people to create and build the queries and calculations and, ultimately, the reports and user experience on the interface.

One thing that will be a bit different for SAP BW on SAP HANA—or one opportunity for things to be different—is that you can change your data model. You can flatten it out. Make sure that you have developers who can handle this process.

Basically, if you are considering SAP BW for the first time and plan to be using SAP HANA, or if you will be building a second instance of SAP BW for specific solutions, then your developers need to be able to look at data modeling requirements and skills quite differently from the "traditional" SAP BW modeling skills. Because they are using SAP HANA as the database, they will be able to design a thinner and leaner data model.

2.4.3 Project Plan Steps

At a very high level, the steps to build a project plan for SAP BW on SAP HANA are as follows (you'll see that these steps are similar to implementing SAP HANA as a data warehouse):

1. Work with your hardware vendor to determine if your existing hardware will be usable for an SAP HANA database and, of course, work with SAP to secure the appropriate licenses for SAP HANA:

   ► Work with your hardware partners and SAP to estimate your compressed database size to determine the amount of hardware necessary.

   ► Secure new hardware if necessary.

   ► If appropriate, look at reworking your SAP BW Accelerator hardware or find alternate uses.

2. Check your SAP BW and SAP BusinessObjects BI versions to make sure they are at the appropriate levels required for SAP HANA. Upgrade if necessary.

3. Migrate the SAP BW database to SAP HANA.

4. Check your data sources and connections. Look to see what you might be able to migrate to SLT connections. (However, be aware that business content data sources have not all been converted at this stage.)

5. If you're planning to extend your solution with any additional data—from SAP or non-SAP sources—you'll want to look at mechanisms to incorporate this data, such as SLT, SAP Data Services, and so on.

6. Work with your data modelers to make basic, necessary adjustments to your SAP BW data model, such as removing aggregates. Work with your ETL developers to match the ETL requirements to the necessary data model and transformation requirements (e.g., for process chains).

7. Start looking for opportunities to flatten out your existing SAP BW model. The actual flattening itself is not necessary at this time, unless you have factored in a certain amount of reduced data redundancy into your compression or if you want to immediately strive for maximum data efficiency.

8. Work with your business analysts and the overall user community to determine what the next set of solutions on your newly enhanced SAP BW solution should be and start mapping those out.

9. Test all of your data feeds and the overall data flow.

When your new system passes the testing phase, it's ready for your users.

As you can see, if you install a fresh SAP BW system with an SAP HANA database, you follow pretty much all of the traditional SAP BW development steps that you normally would, except that you are working with an SAP HANA database and have to make sure you have the right hardware and system versions for that solution. Otherwise, you strategize, design, build, and run as usual (see Table 2.4).

Strategize	Design	Build	Run
▸ Identify bottlenecks and areas for improvement by evaluating existing or future SAP BW solutions. ▸ Analyze the existing SAP BW data model to discover areas that could be leaner. ▸ Determine role and organization impacts.	▸ Recognize additional data or atomic detail that may be required for solutions. ▸ Design lean SAP BW data models. ▸ Create analysis authorizations to restrict user groups.	▸ Migrate database to SAP HANA. ▸ Build new data interfaces as required for new or additional data. ▸ Enable cubes for SAP HANA optimization. ▸ Thin out data models if necessary. ▸ Build new objects if necessary.	▸ Design new backup procedures to protect in-memory applications and data. ▸ Determine the time it will take to reload and restore mission-critical data after failure. ▸ Develop alternative business procedures to run during downtime. ▸ Develop high-availability and disaster recovery capabilities.

Table 2.4 Project Phases for SAP BW on SAP HANA

As with other SAP HANA efforts that we have discussed, migrating your SAP BW database over to SAP HANA is a project that should be undertaken with experienced professionals. The migration itself is only one aspect of this effort. After you've migrated the database, you must make sure that you set up everything in SAP BW that is necessary to take advantage of the power that is now at your fingertips.

Remember that you don't have to make any changes to your SAP BW data model or system (other than the migration and setting of the cubes for the SAP HANA capabilities) until you are ready. Things like deleting your aggregates can be done when you decide that it's the right time.

After you have SAP BW running on SAP HANA, you can start looking at the big data problems that you never before thought you could bring into an SAP BW solution.

2.4.4   Choosing SAP BW on SAP HANA

If you want to empower your *existing* SAP BW system with new, faster, in-memory capabilities and maximize what SAP BW can do for you while taking advantage of the investments your organization has already made, then you're looking at a migration of your SAP BW database to SAP HANA. The key word in that sentence is "existing." For those customers who have invested tens of thousands of hours and maybe millions of dollars into their SAP BW systems, this key step ensures that that SAP BW system will be able to continue to support your business needs today and in the future. You will also be leveraging all of those investments you have already made.

First, however, remember that you need to be on certain versions of SAP BW to do this, so you may need to decide if you're going to upgrade and then migrate or if you're going to install a side-by-side version of SAP BW on SAP HANA with the newest versions and then migrate solutions when you're ready. You can use the side-by-side version of SAP HANA to solve particular use cases or certain high-value analytics that you bring over first and then migrate the rest as you are ready. In this scenario, you don't have to deal with an upgrade right away.

SAP BW on SAP HANA presents you with many opportunities. You can simply migrate your database and immediately gain some good efficiencies and reduce your overall database size. You can speed up your data loading and your reporting. You can bring new solutions, data sets, and use cases into your SAP BW realm. But, remember, you must work to gain all of the efficiencies and benefits that SAP HANA brings to your SAP BW system. Migrating a database to SAP HANA will not deliver all of the benefits. You'll get benefits, but to maximize those benefits, you'll need to go through the exercise of assessing your SAP BW data model and flattening it out. You can also build a fresh installation of SAP BW alongside your existing SAP BW system and design only the key solutions that need the extra power of SAP HANA at this time. Later, you can move over additional solutions as time, money, or desire permits. Many organizations are making this approach work for them.

SAP BW on SAP HANA has definite benefits. The smaller database means less hardware and therefore lower costs. Increased data loads mean you can realistically look at a single global instance with a follow-the-sun loading cycle and actually have a single global instance with acceptable data loading windows and data accessibility for all users. This technology is real, and real customers are seeing dramatic improvements in their SAP BW solutions as they employ SAP HANA. The improvements are not gained without some effort (remember, SAP HANA is not a plug-and-play solution), but the benefits are real and worth evaluating.

> **Note**
>
> We hope this is clear at this point, but we want to clarify that you aren't being forced to migrate your database to SAP HANA. SAP has publicly stated that it will continue to support SAP BW systems that run on other databases.

2.5 SAP Business Suite Powered by SAP HANA

The next implementation option for SAP HANA is SAP Business Suite on SAP HANA, which means implementing SAP HANA as the underlying database for your SAP Business Suite applications but only implementing SAP HANA as the database. At this point, you are not changing any core code or optimizing any transactions as a result of this database change. (Once you implement any optimized transactions, your system will be considered an SAP S/4HANA system.)

Similar to SAP BW on SAP HANA, this implementation of the SAP HANA solution is a technology platform and a database but *not* an application or solution in and of itself. In other words, this platform involves migrating your existing database to an SAP HANA database. This solution doesn't have an option to use SAP HANA-based tools to design, configure, and/or develop your own transaction systems within SAP HANA; you must use native SAP applications.

> **Note**
>
> SAP has made a clear commitment to supporting its customers' choices for database technologies and vendors. They will continue to support and provide innovation for all supported databases and work with the partners who provide those databases. However, the tools SAP is currently launching and future enhancements will assume (and therefore require) you use an SAP HANA platform.

The core applications within SAP Business Suite support processes for finance, human resources, manufacturing, procurement, product development, marketing, sales, service, supply chain management, and IT management. These solutions can be optimized on an SAP HANA platform, including add-on applications such as SAP CRM, SAP ERP, SAP Product Lifecycle Management (SAP PLM), SAP Supply Chain Management (SAP SCM), and SAP Supplier Relationship Management (SAP SRM). A "simple" database migration to SAP HANA does not require that you implement any of the optimized code sets, however. You can simply migrate the database so that you are on the SAP HANA platform and optimize your processes as you and your organization are ready.

Like your options when implementing SAP HANA for analytic solutions, you have two options when implementing SAP Business Suite on SAP HANA:

▶ A full migration, where you move the entire SAP Business Suite to SAP HANA, performing a database (and hardware) migration.

▶ A sidecar implementation, where you create an additional instance of SAP Business Suite and then run that instance on an SAP HANA database and SAP HANA hardware. In this more conservative option, you can optimize specific business processes in a "test" environment while gaining confidence in the SAP HANA-enabled solution for SAP Business Suite.

The SAP HANA platform provides the basis for you to dramatically increase the performance of your SAP Business Suite applications immediately and to continue to innovate without disruption on an open platform. As the customer, however, you have to be ready to embrace the platform.

The architecture of an SAP Business Suite on SAP HANA implementation is shown in Figure 2.15.

This implementation of SAP HANA requires certain minimum version levels and components: SAP NetWeaver 7.3, SAP ERP 6.0 EHP 6, and ABAP AS 7.4. SAP has indicated that customers will be able to upgrade to an SAP HANA-ready SAP Business Suite via a service pack.

You'll also need the appropriate hardware that can support this technology and might require a (potentially) significant hardware migration as well as the database migration. However, whether you need a hardware migration is completely dependent on your current hardware and should be discussed with your hardware vendors and partners. SAP Business Suite data models and SAP BW data models differ in structure and memory utilization; again, this should be discussed with your hardware vendors.

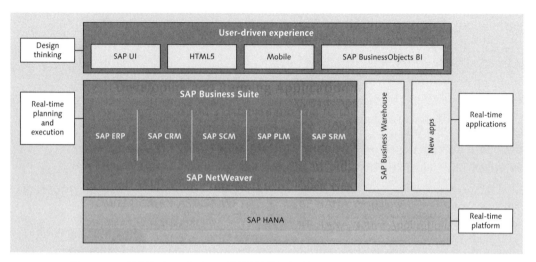

Figure 2.15 SAP Business Suite on SAP HANA: Architecture

When you start looking at SAP Business Suite on SAP HANA and these business critical applications, you won't want to skimp on hardware or memory. You should test and retest all aspects of your hardware to assure yourself and your business leaders that this platform is dependable and reliable.

Instead of going into the discussion of skill requirements and project plans for this effort, let's assume that you know what skills you will require if you are performing a database migration.

Note

For information on getting SAP Business Suite on SAP HANA, you can pick up *Implementing SAP Business Suite on SAP HANA* by Michael Pytel. In addition to the rest of the information contained in this book, you can pursue many avenues when looking for SAP HANA support, including full-service SAP Implementation Partners, the SAP Professional Services Organization, and independent contractors. Be realistic, however, when you put your support requirements out there. If you say that you'll only accept consultants who have 10 years of SAP HANA experience with 30 or more go-lives, you are *not* going to find anyone to fit the bill. SAP HANA has just not been around that long and doesn't have the thousands of live implementations (yet) to justify those high numbers.

With all that said, let's move now to a broader discussion of SAP S/4HANA, which is your SAP ERP system, running on an SAP HANA database, with optimized business processes, code sets, and transactions specifically designed to run with SAP HANA.

2.6 SAP S/4HANA

Finally, we come to a conversation about SAP S/4HANA—the evolution of SAP ERP software. Not just a release or an SPS level, SAP S/4HANA fundamentally moves the SAP ERP system away from SAP R/3. SAP S/4HANA was introduced in January 2015 and is the next iteration of SAP's ERP roadmap from which reaches from SAP R/2 to SAP R/3 to SAP ERP. The **S**implified, **4**th generation of the SAP ERP suite on SAP **HANA** becomes "SAP S/4HANA" once the new business functions are activated. The evolution of the SAP transaction system(s) is shown on the timeline in Figure 2.16.

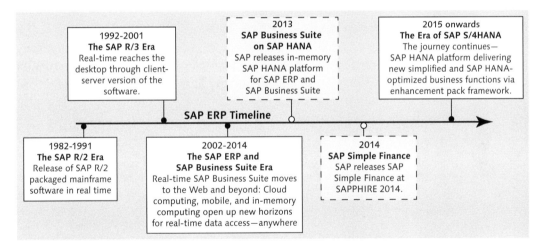

Figure 2.16 SAP S/4HANA Timeline

Note

As discussed previously, if you run an SAP ERP system on an SAP HANA database it is not classified as an "SAP S/4HANA" system. This would be classified as SAP Business Suite on SAP HANA.

Some key points about SAP S/4HANA are as follows:

▶ SAP S/4HANA is built on the advanced SAP HANA in-memory database platform.

▶ New business functionality that is fully optimized (and simplified for SAP HANA) is delivered via *s-innovations* as part of SAP's EHP releases.

▶ In addition to the simplified table structured deployed on an SAP HANA database, and a new set of transactions for these s-innovations, functional and business benefits include a simplified user interface designed with modern principles using the SAP Fiori UX for mobile devices.

▶ SAP S/4HANA offers cloud (e.g., managed cloud through SAP HANA Enterprise Cloud [SAP HEC] or public cloud), on-premise, and hybrid deployment options to provide maximum choice to customers.

▶ SAP Business Suite on SAP HANA will coexist along with the simplified solutions for SAP S/4HANA until SAP redesigns its entire business application suite, step by step. SAP HANA-optimized solutions are available for finance, human resources, sourcing and procurement, supply chain, manufacturing, research and development, asset management, service, sales, and marketing.

▶ The SAP S/4HANA Cloud version will provide some customization options; the public cloud version will provide a limited customization options, while the on-premise version will provide much more flexibility. Versions of various SAP S/4HANA scenarios will typically not be same in the on-premise version as in the cloud version.

▶ SAP S/4HANA is designed to drive business innovation with simplicity by connecting people, devices, and business networks in real time to support the development of new business models as well as to accelerate the adoption of the IoT and big data capabilities. The simplified data model allows customers to reimagine their IT, helping to lower costs and deliver IT efficiency.

Chapter 5 discusses the SAP S/4HANA offering (now also referred to as SAP HANA Enterprise Management), but we hope this general overview is a good start.

2.7   Other SAP HANA Capabilities

With those big topics and use cases introduced, we now want to give you an overview of other functionalities that SAP HANA can bring to your organization. These less commonly known capabilities can help make your SAP HANA-enabled systems extraordinary and can be leveraged to create transformational opportunities for your organizations.

2.7.1   SAP HANA Smart Data Streaming

SAP HANA smart data streaming was first introduced to the SAP HANA suite in SAP HANA SPS 09. SAP HANA smart data streaming processes high-velocity, high-volume event streams in real time, allowing you to filter, aggregate, and enrich raw data before committing it to your database. This includes the fast-paced and highly granular data that come from machine sensors, click streams, social media, transactions, market prices.

With SAP HANA smart data streaming, you can accept data inputs from a variety of sources including data feeds, business applications, sensors, IT monitoring infrastructure and so on; apply business logic and analysis to the streaming data; and store your results directly in SAP HANA (see Figure 2.17).

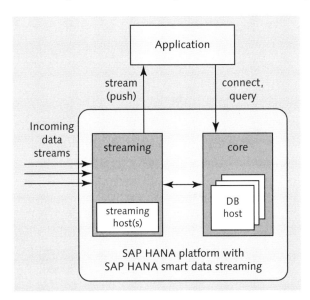

Figure 2.17 SAP HANA Smart Data Streaming

As a result, you can shift from traditional database queries to continuous queries. A traditional database query is a two-step process because you first store the data and then you query the data that has been stored. In a continuous query, first, you define the continuous query and the dataflow. Once the data arrives, it flows through the continuous query and produces immediate results.

The IoT can produce an enormous amount of data that you want to have available to be analyzed and acted upon in real time. SAP HANA smart data streaming allows for this level of real-time analysis and automated action.

This stream capturing allows you to capture data arriving as individual events (that might otherwise be deemed insignificant) at rates of hundreds, thousands, or millions of events per second. This capture is done via micro-batching and parallel processing to optimize load speeds. You can filter, transform, or enrich the data as it comes in so that you are only capturing information that is important to you. Or you can store it all as is and work with it later. You can also prioritize data so that what you deem high-value data goes directly into SAP HANA while lower-value data goes into Hadoop (where you can access it via the other mechanisms as we discussed in Section 2.2.4).

All of this gives you the ability to monitor activity and create immediate responses. You can watch for trends as they develop, monitor correlations, quickly identify if an event or activity is missing, and generate actionable alerts and notifications hours or even days faster than ever possible.

The business applications of this are endless: equipment and safety monitoring, preventative maintenance with minimized downtime and service interruption, consumption analysis, machine and production run optimization, safety and threat detection, and even capital markets fraud detection.

SAP HANA smart data streaming is available as design tool plug-ins to the SAP HANA Studio and are licensed separately (check with SAP or your licensing partner for specific details applicable to your organization). Once licensed, SAP HANA smart data streaming is loaded via the SAP HANA Installer and requires a streaming server on a dedicated host. You administer it via the SAP HANA Studio and SAP HANA Cockpit, and streaming projects are managed in the SAP HANA repository.

Where this starts to really get interesting is when you start thinking about machine learning. You can combine SAP HANA smart data streaming and machine learning algorithms to learn from and make predictions based on incoming data in real time. Smart data streaming offers both supervised and unsupervised machine learning algorithms that are specifically optimized to deal with streaming data and can respond (or alert you) in real time.

2.7.2   SAP HANA Predictive Analysis Library

Our next topic of discussion is predictive analytics with SAP HANA. Predictive analytics have long been a topic of discussion (and debate) with the SAP user community. SAP-based analytics have historically been backward looking—understanding trends and impacts based on past performance. However, with the power and abilities of SAP HANA, we are no longer relegated to this type of analysis.

The SAP HANA's Predictive Analysis Library (PAL) is now available. As of SPS 11, the PAL offers over 3,500 predefined predictive algorithms accessible to you via R integration for SAP HANA. PAL currently includes classic and universal predictive analysis algorithms in nine data-mining categories:

▶ Clustering

▶ Classification

▶ Regression

▶ Association

▶ Time series

▶ Preprocessing

▶ Statistics

▶ Social network analysis

▶ Miscellaneous

The algorithms in PAL were chosen because they were most commonly used in market surveys, were available in other database products, and were determined to be most needed for users of SAP HANA applications. Algorithms are also found here that SAP HANA smart data streaming uses for machine learning.

For a sample of the types of algorithms available, consider the subset in Figure 2.18 (pulled from the PAL).

The goal (and benefit) of these algorithms is to empower your users and data scientists with advanced, predefined capabilities to help them take their analyses to the next level—to understand the business at a fundamentally deeper level, build simulations and models to apply scenarios, forecast potential outcomes (both positive and negative), and define actions that could have a profound impact on the organization.

Category	PAL Algorithm	Built-in Function Name
Clustering	Affinity Propagation	AP
	Agglomerate Hierarchical Clustering	HCAGGLOMERATE
	Anomaly Detection	ANOMALYDETECTION
	Cluster Assignment	CLUSTERASSIGNMENT
	DBSCAN	DBSCAN
	Gaussian Mixture Model (GMM)	GMM
	K-Means	KMEANS VALIDATEKMEANS
	K-Medians	KMEDIANS
	K-Medoids	KMEDOIDS
	LDA Estimation and Inference	LDAESTIMATE LDAINFERENCE
	Self-Organizing Maps	SELFORGMAP
	Slight Silhouette	SLIGHTSILHOUETTE

Figure 2.18 PAL Algorithms

2.7.3 SAP HANA Graph Engine

In simple terms, a graph database is a database that stores both the characteristics and the relationships of a node and can represent them graphically. In practice, graph databases are ideal for highly connected data.

Traditional databases were organized for aggregation, making it difficult to identify and derive relationships and impacts. Graph databases, on the other hand, are optimized for the connections between information. Relationships are known and defined—allowing you be much more precise when defining applications and how you want to use this data.

While originally, graph databases underpinned internet giants like Facebook and Google, SAP HANA leverages the technology for complex data needs. With SAP HANA working with vast amounts of structured and unstructured data, the challenge is how to start identifying, building, and identifying relationships between all of this data in meaningful (impactful) ways. Traditional relational models do not scale and cannot support dense, highly connected data. But the SAP HANA Graph Engine brings new algorithms and paradigms to represent and analyze highly connected data. The SAP HANA Graph Engine passes the ACID tests (previously discussed in Chapter 1) and allows for more powerful querying.

For commercial applications, with the SAP HANA Graph Engine you can quickly and visually identify outliers to connections and relationships. Visual graphs reveal normal flows of money, for instance, and irregularities will pop right out at you.

Graph databases are not going to make traditional databases obsolete any time soon. But, as organizations seek to gain insights from the increasingly complex dynamics at the speed of the Internet, people are looking for new tools. For intricate and complex processes and interconnected systems, graph databases are a great tool.

2.7.4 SAP HANA Sentiment Analysis

We are used to working with structured data that tells us what happened, but what about determining why did those things happened? That "why" can, in many cases, be learned from unstructured data—data that does not neatly fit into predefined rows and columns and does not populate from a dropdown list of pre-selected options.

We have talked previously about incorporating unstructured data into SAP HANA applications—a common big data talking point. We are referring to blogs, emails, Facebook postings, Instagram, surveys, etc. The goal is to extract logic and intelligence from these unstructured postings and analyze it along with the structured data you already have so you can drive relationships. You can understand how customers really felt about your latest ad campaign (did they share the YouTube version on their Facebook page with a positive comment, or did they create a meme out of it?) You can understand product warranty or claim issues based on call center records and feedback comments on Amazon. However, finding a signal in all that noise can be a challenge.

SAP HANA offers full-text searching as a native process across both online transaction processing (OLTP) and online analytical processing (OLAP) use cases. Built-in modeling tools, easy-to-use search definitions, and a rapid development kit are available to help you get started. SAP Predictive Analysis 2.4 has updated the SAP HANA Sentiment Analysis module. Text analytics has been available for several years, but this advancement in sentiment analysis is relatively new, since 2015, thanks to the advances in the technology.

The business applications of sentiment analysis are endless—much like the applications that include big data components are endless. What was required was the computing power to perform these levels of analysis. SAP HANA is continuing to evolve with these advanced capabilities as the technology and platform evolve— and as their customers present them with desired use cases.

2.8   Summary

The benefits of SAP HANA were initially presented as speed and computing power. SAP HANA improves the performance of your existing SAP solutions and applications, running processes in seconds that previously took hours. Take a report that currently runs in 30 minutes and have it execute in 3 seconds or execute business processes (such as Profitability Analysis [CO-PA] or material requirements planning [MRP] processing) in minutes. SAP HANA's speed and power has evolved to become a full-blown development platform that can bring in more volumes and varieties of data than ever before.

Speed for the sake of speed, however, does not translate into business value. Regardless of how you choose to implement an SAP HANA-enabled solution, the true business benefit emerges when you monetize that speed. For example, with your now 3-second report, what changes in *how* you respond to the information in the report? How does a savings of 29 minutes and 57 seconds bring financial benefit to your organization? Delving into that question will identify the monetization opportunities that leverage the speed and power of SAP HANA-enabled solutions.

Thus, your SAP HANA implementation *must* be a business-driven program and not merely a technology or database project. To limit yourself to looking at this as a technology play limits the potential business benefits—the monetization—possibilities.

After reading this chapter, you should now understand the opportunities gained from implementing SAP HANA. Now, you can determine where to start and where you might want to extend your SAP HANA platform. Big data? Predictive analysis? It's all up to you.

In this chapter, we'll explain how you can use SAP HANA as an application platform, and we'll learn about the exciting new features available in the SAP HANA extended application services, advanced model (SAP HANA XSA) as part of SAP HANA SPS 11 and SPS 12.

3   SAP HANA as an Application Platform

We refer to SAP HANA as a platform, but sometimes we forget that the platform is capable of being more than a high-speed database for an SAP ERP or SAP Business Warehouse (SAP BW) implementation. SAP HANA is fundamentally a database platform that can support any type of application, not just SAP-delivered ones, and SAP has been hard at work developing an application platform that is flexible and powerful enough to meet the changing needs of a constantly evolving business landscape.

SAP took the first steps towards unleashing the power of SAP HANA as an application platform when the SAP HANA extended application services were included in the release of SAP HANA SPS 5. At the time of its release, this technology was referred to as the XS engine, or simply as SAP HANA XS; however, we'll refer to this version of the application services as SAP HANA extended application services, classic model (SAP HANA XS Classic), because SAP significantly upgraded and expanded the application platform with SAP HANA SPS 11. The latest version of the application platform is known as SAP HANA extended application services, advanced model, or simply as SAP HANA XSA.

Before the release of SAP HANA XS Classic, in order to connect a web page or application to the data in your SAP HANA database, you needed to connect through another application server, like the SAP ABAP or SAP Java application stack, or you could also connect through ODBC (Open Database Connectivity) or JDBC (Java Database Connectivity). SAP HANA XS Classic simplified this process by adding a lightweight application server as part of the SAP HANA system itself. With SAP HANA XS Classic, you could develop applications that rendered in a browser or on a mobile device and connected through the XS engine in SAP HANA directly to the database layer.

With SAP HANA XSA, SAP added support for Node.js, Java, HTML, and other application programming interfaces, like C++. In an attempt to simplify and unify development between the SAP HANA on-premise and SAP HANA cloud deployments, SAP HANA XSA is based on the Cloud Foundry, which means you can now support multiple languages and multiple runtime instances within the same server. As a result, each deployment of an application or service has its own copy of the Java or Node.js runtime and runs in its own separate instance within the SAP HANA XSA architecture.

In this chapter, you'll learn about SAP HANA XS Classic and SAP HANA XSA. If your SAP HANA platform is on SPS 10 or an earlier release, you'll need to develop your applications with SAP HANA XS Classic. On the other hand, if your platform is on SPS 11 or higher, you can take advantage of SAP HANA XSA, so we'll look at how to use both platforms. We'll also learn how to develop applications using SAP HANA Studio and the SAP Web IDE.

> **Note**
>
> If you start with SAP HANA XS Classic because your system is on SPS 10 or an earlier release and later upgrade your system to SPS 11 or higher, you'll still be able to use the content you developed for SAP HANA XS Classic.

3.1 SAP HANA XS Classic

As part of making SAP HANA more self-reliant, SAP developed SAP HANA XS Classic to enable the development of native SAP HANA applications. If your SAP HANA system is on SPS 5 through SPS 10, you'll need to develop your native SAP HANA applications with SAP HANA XS Classic.

> **Note**
>
> The SAP HANA XS Classic was not available until SAP HANA SPS 5, so you'll need at least SPS 5 to be able to enable the development of native SAP HANA applications with SAP HANA XS Classic. If you're already on SPS 11 or higher, you should be using SAP HANA XSA, so see Section 3.2 and Section 3.3 for information on SAP HANA XSA and how to develop SAP HANA XSA content.

3.1.1 Architecture

As with most things related to SAP HANA, the release of SAP HANA XS Classic marked a paradigm shift in the application programming model. Before SAP HANA XS Classic, in most cases, your application programming was handled using ABAP in the SAP Graphical User Interface (SAP GUI). Rendering, application logic, and database interactions occurred in the ABAP stack, and SAP HANA typically served as an application server for the ABAP stack and a high-speed database only. Figure 3.1 represents the system landscape before the introduction of SAP HANA XS Classic, which was a significant improvement over deployment scenarios prior to SAP HANA but still had room for improvement.

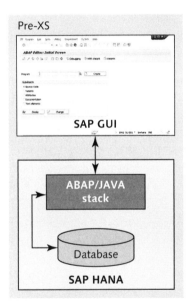

Figure 3.1 System Landscape before SAP HANA XS Classic

The release of SAP HANA XS Classic changed the game. Figure 3.2 displays the system architecture of SAP HANA XS Classic.

As you can see, SAP HANA XS Classic landscape improved the architecture and design options available for connecting applications to data in SAP HANA. The release of SAP HANA XS Classic meant that your company no longer needed to have a separate application server. Instead, the XS engine was included as part of the standard SAP HANA deployment.

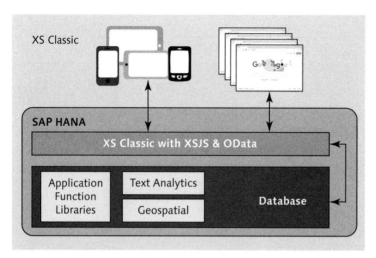

Figure 3.2 SAP HANA Application Landscape with SAP Extended Application Services (SAP HANA XS Classic)

SAP HANA XS Classic also allowed developers to create applications that were easy to deploy via a web browser or mobile device. By combining HTML5 with XSJS (XS JavaScript), you could develop applications that were wholly contained within SAP HANA. The expense and overhead involved in deploying separate application servers could be avoided, and the application logic often could be pushed to the database layer for processing in SAP HANA's in-memory computing engine (IMCE). Furthermore, SAP HANA XS Classic allows for authentication and security through SAP HANA, so there's no need to configure complicated authentication protocols between the application server and the database.

3.1.2 Developing SAP HANA XS Classic Applications

The release of SAP HANA XS Classic prompted the development of a new perspective in SAP HANA Studio called the SAP HANA DEVELOPMENT perspective, which at the time was one of two preferred methods for developing browser- and mobile-based applications and content. (The other is the SAP HANA Web-Based Development Workbench, which we'll discuss in Chapter 8.) The SAP HANA DEVELOPMENT perspective is intended for development of server-side scripting and object development (unlike SAPUI5, which is executed mostly at the client side during runtime). However, it is important to note that SAPUI5 is technically a component of SAP HANA XS.

With SAP HANA XS Classic, you get access to some serious server-side programming as well, including XMLA, OData, and more complex Java scripting with XSJS. You can also access the SAP HANA web server features directly. The functionality in SAP HANA XS Classic provides SAP with an open platform for companies that want to use SAP HANA as a development platform for targeted applications that go far beyond traditional SAP ERP and data warehousing.

A major benefit of SAP HANA XS Classic is that it does not require another application server. The application simply becomes native to SAP HANA and doesn't need another piece of hardware or application server software; in other words, you build and run your application on the SAP HANA platform. The database is the SAP HANA database, with its column and row stores, and at application runtime, your application runs on SAP HANA XS Classic. In this type of deployment, SAP HANA XS Classic serves a dual role as an internal SAP HANA small-footprint application server, including a web server and a core application development platform inside SAP HANA. When you are designing an SAP HANA XS Classic application, you can use the SAP HANA Web-Based Development Workbench, as shown in Figure 3.3, or you can also use the SAP Web IDE (Section 3.3).

Figure 3.3 SAP HANA Web-Based Development Workbench Editor with SAP HANA XS Classic

Unlike development in Eclipse-based SAPUI5 and SAP HANA Studio, you can use either the SAP HANA Web-Based Development Workbench or the SAP Web IDE to create a complete application without installing anything on your desktop. Instead, you'll use your web browser to do all the development for your SAP HANA XS Classic application.

When you develop applications, you can also develop the backend in SAP HANA Studio. To do so, unlike the web interface option, you need to have SAP HANA Studio installed on your local PC, and you need to have a connection, user name, and password set up on an SAP HANA database system. You also need to be assigned an SAP HANA developer role by your system administrator to be permitted to do this kind of native SAP HANA XS Classic development.

Generally, SAP HANA XS Classic mini-application servers inside SAP HANA can assist frontend applications developed in SAPUI5 and SAP HANA XS Classic by merging data from many tables into simple access views.

You can also push application logic, such as a calculation, into the analytical and calculation views inside SAP HANA. This functionality simplifies code execution and lowers processing power requirements on smaller mobile devices because most of the logic is executed in memory at the database layer, instead of on the smaller devices, or even on traditional application servers—which, even if they are somewhat faster, are still extremely slow compared to SAP HANA. You can push much of the mundane application logic to the SAP HANA database server level instead of having to install dedicated external application servers. As a result, you can keep your SAP HANA environments simple and clean, which your SAP Basis support staff will appreciate.

To get started, go to SAP HANA Studio and click the WINDOW menu option. Then select PERSPECTIVE • OPEN PERSPECTIVE • OTHER and select SAP HANA DEVELOPMENT, as shown in Figure 3.4.

From the SAP HANA DEVELOPMENT perspective, you can create a project for your development effort. From the FILE menu, select NEW • XS PROJECT (Figure 3.5) to create a new SAP HANA XS Classic development project. Creating a new project allows you to separate your work from other developers who may be working on other areas of the SAP HANA system.

Figure 3.4 Getting Started with SAP HANA Development in SAP HANA Studio

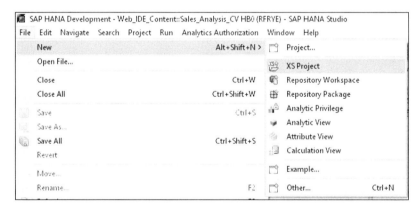

Figure 3.5 Creating a New Project for Development in SAP HANA Studio

Note

If you work in a multideveloper work environment, it is important to take some time to discuss development standards and naming conventions before you start this project to prevent confusion and unintentional interference with the development work of others.

The New XS Project wizard will open, and you'll be prompted to enter a Project Name. You can select the Share project in SAP repository checkbox to allow other developers to collaborate with you on the project, or you can leave this blank. Next, choose the USE DEFAULT LOCATION option to save the files to your working directory for your SAP HANA Studio installation. You can also BROWSE TO THE LOCATION where you'd like to save your project files.

If you browse to a location, you'll also need to choose the file system for the files from the following options:

▶ DEFAULT
This is the default file system on your development machine.

▶ SEMANTIC FILE SYSTEM
Allows you to specify a location within the PROJECT EXPLORER landscape.

If you're saving the project locally, just click FINISH to create the project in the PROJECT EXPLORER.

On the other hand, if you share the project to the repository, you'll need to click NEXT to select the REPOSITORY WORKSPACE for the project (Figure 3.6). You can either select from an existing workspace, or you can click ADD WORKSPACE to create a new one in the repository.

Figure 3.6 Selecting a Workspace for the New SAP HANA XS Classic Project

Click Next to advance to the next window for the SAP HANA XS project wizard (Figure 3.7), where you'll configure the common object names for the project repository. From here, you'll need to provide a Schema name for the new project, a DDL name, and an XS JavaScript name for the objects you'll be adding to the repository. Click Finish to create the new SAP HANA XS Classic project.

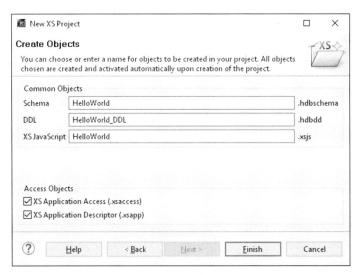

Figure 3.7 Creating Repository Objects for the SAP HANA XS Classic Project

Once the project has been created in SAP HANA Studio, you're ready to start building your application. Please be aware that developing applications in SAP HANA XS Classic and SAP HANA XSA requires a solid background in coding, so you may need to develop or brush up on those skills as you're learning to create applications on SAP HANA. The coding for SAP HANA XS Classic is quite similar to JavaScript, and SAP HANA Studio provides some development wizards to get you started with common tasks. The wizards also allow you to build your own JavaScript library files where you can store your most frequently used controls or custom code extensions. The purpose of these wizards is to make your job as easy as possible.

When your project has been created, the Project Explorer will show the project content in the navigation pane, and you can code your application in the editor, as shown in our simple HelloWorld_XS example in Figure 3.8.

Figure 3.8 HelloWorld in SAP HANA XS Classic with SAP HANA Studio

> **Note**
>
> The steps below assume you've used the package and object names that we've pre-sented in the examples above. If you've selected different names, make sure you update the object names in the code listings below to match your selections.

To duplicate the SAP HANA XS Classic version of the HelloWorld program, you'll need to do the following:

1. Create the SAP HANA XS Classic project as explained earlier.

2. Open the *.xsaccess* file and enter the following line of code to the file:

```
"default_file": "HelloWorld.xsjs",
```

3. Save the *.xsaccess* file.

4. Add a file called *.xsprivileges* to the project.

5. Add the following code to the file:

```
{"privileges" :
     [ { "name" : "Basic", "description" : "Basic usage privilege" } ]}
```

> **Note**
>
> When adding files, you may be able to select the XS file type that matches the object you're adding from the context menu or by navigating to FILE • OTHER; however, if the file type you're looking for is not available, simply right-click in PROJECT EXPLORER to open the context menu and select NEW FILE.

6. Save the *.xsprivileges* file.

7. Add a file named *model_access.hdbrole* to the project and add the following code to the file:

```
role HelloWorld_XS::model_access {
    application privilege: HelloWorld_XS::Basic;}
```

8. Open the *HelloWorld.xsjs* file and add the code from Listing 3.1 to the file.

```
$.response.contentType = "text/html";
var output = "Hello, " + $.session.getUsername() + " <br><br>";
var conn = $.db.getConnection();
var pstmt = conn.prepareStatement( "SELECT CURRENT_USER FROM DUMMY" );
var rs = pstmt.executeQuery();
if (!rs.next()) {
    $.response.setBody( "Failed to retrieve data" );
    $.response.status = $.net.http.INTERNAL_SERVER_ERROR;
}
else {
    output = output + "This is the response from my SQL.
    The current user is: " + rs.getString(1);
}
rs.close();
pstmt.close();
conn.close();
$.response.setBody(output);
```

Listing 3.1 Code for the SAP HANA XS Classic HelloWorld Program

9. Save the *HellowWorld.xsjs* file.

10. Activate all the objects from your project with the ACTIVATE ALL SAP HANA DEVELOPMENT OBJECTS button (Figure 3.9) or by pressing `Ctrl`+`Shift`+`F3` on your keyboard.

Figure 3.9 Activating All Inactive Objects in an SAP HANA XS Classic Project

11. Add the `HelloWorld_XS::model_access` role to your user.

When you've activated all the objects in the project, you should be able to view your simple HelloWorld greeting by navigating to *http://<hana_server>:80 <instance>/helloworld_xs/*. Login to the server with the user with the `HelloWorld_ XS::model_access` role. You should be greeted by your user name as shown in Figure 3.10.

Hello, RFRYE

This is the response from my SQL. The current user is: RFRYE

Figure 3.10 Hello World Program Developed in SAP HANA Studio with SAP HANA XS Classic

This example of creating an application in SAP HANA XS Classic should be enough to get you started. For more information about coding applications in SAP HANA XS Classic and SAP HANA XSA, you can download the following reference guides from SAP:

▸ *SAP HANA XS JavaScript Reference*

▸ *SAP HANA JavaScript API Reference*

▸ *SAP HANA XSUnit JavaScript API Reference*

▸ *SAP HANA XS DB Utilities JavaScript API Reference*

▸ *SAP HANA REST API Reference*

These guides, and many more, are available for download from *http:// help.sap.com/hana_platform*.

SAP HANA XS and SAPUI5

Although SAP HANA XS and SAPUI5 are separate components, it's important to understand how they work together. You could build an SAPUI5 application without SAP HANA XS being directly involved, but if you build an SAP HANA XS-based application, you may be using SAPUI5 as your custom-developed frontend tool, or you can use the SAP Web IDE or the SAP HANA Web-Based Development Workbench.

You can clearly see this relationship if you look carefully under the content folder in your SAP HANA XS project. The subsections correspond to the different components as illustrated in Figure 3.11.

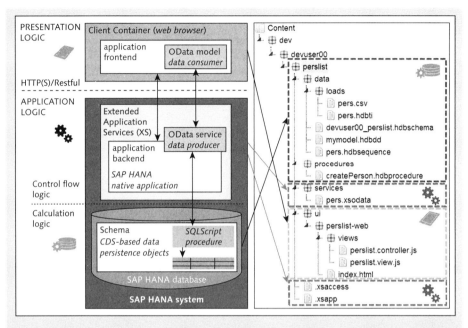

Figure 3.11 Development Achitecture for SAP HANA XS and SAPUI5 on SAP HANA

It is important to note that this type of development is not for those with limited programming skills; some basic training with programming languages such as C++, Java, JavaScript, and VBScript is essential to learn how to do this properly.

3.2   SAP HANA XSA

With SAP HANA SPS 11, SAP released SAP extended application services, advanced model (SAP HANA XSA). SAP HANA XSA builds on the foundation provided by SAP HANA XS Classic, with support for JavaScript, Node.js, and Java, as well as support for GitHub and Maven. As a result, you can create applications with separate components using different programming languages, all on the same SAP HANA server.

SAP HANA XSA uses the micro-services approach where applications and their related, programming language-specific runtime environments are modular, decoupled services that exchange information through RESTful APIs (representational state transfer for application programming interfaces). This micro-service architecture means you can maintain one service without affecting other services. For example, you can apply a patch to one component of the application without causing the rest of the application to crash. As a result, you may potentially be able to avoid downtime, as new versions of an existing micro-service may be deployed and tested on the same SAP HANA instance without requiring a full system outage.

> **Note**
>
> REST is an architecture style used in designing networked applications. REST relies on client-server, cacheable, stateless communications protocols, most often HTTP. Applications based on the REST architecture typically allow the user to advance through the program flow by selecting links that load and render the next page of the application.

SAP HANA XSA also introduced a new runtime controller based on the Cloud Foundry, which enabled the introduction of build packs into SAP HANA development. Build packs include a set of compilers and utilities used in application design, and the new SAP HANA XSA runtime supports build packs with the following languages:

- XSJS (XS JavaScript)
- Node.js
- Java on Apache TomEE 1.7.3
- Java on Apache Tomcat 8.0.32

The runtimes in SAP HANA XSA are decoupled from the database in SAP HANA, which allows for flexible scaling during peak demand. New servers or nodes can be dynamically added or removed as needed to meet your business needs.

> **Note**
>
> You may notice that we've included C++ as one of the available language runtimes with SAP HANA XSA in our landscape diagram (Figure 3.12). While C++ and FastCGI runtimes are available internally, as of August 2016, support for C++ and FastCGI is not in the general release of SAP HANA XSA for SAP HANA SPS 12. In fact, since the SAP HANA XSA architecture is based on the Cloud Foundry, in the future, you may potentially be able to use other Cloud Foundry build packs, such as Go, Ruby, or PHP, as your chosen language or runtime for SAP HANA XSA.

In short, the release of SAP HANA XSA has completed the transformation of SAP HANA from a specialized application server and high-speed database engine into a true next-generation platform for meeting your business needs. It's also important to note that, as of SPS 11, SAP recommends using SAP HANA XSA to develop any new applications for the SAP HANA platform. In this section, we'll take a look at how SAP HANA XSA fits into the rest of the SAP HANA architecture. We'll also provide step-by-step instructions for installing SAP HANA XSA and the SAP Web IDE so you can quickly start building your own applications.

3.2.1   SAP HANA XSA Architecture

Let's take a look at the new SAP HANA XSA landscape (Figure 3.12) and compare it to the SAP HANA XS Classic landscape (Figure 3.2). The new landscape retains support for all of your SAP HANA XS Classic applications, so upgrading your SAP HANA installation to SPS 11 or greater won't cause all of your SAP HANA XS Classic applications to fail, but only new applications can take full advantage of the improvements in SAP HANA XSA.

The application router accepts service requests from browser-based applications and mobile applications and routes these requests to the correct micro-service. A separate micro-service container is created for each application component, and these components exchange data through the RESTful APIs. Multiple containers may be created for any given runtime, allowing you to develop multiple application components using different languages.

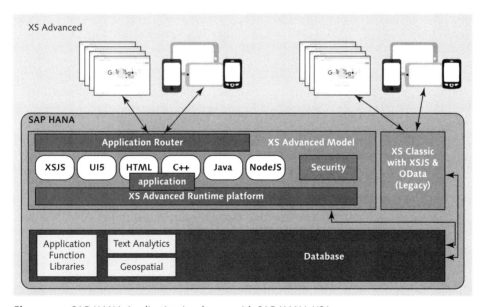

Figure 3.12 SAP HANA Application Landscape with SAP HANA XSA

Each micro-service container has a complete copy of the entire Node.js, Java, or XSJS runtime, which locks each component into using the version with which it was deployed. As a result, the upgrade path for future revisions is much more stable, since a deployed component will continue to use its original runtime library until it's individually deployed with an updated version in a future revision.

The micro-service approach is also applied at the level of the operating system, since each deployed instance of a given runtime will have its own dedicated operating system process. This decoupled runtime architecture means that the failure of one service will not cascade outward to other application components or services.

Next, we'll take a closer look at some of the key components of the SAP HANA XSA architecture, including the role of multi-target applications and how they're handled by the runtime platform. We'll also explain how user accounts and authentication are handled in the landscape, as well as the role of OData services, and then we'll finish this section with a look at the administration tools available for use in SAP HANA XSA.

Multi-Target Applications

SAP HANA SPS 12 introduced support for multi-target applications (MTAs). MTAs use what is commonly known as a *blue-green deployment technique*, which designates two identical target environments, the blue and green environments. In this deployment scenario, only one of the two environments will be live at any given time. Development and testing can therefore take place in the other environment, and switching between the environments can be as easy as updating the routing within your network to identify the development environment as the live version.

By making switching between environments easy, you can quickly and easily switch back to the known good environment in the event of an unexpected failure in the other. Once the new environment has been certified as stable through your company's risk management processes, you can save the old environment to an archive and copy the new environment for use as the next development environment.

An MTA will consist of one or more application modules, each of which is considered a micro-application. These micro-applications may be bound to required services and pushed to a deployment platform. Each module may expose attributes for use in other modules and may also be dependent on other modules.

An MTA deployment descriptor file specifies the modules and dependencies for an application, including the technical types, dependencies, and any parameters required for the modules. The descriptor file is used to verify that the required dependencies exist and that the modules are deployed in the correct order and also to set up any necessary connections between modules. All the application files for the MTA, including manifests, descriptors, and service configuration information, are gathered into an archive package, and this package may be used to deploy the MTA. An MTA archive typically contains a folder for each module in the application. The exact folder structure (as specified in the MTA manifest) will depend on the structure of your application but may contain folders such as:

▶ **java/**
Java application files

▶ **web/**
State web content and application routing configuration

▶ **db/**
Views, tables, procedures, calculation views, etc. common to an SAP HANA database

▶ **js/**
Node.js application and XSJS files

When you develop your applications using the micro-service architecture and MTAs, you should adhere to the following guidelines:

▶ **Isolated and independent**
Services must be isolated and not share any libraries and components with each other. Common libraries and frameworks are embedded in each service container, which facilitates the goal of isolating each service from another. Redundancies will exist, and different services may be running on different versions of the same libraries.

▶ **Languages and runtimes**
Services may be implemented in any language and run in an available runtime environment, regardless of the languages and runtime environments implemented in other services.

▶ **Lifecycle**

Each service has a lifecycle that is independent of all other services, allowing for stable integration with other services and facilitating isolated upgrading or replacement of the service.

▶ **Extensibility**

Services may wrap, replace, or extend existing services and may be aggregated with new and existing services to provide a "mashup" service.

For more information about developing with MTAs, see the SAP HANA XS ADVANCED MULTI-TARGET APPLICATIONS subsection of the INTRODUCTION TO APPLICATION DEVELOPMENT AND DEPLOYMENT (XS ADVANCED MODEL) site on *http://help.sap.com*.

Runtime platform

The runtime platform is the framework that makes the entire micro-services architecture of SAP HANA XSA work properly. Each micro-service container for each of your multi-target applications relies upon the runtime platform to manage a vast array of functions within the landscape, including:

▶ Routing

▶ Load balancing

▶ Identity and access management

▶ Lifecycle management

▶ Elastic, on-demand scaling

▶ API management for each container

The XS platform starts and stops each micro-service container as required and enables monitoring of each container instance and application, as well as CPU, memory, network, and file system resources used by each container.

Without the coordination and management activities carried out by the SAP HANA XSA runtime platform, the entire landscape would require multiple application servers, each dedicated to one application, and would lack the benefits of the micro-services approach, especially those pertaining to lifecycle management. Without the runtime platform, updating one component of an application would require redeploying the entire application. Instead, with SAP HANA XSA, you can update and deploy changes that are isolated to their respective containers, and you don't need separate application servers for each application.

User Account and Authentication Service

The User Account and Authentication (UAA) service handles any unauthenticated request to an SAP HANA XSA application or the XS Application Router. UAA relies on an external user store, such as SAP Cloud Identity, Lightweight Directory Access Protocol (LDAP), or the SAP HANA database, and can process different authentication methods, such as Security Assertion Markup Language (SAML) assertions, X.509 certificates, and basic user names and passwords.

When the UAA successfully processes a login, an OAuth token is issued. This token can be used in all other calls to application services for the user and can also be forwarded to another service for user-based authorization. For example, the UAA could provide an OAuth token to the SAP HANA database for authorizations based on SAP HANA database users. The OAuth token provides a unified authentication approach while also specifying the scope of the user's permissions, thus allowing functional authorization checks, based on the scope, for every service layer in an application.

OData Services

OData is the SAP-recommended protocol for RESTful data access. To enable support for OData services, SAP included OData server libraries for use with SAP HANA XSA, including the libraries for Java and Node.js. Your SAP HANA XSA applications may define their own data providers using the OData libraries or may define `xsodata` metadata artifacts or core data services (CDS) views as generic data providers.

> **Note**
>
> CDS views are not covered in detail in this book, but they provide developers with the ability to define entities and the relationships between those entities using an SQL-based data definition language (DDL). This SQL-based DDL has been extended to allow for the definition of relationships between CDS views, annotations regarding the specific use of CDS objects, and aggregation expressions, to name a few. For more information about CDS views, consider reading "Enhanced ABAP Development with Core Data Services (CDS) – How CDS Brings a Modern Data Modeling Approach to ABAP" by Karl Kessler, published on October 8, 2015 in Volume 16, Issue 4 of *SAPinsider*.

Administration Tools

To monitor your SAP HANA XSA landscape, as well as any applications you develop, SAP has provided administration tools for SAP HANA XSA. These tools are available for easy integration with the SAP HANA Cockpit (see Chapter 10 for detailed instructions about adding tools to the cockpit). The following administration tools are available for integration with the SAP HANA Cockpit:

- **Application Monitor**
  Monitors SAP HANA XSA applications.

- **Organization and Space Management**
  Create, list, and delete user spaces and organizations in SAP HANA XSA.

- **Application Role Builder**
  Manage and maintain user roles and collections in SAP HANA.

- **SAML Identity Providers Configuration**
  Allows configuration of SAML identity providers for SAP HANA XSA model applications that use SAML.

- **User Management**
  Manage and create business users for SAP HANA XSA.

- **SAP HANA Logical Database Configuration**
  Manage database instances for SAP HANA XSA applications.

- **SAP HANA Service Brokers**
  Monitor and manage SAP HANA XSA service brokers.

- **Job Scheduler Service Dashboard**
  Schedule, create, and manage long-running SAP HANA XSA jobs.

3.2.2   Installing SAP HANA XSA Runtime

Before you begin installing the SAP HANA XSA runtime server, you need to determine if your SAP HANA server is a single-host or multihost system. The single-host installation is the easiest to install and configure, and this installation can be scaled up as needed. The host system will need both the database worker and xs_worker host roles in a single-host installation. See Figure 3.13 for an example of the system service landscape in a single-host system.

Note

The SAP HANA XSA runtime is currently being modified and is updated frequently. As a result, any installation should begin with a thorough examination of the SAP Notes on SAP HANA XSA. See Table 3.1 for a list of relevant notes on the subject before beginning your installation.

Furthermore, be aware that each update of the SAP HANA XSA server may cause compatibility problems with the SAP HANA XS client. For this reason, if you're upgrading your server, go ahead and get the latest version of the client from the SAP HANA installation media before attempting to connect.

SAP Note	Description
2242468	Setting up SAP HANA extended application services, advanced model command-line client from SAP HANA installation DVD
2303772	SAP HANA XS Advanced Model SPS 12 Release Note
2324508	Uninstallation of software components in SAP HANA XS Advanced Model
2245631	Domains and routing configuration for SAP HANA extended application services, advanced model
2304873	SAP Web IDE for SAP HANA SPS 12 – Central Release Note
2300937	Backup and restore for SAP HANA extended application services, advanced model
2300936	Failover & High Availability with SAP HANA extended application services, advanced model
2298750	SAP HANA Platform SPS 12 Release Note
2243019	Providing SSL certificates for domains defined in SAP HANA extended application services, advanced model
2239095	SAP HANA XS ADVANCED DEMO MODEL – SHINE XSA Release & Information Note
2326004	How to uninstall SAP HANA XS advanced manually
2313789	Restrictions of SAP HANA XS advanced SPS 12
2243156	Secure user setup for SAP HANA extended application services, advanced model
2244998	Restrictions of SAP HANA XS advanced SPS 11

Table 3.1 SAP Notes with Information about SAP HANA XSA

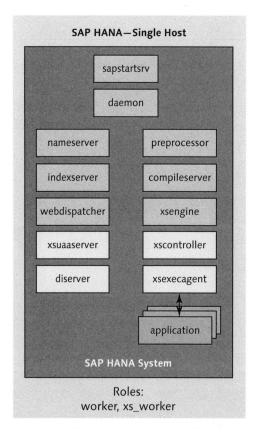

Figure 3.13 Single-Host Deployment of SAP HANA XSA

A multihost installation of SAP HANA XSA will allow for load balancing between different hosts. For this installation, the server software is installed in a shared file system, and the file system must be mounted by all the hosts in the distributed system. In this configuration, the system hosts may be active, or they may be idle and only activated when the load on the system increases. See Figure 3.14 for an example of the SAP HANA XSA system landscape in a simple multihost system.

You can also perform an advanced installation of your SAP HANA XSA runtime server, in which your worker, xs_worker, standby, and xs_standby roles are distributed across multiple systems. In this type of installation, the role for each system must be determined and assigned during the installation of SAP HANA XSA. For an example of an advanced multihost deployment, including a worker system, xs_worker system, and a standby system, see Figure 3.15.

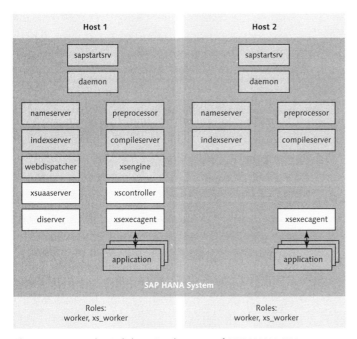

Figure 3.14 Simple Multihost Deployment of SAP HANA XSA

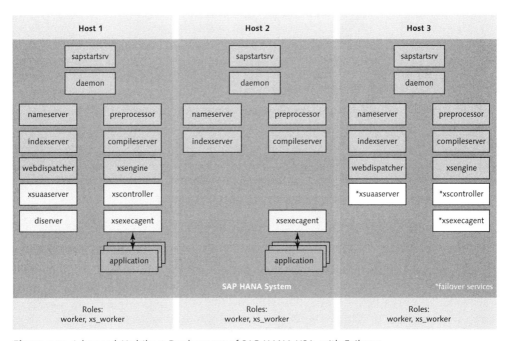

Figure 3.15 Advanced Multihost Deployment of SAP HANA XSA, with Failover

Installing the SAP HANA XSA runtime is a fairly simple process, regardless of the version of SAP HANA lifecycle manager (SAP HANA LCM) you choose to use, so we'll describe the steps to install the runtime using both the graphical and command line versions of the SAP HANA LCM in the following sections. Then, we'll finish this section with a detailed look at installing the SAP Web IDE.

Before You Begin...

As you should be using the SAP Web IDE to develop any SAP HANA XSA applications, you should download the SAP HANA XSA components you want to install prior to beginning the installation. The components can be downloaded from the SAP Marketplace at *http://launchpad.support.sap.com/*.

Click the SOFTWARE DOWNLOADS tile, then select BY ALPHABETICAL INDEX (A-Z) • H • SAP IN-MEMORY (SAP HANA) • HANA PLATFORM EDITION • SAP HANA PLATFORM EDITION • SAP HANA PLATFORM EDIT. 1.0. Click the SUPPORT PACKAGES AND PATCHES button in the upper right, then select ENTRY BY COMPONENT to find the components listed below:

- XS ADVANCED RUNTIME
- HANA SHINE CONTENT FOR XSA (optional)
- XS ADVANCED SERVICES
- XS ADVANCED MONITORING
- SAP WEB IDE 4 SAP HANA
  - DI CORE 1
  - SAP WEB IDE 1
- SAP HANA RUNTIME TOOLS

When you've downloaded all the components, you need to create a folder on the Linux host of the SAP HANA system to contain the installation media. For convenience, you may also consider creating a separate directory within this directory to hold the extracted SAP HANA XSA runtime components.

You can then extract all the installers to this installation directory and simply point the lifecycle manager to this location with the option to INCLUDE SUBDIRECTORIES when adding components. Then you simply need to choose the components to install in the order recommended later in this section, and the SAP HANA XSA runtime will be detected properly as a component to install each time. See Figure 3.16 for an example of the installation directory we used to install our components.

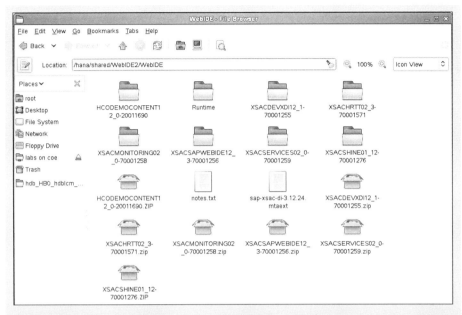

Figure 3.16 SAP HANA XSA Components in One Installation Path

When you install the SAP HANA XSA runtime, you should specify the fully qualified domain name for you SAP HANA system. If you fail to do so, and instead you select the local domain, you may have authentication problems when you use the SAP HANA XS command line interface (XS CLI) to obtain the URLs for accessing the SAP Web IDE, as described in Section 3.3.

Installation with the SAP HANA Lifecycle Manager Web Version

To install the SAP HANA XSA runtime, you'll need to use the SAP HANA LCM. You can use the graphical user interface (GUI), web-based interface, or the command line version of the lifecycle manager; however, the GUI lifecycle manager or web-based lifecycle manager is generally easier to use.

You can find a complete description of the installation process in the *SAP HANA Server Installation and Update Guide*, available for download in PDF format from *http:// help.sap.com/*. Also, the installation steps are nearly identical between the web-based and GUI versions of the lifecycle manager, so we'll be giving examples with the web-based version in this section.

You'll need to use the following process to install the SAP HANA XSA runtime:

1. Login to the SAP HANA system as the root user.

2. Navigate to the directory containing the installation medium.

3. Enter /<install_path>/<sid>/hdblcmweb from the command line to open the web-based version of the SAP HANA lifecycle manager (LCM).

4. Select INSTALL NEW SYSTEM and then click NEXT.

5. Click ADD SOFTWARE LOCATIONS (Figure 3.17).

Figure 3.17 SAP HANA Lifecycle Manager: Web Version

6. Navigate to the location of the installation media and click OK.

7. Confirm the DETECTED SOFTWARE COMPONENTS by clicking NEXT.

8. Check the INSTALL SAP HANA XS ADVANCED RUNTIME checkbox and click NEXT.

9. Select a system from the EXISTING HOSTS in the SAP HANA System list and click NEXT.

10. (Optional) Select ADD HOST to specify parameters for additional hosts in a multihost installation. You'll also need to specify:

▸ INSTALLATION PATH: path to the SAP mount directory (see your system administrator to get this information).

▸ NON-STANDARD SHARED FILE SYSTEM: usually used when the SID is included in the mount point.

▸ HOST NAME: fully qualified host name of the machine.

▸ ROLE: purpose of the host, selected from the options in Table 3.2.

Role	Role name	Description
Database Worker	`worker`	Worker host used for database processing.
Database Standby	`standby`	Idle and available for failover in high-availability.
Dynamic Tiering Worker	`extended_storage_worker`	Host for dynamic tiering.
Dynamic Tiering Standby	`extended_storage_standby`	Standby host for dynamic tiering.
Accelerator for SAP ASE Worker	`ets_worker`	Worker host for SAP ASE accelerator.
Remote Data Sync	`rdsync`	Remote data sync host.
Smart Data Streaming	`streaming`	Host for smart data streaming.
XS advanced runtime worker	`xs_worker`	Host for SAP HANA XSA.
XS advanced runtime standby	`xs_standby`	Available for failover/dynamic scaling.

Table 3.2 SAP HANA Host System Roles

11. For the SYSTEM TYPE, select either a SINGLE-HOST SYSTEM or MULTIPLE-HOST SYSTEM. (This prompt won't appear in single-host system landscapes.)

12. Select YES or NO in the AUTOMATIC ASSIGNMENT OF XS RUNTIME roles window. This option will determine whether or not you want to assign the SAP HANA XS runtime role to the host of the database you selected. If not, you'll need to specify a different host for the runtime role.

13. Enter the SYSTEM ADMINISTRATOR (<SID>ADM) PASSWORD, DATABASE USER NAME, and DATABASE USER PASSWORD and click NEXT.

14. The CONFIGURE XS ADVANCED RUNTIME screen (Figure 3.18) will require you to provide the:

- XS ORGANIZATION MANAGER user (XSA_ADMIN by default)
- XS ORGANIZATION MANAGER USER PASSWORD
- CUSTOMER ORGANIZATION NAME
- CUSTOMER SPACE NAME
- ROUTING MODE
  - PORTS: SAP HANA XSA system services will be assigned to the host domain with different ports for each service (e.g., *www.<domain>.<extension>:3<instance>32* is usually the link for the uaa-security service).
  - HOSTNAMES: SAP HANA XSA system services will be assigned to the host domain with different domain prefixes (e.g., *http://uaa-security.<domain>.<extension>* and *http://webide.<domain>.<extension>*).
- DOMAIN NAME (a fully qualified domain name is recommended)

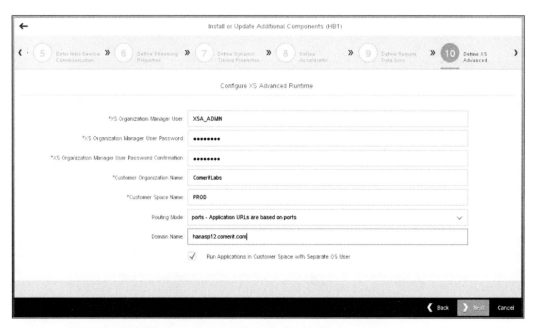

Figure 3.18 Configuring SAP HANA XSA Runtime Settings

15. Click NEXT to confirm the settings.

16. Designate user IDs for the XS ADVANCED SAP SPACE OS USER ID and the XS ADVANCED CUSTOMER SPACE OS USER ID.

17. Click NEXT to confirm the user IDs.

18. (Recommended) Select the XS MONITORING 1 and XS SERVICES 1 updates as part of the installation, if available, and then click NEXT.

19. Confirm the system settings you entered on the REVIEW AND CONFIRM ENTERED DATA screen (Figure 3.19).

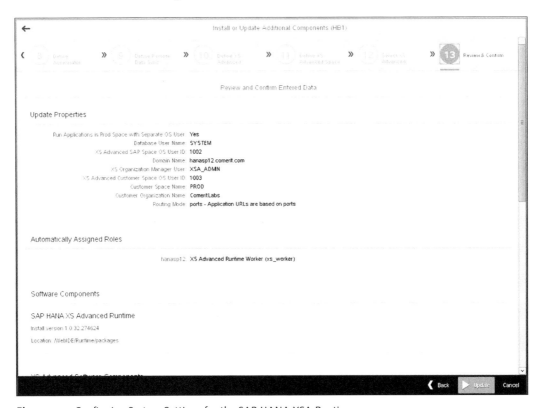

Figure 3.19 Confirming System Settings for the SAP HANA XSA Runtime

20. Click UPDATE to install the runtime.

The installation will proceed, and you'll be notified of a successful installation, as shown in Figure 3.20.

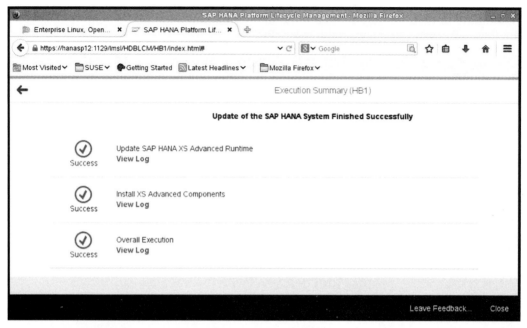

Figure 3.20 SAP HANA XSA Runtime Successfully Installed

Installation with the SAP HANA Lifecycle Manager Command Line Interface

In order to install SAP HANA XSA from the command line interface, you'll need to do the following:

1. Login to the SAP HANA system as the root user.

2. Browse to the location where the installation media is located.

3. Execute /<install_path>/<sid>/hdblcm from the command line in the installation media directory.

4. Select the UPDATE option from the command line interface. In our example (Figure 3.21), our SID is HB1, so we selected 1 and pressed Enter.

5. Select the UPDATE SAP HANA XS ADVANCED RUNTIME option and press Enter.

6. Enter the credentials for the system administrator, the system user, and the SAP HANA XSA administrator (Figure 3.22).

7. Select the components you want to install. Use comma-separated indices for multiple selections, or enter "1" for all.

8. Enter "y" on the keyboard and press Enter to confirm the selected components.

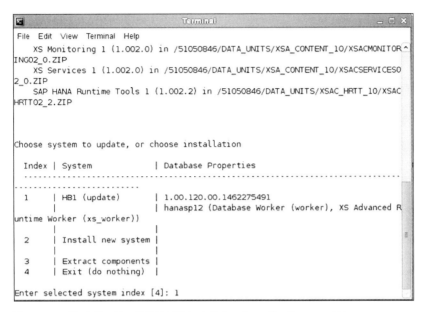

Figure 3.21 Updating the SAP HANA Installation from the Command Line

```
[Terminal]
File  Edit  View  Terminal  Help

  Index | Components | Description
  ------------------------------------------------------------------
  -------------------------------------------
    1   | all       | All components
    2   | server    | Update SAP HANA Database from version 1.00.120.00.1462275
491 to version 1.00.120.00.1462275491
    3   | client    | Install SAP HANA Database Client version 1.00.120.024.146
1933179
    4   | afl       | Install SAP HANA AFL (incl.PAL,BFL,OFL,HIE) version 1.00.
120.00.1462291682
    5   | smartda   | Install SAP HANA Smart Data Access version 1.00.6.001.0
    6   | studio    | Install SAP HANA Studio version 2.3.5.000000
    7   | trd       | Install SAP TRD AFL FOR HANA version 1.00.120.00.14622916
82
    8   | xs        | Update SAP HANA XS Advanced Runtime from version 1.0.24.2
68783 to version 1.0.24.268783

Enter comma-separated list of the selected indices [2,3]: 8
Enter System Administrator (hb1adm) Password:
Enter Database User Name [SYSTEM]:
Enter Database User (SYSTEM) Password:
Enter XS Advanced Admin User [XSA_ADMIN]:
Enter XS Advanced Admin User Password:
```

Figure 3.22 Entering the System Credentials for SAP HANA XSA Installation

SAP HANA XSA should begin to install. When the installation has completed, you can navigate to the Administrator Console in SAP HANA Studio and verify that the SAP HANA XSA components are ACTIVE, as shown in Figure 3.23.

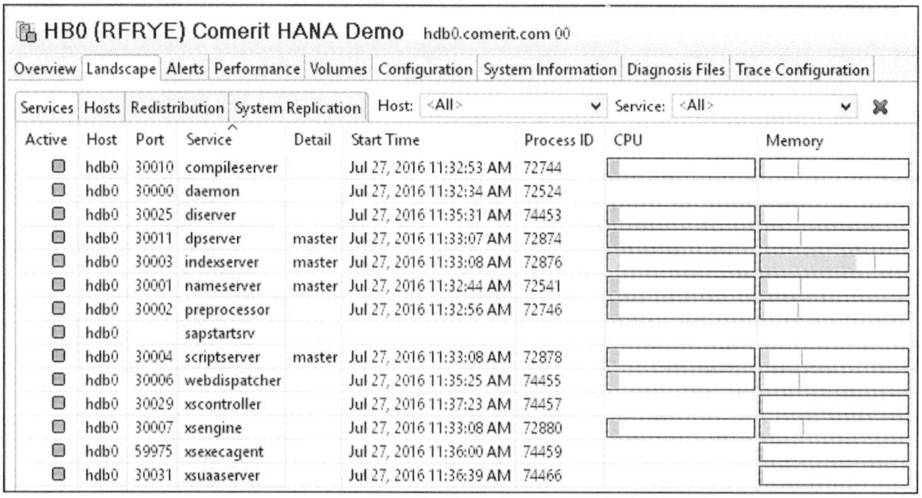

Active	Host	Port	Service	Detail	Start Time	Process ID	CPU	Memory
	hdb0	30010	compileserver		Jul 27, 2016 11:32:53 AM	72744		
	hdb0	30000	daemon		Jul 27, 2016 11:32:34 AM	72524		
	hdb0	30025	diserver		Jul 27, 2016 11:35:31 AM	74453		
	hdb0	30011	dpserver	master	Jul 27, 2016 11:33:07 AM	72874		
	hdb0	30003	indexserver	master	Jul 27, 2016 11:33:08 AM	72876		
	hdb0	30001	nameserver	master	Jul 27, 2016 11:32:44 AM	72541		
	hdb0	30002	preprocessor		Jul 27, 2016 11:32:56 AM	72746		
	hdb0		sapstartsrv					
	hdb0	30004	scriptserver	master	Jul 27, 2016 11:33:08 AM	72878		
	hdb0	30006	webdispatcher		Jul 27, 2016 11:35:25 AM	74455		
	hdb0	30029	xscontroller		Jul 27, 2016 11:37:23 AM	74457		
	hdb0	30007	xsengine		Jul 27, 2016 11:33:08 AM	72880		
	hdb0	59975	xsexecagent		Jul 27, 2016 11:36:00 AM	74459		
	hdb0	30031	xsuaaserver		Jul 27, 2016 11:36:39 AM	74466		

Figure 3.23 SAP HANA XSA Model Services Installed and Active

Installing SAP Web IDE

The SAP Web IDE is a component of the SAP XSA platform, as is reflected in some of the documentation for SAP HANA XSA. However, you should consider it a separate installation that requires many of the same components as the SAP HANA XSA runtime, because the SAP Web IDE will not install without including the SAP HANA XSA runtime as a DETECTED SOFTWARE COMPONENT at the beginning of the installation process.

Warning!

If you don't navigate to the location where the runtime package is extracted and add it as a component in the lifecycle manager process, you will receive an unhelpful error message stating that the runtime is required to install the other components regardless of whether or not the platform has already been installed. Again, the installation process currently requires the installation files for the runtime platform as part of any component installation, so make sure you select the SAP HANA XSA platform as part of any component installation.

The order in which you install the SAP XSA components matters a great deal. You cannot simply select all the components and install them all at once, as we experienced unrecoverable failures whenever we attempted to do so. (We had to roll back to an earlier snapshot of our virtual machine.) Regardless of which method is chosen, you should install the components in the following order:

1. Install the SAP HANA XS ADVANCED RUNTIME, as well as the XS SERVICES 1 and XS MONITORING 1 components.
2. Install the SAP HANA RUNTIME TOOLS.
3. Install the SAP WEB IDE DEVELOPMENT INFRASTRUCTURE.
4. Install the SAP WEB IDE WEB CLIENT.
5. Install the SAP HANA DEMO MODEL FOR XS ADVANCED 1.0 (optional training content).

Each of these installation steps should be completed as a separate installation cycle of the SAP HANA lifecycle manager.

See Table 3.3 for a description of the SAP HANA XSA components.

SAP HANA XSA Component	Description
SAP Web IDE web client	Comprehensive browser-based integrated development environment for complex applications using web-based or mobile user interfaces, business logic, and SAP HANA data models.
SAP Web IDE development infrastructure	Core component of the SAP Web IDE, required to enable the SAP HANA Web-Based Development Workbench in your environment.
XS Monitoring	Allows the maintenance of the application environment, including security, authentication, and resource monitoring.
XS Services	Enables using a catalog of services managed by the SAP HANA Service Broker, including OAuth clients, user accounts, and job scheduling.
SAP HANA runtime tools	Tools that help in design-time development and runtime administration of MTAs with SAP HANA XSA.
SAP HANA Demo Model for XS Advanced	SAP HANA Interactive Education (SHINE) content for SAP HANA XSA.

Table 3.3 SAP HANA XSA Installation Components

3.3   Developing SAP HANA XSA Applications with SAP Web IDE

SAP HANA XSA applications may be developed using either the XS CLI or with the SAP Web IDE. In this section, we'll provide an overview for creating SAP HANA XSA applications using both approaches. We'll begin with a brief overview of using XS CLI, and then we'll move on to develop a sample SAP HANA XSA application using the SAP Web IDE.

Before we jump right into developing with SAP Web IDE, let's take a moment to understand the overall process for developing applications using SAP HANA XSA. To be successful in any SAP HANA XSA application project, you'll need to apply the steps in the process below:

1. Create the folder infrastructure for your application files.
2. Create the deployment descriptor files.
3. Add database artifacts and content as needed.
4. Add business logic to work with the database artifacts.
5. Create OData service definitions as needed.
6. Create the user interface (UI).
7. Add security to the project.
8. Define application routes.
9. Create service instances for the application.
10. Add scheduled jobs as needed.
11. Deploy the application.
12. Test the application.

In this section, we'll offer some simple examples to get you started on the path to developing your own SAP HANA XSA applications. Much of the content in this section, including the development of the Tiny World application, is contained in the *SAP HANA Developer Guide for SAP HANA XS Advanced Model*, available for download from SAP at *http://help.sap.com*.

As the SAP Web IDE is the preferred application for unlocking the power of SAP HANA as an application platform, we'll cover the following steps in this section:

1. Getting the SAP Web IDE address.

2. Setting up a project.

3. Developing and running application modules.

These topics should be enough to get you started with using SAP HANA XSA as your preferred application development platform; however, this section is not intended to be a comprehensive guide. For many more related subjects, including debugging, packaging modules, and deploying your application, you should consult the *SAP HANA Developer Guide for SAP HANA XS Advanced Model* for a complete guide to developing applications with SAP HANA XSA.

3.3.1 Getting the SAP Web IDE Address

The first step in your SAP HANA XSA development efforts will be opening the SAP Web IDE. The XS CLI that we referred to earlier is essential because you'll need to use the XS CLI to determine the URL for your SAP Web IDE installation. For a guide to extracting the SAP HANA XS client, see SAP Note 2242468.

First, you need to obtain the SAP HANA XS client for your system. To get the client, you'll need to extract the SAP HANA Platform installation media to your computer and then navigate to the DATA_UNITS • XSA_CLIENT_10 folder (Figure 3.24).

Select the ZIP file that matches your system (for example, the Windows client is in the *xs.onpremise.runtime.client_ntamd64.zip* file) and extract it to a folder on your system. If you're on a Windows system, you can navigate to the folder where you extracted the files and hold [Shift] while right-clicking on the BIN folder to open the alternate context menu for the folder. Select OPEN COMMAND WINDOW HERE from the context menu to open a command prompt in the bin folder.

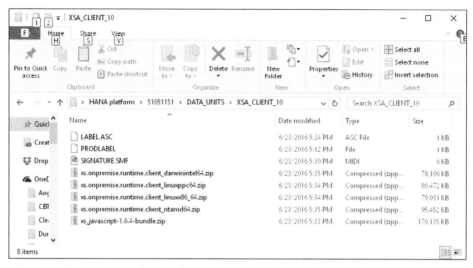

Figure 3.24 SAP HANA XS Client in the SAP HANA Platform Installation Media

---

Note

The command line options in the following section will work regardless of whether you're using a Windows or Linux system. For Linux, you need to open the TERMINAL window in the BIN location and add the "./" prefix to all of the commands.

From the command prompt, you can use the XS CLI client to obtain the URLs for the SAP HANA XSA platform components, but first you'll need to set the client environment and login. To set the client environment and configure a secure SSL connection between your system and the SAP HANA XSA platform, you'll need to configure SSL for your system. See SAP Note 2242468 for information about configuring your system for SSL, or see your system administrator to obtain the SSL certificate for your server. With the certificate available, you can now connect your client to the server with the following command:

```
xs api https://<FQDN>:3<instance>30 -cacert <path/certificate>
```

Next you'll need to login to the platform. To do so, enter xs login at the command prompt. You'll be prompted to enter your user name and password, and you should be notified that your authentication was successful by the return of the system connection information, as shown in Figure 3.25.

Figure 3.25 Connection Established to the SAP HANA XSA Runtime Platform

To get the URL for your SAP Web IDE connection, enter `xs app webide -urls` at the command prompt. The web address for your SAP Web IDE connection will be displayed in the COMMAND PROMPT window.

You should use command `xs -v` in the XS CLI to obtain the addresses for other important components in your SAP HANA XSA system. In particular, you're going to want the address for the XS ADVANCED ADMINISTRATION AND MONITORING TOOLS portal, where you'll need to create spaces for your applications, add developer users, and assign users to development spaces. The `xsa-admin` service has the address for this portal, as shown in Figure 3.26.

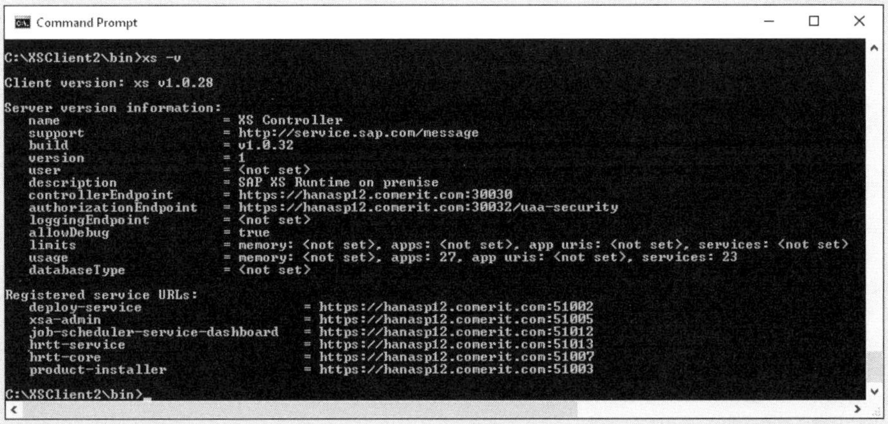

Figure 3.26 Addresses for SAP HANA XSA Service Portals

3.3.2 Project Setup

With the address for the SAP Web IDE in hand, you're ready to set up your project. Navigate to the web address you found using the directions in the previous section and login to the platform with your SAP HANA XSA developer user. The SAP Web IDE will open (Figure 3.27), and you'll be ready to set up your project.

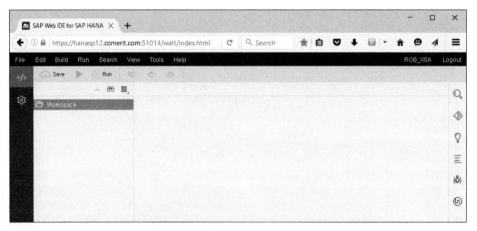

Figure 3.27 SAP Web IDE for SAP HANA XSA Application Development

From the SAP Web IDE, select FILE • NEW • PROJECT FROM TEMPLATE. The TEMPLATE SELECTION window will open, and you should be able to select the template for a MULTI-TARGET APPLICATION PROJECT (Figure 3.28). Select the template and click NEXT.

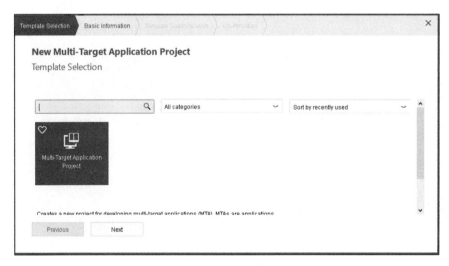

Figure 3.28 Creating an SAP HANA XSA Application from a Template

Enter a name for the project and click NEXT. Since we're using the tutorial from the developer guide, we entered "TinyWorld" for our PROJECT NAME (Figure 3.29). Click NEXT to advance to the TEMPLATE CUSTOMIZATION tab.

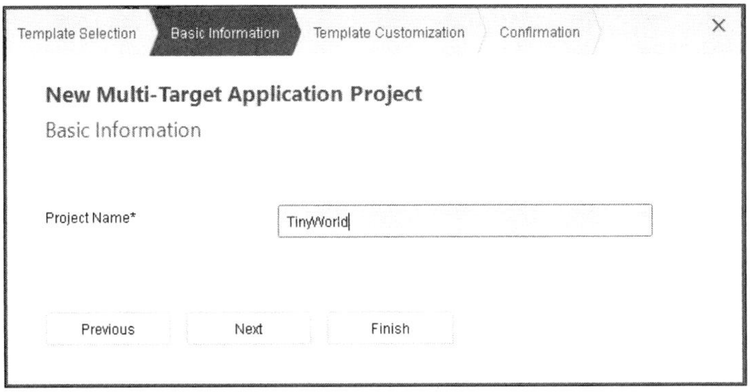

Figure 3.29 Creating the TinyWorld Application

On the TEMPLATE CUSTOMIZATION tab, you can specify the APPLICATION ID, APPLICATION VERSION, DESCRIPTION, and development SPACE for the new application (Figure 3.30). Enter the required information and click NEXT to advance to the CONFIRMATION tab. Click FINISH to create the new project.

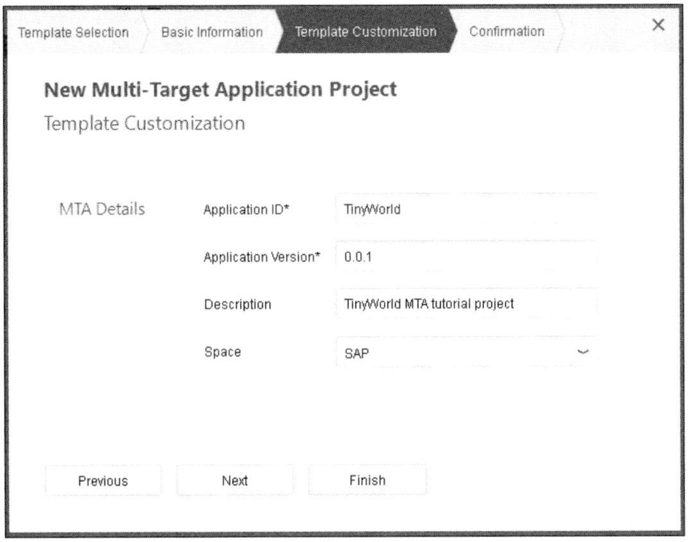

Figure 3.30 Assigning Descriptive Information to Your SAP HANA XSA Project

The new application will appear in the WORKSPACE folder in the SAP Web IDE, and a filed named *mta.yaml* will be the only file in the new project. This file is the MTA descriptor file, which contains a record of any dependencies or prerequisites required when the application is ready for deployment. This file will grow as you add code and modules to your project. With the project created, you're ready to begin developing the new project.

3.3.3   Developing and Running Application Modules

Next, we're going to add a database module to the project. To add this module, right-click the TINYWORLD project folder and select NEW HDB MODULE from the context menu. The NEW • HDB MODULE window will open, and you'll need to provide a MODULE NAME for the project. In our example (Figure 3.31), we've named our module the "tinyWorldDB." Click NEXT to advance to the TEMPLATE CUSTOMIZATION tab.

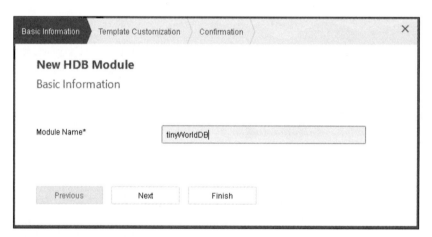

Figure 3.31 Creating a New SAP HANA Database Module

Confirm the INITIAL VIEW DETAILS for the NAMESPACE. If you've been following along with our example, you should have `TinyWorld.tinyWorldDB` already entered here. Click NEXT to advance to the CONFIRMATION tab and click FINISH to create the new database module. The TINYWORLDDB object folder will be added to the TINYWORLD project folder, and the new object folder will contain a folder named SRC, which will appear to be empty upon first inspection; however, if you'll select VIEW • SHOW HIDDEN FILES from the SAP Web IDE menu, you'll see that the src folder actually contains files named *.hdiconfig* and *.hdinamespace*. The *.hdiconfig* file is required for SAP HANA XSA projects and specifies the plug-ins used by SPA HANA to create a catalog object. The *.hdinamespace* file specifies rules for runtime namespaces and is optional.

Next, we'll need to create a simple database table in our project using core data services (CDS) programming, an enhanced and extended version of SQL used to define and consume data models. Use the following steps to create the new data model:

1. Right-click the src folder in the tinyWorldDB folder and select New CDS Artifact from the context menu.

2. Enter "tinyTable" as the name in the Create New CDS file window (Figure 3.32).

Figure 3.32 Creating a New CDS Data Model

3. Select Graphical as the Editor and make sure the With Context checkbox is selected.

4. Click Create to create the new data model and verify that the file named tiny-Table.hdbcds is created in the src folder.

5. Double-click the new file to open the editor.

6. Enter the code from Listing 3.2 into the editor pane.

```
namespace TinyWorld.tinyWorldDB;
context tinyTable{
    entity world {
        key continent: String(100);
    };
};
```

Listing 3.2 Code for the tinyTable.hdbcds File

> **Note**
>
> The code in Listing 3.2 defines a table named "world" with a field named "continent." and a field type of up to 100 characters in a string.

7. Save the HDB module with the SAVE icon or with Ctrl+S on the keyboard.
8. Select BUILD • BUILD from the file menu in the SAP Web IDE.

You should receive a message stating that the build was completed successfully in the console window, which indicates that your simple data model has been activated in the SAP HANA database and can be used for storing and retrieving data.

Next, we'll create a Node.js module based on the XSJS library. Use the following directions to build a simple Node.js module:

1. Right-click the TINYWORLD folder to open the context menu.
2. Select NEW NODE.JS MODULE from the context menu.
3. Name the module "tinyWorldJS."
4. Select the checkbox to ENABLE XSJS SUPPORT.
5. Click FINISH.
6. Double-click the *lib/index.xsjs* file to open the file in the JavaScript editor.
7. In the JavaScript editor, replace the default code with the following:

    ```
    $.response.contentType = "text/html";
    $.response.setBody("Welcome to the tiny JS World!");
    ```

8. Save the file with Ctrl+S.
9. Right-click the TINYWORLDJS folder to open the context menu.
10. Select RUN • RUN AS • NODE.JS APPLICATION.

A new browser tab will open with the address for the new XSJS module (or in a new window, depending on your browser settings). By choosing to run the application, we implicitly tell the editor to build the application and then run it, so you can return to the SAP Web IDE console to monitor the progress. You should soon see the application status change to STATUS: RUNNING, and you should have the message, "Welcome to the tiny JS World!" in the browser window for the application.

Finally, the process to add an HTML5 module to your new application is nearly identical to the one used for Node.js, with the obvious exception being the difference in programming languages between HTML5 and Node.js. Follow the process below to add an HTML5 module:

1. Right-click the TINYWORLD folder to open the context menu.

2. Select NEW HTML5 MODULE from the context menu.

3. Name the module "tinyWorldUI."

4. Click FINISH.

5. Double-click the *resources/index.html* file to open the file in the editor.

6. Replace the default code with the following:

```
<!DOCTYPE html>
<html> <body> Welcome to your Tiny HTML World! </html>
```

7. Save the file with Ctrl + S .

8. Right-click the TINYWORLDJS folder to open the context menu.

9. Select RUN • RUN AS • WEB APPLICATION.

As with Node.js modules, a new browser tab or window should open, and the text "Welcome to your Tiny HTML World!" should appear in the new window.

We'll wrap up our discussion of SAP Web IDE here for now, as this should be enough to get you started. For a more in-depth exploration of creating SAP HANA XSA applications, you can download the *SAP HANA Developer Guide for SAP HANA XS Advanced Model*, or you can access the excellent series of blogs by Chaim Bendelac on the subject called *Developing with XS Advanced: A TinyWorld Tutorial*, which covers both basic and advanced development with SAP HANA XSA. Part 1 of the blog can be accessed at *http://scn.sap.com/community/developer-center/hana/blog/2016/03/28/developing-with-xs-advanced-a-tinyworld-tutorial*.

3.4   Summary

In this chapter, we explored the capabilities you can unlock with SAP HANA as your application platform. You can develop basic applications through the SAP HANA Web-Based Development Workbench, but the SAP Web IDE is the latest development interface for creating customized, high-performance web applications. The development interface you choose will depend on the support package stack of your SAP HANA system, and the SAP Web IDE is frequently updated to enhance its effectiveness and ease of use. The combination of SAP HANA as your application platform and the new, powerful web-based development tools provides you with the flexibility to build anything you want with virtually no limitations on one of the fastest database systems in the world: SAP HANA.

SAP HANA Cloud Platform (SAP HCP) is a platform as a service (PaaS) offering that allows you to develop new applications.

4   SAP HANA Cloud Platform

A platform as a service (PaaS) is a cloud computing model that delivers applications over the Internet—from any cloud your organization has access to or pays for. In a PaaS model, a cloud provider (IBM, SAP, Google, etc.) delivers hardware and software tools (usually those needed for application development) to its users as a service. A PaaS provider hosts the hardware and software on its own infrastructure. As a result, PaaS frees users from having to install in-house hardware and software to develop or run a new application. PaaS arrangements can be for "private" clouds, meaning only your organization has access to anything on this cloud, or multitenant/public clouds, which are similar to a time share: you pay for a piece of it and have your own little area, but you share the common resources.

The SAP HANA Cloud Platform is SAP's PaaS offering that allows its customers, partners, and developers to build, extend, test, and run applications built for SAP HANA "on the cloud." Subscription models and services are available that let each organization dictate how much, what kinds, and what levels of service are included with this model. The "as a service" concept also means that you pay for what you need as you need it—so you can rent a room instead of buying the whole house.

SAP HANA Cloud Platform allows you to both build standalone applications and add enhancements from the cloud to your existing SAP applications. This chapter starts with an introduction to SAP HCP, including information regarding the different editions available to customers. Then, we'll walk through some of SAP HCP's most important features, from enablement services to its Content Management Interoperability Service (CMIS).

We then provide a brief introduction to the SAP HANA Platform Cockpit and the SAP HANA Cloud Portal, before closing with an overview of the steps necessary to get started in the SAP HANA Cloud Platform.

4.1 Overview

Using the SAP HANA Cloud Platform, users can develop and operate their own solutions. A Java Runtime Environment (JRE); SAP HANA extended application services, classic model (SAP HANA XS Classic); SAP HANA extended application services, advanced model (SAP HANA XSA); and an HTML5 runtime environment are some of the available runtime environments. SAP HANA XS Classic and SAP HANA XSA were covered in detail in Chapter 3.

Arguably, the biggest benefit of the SAP HANA Cloud Platform is that there are no investment costs because the SAP HANA database is operated in the cloud. SAP is responsible for supporting and maintaining the SAP HANA databases and the entire platform including regular updates and patches. Furthermore, SAP assumes responsibility for data security and secure communication channels.

Existing on-premise and cloud solutions from SAP and other providers can be integrated with SAP HCP to map consistent processes. To help with this, SAP HCP provides adapters and integration flows. For simple user management, SAP HCP allows you to define roles and assign authorizations.

SAP HCP is mainly based on established standards. Some of the web development standards supported by SAP HCP are Apache Maven, Eclipse Memory Analyzer, JRebel, Gerrit, and Git. These tools can help you with revision control, facilitating collaboration, reducing data leaks, and modifying code in running applications, among their many functionalities.

When discussing the cloud, one topic that always comes up is data security. Enterprises can lose control over their data because the data might not be physically located in the same country as the customer. Sometimes, how the cloud provider manages customer data is not always clear.

SAP HANA Cloud Platform is certified according to ISO 27001. All hosts are operated in SAP HCP in isolation from one another in what are called *application sandboxes*. Data can only be accessed via an application programming interface (API), which is coupled to user-specific authorization concepts. As a result, your data is isolated from the data of other customers on SAP HCP.

Additionally, an auditing trace is installed that allows for the permanent tracing of all user actions, enabling you to track what changes were made by which users. The data is stored and encoded using encryption algorithms, such as AES, RSA, or SHA-256. Data is transferred using encrypted communication according to the

HTTPS protocol. In addition, protection against SQL injection and scripting attacks is ensured.

SAP HCP is offered in different editions that differ in storage, CPU, and RAM. Generally, the following applies: The more complex your application, the more RAM should you select. For fast implementation of SAP HCP, you can try the trial edition. The editions differ as follows:

▶ **Developer edition**
The developer edition includes a free SAP HANA instance on a shared database. This edition includes development tools like Eclipse, the SAP Web IDE, SAP HANA XS Classic, SAP HANA XSA, and HTML5. Only one user is allowed, and this edition provides 2 GB RAM (on a shared database instance) and 1 GB of storage. Support is not available for this edition.

▶ **Starter editions (32 GB and 64 GB)**
Two starter editions are available, one with 32 GB of storage and 4 GB RAM and one with 64 GB of storage and 6 GB of RAM. The starter editions do not operate on a shared SAP HANA database. The starter edition is ideal for developing large SAP applications or enhancements for existing SAP and non-SAP systems.

▶ **Medium business packages**
Three editions fall within this offering, as follows:

  ▹ SAP HANA Cloud Platform, professional edition: minimum of 30 users, 4 GB RAM, and 10 GB of storage

  ▹ SAP HANA Cloud Platform, single application edition: minimum of 10 users, 8 GB RAM, and 2 GB of storage per end user

  ▹ SAP HANA Cloud Platform, multiple application edition: minimum of 10 users, 24 GB RAM, and 2 GB of storage per end user

The main goal of these editions is for developing extensions for existing (on-premise) SAP and non-SAP applications. These editions provide SAP support.

▶ **Enterprise packages**
Three editions fall within this offering, as follows:

  ▹ SAP HANA Cloud Platform, app services package, standard edition: 8 GB RAM and 100 GB of storage

  ▹ SAP HANA Cloud Platform, app services package, professional edition: 16 GB RAM and 200 GB of storage

▶ SAP HANA Cloud Platform, app services package, premium edition: 32 GB RAM and 400 GB of storage

The enterprise package editions are ideal for developing Java or SAP HANA applications using SAP HANA XS or SAP HANA XSA. This edition includes SAP support.

For a full comparison of all the editions, visit *https://hcp.sap.com/content/dam/website/skywalker/en_us/PDFs/SAP_HANA_Cloud_Platform_Pricing_and_Packaging.pdf*.

To register for one of these editions, go to *https://account.hanatrial.ondemand.com/*. After selecting an edition, follow the steps on the screen to register. You will need to provide your personal data and accept the usage guidelines. Now, you can start developing your first application as a registered SAP HCP user.

4.2   Features

This section will provide an overview of SAP HCP's most critical features including access and authorizations, enablement services, schema, content management, and mobile services.

4.2.1   Access and Authorizations

The most important SAP HCP function is the creation of an application platform with database calls and data manipulation. SAP provides several interfaces to access data, the most relevant of which are the Java Database Connectivity (JDBC) interface and the Java Persistence API (JPA) 2.0. Each has the following characteristics:

▶ **JDBC**
This is designed for relational databases and is a universal and manufacturer-independent database interface. JDBC establishes and manages database connections, forwards SQL requests to the database, and converts the results into a format that can be processed by the application. You can use JDBC to read data from the database and to update data.

▶ **JPA**
This is an interface for Java applications that provides support for assigning and transferring Java objects and that describes how relational data in applications is managed. You can also use JPA with SAP HANA Enterprise Cloud (SAP HEC).

You can manage access authorizations in the SAP HCP Cockpit. However, because users should not be managed for each application separately, SAP uses the open SAML (Security Assertion Markup Language) 2.0 standard to manage the authentication process and identities. As such, you can authenticate users via the SAP ID service, SAP Single Sign-On, or third-party applications. The SAML standard defines the authentication procedure. The external identity manager authenticates the user according to a specified mechanism (e.g., user name and password, SAP login ticket, certificate, etc.). After the central management system has verified the identity, the identity manager returns an SAML response that includes the user's access. If the response is positive, the user is granted access. The SAP ID service is set as the user management option by default.

4.2.2 Enablement Services

SAP HCP includes a series of enablement services for access to and consumption of cloud-based resources. The following is a list of the most important services provided by SAP HCP. We recommend checking the SAP HANA cloud documentation for the most up-to-date information, as offerings are continually being expanded.

▶ **Persistence Service**
This service provides an abstraction on top of relational database instances deployed in the cloud. This abstraction provides developers with a common interface for accessing database instances while at the same time shielding them from the underlying complexities of scaling databases in the cloud.

▶ **Connectivity Service**
This service provides developers with a means of transparently communicating with remote services that could be hosted either on-premise or elsewhere on the Internet.

▶ **Document Service**
This service provides access to a content repository for storing unstructured content and can also be used to implement a sort of virtualized file system as needed.

▶ **Identity Service**
This service encompasses a series of security-related services or features integrated into SAP HCP. Some highlights in this offering include support for single sign-on (SSO) scenarios, identity federation with SAML, and authorization based on the OAuth protocol.

► **Feedback Service**
This service provides a framework for implementing user feedback scenarios in cloud applications.

4.2.3 Schemas

You can coordinate numerous applications and internal and external providers using SAP HCP. In general, you access the database in SAP HCP using either JDBC or JPA, discussed in Section 4.2.1. At the database level, different schemas are maintained. Each application usually has its own schema, which you can also manage in the SAP HANA Cloud Cockpit (see Section 4.3). One schema is assigned to exactly one application, and SAP HANA Cloud Platform automatically creates the bindings between schemas and applications.

You can change the default settings, however. For example, several applications can share a schema, or one application can use several schemas. In the first case, data stored in tables in the schemas can be used by several applications. This sharing enables you to implement highly complex use cases.

You can use several locations (computer, server, etc.) to test applications consistently. For example, you could develop new applications on local computers and then test them on local computers and on the corresponding servers in the data center.

4.2.4 Content Management

For unstructured data, SAP provides the Content Management Interoperability Service (CMIS), which enables you to process and store documents. CMIS defines semantics and protocols, and its tasks include data management and folder management as well as management of the corresponding metadata and properties. The data is stored via SAP HCP. In SAP HCP, CMIS is charged according to a pay-per-use model.

CMIS includes versioning and rights management. Lifecycle management allows you to define the maximum or minimum age of a database entry. You can also create custom queries with CMISQL. For these queries, metadata and properties are browsed. Predefined metadata includes name, description, created by, changed by, created on, changed on, and so on. In addition, you can create property fields (sap-tags) that contain any number of values. You can use CMISQL to access metadata and properties.

SAP makes extensive use of security mechanisms like encryption. Content in the repository is encrypted, for example, and documents are always scanned for viruses when they are uploaded. Data is backed up at regular intervals.

You can also utilize data from the repository through external solutions, that is, using an external application. Normally, the documents in the cloud are solely available for applications in a specific account. A proxy bridge enables you to access data from external solutions and guides external CMIS requests to the document service. To protect documents against unauthorized access, roles and filters are used to provide security. Only users with the right roles can access data through CMIS tools. Access Control Lists (ACLs) are another means of providing security; they create access lists at the folder and document levels.

4.2.5 Mobile Services

With Mobile Services, SAP HCP enables you to create and manage mobile applications. With a focus on business applications, you can include a variety of functions in your applications, such as notifications, reporting, or logging. It also allows your mobile applications to connect with the backend system and to access data via SAP HANA Cloud Integration (SAP HCI) OData services.

SAP HCP provides a central cockpit for mobile applications. The Mobile Service Cockpit contains many options for managing mobile applications. You can perform the following activities:

▸ Creating applications

▸ Configuring applications

▸ Defining and configuring push notifications

▸ Configuring OData services

▸ Logging and tracing

To create a new application, only a few steps need to be performed. First, you require some information regarding configuration, such as integration or security information. Then, you can register the application. Only if you register the application can you use the data from the backend system (e.g., data from SAP ERP). Then, you can actually develop the application. The Mobile Service Cockpit displays the entire data traffic and which end devices are logged on to the application.

4.3 SAP HANA Cloud Platform Cockpit

The SAP HCP Cockpit is the central hub of SAP HCP and is required for all applications. The dashboard is illustrated in Figure 4.1, which shows several available options.

The initial screen shows the DASHBOARD of your account as well as an overview of the current state of applications that are running. As you can see in Figure 4.1, the system can display the status of applications on the SAP HANA XS engine and on HTML5 and JREs. You can also view the error log here.

In the fee-based editions, the DASHBOARD provides access to 24/7 monitoring including the option of email notifications for certain events. You can also access logging tools with which you can monitor the application's traffic.

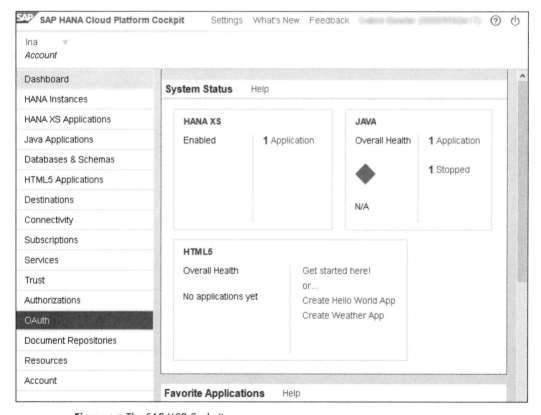

Figure 4.1 The SAP HCP Cockpit

Each tab has the following attributes:

▸ The HANA INSTANCES tab shows all running instances of the SAP HANA application as well as their current health (see Figure 4.2). You can also add further instances here. This tab also provides information on the database version, the number of applications operating on this database, and when this instance was created.

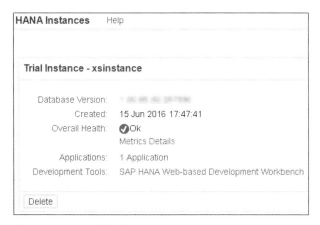

Figure 4.2 An SAP HANA Instance

▸ The application list on the HANA XS APPLICATIONS tab shows all SAP HANA XS applications that have been created for your account.

▸ The JAVA APPLICATIONS tab lists all of your Java applications. For each application, you can view its current state, its name, and the number of currently executed processes. You are also provided with information on when the processes were started (date and time).

▸ The DATABASE & SCHEMAS tab shows all databases and schemas that are currently being used. For each database, the respective version and type are listed. This tab also lists applications that have access to the database.

▸ The HTML5 APPLICATIONS tab shows what HTML5 applications are running as well as their names, states, and version numbers. In this context, you can find various labels that describe the state of applications.

Your applications can have various states, such as the following:

▸ *Started*: Your application was started successfully and is available.

▸ *Starting*: Your application is still starting and is not available yet.

> ▹ *Stopping*: Your application is currently stopped and is no longer available.

> ▹ *Infrastructure error*: Due to an error in the underlying infrastructure, your application cannot be started.

> ▹ *Stopped*: Your application was created but has not been started yet.

> To change the state of the application, you can either start or stop the files. If you delete an application, you remove the application from the SAP HCP repository. You can no longer use or start the application afterwards.

▶ You can create new connections in the DESTINATIONS tab. Your application can then use these connections to access an Internet service or an on-premise system. You can also import connections from other projects.

▶ The SUBSCRIPTIONS tab contains all HTML5 applications for which you have a subscription in SAP HCP.

▶ The SERVICES tab lists all services that you can access in SAP HCP. Cloud administrators can select and activate additional services here. For example, mobile services are available that would enable you to develop mobile applications or create a portal for a website. Services include many basic SAP HCP functions, which were described in detail in Section 4.2.

▶ On the TRUST tab, you can define relationships between SAP HCP and other systems (on-premise systems, for example). Here, SAML 2.0 is used to configure communications between SAP HCP and the identity provider.

▶ The AUTHORIZATIONS tab is used to manage authorizations. Initially, you define roles and assign them to users. For authorizations, you can also use an external user management system (for example, SAP ID) to identify users. As with many IT tools, you can combine several roles into groups.

▶ The OAUTH tab enables API authorization for applications. The advantage of the open OAuth protocol is that access can be granted without having to explicitly exchange access data. This functionality is ideal, for example, for mobile applications that are not supposed to store authentication logics or for centralizing user management processes.

▶ Via the DOCUMENT REPOSITORIES tab, you can store unstructured or semistructured data.

Unstructured versus Semistructured Data

Unstructured data usually includes text (i.e., blogs, forum posts, and documents); videos; or graphics, whereas semistructured data maps input fields or XML files, for example.

▸ The DOCUMENT REPOSITORIES tab enables you to provide data for exchanges over the Internet. Provisioning actually takes place via the standard OASIS protocol, for example, through Content Management Interoperability Services (CMIS).

▸ The RESOURCES tab shows a detailed overview of available resources, such as network (data transfer), persistency (storage space), and computer units. The limitations of each resource depend which edition you are using.

▸ On the last tab, the ACCOUNT tab, you can manage information on your SAP HCP account, such as the account name or your user name.

Thus, the SAP HCP Cockpit provides a detailed overview about the edition you are using and all relevant applications. Furthermore, you can use the cockpit to manage and control access options and essential SAP HCP functions.

For SAP HCP, SAP provides comprehensive online help with numerous sample scenarios and step-by-step instructions. You can navigate to the corresponding online help sections from each tab. To do so, simply click on the question mark icon or HELP links, which will take you to the online help. You can also directly access the help at *http://help.hana.ondemand.com*.

SAP's large developer community is a good supplement to the official online help. The community comprises a vast number of blogs, podcasts, and forum posts. The direct link to the community is *http://developers.sap.com/cloud*. Alternatively, you can also click on COMMUNITY in the SAP HCP Cockpit.

4.4   SAP HANA Cloud Portal

SAP HANA Cloud Portal allows you to create websites. These websites can be extensions of local applications, such as support websites. SAP HANA Cloud Portal is a cloud-based solution that can be used from a web browser. You can easily manage these websites via a graphical interface. Internally, you can use HTML5 and SAPUI5 to manage them.

To create a website, navigate to the SERVICE tab in the SAP HCP Cockpit and click on SAP HANA CLOUD PLATFORM. In the new window, click on GO TO SERVICE. The system then generates an empty portal, as shown in Figure 4.3.

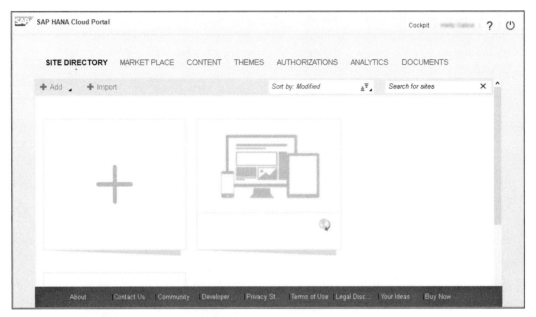

Figure 4.3 SAP HANA Cloud Portal

You can purchase specific templates from the marketplace, modify website content, edit templates and images, define authorizations, or analyze your website. In the DOCUMENTS tab, you can upload documents to make available on the website.

The SAP Marketplace contains various sample websites that you can easily add to your account and then adapt. To do so, select a website on the MARKET PLACE tab in SAP HANA Cloud Portal and click on +GET THIS SITE. This site is then added to your site directory, and you can edit it from the SITE DIRECTORY tab. To edit the template, click on EDIT in the tile of the selected template. The system opens a new editing window where you can change text, images, and videos in the template. Editing is quite user friendly because you can simply click on the ⚙ icon in each field and then on EDIT in the context menu. The text field opens in edit mode (see Figure 4.4).

Figure 4.4 Creating Sites in SAP HANA Cloud Portal

You can also create sites without templates by clicking on the large plus icon in the SITE DIRECTORY tab and assigning a name to the site. You can then create the site graphically, in a way that is analogous to creating sites with templates.

When the site is complete, you can view it offline before going live. Additionally, to access the site via a web browser, you can also preview the site on mobile end devices, such as tablets and smartphones. To do this, click on the ▣ icon in the menu bar at the right.

Next, you can click on the ▣ icon in the menu bar on the right and then on the PUBLISH button. Now, your site has been published online and can be accessed from any device. If you want to delete the website, you must first take it offline.

4.5 Getting Started

To use SAP HCP for development purposes, you install the local components on your computer. The developer tools you'll need are available via *https:// tools.hana.ondemand.com*. Here, you can also find Eclipse versions to develop with SAP HCP. SAP extensions for Eclipse are available for the two Eclipse versions: Eclipse Mars (4.5) and Eclipse Neon (4.6). Links for these extensions are available at: *https://tools.hana.ondemand.com/#cloud*.

Installing the local components involves three required steps and one optional step:

1. **Install Eclipse**
   For this purpose, navigate to the TOOLS tab in the SAP HCP Cockpit. Installing Eclipse is rather simple, and a setup wizard will guide you through each individual step. To use SAP HCP for development purposes, you should install Eclipse IDE for Java EE Developers.

   During this step, you must also must install the add-ons for SAP HCP. To do this, open Eclipse and navigate to HELP • INSTALL NEW SOFTWARE. The system displays a dialog window in which you must enter the path to your add-ons. To do so, click on ADD... and enter any name and the corresponding path. Depending on whether you downloaded the Mars or Neon version, you must enter one of these two paths:

   ▶ Eclipse Mars (4.3): *https://tools.hana.ondemand.com/mars*

   ▶ Eclipse Neon (4.4): *https://tools.hana.ondemand.com/neon*

   Select the SAP HANA CLOUD PLATFORM TOOLS and SAP HANA TOOLS options. Confirm your selection with NEXT and accept the license. Then, click on FINISH. Installing these SAP HANA development tools should take several minutes.

2. **Install Java**
   In most cases, Java will already been installed on your machine. To confirm, open the administration console (for Windows operating systems, the console is under START • CMD; for Mac OS X, open the Terminal app) and enter "java -version." If Java has been installed, the system now displays what version you have. If no Java version has been installed on your local computer, you can download the latest version from the official website at *https://java.com/en/download*. A setup wizard will guide you through the necessary steps to install Java.

3. **Install the software development kit (SDK)**
   You can download the SDK from the official SAP website or directly at *https://tools.hana.ondemand.com/#cloud*. You can select between different SDK versions for various runtime environments (see Figure 4.5).

SAP HANA Cloud Platform SDK	Comment	Version	File Size	Download	Show old versions
Java Web		1.110.17.1	79.9 MB	neo-java-web-sdk-1.110.17.1.zip	
Java Web Tomcat 7		2.57.7.1	60.9 MB	neo-java-web-sdk-2.57.7.1.zip	
Java EE 6 Web Profile		2.92.5.2	99.7 MB	neo-javaee6-wp-sdk-2.92.5.2.zip	
Java Web Tomcat 8		3.11.5.1	61.2 MB	neo-java-web-sdk-3.11.5.1.zip	

Figure 4.5 Selecting the SDK Version

For installations on your local computer, the version is irrelevant. Click on a version, accept the license agreement, and download the SDK. After downloading the file, you have to unpack it (using ZIP or similar) and install the SDK.

4. **(Optional) Install SAP Java Virtual Machine (SAP JVM)**
The SAP JVM can be downloaded from the same downloads page we used to download the SAP HCP SDK: *https://tools.hana.ondemand.com/#cloud*. In the SAP JVM section of the page, simply download the appropriate bundle for your OS configuration. You can find installation instructions for your particular OS in the SAP HANA cloud documentation available at *https://help.hana.ondemand.com/help/frameset.htm*. Here, browse to Java Development • Getting Started • Installing Java Tools for Eclipse and SDK • Installing SAP JVM. After the SAP JVM is installed, you will need to associate it with the set of installed JREs in Eclipse

4.6   Summary

This chapter provided you with a detailed overview of SAP HCP. SAP HCP is a PaaS offering from SAP. SAP HCP enables you to access an SAP HANA database and a programming platform, which are provided by SAP and enhanced by a broad range of additional services and solutions. Regarding usage scenarios, SAP mainly focuses on hybrid and mobile scenarios. Regardless of the specific scenario, SAP HCP reduces time to market and enables you to create and use a vast number of applications.

SAP continuously promotes the development of SAP HCP, and complex integration scenarios are supposed to motivate customers to take the step towards adopting hybrid clouds.

SAP S/4HANA is SAP's answer to the much-hyped "digital transforma-
tion." In this chapter, we will look at what SAP S/4HANA brings to the
table in terms of functionality and innovation by looking at a few finan-
cial and logistics use cases.

5   SAP S/4HANA

In Chapter 2, we briefly introduced the topics and concepts around SAP S/4HANA—
the new and improved ERP solution from SAP. In this chapter, we want to delve
into this discussion in further detail. SAP S/4HANA Enterprise Management requires that you have SAP HANA as the underlying database/platform; it will not
execute on any other vendor's database even if that database is another in-memory
platform.

Let's start with understanding the fundamentals and the thought process that went
into SAP S/4HANA and what, exactly, SAP S/4HANA Enterprise Management is.
Next, we'll take a look at the two most significant areas where SAP S/4HANA currently delivers new functionality: finance and logistics.

We will also discuss business cases for moving to SAP S/4HANA. Finally, we will
take a quick look at what migrating to and implementing SAP S/4HANA would
look like.

5.1   Overview

We are in an age where we, as a community, create more data every two days
than all of the information created in history until recent times. However, we
struggle to separate information from data—value from the noise. Businesses
need a way to capture this level of information, make sense of it all, and then use
it to their competitive advantage.

Modern solutions must enable real-time decision making—from any device at any time. Information itself, the systems themselves, must be more integrated and connected. Having all your data in an SAP system is not enough if you can't access all the data or make sense of it. Solutions must empower your user communities—internally and externally—to make better decisions.

SAP answers these problems with SAP HANA. Starting with SAP HANA as an in-memory database (IMDB) for existing SAP ERP systems, they addressed the need for more real-time access to information and laid the foundation for the connected solutions of the future. They then rewrote and simplified their applications to take advantage of SAP HANA as an in-memory business platform. This new and unique enterprise application is called SAP S/4HANA, which we introduced in Chapter 2.

> **Note**
>
> For those who are not ready to move to SAP S/4HANA, SAP Business Suite on SAP HANA is still a valid option. Although you will not see all the new functionality brought by SAP S/4HANA, you will still see significant performance improvements.

So what is SAP S/4HANA? The short, nontechnical answer is that SAP S/4HANA is SAP ERP redesigned and rewritten to take advantage of SAP HANA. SAP is changing the core code and rewriting modules one by one, the biggest change to the core SAP systems since moving from SAP R/2 to SAP R/3. SAP S/4HANA leverages SAP Fiori to provide a new user experience, maximizes the capabilities of SAP HANA for speed and power, and brings together the possibility of a single database for both online transaction processing (OLTP) and online analytical processing (OLAP). As a result, your users are closer to their data and can gain insights from that information.

The solution today is referred to as SAP S/4HANA Enterprise Management, but most people still simply refer to it as SAP S/4HANA. An overview of SAP S/4HANA's product landscape can be seen in Figure 5.1.

Your first introduction to SAP S/4HANA was likely SAP Simple Finance in 2014, which was renamed to SAP S/4HANA Finance in 2015. SAP S/4HANA Finance was the first module rewritten to maximize (and require) the SAP HANA foundation. However, as you can see from Figure 5.2, SAP S/4HANA Finance was only the first module to be redesigned.

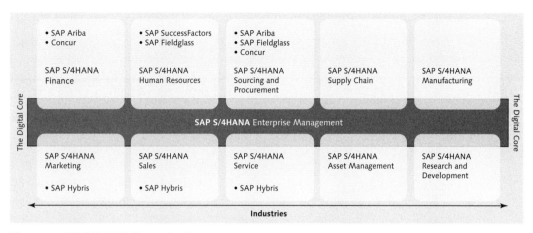

Figure 5.1 SAP S/4HANA Enterprise Management

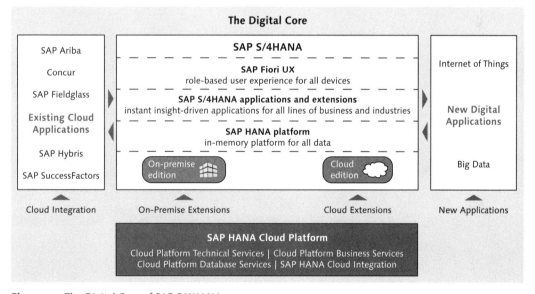

Figure 5.2 The Digital Core of SAP S/4HANA

SAP S/4HANA Enterprise Management is the next major update of SAP S/4HANA, release 1511. SAP S/4HANA Enterprise Management broadened already-supported functionality beyond financials and into area of logistics, such as production planning and inventory management. What is in SAP S/4HANA Enterprise Management, and how does it relate to the software we currently know: SAP ERP

6.0? How does everything fit together? How is SAP S/4HANA Enterprise Management implemented? Does it require an SAP HANA database?

First things first, SAP S/4HANA Enterprise Management's features and functions are similar to the scope of SAP ERP 6.0. Although yet not a complete rewrite of SAP ERP, a significant part of the core SAP ERP system has been rethought and reimagined to take advantage SAP HANA's capabilities and to eliminate the restrictions that the existing relational databases imposed.

SAP S/4HANA Enterprise Management also organizes processes differently, even thinking of them differently. Gone are the traditional modular concepts of SAP ERP Financials (FI) and Controlling (CO), Sales and Distribution (SD), Materials Management (MM), Warehouse Management (WM), etc. SAP S/4HANA Enterprise Management is organized the way your business is organized—by processes. Think of SAP S/4HANA Enterprise Management in terms of processes: procure-to-pay, plan-to-produce, order-to-cash, request-to-service, as well as human resources (HR), human capital management (HCM), and finance. This structure is more in line with how you would likely choose to implement a new system or to roll out new functionality than the previous modular concept. Some of the most important process areas, and their most significant functionality, are as follows:

- Procure-to-pay
  - Operational procurement
  - Inventory and basic warehouse management
  - Invoice and payables management
  - Sourcing and contract management
  - Supplier information and master data
- Plan-to-produce
  - Production planning
  - Manufacturing execution
  - Inventory and basic warehouse management
  - Product development and project control
  - Maintenance
  - Quality management and compliance

- Order-to-cash
  - Order and contract management
  - Inventory and basic warehouse management
  - Receivables processing
- Human resources
  - Cross-application time management
- Finance
  - Accounting and financial close
  - Cost management and profitability analysis
- Request-to-service
  - Service master data management
  - Service management
  - Service parts management
  - Service agreement management

From the business perspective, with SAP S/4HANA Enterprise Management, organizations can connect to people, devices, and other networks via any channel—especially with the Internet of Things (IoT) and big data inputs now accessible and integral to creating and driving value for your organization. Real-time processing will become more and more prevalent, and batch processing will be the exception—an exception that you choose to do instead of being constrained by the system's capabilities.

Additional technological changes and improvements are the result of how SAP S/4HANA leverages an open platform—SAP HANA Cloud Platform (SAP HCP)—for advanced development scenarios (therefore leaving existing investments untouched). SAP S/4HANA can be deployed on-premise, in the cloud, or potentially supported in a hybrid model—offering more savings potentials for customers.

The scope of the SAP S/4HANA Cloud addresses business scenarios for the marketing and professional services lines of business (LOBs) as well as most of the essential scenarios to run a business via the cloud. This digital core includes finance, procurement, sales, inventory management, project systems, and product lifecycles.

Other SAP tools are also integrated, such as SAP SuccessFactors Employee Central, the SAP Ariba Network, and SAP Hybris.

The on-premise version of SAP S/4HANA Enterprise Management is designed for organizations across industries that require a broad level of functionality combined with the flexibility to configure and customize their implementation to their exact requirements.

We are still in the early days of SAP S/4HANA Enterprise Management, and as with any early release, the functionality will continue to evolve, and the product itself is evolving along with it. Customer feedback and demand for new functionality will be significant drivers for future directions and capabilities. Partners, as well as customers, are driving additions as an extensive ecosystem of partners leveraging SAP HANA's capabilities for their own offerings and additions to SAP's core products.

Early adopters have spanned many different countries and industries—with no one group or region standing out as the dominant. Industries and organizations that are data driven and/or more entrenched in the digitization have seen more movement towards SAP S/4HANA than some others, but all industries can take advantage of the different features and functions offered.

All of the functionality featured in SAP S/4HANA Enterprise Management requires that SAP HANA be at the core of the system. Although this requirement is not optional, you are not being forced to transition to SAP HANA. However, if you want to use the new features and functions of SAP S/4HANA Enterprise Management, you must use SAP HANA. With that in mind, the question is no longer *if* your organization will have an SAP HANA footprint but has become a question of *when* your organization will have an SAP HANA footprint and how large that footprint will be.

5.2 SAP S/4HANA Finance

SAP S/4HANA Finance is highly focused on the need to run a real-time business to better facilitate decision making. SAP S/4HANA Finance enables this vision by removing technical barriers, but this is only one part of transforming business processes. Note that SAP S/4HANA Finance started out as an add-on to SAP ERP, which means that it was/is a standard product designed to work on top of—and in concert with—SAP ERP.

SAP S/4HANA Finance should not be interpreted as a simplified version of SAP ERP FI and CO. Instead, SAP S/4HANA Finance is a new, rewritten financial package from SAP that has been engineered to help meet the evolving business needs of finance departments. A broad offering covering end-to-end solutions for finance with data architectural changes, SAP S/4HANA Finance includes a set of new functionalities previously not available in SAP Business Suite on SAP HANA. (Remember that SAP Business Suite on SAP HANA is really "just" SAP ERP running on an SAP HANA database.) SAP S/4HANA Finance fully leverages the latest in-memory and real-time capabilities of SAP HANA with a new user experience written in SAP Fiori, usable on nearly any device with a simpler data model and real-time reporting capabilities.

On the technical side, implementing SAP S/4HANA Finance redefines traditional data aggregation using the in-memory capabilities of SAP HANA. As a result, calculations can be performed ad hoc for financial transactions. On the functional side, new capabilities were made available with the second release of SAP S/4HANA Finance, which we will discuss in the following sections. While by no means exhaustive, this list of SAP S/4HANA Finance's features and functions can start your discussions and evaluation of the tool.

5.2.1 Universal Journal

The biggest, and to many the most important, feature of SAP S/4HANA Finance is the new Universal Journal table. The Universal Journal table combines the previous financial tables from SAP General Ledger (G/L), Profitability Analysis (CO-PA), SAP Material Ledger (ML), Asset Accounting (FI-AA), and Controlling (CO) into a single table, as can be seen in Figure 5.3. This consolidation brings the benefits of having a single line-item table with full detail available for all your applications. Rather than having to source six different places and create joins, lookups, and references, data will be stored only once, which will reduce or eliminate the need for reconciliations. As a result, you will have a smaller footprint for your database size (and enjoy the resulting costs savings associated therein). You will also be able to create multidimensional reporting without having to replicate or move the data to an external database like SAP Business Warehouse (SAP BW).

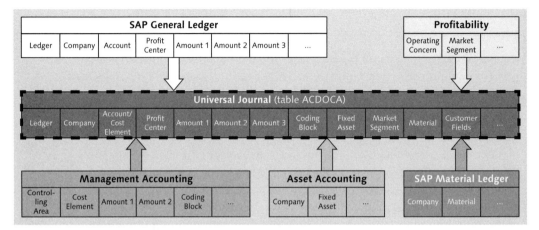

Figure 5.3 Universal Journal

SAP's new definition of "single source of truth" uses a new data model that combines CO, FI, CO-PA, and other financial data into one Universal Journal entry, all represented in one line-item table with full detail available for all components. Providing all data in real time from this single journal reduces effort on period-end reconciliations and financial reporting preparation.

The new Universal Journal allows ad-hoc, on-the-fly computations for converting periodic transactions, such as month-end activities, using real-time processing instead of batch processing, without needing the data to be replicated first to other systems like SAP BusinessObjects Business Intelligence (SAP BusinessObjects BI).

5.2.2 Period Close

SAP S/4HANA Finance also offers an accelerated period close, which gives you the ability to move away from batch to event-based processing and enables period-end processes to be run on a daily or weekly basis. As a result, your organizations will get a more real-time view of their profits and losses (P&L), providing the business with early visibility of emerging trends. This visibility will facilitate prompt remedial action where necessary, rather than forcing you to wait until after period end.

Because FI and CO data now both reside in the Universal Journal, SAP S/4HANA Finance also removes the need to reconcile FICO data before performing period-end closing. A soft closing process is also available.

5.2.3 Asset Accounting

The new Asset Accounting (FI-AA) is the mandatory replacement for the old Asset Accounting with simplified posting logic and tight integration with Universal Journal. As with other elements, FI-AA no longer needs to be reconciled with the SAP General Ledger (G/L) due to the Universal Journal.

With the new FI-AA, depreciation values are posted in real time, reducing the length of the asset depreciation run. Depreciation values are no longer part of the depreciation run itself. Balance carryforward is also performed by default on FI-AA balances. Overall, the depreciation posting run is executed faster due to simple processing logic, new data structures, and parallel processing.

5.2.4 SAP Cash Management

SAP Cash Management powered by SAP HANA is the replacement for SAP Cash and Liquidity Management. With bank account management, short-term cash position and forecast reports, and real-time liquidity planning, SAP Cash Management allows for tighter cash management (for optimizing working capital).

SAP Cash Management also provides on-the-fly reporting capabilities about cash position and liquidity forecast. The three major components of SAP Cash Management are as follows:

- Bank Account Management
- Cash Operations
- SAP Liquidity Management

5.2.5 SAP Material Ledger

The new SAP Material Ledger (ML) allows for multiple currencies. Traditionally, inventory was mainly valuated in a single currency in SAP ERP. The new SAP Material Ledger features allow for valuation in two additional currencies for today's global organizations who desire to valuate inventory in multiple currencies. This functionality became available in SAP S/4HANA, release 1511.

ML also allows for multiple valuations on three different levels (legal, group, and profit center). Generally, legal valuations are stored in local currency, while group and profit center valuations are stored in group currency. Parallel valuations support transfer pricing for internal sales between legal entities or profit centers within the group for a worldwide supply chain.

Finally, ML allows for actual costing. Inventory and material movements are generally valuated either at a standard price that is constant over a period of time or a moving average price that gets adjusted (calculated) automatically based on every goods receipt or invoice receipt. Actual costing combines the advantages of standard price with advantages of using a moving average price.

ML captures all price variances (like purchase price variances, production variances, etc.) and allows (as an optional period-end activity) the revaluation of ending inventories at period end and releases it as standard price (generally) for next period. Actual costing is optional in SAP S/4HANA.

5.2.6   SAP BPC for S/4HANA Finance

SAP BPC for S/4HANA Finance (formerly SAP Integrated Business Planning) leverages the power of SAP HANA and the embedded planning engines to create a more powerful planning experience. Figure 5.4 shows how this integration occurs.

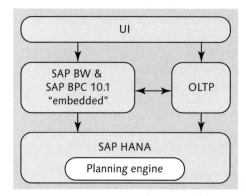

Figure 5.4 SAP Business Suite Powered by SAP HANA with SAP S/4HANA Finance

Planning applications are built as embedded content, with this content available as part of SAP S/4HANA Finance, not as part of the SAP BW content that historical customers are used to seeing. As a result, direct access to actual and master data via SAP HANA views replaces the data replication that we used in previous versions of SAP BPC and planning functions.

Supported planning functions include:

- Cost center planning
- Internal order planning
- Project planning
- Profit center planning
- P&L planning
- Market segment planning
- Balance sheet planning

These supported planning functions are just some of the features that can be potentially appealing to SAP customers as they evaluate SAP S/HANA Finance and determine if, how, and when to move forward.

5.3   SAP S/4HANA Materials Management and Operations

Similar in logic and intentions to SAP S/4HANA Finance, SAP "Simple Logistics" was to be a rewrite of the logistics modules of the core SAP ERP system, taking advantage of the new capabilities of the underlying SAP HANA system.

So, is there an SAP Simple Logistics? Yes and no.

Although intended to be a standalone product, the capabilities of SAP Simple Logistics have been incorporated into SAP S/4HANA, release 1511, which debuted in November 2015, carrying the umbrella name SAP S/4HANA Enterprise Management. Specifically, the logistics functionality falls under the SAP S/4HANA Materials Management (MM) and Operations umbrella. This functionality combines LOB capabilities for manufacturing, supply chain, sourcing, and procurement and sales.

Innovations and improvements in SAP S/4HANA Materials Management and Operations fall into three categories, as follows:

- The first category is a role-based user experience with a new design. The user interfaces (UIs) run on any device (desktops, tablets, smart phones, and even smart watches) and have been redesigned for exception-based issue handling, helping to shift from historical management by inspection to management using an exception approach.

▶ The second category is a set of innovations that make up the SAP S/4HANA core itself. The fundamentals of the system have a more modern, simplified, and optimized technology footprint courtesy of the SAP HANA footprint. Additionally, by collapsing the barriers between OLTP and OLAP processes and systems, functionality is more intuitive and relevant to today's businesses and business demands.

▶ The third category is the elimination of functional redundancies that have been built into the SAP Business Suite over the years. This elimination of redundancies will continue to evolve over time as more and more pieces of the system are redesigned and optimized for improved business processes leveraging SAP HANA.

In the following sections, we will look at two important pieces of SAP S/4HANA Materials Management and Operations: the manufacturing and supply chain functionalities.

5.3.1 Manufacturing

SAP HANA offers innovations to address business challenges in the manufacturing and material requirements planning (MRP) areas. These areas of innovation include, but are not limited to:

▶ **Faster MRP**
Much of the time that it takes to run an MRP process comes from the time required to read the many different material receipts and movements. By running MRP in SAP HANA, you can leverage significant advances in speed to collect this information and run net requirements calculations; lot sizing, sourcing, scheduling; and BOM (bill of material) explosions directly in SAP HANA and benefit from the speed of SAP HANA. With faster MRP processing, you can run different scenarios and options to find the optimal mix of product manufacturing.

▶ **Simple MRP**
By running MRP on SAP HANA, you are no longer required to plan within the planning horizon only and specify application servers for parallel processing.

▶ **Cross-plant MRP**
SAP HANA-powered MRP functions use special keys to determine the planning sequence for multiple plants. The MRP run can then create plans for supplying plants after receiving plants so that stock transfers and levels are optimized.

These benefits, combined with others, will allow you to have more current and optimized supply-and-demand information to ensure that you meet your customers' needs and therefore get higher customer satisfaction ratings. You will reduce the potential of stock-outs with better planning and replenishment plans and will identify issues sooner—therefore allowing you to address issues quickly.

5.3.2 Supply Chain

Your organization's supply chains are under constant pressure to meet the complex supply and demand of a changing marketplace. Expectations are growing steadily, and greater revenue opportunities are possible—if you can respond quickly to market changes. But preventing quick change and adaptation are supply chains that are often spread across global networks. Lack of visibility and lengthy decision-making processes make it difficult to plan and execute with speed and precision.

Supply chain optimization via SAP HANA provides companies a clear understanding of their customers, the ability to respond with flexibility, and the capacity to maximize opportunities.

This topic can encompass a huge array of information, but some of the features and benefits of supply chain optimization with SAP HANA are as follows:

▶ **Sales and operations planning**
Sales and operations planning (S&OP) leverages the power and speed of SAP HANA to run real-time comprehensive processes that optimize plans for better business results.

▶ **Big data**
The SAP HANA platform enables real-time planning and analysis at any level of granularity and dimension with a unified model of demand, supply chain, and financial data.

▶ **Social networking**
Embedded, context-aware social collaboration enables rapid planning, decision making, and execution across the organization and along the supply chain.

- **Cloud computing**
  SAP HANA Cloud Platform (SAP HCP) makes state-of-the-art technology easier to deliver, consume, and share—creating a new order of simplicity.

- **Mobile**
  Users can access S&OP via mobile devices such as smart phones and tablets.

With the unified S&OP model powered by SAP HANA, you can run simulations and planning scenarios quickly to make more real-time decisions. You can also "fail fast" to identify financial and strategic scenarios that will not meet your goals and objectives—and run new scenarios with new parameters.

5.4   Business Case for SAP S/4HANA

SAP S/4HANA Enterprise Management enables you to simplify your overall SAP landscape as well as to reduce the associated total cost of ownership (TCO). Your data footprint will be smaller with SAP S/4HANA because of the reduced or eliminated redundancies of data, required aggregation tables, etc., which means you will need less hardware.

> **Note**
>
> You may be required to obtain new or different hardware, however, depending on the systems that you have in place today and whether or not they are certified for SAP S/4HANA. SAP and your hardware vendors are the best sources for the most up-to-date information on that subject.

Implementing SAP S/4HANA will allow users to access a variety of reports/dashboards on their mobile devices. While a great feature, training will be needed both for how to use these tools on mobile devices and for the bigger question— how to change the thinking of your users. Suddenly, the business will have real-time data, which also requires business functions, processes, and behaviors necessary to facilitate real-time exploitation to derive maximum benefit. Behavioral and/or organizational changes, therefore, would be required to exploit the available information to create "value" for the organization. This larger dimension needs to be managed effectively through an organizational plan for change.

A variety of possible combinations to optimize the licensing costs associated with adopting SAP S/4HANA are available. Clarity in terms of your business requirements and mapping them to functionalities in SAP S/4HANA are key when optimizing the business case value for SAP S/4HANA.

From a business perspective, the following are some of most important points in a business case for SAP S/4HANA:

▸ Greater engagement with the business through real-time analytics and a centralized, single source for data (in SAP terms, a "single version of the truth")

▸ Process improvements, from general simplifications (like those seen with the Universal Journal) to all-new functionality like advanced cash and liquidity management

▸ Increased compliance due to faster close and reconciliation and real-time insights into risk

From a technical perspective, the following are some of most important points in a business case for SAP S/4HANA:

▸ A modernized platform with in-memory speed and power and a reduced footprint

▸ A simplified landscape that reduces data movement and redundancy

▸ The availability of multiple deployment options: on-premise, cloud, or hybrid

▸ An improved user experience that leads to higher adoption and is compatible with multiple devices

Implementing SAP S/4HANA is a significant strategic decision, both for IT and for the business. Making this decision, therefore, has to be specific to the customer environment. By doing so, you can reap the benefits of SAP HANA without having to make the full transition to a fully enabled SAP ERP system just yet.

With that in mind, what is the business case for SAP S/4HANA? SAP S/4HANA is a major step forward in changing how enterprise software is deployed and used across organizations. The ease of cloud-based deployment (or on-premise or hybrid) is combined with a full set of standard financial functions and new functionalities that enable an organization to, for example, conduct a soft financial close and to model different financial scenarios.

Business Case: SAP S/4HANA Finance

SAP S/4HANA Finance can provide the following benefits to support the business case:

▶ A further reduction in database size due to the reduction of the aggregation tables, thus reducing the costs of the SAP HANA license(s) and associated hardware costs.

▶ All of the newly developed SAP Fiori apps are only available via SAP Business Suite on SAP HANA. (The first release of SAP Fiori apps can be consumed on non-SAP HANA Business Suite solutions, however.)

▶ The new capabilities enabled within SAP S/4HANA Finance improve usability and reduce reliance on data warehouse systems for reporting and analysis by using a single database and a "single version of the truth" that allows for OLTP and OLAP processes off the same data set.

▶ Reconciling FICO data is no longer needed because all of the data is held in a common structure, thus further reducing the need for and size of aggregation tables (a cost savings) and allowing for faster period-end processes.

▶ In-application reporting and analysis provide immediate insights.

▶ A single source of truth between transactions and analytics streamlines and eliminates cycle times and reconciliations of the data, thus reducing time, errors, and costs.

▶ New ad-hoc computational capabilities for moving finance processing, such as month-end activities, from batch processing to real-time processing.

▶ Rapid planning and forecasting, combined with predictive analysis, to explore new business models and immediately assess potential effects on the bottom line.

▶ Connections to business networks in real time to establish an integrated business ecosystem and help drive optimal collaboration with customers, suppliers, banks, and government authorities.

▶ Global regulatory compliance capabilities across currencies, languages, and industries with built-in legal compliance capabilities and continuous risk assessment along all enterprise processes.

5.5   Migration from SAP ERP to SAP S/4HANA

The high-level technical path to get from SAP ERP 6.0 to SAP Business Suite powered by SAP HANA to SAP S/4HANA can be seen in Figure 5.5.

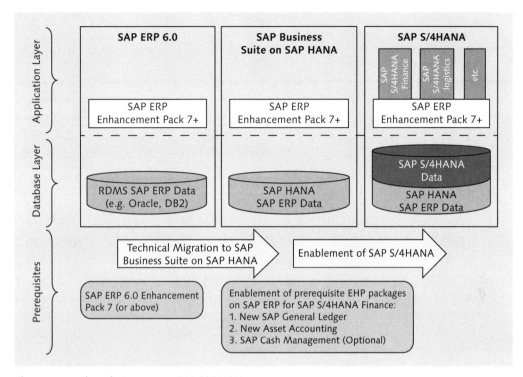

Figure 5.5 Technical Migration to SAP S/4HANA

In more detail, if an SAP ERP 6.0 system was used with the classic G/L functionality, a new G/L migration project needs to be undertaken ideally before the start of the upgrade because the classic G/L functionality has been discontinued in SAP S/4HANA Finance. Additionally, during the upgrade, the new Asset Accounting needs to be enabled with the relevant enhancement packages. SAP Cash Management for SAP HANA could be enabled during the upgrade or at a later stage.

You can also perform a new G/L migration while migrating to SAP S/4HANA Finance. However, this migration provides less functional options and features compared to undertaking a separate migration.

With these considerations in mind, the logical progression for clients who are on SAP ERP 6.0, on any non-SAP HANA database, would be to move to the SAP Business Suite on SAP HANA (with or without SAP S/4HANA Finance). SAP S/4HANA would be the next step further. Two approaches to migrate from an SAP ERP 6.0

system running on a relational database management system (RDBMS) to the SAP S/4HANA environment are available:

▶ **Two-step approach**
In this approach, you would follow an EHP 7 upgrade with a migration to SAP S/4HANA. While this approach is less risky, the disadvantages include a longer overall project and higher cost.

▶ **One-step approach**
In this approach, you would upgrade EHP 7 and migrate to SAP S/4HANA at the same time. While this approach is faster and cheaper, including in terms of testing, the project is more complex.

Any custom code that is database dependent may have to be tested—and possibly rewritten. An SAP check program can validate "noncompliant" SAP HANA code as part of the migration process.

Remember that migrating to SAP S/4HANA is optional. While there are risks to adopting a new solution, the benefits can potentially transform your business. Change is never easy, but it can be liberating.

5.6   SAP Activate

With all of these "new" solutions and advances in integrated solutions, SAP has updated their implementation methodology to reflect this new environment. SAP Activate is an innovation adoption framework that combines best practices, methodologies, and guided configuration. SAP Activate is designed to helpful to both business and IT leaders involved in the process of implementing or migrating to SAP S/4HANA.

SAP Activate offers an approach that can be used for cloud-based or on-premise implementations, hybrid or mobile solutions. Some of the benefits of SAP Activate are as follows:

▶ **Start with best practices**
Leverage Rapid Deployment Solutions (RDS), SAP Best Practices, model companies, and other prebuilt assets.

▶ **Preassembled and cloud ready**
Rapidly build your solution environment in the cloud based on best practices to accelerate validation activities.

▶ **Validate solution**

Guide customers through standard functionalities with show-and-tell sessions, identify and validate delta requirements and gaps, design solutions that minimize modifications to standard programs, and enable faster innovation.

▶ **Agile build**

Use iterative building of capabilities, prototyping, and frequent validation of results with business users to ease adoption and to release solutions faster.

▶ **Premium engagement**

Customers under SAP MaxAttention and SAP Active Embedded agreements will find guidance for using control centers and related services in the methodology (e.g., Innovation Control Center, Operations Control Center, and Mission Control Center).

▶ **Quality management**

Formal risk and quality management with structured quality management plans and predefined Q-Gates are built into the project from the start.

What will or what has happened to ASAP, the tried and true SAP implementation methodology? The SAP Activate methodology supersedes ASAP methodology for implementation. SAP will continue to provide access to the last version of ASAP 8 in the SAP Service Marketplace for project teams that are using it today. No further content enhancements will be made to ASAP 8 going forward because all the new implementation methodology assets will be made available through SAP Activate framework.

5.7   Summary

This chapter has introduced many enhancements and advances that are possible with SAP S/4HANA. You are not required to move your existing SAP ERP implementations to SAP S/4HANA—but you may want to strongly consider the possibility if you are reaching a point of inflection with your existing systems either due to system capacity issues, licensing renewals, database renewals, or hardware renewals.

An entirely new (greenfield) implementation of the SAP suite of transactional systems, with SAP S/4HANA first, would likely benefit you overall—for today and as a foundation for the future.

SAP S/4HANA is the future of ERP systems for SAP, and the advances and innovations coming from SAP and its partners will all be based on the assumption that you are on the SAP S/4HANA platform.

Before you embark on an SAP HANA implementation, you need to know some key pieces of information. This chapter will guide you through hardware, software, sizing, and migration considerations for SAP Business Warehouse (SAP BW) powered by SAP HANA and SAP Business Suite, specifically SAP ERP, powered by SAP HANA.

6   Planning an SAP HANA Implementation

This chapter will guide you through planning an SAP HANA implementation. First, we begin with an overview of the SAP HANA environment and the hardware options available to you. Then, we look at how to implement SAP HANA for a standalone data warehouse, SAP Business Suite, and SAP S/4HANA and, finally, how to migrate to or implement SAP Business Warehouse (SAP BW) on SAP HANA.

6.1   Technical Basics

In this section, we'll walk you through the technical aspects and components you need to understand when planning an SAP HANA implementation. We'll also look at SAP HANA's in-memory computing engine (IMCE), the software components of an SAP HANA system, including their editions and installation best practices, and we'll conclude the section with some considerations regarding network speed.

6.1.1   In-Memory Computing Engine

To many, the components of SAP HANA may be a bit confusing. After all, SAP HANA is supposed to be an "appliance" with all its components hidden from the users. However, inside the IMCE of SAP HANA, many different components manage the access and storage of the data. For a look at the core components of the IMCE, see Figure 6.1.

First, the disk storage is typically a file system that allows for data security and logging of activities, which is managed in the persistence layer. The persistence layer is basically a normal set of disks which stores a copy of what is in memory on the hardware. As a result, if a memory bank fails, the data is not lost but can be read into other memory banks or to a standby system. Logging data is stored on disk hardware as well.

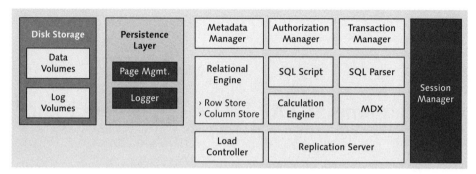

Figure 6.1 Core Components of the In-Memory Computing Engine

In a typical SAP HANA system, we tend to see about five times the memory being reserved on hard disk for persistence and logging. Some hardware vendors such as Lenovo also offer to store these files in separate memory banks for even faster recovery in case of a (highly unlikely) core memory failure. Whether or not to take advantage of such options is basically a question of how much you can afford and how mission critical your SAP HANA system is to your organization. For most companies, the default disk option for logging and persistence is the correct answer, and your hardware vendor will help you size this correctly.

A relational engine manages the row or column store. Whether your implementation will use a row or column store depends on the content you're implementing as well as the system you're placing on top of SAP HANA (e.g., SAP BW or SAP Business Suite).

All systems will use a combination of row and column stores, and your migration tool will automatically select the appropriate row or column store type for each table during the migration process. However, when you're building your new data mart or data warehouse on SAP HANA, you'll have the option to select either row or column store table types. A quick way to remember which type to pick is that column stores have higher compression and are optimized for faster data reads (great for reporting systems). Row store-based tables, on the other hand, are optimized for updates. For more on row and columns stores, see the earlier discussion in Chapter 1, Section 1.2.

Several tools to move data within SAP HANA are available. For example, using SAP (Sybase) Replication Server (RS) and SAP HANA Load Controller (LC), you can provide log-based replication, or you can leverage the SAP Landscape Transformation (SLT) trigger-based data replication. SAP Data Services is another option that provides traditional scheduled data movement as well as complex data transformations during the load process. We'll take a closer look at each of these options in Chapter 9.

For access to data in frontend tools, SAP HANA provides support for SAP HANA SQLScript and multidimensional expressions (MDX) as well as an SQL parser. In addition, a hyper-fast calculation engine can perform in-memory calculations. In Chapter 7, we'll look at all of the options for accessing the SAP HANA system with business intelligence and reporting tools.

Internally, the SAP HANA system also manages security, transactions, and metadata (data about the data) in three IMCE components that are integrated with the session manager, which keeps an eye on who is accessing the system and how the result set and dialogues are managed. Overall, the IMCE is a complex internal SAP HANA component that is easy to use by being bundled together as an appliance to simplify installs and management.

6.1.2 Software Specifications

Currently, SAP has three different editions of SAP HANA (not to be confused with the three different implementation options that we discussed in Chapter 2 through Chapter 5):

- SAP HANA appliance software platform edition
- SAP HANA appliance software enterprise edition
- SAP HANA appliance software extended enterprise edition

The editions simply determine what components are included in the software license and how you want to extract, move, and replicate the data. For any implementation of SAP HANA—standalone analytics, SAP BW, or SAP Business Suite—you then have the additional choice of which edition of SAP HANA is right for you.

To better understand this, think of how you would migrate an SAP ERP system to SAP S/4HANA. You first have the option to migrate the system as is, and depending on your licensing agreement, you most likely will buy a platform edition of SAP HANA. However, if you also plan to use your SAP HANA database to load non-SAP data, to build data marts, or to integrate external data, you would often be better off buying an enterprise license for SAP HANA. This license would give you access to a variety of data load tools such as SLT, SAP HANA Direct Extractor Connection (DXC), or SAP Data Services, to name a few.

> **Note**
>
> Editions are also available for the Rapid Deployment Solutions (RDS). As mentioned previously, we don't go into detail about Rapid Deployment Solutions in this book.

Again, the enterprise edition is great for companies who want to use their SAP HANA system with real-time, trigger-based data replication or use SAP Data Services, so you can actually invoke both extract, transform, and load (ETL) and trigger-based data replication in the same system. We'll cover trigger-based data and table replication in more detail in Chapter 9, Section 9.2.

Finally, the SAP HANA appliance software extended enterprise edition is for those who want it all. This license adds the log-based replication of data to the features of the other editions. Most large-scale organizations that already have SAP ERP or a business intelligence (BI) software in their landscapes should consider this extended edition.

The components included in the editions are summarized in Table 6.1.

Software Component	Enterprise Extended Edition	Enterprise Edition	Platform Edition
SAP HANA Studio	X	X	X
SAP HANA Information Composer	X	X	X
SAP HANA client	X	X	X
SAP HANA client for Excel	X	X	X
SAP HANA UI for Information Access (INA)	X	X	X
SAP HANA database	X	X	X
SAP Host Agent	X	X	X
Software Update Manager (SUM)	X	X	X

Table 6.1 The Different Editions of SAP HANA

Software Component	Enterprise Extended Edition	Enterprise Edition	Platform Edition
SAP HANA Advanced Functions Library (AFL)	X	X	X
Diagnostics agent	X	X	X
SAP Data Services	X	X	
SAP HANA Direct Extractor Connection (DXC)	X	X	
SAP Landscape Transformation Tool (SLT)	X	X	
Landscape Transformation Replication Server	X	X	
SAP HANA Load Controller (LC)	X	X	
SAP (Sybase) Replication Server (RS) and Agent (RA)	X		
SAP Adaptive Service Enterprise (ASE)	X		

Table 6.1 The Different Editions of SAP HANA (Cont.)

6.1.3 Software Editions for Specific Purposes

In addition to the platform, enterprise, and extended enterprise editions of SAP HANA, special software editions for specific purposes are available. For example, a database edition for SAP BW would be appropriate for customers who have an EDGE-type license (typically purchased by small- and medium-sized businesses), while a limited edition allows only applications and accelerators to be developed. These editions are targeted solutions based on the SAP HANA platform. Through these offerings, smaller companies, or those with a limited need for the complete capabilities of SAP HANA can buy a smaller subset of what they need in these appliance editions.

The operating system installed on your system will be SUSE Linux Enterprise Server (SLES) or Linux from Red Hat. From a technical standpoint, many subcomponents can be installed or connected to SAP HANA. As you start working with SAP HANA, knowing the technical name of each component can be quite useful, so that you can search for more information, such as installation and administration guides for each component on the SAP Marketplace or the SAP Community Network (SCN) at *http://scn.sap.com*. The technical name of each component can be found in Table 6.2.

Area	Component ID	Technical Name
Lifecycle management	HAN-LM-INS	SAP HANA Installation
	HAN-LM-INS-DB	Installation of HANA Database
	HAN-LM-INS-SAP	Installation of SAP Systems on HANA
	HAN-LM-UPG	SAP HANA Upgrade
	HAN-LM-UPG-DB	Upgrade of HANA Database
	HAN-LM-UPG-SAP	Upgrade of SAP Systems on HANA
	HAN-LM	SAP HANA Lifecycle Management
	HAN-LM-APP	SAP HANA Application Lifecycle Management
	HAN-LM-PLT	SAP HANA Platform Lifecycle Management
SAP HANA database	HAN-DB	SAP HANA Database
	HAN-DB-AFL	Application Function Library New: See note 2198403
	HAN-DB-AFL-DQ	Data Quality Library
	HAN-DB-AFL-GEN	AFL Shipment and general AFL topics
	HAN-DB-AFL-HIE	AFL Hierarchies
	HAN-DB-AFL-PAL	Predictive Analysis Library
	HAN-DB-AFL-POS	On-Shelf Availability
	HAN-DB-AFL-SAL	Self Service Analytics Library
	HAN-DB-AFL-SCA	Supply Chain Algorithm Library
	HAN-DB-AFL-SOP	Sales and Operations Planning
	HAN-DB-AFL-TEC	AFL Technology and SDK
	HAN-DB-AFL-UDF	Unified Demand Forecast
	HAN-DB-BAC	Backup and Recovery
	HAN-DB-CDS	Activation of HDBDD-files -CDS Definitions
	HAN-DB-CLI	Clients -JDBC, ODBC
	HAN-DB-ENG	DB Engines
	HAN-DB-ENG-BW	BW Engine
	HAN-DB-ENG-GPH	Graph Engine
	HAN-DB-ENG-GPH-API	Graph Engine API

Table 6.2 SAP HANA Software Components and Technical Names

Area	Component ID	Technical Name
SAP HANA database (Cont.)	HAN-DB-ENG-GPH-GEM	Graph Exploration and Manipulation -GEM Language
	HAN-DB-ENG-IM	Use new Smart Data Quality: HAN-DB-SDQ
	HAN-DB-ENG-PLE	Planning Engine
	HAN-DB-ENG-SPA	Spatial Engine
	HAN-DB-ENG-TXT	Text Engine
	HAN-DB-ENG-VE	Velocity Engine
	HAN-DB-EPM	Enterprise Performance Management Platform
	HAN-DB-EPM-PLT	EPM Platform
	HAN-DB-EPM-XSL	EPM XSJS library
	HAN-DB-HA	High Availability
	HAN-DB-LVC	Integrated LiveCache
	HAN-DB-MDX	MDX Engine/Excel Client
	HAN-DB-MON	SAP HANA Monitoring
	HAN-DB-PER	Database Persistence
	HAN-DB-R	SAP HANA Integration with R library - Statistics
	HAN-DB-SCR	SAP HANA SQL Script
	HAN-DB-SDA	SAP HANA Smart Data Access - SDA
	HAN-DB-SDQ	Info Mgmt Platform Smart Data Quality - SDQ
	HAN-DB-SEC	Security and User Management
SAP HANA application services	HAN-AS	Application Services
	HAN-AS-INA	Tools and Infrastructure
	HAN-AS-INA-FL	File Loader
	HAN-AS-INA-FLY	Firefly
	HAN-AS-INA-SVC	Service
	HAN-AS-INA-UI	Toolkit, Fiori Search UI
	HAN-AS-MDS	SAP HANA Multidimensional Service

Table 6.2 SAP HANA Software Components and Technical Names (Cont.)

Area	Component ID	Technical Name
SAP HANA application services (Cont.)	HAN-AS-RPO	SAP HANA Repository
	HAN-AS-RST	Development Environment REST API
	HAN-AS-RUL	Rules Framework
	HAN-AS-XS	Extended Application Services -XS Classic
	HAN-AS-XS-ADM	XS Administration
	HAN-AS-XS-JOB	XS Scheduled Jobs
	HAN-AS-XSA	XS Basis Applications
	HAN-AS-XSA-LIB	New: HAN-AS-XS
	HAN-AS-XSA-SHN	SAP HANA Interactive Education -SHINE Model
	HAN-AS-XSA-TM	SAP HANA Task management
	HAN-AS-XSA-WF	SAP HANA Workflow
SAP HANA native applications	HAN-APP	SAP HANA Native Applications
	HAN-APP-DCI	Data Center Intelligence
	HAN-APP-DWS	Data Warehouse Services
	HAN-APP-DWS-DDO	Data Distribution Optimizer
	HAN-APP-DWS-DLM	Data Lifecycle Manager
	HAN-APP-IOA	SAP IT Operations Analytics
SAP HANA XS Advanced	BC-XS	Engine - XS Advanced Dev
	BC-XS-JAS	Java Runtime
	BC-XS-JS	JavaScript runtime
	BC-XS-SEC	UAA and Security for XS engine
	BC-XS-SRV	XS Engine Services and Administration
SAP HANA Studio - Eclipse	HAN-STD	SAP HANA Studio -Eclipse
	HAN-STD-ADM	SAP HANA Administration
	HAN-STD-ADM-BAC	Backup and Recovery -Studio
	HAN-STD-ADM-DBA	Database Administration and Monitoring
	HAN-STD-ADM-PVZ	Plan Visualizer
	HAN-STD-ADM-SEC	Security and User Management -Studio
	HAN-STD-DEV	Development Tools

Table 6.2 SAP HANA Software Components and Technical Names (Cont.)

Area	Component ID	Technical Name
SAP HANA Studio - Eclipse (Cont.)	HAN-STD-DEV-CDS	CDS Tools
	HAN-STD-DEV-CDS-GRA	CDS Graphical Modeler
	HAN-STD-DEV-DP	Data Provisioning Modeler
	HAN-STD-DEV-EPM	EPM Modeler
	HAN-STD-DEV-MOD	Analytical Modeling
	HAN-STD-DEV-MOD-CLT	Analytical Modeling - Client Component
	HAN-STD-DEV-MOD-SRV	Analytical Modeling - Server Component
	HAN-STD-DEV-REF	Tools for Where-used, Refactoring and Mass Copy
	HAN-STD-DEV-RUL	Rules Editor
	HAN-STD-DEV-SCR	SAP HANA SQL Script Editor/Debugger
	HAN-STD-DEV-TP	SAP HANA Tools Platform/Team Provider
	HAN-STD-DEV-TP-CM	Development Change Management
	HAN-STD-DEV-UIS	UI Integration Services
	HAN-STD-DEV-UIS-FLP	SAP HANA Fiori Launchpad
	HAN-STD-DEV-XS	SAP HANA XS Editors and Wizards
End user clients	BI-BIP,BI-BIP-CMC	Business intelligence platform -before: BOE
	BI-RA-EXP	SAP BusinessObjects Explorer
	BI-RA-CR,BI-BIP-CRS	SAP Crystal Reports
	BI-RA-XL	Dashboard Designer
	BI-BIP-IDT	Information design tool
	BI-RA-WBI	Web Intelligence
	BI-RA-AO-XLA	MS Excel Add-In
SAP HANA data services	HAN-DP-DS	SAP Data Services
	HAN-DP-DXC	Direct Extractor Connector
	HAN-DP-ESS	Enterprise Semantic Services -ESS
	HAN-DP-LTR	SAP Landscape Transformation Replication Server
	HAN-DP-REP	SAP Sybase Replication Server
	HAN-DP-SDI	Smart Data Integration - SDI

Table 6.2 SAP HANA Software Components and Technical Names (Cont.)

Area	Component ID	Technical Name
SAP HANA Cockpit	HAN-CPT	SAP HANA Cockpit
	HAN-CPT-ADM	Administration Core
	HAN-CPT-ASE	Accelerator for SAP ASE Administration
	HAN-CPT-BAC	Backup and Recovery
	HAN-CPT-DCC	SAP DB Control Center
	HAN-CPT-DP	New: HAN-DP-SDI
	HAN-CPT-DYT	SAP HANA Dynamic Tiering Administration
	HAN-CPT-SDS	SAP HANA Smart Data Streaming Administration
	HAN-CPT-SYN	SAP HANA remote Data Sync Cockpit
	HAN-CPT-UM	User Management
	HAN-AS-XS-ADM	XS Admin
Other	BC-DB-HDB-CCM	CCMS for SAP HANA
	BC-DB-HDB-POR	DB Porting for SAP HANA
	BC-DB-HDB-SYS	Database interface/DBMS
	HAN-ASE	Accelerator for SAP ASE
	HAN-DYT	SAP HANA Dynamic Tiering
	HAN-IC	Information Composer
	HAN-SDS	Smart Data Streaming
	HAN-WDE	Web IDE

Table 6.2 SAP HANA Software Components and Technical Names (Cont.)

To help you keep up to date with what's going on, SAP has created a set of key SAP Notes that are appended and modified with important information with each new release or service pack. Partners and hardware vendors should read these key notes carefully and check back periodically for updates. A subset of these SAP Notes is also outlined in Table 6.3.

SAP Note Number	SAP Note Name
2000003	Frequently Asked Questions on HANA
1514967	SAP HANA: Central Note
1523337	SAP HANA Database: Central Note

Table 6.3 Key SAP Notes for the SAP HANA Install

SAP Note Number	SAP Note Name
1514966	Sizing SAP HANA Database
1637145	Sizing SAP HANA Database - BW
1793345	Sizing SAP HANA Database - Suite
1018839	Admin (HANA)
1599888	SAP HANA: Operational Concept
1598623	Security
1729988	SAP BW Check for HANA Migration

Table 6.3 Key SAP Notes for the SAP HANA Install (Cont.)

6.1.4 Network Speed between Servers

The network connections between nodes in a scaled-out SAP HANA system should be 10 GB/sec to ensure that the data dialogs and replication are efficient. Because a substantial amount of data will be moving between these servers, be sure that the connection isn't shared with other components such as shared routers. While 10 GB/sec is recommended between the servers in a scaled-out hardware scenario, you can actually migrate a legacy system to SAP HANA over a 1 GB/sec connection, but a lot of network latency (35+ ms) or lots of network jitter may result in significant slowdown. In order to mitigate the risk to your project, test your network connection speed and performance before committing to a migration to SAP HANA across data centers.

For data replication between systems, SAP recommends that these connections be as dedicated to the servers only as possible and that these environments are not far from each other (e.g., servers in Europe and the Americas with an SAP HANA system in Asia where jitter and latency can become significant issues). While this recommendation doesn't prevent such architecture from being implemented, it's important to note that any slow network connection can also slow down the replication of data to systems such as SAP BW on SAP HANA, thereby defeating some of the great data load benefits of this in-memory platform.

6.1.5 Software Install

After you've decided which version to install, your hardware partner can start the install. To simplify the install, SAP provides a software tool to its partners called the SAP HANA Unified Installer. With the install, you also get the Software Logistics

Toolset (SL), which includes the Software Update Manager (SUM). This tool provides software updates to the components of SAP HANA to help make sure they stay compatible over time. (More details on the automated software update process are given in Chapter 10.)

It's important to note that only hardware vendors and installation partners should install the SAP HANA SL software and the components of SAP HANA. Given that SAP HANA is an emerging technology, the SAP Basis staff in your organization will likely not have the required skills to make this work. While SAP does provide a detailed online guide for the SAP HANA Unified Installer, we strongly recommend that customers leave the responsibility for the SAP HANA software installation to hardware vendors and certified partners. We recommend that the roles and responsibilities of SAP, the hardware vendor, and the customer be assigned as shown in Table 6.4.

Area	Task	Hardware Vendor	Customer	SAP
Initial Setup	Hardware installation and health check	X		
	Linux OS installation	X		
	SAP HANA platform installation	X		
	Data source connectivity		X	
	Adding database instances (Multiple Components in One System [MCOS])		X	
	SMD agent installation		X	
Operations	SAP HANA database admin		X	
	Third-party software installations		X	
	SAP HANA system monitoring		X	
	SAP HANA database monitoring		X	
	Backup and recovery		X	
	"Bare metal" recovery		X	
Maintenance	Firmware patching	(X)*	X	
	Linux OS upgrades and patching	(X)*	X	
	Peripheral components patching		X	
	Platform components updates and patching		X	

Table 6.4 Roles and Responsibilities of an SAP HANA Installation

Area	Task	Hardware Vendor	Customer	SAP
Support	Issue resolution process	(X)*	X	X
* depending on support contract				

Table 6.4 Roles and Responsibilities of an SAP HANA Installation (Cont.)

Note

SAP HANA is also integrated into the standard solution monitoring and diagnostics of SAP Solution Manager just like other SAP software servers such as SAP BW and SAP Business Suite.

6.2   Hardware Specifications and Options

SAP HANA is sold as an in-memory appliance, which means that both software and hardware are included from the vendors. As of August 2016, you can buy certified SAP HANA hardware solutions from Bull, Cisco, Dell, Fujitsu, Hitachi, HP, Huawei, IBM, Lenovo, NEC, Silicon Graphics, and Unisys.

A major change for 2016 was the availability of Intel's new E7 CPUs, also known as Haswell CPUs, which replaced the older IvyBridge processors. What makes these new chips so fast is that they have 18 cores, instead of the 15 cores available in the previous versions. While there are actually several models of the E7 CPU, known as 2880/90, 4880/90, 8880/90, only the latter four (4880/90, 8880/90) are normally used in certified SAP HANA appliances. The differences between the processors are generally faster clock speeds, ranging from 2.3 to 2.8 GHz, so some processors are faster than others.

In 2017–2018, you should expect newer certified SAP HANA systems based on Intel's latest Xeon E7-889x version 4 Broadwell processors with up to 24 cores and speeds up to 3.2 GHz, resulting in even faster systems and more scalability options for SAP HANA.

SAP HANA hardware servers can either increase in size (scale-up), or multiple smaller servers can be linked together (scale-out). One benefit of a scale-up solution is that you have fewer servers to manage and purchase, while the core benefit of a scale-out solution is the ability to create extremely large SAP HANA systems.

In the following sections, we will take a closer look at both scenarios, before diving into the hardware platforms available for SAP HANA.

6.2.1 Scaled-Up SAP HANA Systems

Whether you should go with a scale-up or scale-out approach deserves some serious consideration by the SAP Basis team in your organization planning an SAP HANA implementation. The benefits of a single system include simplified maintenance, somewhat lower costs, a smaller hardware footprint, and ease of installation.

However, in large and rapidly growing organizations with SAP BW, or in a large enterprise data warehouse (EDW), a single node with only 3 TB of memory may not be enough for long-term needs. To determine if this is going to suffice for your company, you have to consider data growth. A 3 TB system may be able to handle 6–8 TB of uncompressed data.

You also need to consider the number of active concurrent users (ACU). If you are using your SAP HANA system for reporting and analytics, a nice rule-of-thumb is 0.2 cores per ACU. So a 3 TB system like Lenovo's x3950 X6 with 8 Haswell CPUs x 18 cores could support up to 720 ACUs (8 × 18 ÷ 0.2) from a CPU perspective. If you plan for 20% concurrency of your users, that could be equal to 3,600 named users. Of course, you should spend more time on a detailed sizing effort with your hardware partner using real usage data from your own system, but this example gives you the basic idea of the capacity of a scaled-up system.

As of August 2016, all hardware vendors with certified SAP HANA solutions on Haswell processors use Linux SLES or Red Hat as their operating system. For a list of certified vendors and their hardware options, see Table 6.5.

Vendor	Certified System	Memory SAP HANA Certified	CPU		Target Use			
			Max Number	Max Cores	Scale-Out	Scale-Up	SoH/ S4	BW/ EDW
Bull SAS	bullion S2	512-1536 GB	2	36	-	X	X	X
	bullion S4	1024-3072 GB	4	60–72	X	X	X	X
	bullion S8	2048-6144 GB	8	144	X	X	X	X

Table 6.5 SAP HANA Hardware Options

Vendor	Certified System	Memory SAP HANA Certified	CPU		Target Use			
			Max Number	Max Cores	Scale-Out	Scale-Up	SoH/S4	BW/EDW
Cisco	UCS B260	128-1536 GB	2	36	-	X	X	X
	UCS B460	512-3072 GB	4	72	X	X	X	X
	UCS C460	128-3072 GB	4	72	X	X	X	X
	UCS C880	2048-6144 GB	8	144	X	X	X	X
Dell	PowerEdge R930	128-3072 GB	4	72	X	X	X	X
Fujitsu	PQ 2400 E2/S2	128-3072 GB	4	72	-	X	X	X
	PQ 2800 B2/E2	128-6144 GB	8	144	X	X	X	X
	RX4770	128-3072 GB	4	72	X	X	X	X
HP	CS-500	128-3072 GB	4	72	X	X	X	X
	CS-900	256-12288 GB	16	288	X	X	X	X
IBM* Power8 (supported systems)	E850	128-4096 GB	Max/LPAR	32	X	X	X	X
	E870	128-6144 GB	Max/LPAR	80	X	X	X	X
	E880	128-6144 GB	Max/LPAR	96	X	X	X	X
	S822	128-1024 GB	Max/LPAR	20	-	X	X	X
	S822L/ S824/ S824L	128-2048 GB	Max/LPAR	24	X	X	X	X
Hitachi	CB 520X	128-6144 GB	8	144	X	X	X	X
	HA8000/ RS440xN	128-1536 GB	4	72	-	X	X	X
Huawei	RH-5885H	128-3072 GB	4	72	X	X	X	X
	RH-8100	512-4096 GB	8	144	X	X	X	X
Lenovo	x3850 X6	128-3072 GB	4	72	X	X	X	X
	x3950 X6	256-6144 GB	8	144	X	X	X	X

Table 6.5 SAP HANA Hardware Options (Cont.)

| Vendor | Certified System | Memory SAP HANA Certified | CPU | | Target Use | | | |
			Max Number	Max Cores	Scale-Out	Scale-Up	SoH/ S4	BW/ EDW
NEC	Exp. 5800/ A2040	128-2048 GB	4	72	-	X	X	X
	NX7700x/ A2080	1024-6144 GB	8	144	X	X	X	X
Silicon Graphics	UV 300H	256-6144 GB	8	144	X	X	X	X
Unisys	Forward! 4150-B	128-3072 GB	4	60* (E7v2)	-	X	X	X

Table 6.5 SAP HANA Hardware Options (Cont.)

6.2.2 Scaled-Out SAP HANA Systems

Scaled-out SAP HANA systems consist of several nodes connected together via a network that has at least 10 GB/sec speed to avoid data transfer bottlenecks between the servers. Most SAP HANA systems can be configured to accommodate this setup. The benefit of the scale-out solution is the ability to create very large SAP HANA systems with hundreds of CPU cores that can handle tens of thousands of users. This capability makes SAP HANA truly the big data platform for the future.

Currently, many interesting approaches exist to scale out a system. For example, Lenovo's 3 TB x3950 X6 system in a scale-out solution can, as of June 2016, be configured with up to 56 nodes, thereby creating a system with 168 TB of memory and 8,064 CPU cores. Another approach to scale out a system is to use blades, instead of "standalone" server nodes. Cisco has UCS B260/B460 and Hitachi has HA8000 blade servers for this purpose. As you can see, scaled-out SAP HANA systems have many options.

For comparison, HP's Converged System 500, another SAP-certified platform, can scale up to 16 TB in a single node (this may increase in the near future). In general, the scale-out approach is used by SAP Business Suite on SAP HANA and SAP S/4HANA, while the scale-up approach is sometimes used by very large SAP BW or EDW solutions.

It is important to note that some hardware vendors provide what is referred to as *investment protection*, which allows you to use some older hardware together with newer boxes as your environment grows. For example, if you bought a 15-core system like IBM's 3950 a couple of years ago, you can now add new 18-core, Haswell processor-based server nodes to your system, which will work together as compatible units with the older 15-core nodes. Only when your new nodes account for more than 50% of your overall SAP HANA system are you required to switch over. As a result, you can save thousands of dollars and can rest assured that your hardware investments will last much longer than before.

Since these considerations can be quite confusing, we recommend that you involve SAP HANA experts from your consulting partner and work together with them and your hardware vendor to find the right solution for your company. However, since hardware options are also rapidly changing, you should avoid relying on resources that don't deal with SAP HANA hardware deployment and integration on a daily basis. Buying the wrong hardware can be quite costly, so spend some time before you commit to a scale-out solution.

6.2.3 Hardware Platforms

SAP HANA hardware is unique in many respects and is optimized by each vendor to correctly support your chosen SAP solution. Vendors have also acquired expertise in installing and supporting the SAP HANA landscape, so you should not expect noncertified hardware vendors to be able to install, run, and support your SAP HANA appliance.

As part of writing this book, we worked with Lenovo Labs in installing and testing its high-end x3850 X6 server (Figure 6.2). Because we only needed a medium-sized system, we decided on 256 GB memory and a mid-sized file system.

In 2012, when we first started working on the new x3850 4th generation modular SAP HANA system, we had 10 core processors; then, with the 5th generation, we had 15 cores, and now, we have 18 cores in the 6th generation of this hardware platform. The hardware is now completely rearranged into units with flash memory banks and a combination of self-contained compute books and a storage book for persistent SAP HANA data logs and the data files. The new system also had 18 core processors that were much faster than the X5 2014 system. In fact, we benchmarked the system against 1.22 billion rows and saw the query speed increase by more than 296%, almost 3 times faster in only 2 years, so getting the latest version of the SAP HANA hardware can really make a difference.

Although this hardware example is specific to Lenovo's high-end x series boxes, the components of other vendors are often quite similar.

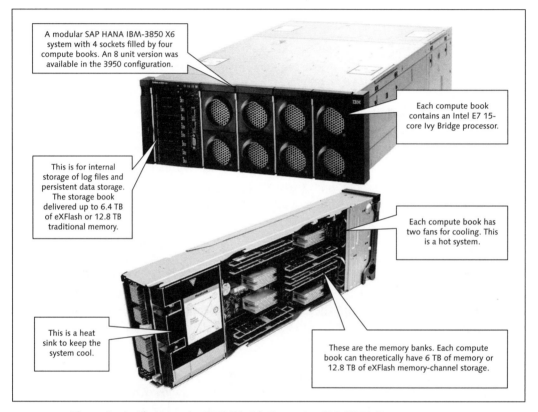

A modular SAP HANA IBM-3850 X6 system with 4 sockets filled by four compute books. An 8 unit version was available in the 3950 configuration.

Each compute book contains an Intel E7 15-core Ivy Bridge processor.

This is for internal storage of log files and persistent data storage. The storage book delivered up to 6.4 TB of eXFlash or 12.8 TB traditional memory.

Each compute book has two fans for cooling. This is a hot system.

This is a heat sink to keep the system cool.

These are the memory banks. Each compute book can theoretically have 6 TB of memory or 12.8 TB of eXFlash memory-channel storage.

Figure 6.2 Inside Lenovo's x3850 X6: 6th Generation SAP HANA Box

6.3   SAP HANA as a Standalone Data Warehouse

Implementing a standalone data warehouse on SAP HANA is one of the least complicated ways of leveraging the speed of this platform, though there are some design considerations that should be factored into the planning for your implementation project. The two most important considerations are data modeling and sizing, which we'll discuss in this section.

6.3.1   Data Modeling

When modeling data for SAP HANA as a data warehouse, we have to make sure that the approach keeps two things in mind: First, it should take advantage of the speed of SAP HANA. Second, it should not try to optimize for speed when speed is not required.

To understand these points more practically, let's consider the traditional star-schema and snowflake modeling techniques, which may not be appropriate in an in-memory data warehouse. These two techniques were primarily designed to reduce table joins and data volumes in a data warehouse. These techniques took the third normal form models in the transaction system and denormalized them by creating event tables (facts) and dimension tables (descriptions). This modeling approach had two benefits: First, costly table joins when querying master data spread in dozens of tables and when trying to link this to transactional data were removed. Conformed dimension tables simply created denormalized tables of all customers, vendors, and products and allowed the modeler to join this data to transactions such as sales, deliveries, and billing data. Second, this approach removed the costly overhead of recording all events and master data in a single table as is the case of first normal form models or transaction files.

To get more speed from the system, dimensional modelers would create summary tables and make sure that slower queries needing summary data could be routed to these tables instead of to the fact tables containing more detailed transactions. Other modelers would create summary star schemas with different granularity (i.e., total sales by products, by store per day). Finally, to get even faster results, prerunning queries and keeping temporary result sets on application servers in memory caches became the norm. In each of these approaches, the goal was to get more speed from a hard disk-based data warehouse.

Many of these approaches are inappropriate in a standalone data warehouse based on SAP HANA. For example, column store compression drives out most of the data redundancies from first or second normal form models, so the overhead of these approaches can often be minimal. SAP HANA does not have any "real" tables. Instead, we have compressed, index-based row and column stores that are displayed as tables for simple access and modeling. In the standalone data warehouse, we will have mostly column store data and table joins, which are just semantic ways of looking at what really occurs in the new database. In other words, the costly table joins we tried to avoid in the traditional dimensional models are no longer needed.

Furthermore, the use of summary tables does not, in most cases, make sense when the system is already extremely fast. Caching to memory of temporary query results (i.e., via broadcasting to cache) only makes sense in extremely rare cases.

SAP HANA even changes our approach to ETL data. Traditional data warehouses rely on transformations occurring during extraction from the source system or in the application server layer where ETL tools are installed. With SAP HANA, you can simply load the data as is and do the transformations inside SAP HANA through calculation views or procedures and function tables when data is moved between the staging and reporting layers in the models. This approach can be a substantially faster way of doing transforms rather than relying on smaller, slower servers on the ETL or the application layer.

In short, while not required, one should reconsider the modeling approaches to the data warehouse when working with SAP HANA because the older methods may not make sense anymore. Many great resources are available on the Internet and in bookstores on understanding how the Operational Data Store (ODS) has become more important than the star schemas in this new paradigm.

> **Additional Reading and Resources**
>
> For those new to modeling in SAP HANA, we recommend you take the HA-300 class "SAP HANA - Implementation and Modeling" from SAP Training.
>
> For more information about ODSs and how they are used in SAP HANA, see the OPEN OPERATIONAL DATASTORE LAYER content at *http://help.sap.com*.
>
> To better understand how traditional data warehouse design has been changed to leverage the concept of a virtual data mart in SAP HANA, download Juergen Haupt's excellent presentation about the future of data warehousing with SAP HANA. Search the web for "Juergen Haupt - Modern DWH based on HANA Platform" to download a PDF of his presentation to the ISR Kompetenztage 2016 conference. (Don't worry, it's available in English!)

6.3.2 Sizing

Whether you are planning to move data from a transaction system or converting data from an existing system, a key thing to keep in mind when sizing an SAP HANA system is the compression ratio of the data being moved to the in-memory platform. Some customers have seen very high compression ratios (8–10 times), while others have experienced "only" 3.8 times data reduction. Therefore, SAP has recommended that you start your high-level planning assuming a compression factor of 3–5 times when sizing your system and then do an in-depth sizing effort.

The differences in these compression numbers come from the fact that some organizations are already using relational databases with extensive compression methods (e.g., DB2 v10 or native compression turned on in Oracle's 12g database), while others are using databases with less compression capabilities. Naturally, we expect to see higher compression numbers in databases that have little compression already. In addition, different data types are compressed differently (i.e., strings are actually arrays in most databases), while numbers are already compressed up to 50% in most versions of Oracle databases. Finally, indexes in a row-based store are generally larger versus those that are column based. To get a rough estimate, going by the 3–5 times estimate is a reasonable first step.

Sizing your SAP HANA system is a bit of an art, a combination of sizing the memory needed (for column stores, row stores, caches, and components); disk sizing (for logs and persistence); and CPU sizing for processing power. Thankfully, the SAP QuickSizer is a great tool to help you size a system. This tool is most appropriate for those companies that do not yet have an SAP ERP or SAP BW system, that want to use a Rapid Deployment Solution, or that are building a standalone data warehouse.

SAP QuickSizer for SAP HANA is available at *http://service.sap.com/quicksizer* (requires an SAP Service logon). Three versions of the tool are available for each of the different versions of SAP HANA, as shown in Figure 6.3.

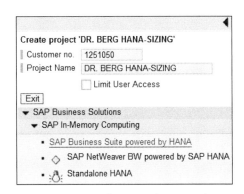

Figure 6.3 Types of SAP QuickSizer Tools

SAP QuickSizer for the SAP Business Suite on SAP HANA allows you to size for specific supported SAP ERP components. The second SAP QuickSizer version is for SAP BW on SAP HANA, and the last version is for those who want to use SAP HANA as a standalone platform for analytics. Since we're discussing building a standalone data warehouse on SAP HANA, let's take a closer look at that version.

To start the sizing of your standalone data warehouse, you should enter your project data, number of users, and the footprint of the data you are planning to bring over to SAP HANA. It is important that you enter this number as uncompressed data. For example, if your source system has compression turned on that achieves 30% compression, you should add 30% to the data size you are seeing in the source system. You should also select the start and end time of your system's normal workday (see Figure 6.4).

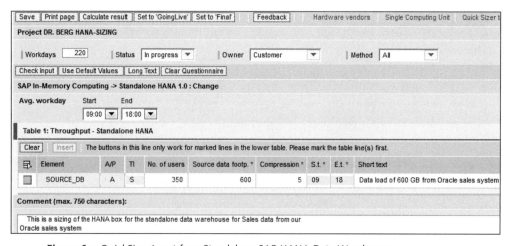

Figure 6.4 QuickSizer Input for a Standalone SAP HANA Data Warehouse

In our example, we are estimating 350 users and 600 GB of data to be loaded from an Oracle database. It is important to note that we should size for the data that was available (300 GB) as well as the expected growth over 3 years (planned at 100 GB per year). So, our input is 600 GB total. Our start and end times are 9:00 in the morning until 6:00 in the evening.

We can add new source systems by highlighting a line and clicking the INSERT button, which allows us to size for multiple source systems. Once we have completed our selections, we simply click Calculate result from the top bar, and we can start analyzing the sizing results.

In this example, we need 246 MB of RAM in our system and support for 70,000 SAPS, as you can see in Figure 6.5.

> **Note**
>
> The term *SAPS* is a unified system performance measure that any hardware vendor should be able to translate into a system sizing. Originally, SAPS was meant to measure the ability to process orders. SAPS was calculated as 2,000 fully processed, business order line items per hour equating to 100 SAPS but is more of a standard measure that tells the hardware vendor how to size the application servers as well as the SAP HANA database server.

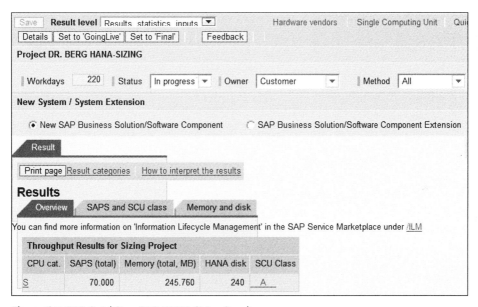

Figure 6.5 SAP QuickSizer SAP HANA Sizing Results

When your sizing estimate is complete, you can simply print out the sizing results for your selected hardware vendors and request a hardware quote. Remember to do a similar exercise for any sandbox, development, quality assurance, and high-availability system that your organization may require, since the size for each of these may be somewhat different.

6.4   SAP Business Suite on SAP HANA

SAP has supported the implementation of SAP Business Suite on SAP HANA since the release of EHP (enhancement package) 6 for SAP ERP 6.0, version for SAP HANA. As a result, you can install a new SAP ERP system on SAP HANA or migrate your existing system to SAP HANA to take advantage of the simplified architecture and the significant performance benefits of SAP HANA. Currently, many companies have installed or moved their SAP ERP systems to SAP HANA, which is becoming increasingly common. However, some key technical considerations must be accounted for when planning a migration of an existing SAP Business Suite system to SAP HANA.

The most current version (as of August 2016) of SAP Business Suite on SAP HANA is EHP 8. EHP 8 included numerous updates to the business content available, with updates to the following functionality:

► Accounting
► Treasury and risk management
► Logistics
► Materials management
► Retail
► Human capital management

Also, numerous fixes and enhancements for the Industry Solutions added in EHP 7 were included in the three support package stacks of EHP 8. The comprehensive list of fixes and enhancements in EHP 8 can be downloaded in the enhancement package release notes. From *http://help.sap.com*, navigate to ENTERPRISE MANAGEMENT • SAP ERP • 6.0 EHP8 • WHAT'S NEW IN SAP ERP for more details.

EHP 7 was another important enhancement package for SAP Business Suite, which included support for more than twenty new Industry Solutions, as well as the following three new key features:

► SAP Fiori applications
► Fast material resource planning (MRP) runs
► Data aging

Let's take a closer look at these new features, so you can better understand what they mean for your business.

6.4.1 New Features

The most significant new features available with EHP 7 and EHP 8 for SAP Business Suite on SAP HANA are the following:

▶ **SAP Fiori applications**

EHP 7 included twenty-five new role-based applications designed to increase user productivity and mobility. These SAP Fiori apps are meant to enhance your user's performance of recurring tasks and are designed to work on your laptop, desktop, tablet, or smart phone. The complete catalog of available SAP Fiori apps is available for download from *http://help.sap.com*. Search for "Catalog of SAP Fiori Apps" and download the catalog using the DOWNLOAD link.

▶ **Faster MRP runs**

Material resource planning is a key element of manufacturing, so SAP added the ability to check material availability and inventory days of supply in bill of materials (BOM) explosion calculation views in SAP HANA Live. You can even perform some ad-hoc simulations, which can greatly enhance your understanding of the MRP process.

> **Warning!**
>
> We implemented SAP HANA Live for one of our clients in an SAP HANA sidecar deployment and found that the BOM explosion views in SAP HANA Live are a work in progress. While a single-level BOM explosion is fully implemented, multilevel BOM explosion was not yet available in the SAP HANA Live distribution package for SAP Product Lifecycle Management (SAP PLM) as of August 2016.

▶ **Data aging**

Data aging is a key requirement for helping business users understand the flow of their business over time. For example, a business user may be interested in comparing the current period's sales to the same period from a prior year. With EHP 7, SAP added the capability to flag the most current raw data from the ERP system to load into memory for rapid use in queries and calculations, while storing older data in the database for historical comparison.

Preparing for Your SAP Business Suite implementation

When you start your migration, you should apply EHP 8 for SAP ERP 6.0, version for SAP HANA. EHP 7 included support for more than twenty new Industry Solutions, and EHP 8 provided fixes and enhancements to these modules, so read carefully through SAP Notes 1774566 (SAP Business Suite Powered by SAP HANA – Restrictions), 1865866 (EHP 7 Release Information), and 2171334 (EHP 8 for SAP ERP 6.0 SP Stacks – Release & Information Note) before you start this process. If you decide to proceed, a separate agreement that outlines any restrictions from the SAP license and maintenance agreement needs to be signed. You can find more information about this requirement in SAP Note 1768031 (SAP EHP 6 for SAP ERP 6.0, version for SAP HANA). In addition, many of the notes regarding SAP Business Suite on SAP HANA are listed in Table 6.6; however, this list is hardly exhaustive, so check the release note for the most recent enhancement package for complete details.

SAP Note	Name	Description
2171334	EHP8 for SAP ERP 6.0 SP Stacks – Release & Information Note	Information about the new industry solutions included in EHP 8
774615	Support package levels for SAP ERP/SAP ECC Installation and Upgrades	List of required support packs
855498	Installation Prerequisite Checker	SAP software on UNIX, Windows, and IBM i; checking OS dependencies
998833	Release Restrictions: SAP ERP 6.0 – Enhancement Packages	Information about the limitations for SAP enhancement packages for SAP ERP 6.0
1730095	EHP6 FOR SAP ERP 6.0 ON HANA – Release Information	Describes release information and support pack equivalence levels
1760306	SAP EhP6 for SAP ERP 6.0, version for SAP HANA 1.0: Add-ons	Explains what you need to consider when running SAP EHP 6 for SAP ERP 6.0, version for SAP HANA together with an add-on on the same system
1768031	SAP EHP 6 for SAP ERP 6.0, version for SAP HANA	Describes limitations concerning the Productive use of SAP EHP 6 for SAP ECC 6.0, version for SAP HANA
1774566	SAP Business Suite Powered by SAP HANA – Restrictions	Describes the restrictions for SAP ECC on SAP HANA

Table 6.6 Key Notes for SAP Business Suite on SAP HANA

SAP Note	Name	Description
1785057	Preparatory steps for database migration to SAP HANA.	Information about preparatory steps for database migration to SAP HANA
1789632	EHP6 for SAP ERP 6.0 on HANA – HANA Content Activation	Information about content that must be activated manually
1865866	EHP 7 for SAP ERP 6.0 – Release information	Information about the new industry solutions included in EHP 7

Table 6.6 Key Notes for SAP Business Suite on SAP HANA (Cont.)

6.4.2 Implementation Options

Three basic implementation options are available for getting an SAP Business Suite system on SAP HANA in your organization:

- New installation (greenfield)
- In-place migration
- Copy, upgrade, and migrate

New Installation

Known as a *greenfield implementation*, a new installation is the simplest approach although the most expensive and time intensive. Under this scenario, you buy and install a fresh, new SAP HANA system with SAP Business Suite on top of it. While not a good way to migrate a production system, you can do some data migration to the SAP HANA system (i.e., master data and open orders) to take advantage of the new capabilities of SAP HANA.

This approach is more appropriate for those who want to clean up older implementations while avoiding an upgrade to newer versions of SAP Business Suite as well as those who are implementing SAP Business Suite for the first time. For this implementation, you should start with the Software Provisioning Manager (SWPM) 1.0, SAP's installation tool, and follow the steps in the *SAP Installation Guide*.

To prepare for the installation, you should:

1. Disable the Windows Server Firewall.

2. Check that the Windows file system is on an NTFS (not FAT) drive.

3. Check the Windows domain structure. For domain installations, all SAP system hosts should be members of a single domain.

4. Change Windows Server to high-performance power plan.

5. Make sure that the user has the authorization for installing the software in the domain. (Do not use the <SID>adm user for the installation of the SAP system.)

6. Create the directory \usr\sap\trans on the host to be used as the transport host, share the \usr\sap directory on the transport host as SAPMNT, and set the permission for EVERYONE to FULL CONTROL for this share. The installer can now address the transport directory in the standard \\SAPTRANSHOST\SAPMNT\ trans.

7. Grant EVERYONE the permission FULL CONTROL for the transport directory.

8. Obtain the physical installation media as part of the installation package. You can use SWPM 1.0.

9. Identify components for your install, such as the central services instance for ABAP (ASCS), the database instance, the enqueue replication server, and the primary and additional application server instance(s).

10. Make sure that the application servers and the SAP HANA database servers are set up for the same time zone.

The steps for the installation include:

1. Make sure that ports 2100, 4239, and 21212 are not blocked. SWPM 1.0 uses port 21200 to communicate with the SAP GUI server. The SAP GUI server uses port 21212 to communicate with the SAP GUI client and port 4239 of the HTTP server, so all these ports must be open.

2. Make sure you have at least 300 MB of space in the installation directory for each installation option, as well as 300 MB free space for the installer executable.

3. Apply SAP Note 1697164 and make sure that the database is up and running before starting the installation.

4. Double-click *sapinst.exe* from the directory where you unpacked the file *SWPM10SP<support package number>_<version number>.SAR*. The install process will start; simply follow the questions on the prompt screen (see Figure 6.6).

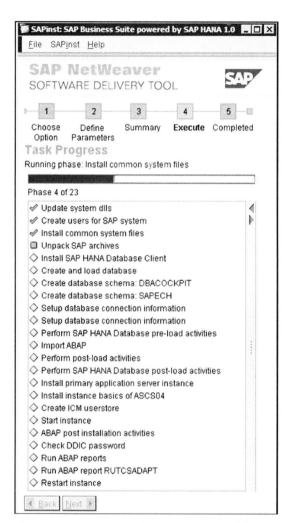

Figure 6.6 SAP HANA Application Server Install for SAP Business Suite

In-Place Migration

An in-place migration is the most common approach for those who already have a functioning SAP Business Suite system and who want to move to SAP HANA. The goal of this approach is to avoid most changes to the overall landscape by keeping SID, host name, application servers, and connectivity the same. With this approach, only the database server is changed during the migration, and the rest of the landscape is, for the most part, left intact. The downtime during the migration is primarily used to move data files between the legacy database and the SAP HANA database, so the downtime required is often a function of the size of the SAP Business Suite system. The first SAP Business Suite systems that migrated to SAP HANA did this migration as a traditional upgrade. This process included first patching up the system, then upgrading the application to the required level, implementing Unicode, and then migrating to SAP HANA.

Today, you can use the Database Migration Option (DMO) and do all these tasks in one step with minimal outage of the system. If you are on an older ERP version, DMO is a great tool to conduct the upgrade and the migration at the same time. DMO is also the recommended approach for all SAP in-place migrations. DMO is not actually a separate tool; rather, it is an option available since SUM 1.0 Service Pack 8. (The latest version is SP 17.) The DMO option can be used for systems that are part of SAP Business Suite 7.0 to migrate to a level corresponding to SAP Basis 7.40, including migrations of SAP ERP version 6.0 EHP 7. DMO is also used to migrate SAP BW to SAP HANA.

The DMO tool can simply create a shadow system, known as a *shadow repository*, inside your SAP Business Suite. This shadow system contains a minimal amount of data and does not impact the existing system if you have enough system resources. You can work with your implementation partner to determine the possible performance impact of your migration before the upgrade begins. In the second step of the configuration phase, you will get three options for the DMO migration (see Figure 6.7). The standard option should be selected by default, unless you know that you have enough system resources in your existing SAP ERP system to accommodate a low-outage database migration.

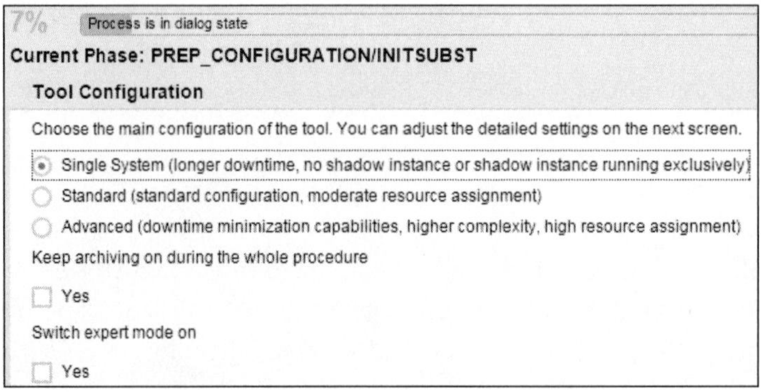

Figure 6.7 Database Migration Option (DMO): Single System

If you selected the advanced option, you can now proceed with the rest of the configuration tasks and all precheck tasks. The DMO tool will guide you through each step. Once you reach Step 4, known as *preprocessing*, the shadow repository will be created. At that stage, you can no longer make changes to the configuration of your system. If you did, the shadow and the real system may no longer have matching configurations. However, users can still access the system and post transactions; you just cannot make new transports into the environment.

The subsequent upgrade steps are done on the shadow system while the real system is still running. Once the upgrade of the shadow system is completed, the DMO moves the shadow system to the SAP HANA box. The actual data movements occur as exports and imports. For large SAP Business Suite systems, we advise splitting up very large tables before the move and, in some cases, adding indexes to speed up the process. The data exports and imports occur after the preprocessing is done in Step 4.

The system must now be locked for further data updates until the data has been migrated to SAP HANA. This migration includes data load jobs; financial allocations; depreciations; user entries; and any jobs that may change, update, or append new data to the system. Once ready to proceed, usually over a weekend, you can lock the system and start the data transfer.

After the data has been migrated to the new SAP HANA system, you now have a working system, and users can be allowed into the new environment. The *SAP HANA Master Guide* on the SAP Marketplace recommends several postprocessing steps, and you should consult an updated version for what may be required for your system and what postprocessing steps are optional.

> **Additional Resources**
>
> More information on DMO is found in SAP Note 2257362 (Database Migration Option [DMO] of SUM 1.0 SP17) and in SAP Note 1813548 (Database Migration Option). You can also take HA-250 (Migration to SAP HANA using DMO), a two-day training class on DMO that SAP Basis team members should attend.

Copy, Upgrade, and Migrate

For those who are extremely risk adverse, you can copy the system over to another system using traditional SAP Basis tools. Then, the copy is upgraded using the same step as in the previous section. This approach requires more hardware and steps than an in-place migration but also removes much of the risk from the project. The copy, upgrade, and migrate approach may also be a good approach for those who want to conduct a proof-of-concept before committing to the overall migration.

6.4.3   Sizing

In the following sections, we will look at the three main options for sizing your new SAP HANA environment for an SAP Business Suite on SAP HANA implementation: the SAP QuickSizer, using an ABAP report, and third-party vendor tools.

SAP QuickSizer

When you start sizing your SAP HANA environment, you should first read the database sizing guidelines from SAP, which are found in SAP Note 1514966 (SAP HANA 1.0: Sizing SAP In-Memory Database). After you understand the basics, you can take your first stab at sizing using the SAP Business Suite powered by SAP QuickSizer tool. You find this tool at *http://service.sap.com/quicksizer*.

You first start by creating a project and entering as much information as possible in the project data, customer data, platform and communication, system availability, and network infrastructure areas of the screen (see Figure 6.8). Most of this data is not used for sizing but gives SAP and your hardware partner valuable information when you are ready to share the sizing output with them.

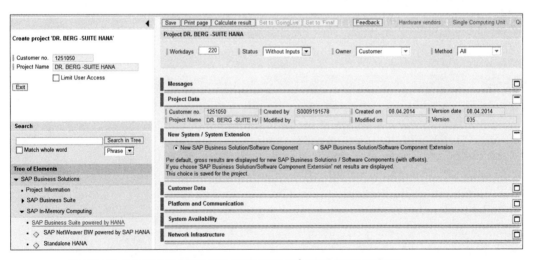

Figure 6.8 Creating an SAP HANA Sizing Project for SAP Business Suite

In this example project, we are simply planning to implement a new SAP ERP Financials (FI) system for SAP Business Suite on SAP HANA. In this scenario, SAP QuickSizer will operate in the same way as sizing a traditional hard disk based system. Only after we complete the sizing effort will we use SAP guidelines to transform the output from the classic sizing to the equivalent SAP HANA sizing, so we must select the module we want to implement (in our example, FICO).

First, we have 940 users divided into low-, medium-, and high-activity users. As shown in the first line of our planned data volumes (Figure 6.9), we plan to process, on average, 5 million billing documents with an average of 2 line items per day. Of these documents, we plan that about 5% of these will be changes every year, and 25% of these changes will be displayed.

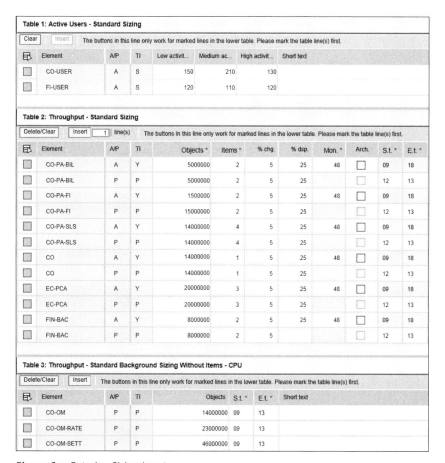

Figure 6.9 Entering Sizing Input

Overall, we plan to retain 48 months of data in our system and have no archiving turned on. In Figure 6.9, the first line of each ELEMENT is the normal average load between 9 am and 6 pm. In the second line for each, we also record our peak loads between noon and 1 pm (you can change the times if your peak load occurs differently). We also enter the estimated number of records for the record types without line items in TABLE 3. Once completed, we can click the CALCULATE RESULT button on top of the page, and we will get the sizing results (Figure 6.10).

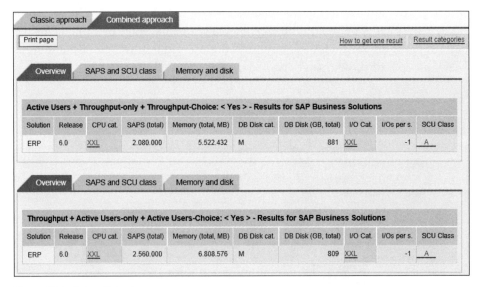

Figure 6.10 Sizing Output

Our output indicates that we have a very large system with system requirements of at least 2,080,000 SAPS and over 5 TB of memory. Remember that this sizing approach is only for a traditional disk-based system and that SAP's guidelines are required to translate this into meaningful and comparative SAP HANA system sizes. The information on how to transform this sizing estimate to SAP HANA is found in the PDF attachment to SAP Note 1779345.

Generally, we advise using throughput-based sizing, instead of number-of-user-based sizing, since you have the ability to control the data retention periods and reduce the required memory better. Of course, you can also keep data on nearline storage (NLS) and still have access to the data, even if it is not physically stored in SAP HANA.

ABAP Report

While the effort of sizing SAP Business Suite on SAP HANA using the SAP Quick-Sizer tool can give you a great starting point for new implementation, SAP also provides a sizing program based ABAP that can be used by existing customers who already have an SAP ERP system. The program is attached to SAP Note 1872170 (Suite on HANA Memory Sizing). You can download the tool (Figure 6.11), following the instructions in the note and execute it to get quite detailed SAP HANA sizing estimates for your SAP Business Suite migration project.

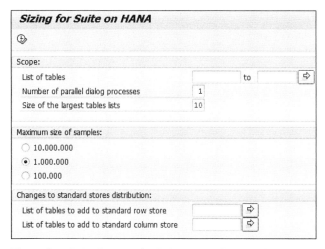

Figure 6.11 Sizing Program for SAP Business Suite on SAP HANA

This program generates an output report that gives you good information on memory requirements for the database tables. The ABAP program is so advanced that it also looks at what will happen during migration, including depooling, indexes, declustering, and LOBs (large objects). In the tool, you can also use filter selections to select certain areas you want to size. As a result, you can select specific tables for SAP HANA sizing or even individual modules such as FI and SAP ERP Material Management (MM) in a sidecar implementation of your SAP HANA system.

Once you execute the program, you will be presented with a screen that shows its progress. Based on the number of parallel dialog processes you assigned in the first input screen, sizing can take some time and may require over an hour in large systems. For many companies, we advise running this during off-hours when more resources can be assigned and when impact to any users is likely to be minimal.

As we can see in this example (Figure 6.12), we are estimating that our SAP Business Suite on SAP HANA will require approximately 7.75 TB of memory overall. Armed with this initial sizing estimate, you can approach vendors and request bids for the necessary SAP HANA hardware.

```
SIZING RESULTS IN GB

Based on the selected table(s), the anticipated maximum requirement are
for the analysed database:
- Memory requirement                                            7,759.6
- Net data size on disk                                         4,685.8

- Estimated Memory requirement after data clean-up              7,374.1
- Estimated net data size on disk after data clean-up           4,685.8

Check the FAQ document attached to SAP Note 1872170 for explanations on how
to interpret the sizing terms and calculations.

Sizing report:                                             ZNEWHDB_SIZE
Version of the report:                                               56
Date of analysis:                                           02-26-2016
Selected accuracy:                                                    H
Number of work processes used:                                       15

SID                                                                 PRD
NW release:                                                   731 SP 16
Type of analyzed database:                                       ORACLE
Database version:                                            11.2.0.3.0
Unicode system                                                       No

Number of tables successfully analyzed:                          94,573
Number of tables partially analyzed:                                  0

MEMORY SIZING CALCULATION DETAILS                     HANA SIZE IN GB

  Column store data                                             3,586.1
+ Row store data                                                  216.2

= Anticipated memory requirement for the initial data          3,802.3
+ Cached Hybrid LOB (20%)                                         104.9
+ Work space                                                    3,802.3
+ Fixed size for code, stack and other services                   50.0

= Anticipated initial memory requirement for HANA              7,759.6
```

Figure 6.12 Output from SAP HANA Sizing Program for SAP Business Suite

Additional Resources

The SAP Note SAP Note 1872170 (Suite on HANA Memory Sizing) also contains a detailed PDF document called *Frequently Asked Questions* that provides detailed instruction on how to download the program, how to execute it, and how to interpret the results.

Vendor Tools

In addition to the SAP QuickSizer and ABAP sizing tools, many hardware vendors have created their own spreadsheets for calculation, or verifying, hardware sizing efforts. Some companies, such as HP, have also created software programs that you can download to assist in the overall SAP HANA sizing effort. The sizing tool from HP may be downloaded from *https://sizersllb.itcs.hpe.com/sb/installs/SAP_HANA_Sizer.zip* and can be installed on your desktop in a few minutes (Figure 6.13).

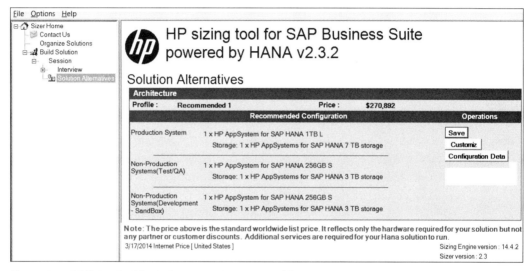

Figure 6.13 HP Sizing Tool for SAP Business Suite Powered by SAP HANA

Other sizing tools and spreadsheets from companies such as Fujitsu, IBM, Dell, Huawei, NEC, Hitachi, and Cisco/EMC may be obtained by contacting the respective vendors.

6.5 SAP S/4HANA

What exactly is SAP S/4HANA? We've been asked this question many times, and the answer is that S/4HANA is simplicity itself. Whether your business data will be managed on-premise or in the cloud, S/4HANA has the flexibility, speed, and simplicity to meet your needs. Let's inform this discussion by taking a look at the landscape for an SAP S/4HANA implementation, as shown in Figure 6.14.

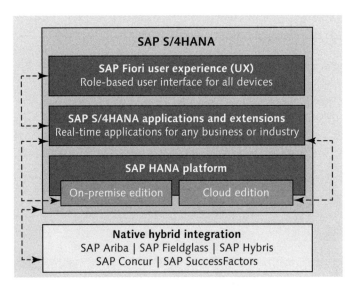

Figure 6.14 SAP S/4HANA Overview

As you can see, the SAP HANA platform can be on-premise, cloud-based, or even a hybrid of these two approaches. The application layer is based on the SAP HANA extended application services, advanced model (SAP HANA XSA), as discussed in Chapter 3. Meanwhile, the presentation layer for S/4HANA is based on the familiar SAP Fiori user experience (UX) and allows for role-based user authentication and access from a multitude of mobile devices.

In the following sections, we'll briefly discuss moving to SAP S/4HANA Cloud before taking a look at your options for implementing the on-premise edition of SAP S/4HANA.

> **Note**
>
> See Chapter 5 for more information on SAP S/4HANA or check out *SAP S/4HANA: An Introduction*, available from SAP Press.

6.5.1 Moving to SAP S/4HANA Cloud

The process of moving to SAP S/4HANA will vary based on the details of your company's current landscape. If you've chosen SAP S/4HANA Cloud, you will typically choose from one or more specific business scenarios, including finance, controlling, accounting, sales, procurement, manufacturing, plant maintenance, product lifecycle management, project systems, marketing, and professional services. As of August 2016, the following offerings were available for SAP S/4HANA:

▸ SAP S/4HANA, on-premise edition 1511 FPS 02

▸ SAP S/4HANA, on-premise edition 1511 FPS 01

▸ SAP S/4HANA, on-premise edition 1511

▸ SAP S/4HANA Cloud 1605

▸ SAP S/4HANA Cloud 1603

▸ SAP S/4HANA Finance, on-premise edition 1503

More information about each of these offerings is available at *https://help.sap.com/s4hana*.

Regardless of your chosen implementation options, implementing SAP S/4HANA Cloud will most likely require two steps. First, you will need to implement the SAP S/4HANA system in the cloud. Then, you will migrate your data from your legacy environment to the cloud using either SAP Landscape Transformation (SLT) or the Data Migration Server (DMIS).

6.5.2 Moving to On-Premise SAP S/4HANA

The scenarios for moving to the on-premise edition of SAP S/4HANA may be generalized into one of the following categories:

▸ System conversion

▸ Landscape transformation

▸ New implementation

We'll take a closer look at each of these scenarios in the following sections.

System Conversion

Existing SAP Business Suite customers who want to move to SAP S/4HANA fall into this category. In this case, you will typically be transitioning to the on-premise edition of SAP S/4HANA. To complete the conversion, you'll need to complete the following steps:

1. Update the SAP NetWeaver Application Server to ABAP stack 7.5.

2. Migrate the database to SAP HANA (if not already using SAP Business Suite on SAP HANA).

3. Install the on-premise edition of the SAP S/4HANA core components.

4. Install SAP Fiori for the on-premise edition of SAP S/4HANA.

5. Migrate data from old data structures to the new simplified data structures.

Let's talk a bit about the migration step. Whether you're planning a system conversion or landscape transformation, the tool of choice will be the SUM. If your database is not already on SAP HANA, use SUM with DMO. If your system database is already on SAP HANA, you can simply use SUM. In either case, make sure you're using SUM 1.0 SP 16 or higher, since SPs 14 and 15 were both specialized to work for specific scenarios.

Figure 6.15 can help you choose between SUM alone or SUM with DMO for your move to SAP S/4HANA. You should be aware that versions of SAP ERP prior to 6.0 may need to be upgraded prior to the move, since they may be using Unicode, but they will not have the Customer Vendor Integration (CVI), which must be present to use SUM.

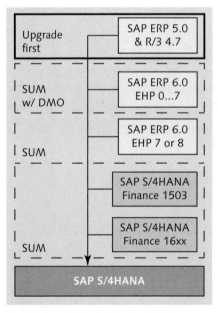

Figure 6.15 Paths to Move to SAP S/4HANA

The process of converting your system using SUM with DMO is quite similar to migrating SAP Business Suite with DMO. If you're system is already on SAP ERP

6.0, EHPs 0 through 8, including SAP Business Suite on SAP HANA with the SAP S/4HANA Finance add-on, you can convert the entire system to SAP S/4HANA in one step.

If your system is on an older release of SAP Business Suite or SAP ERP, you can use a two-step process to convert the system. The first step may consist of a Unicode and business partner conversion, and the second step will install the SAP S/4HANA core.

> **Note**
>
> In some scenarios, especially for moving highly complex systems to SAP S/4HANA, you may require more than two steps to complete the move. For this reason, you should work closely with your chosen implementation partner to find the path that best suits your business needs.

Landscape Transformation

For more complex migration scenarios, such as consolidating multiple systems into one global system, a landscape transformation is required. A landscape transformation will typically require you either to install a clean installation of SAP S/4HANA or to convert an existing system. Then, you'll need to merge the systems or migrate only selected parts of the system (for example, an entire organizational unit).

As part of a landscape transformation effort, you may need to use SLT to replicate data from the old system to the new SAP S/4HANA environment. This stage is also the perfect time to clean up and archive old data to reduce the overall data footprint of your system. These archives can often be stored on nearline storage, which can reduce the licensing and hardware costs for your new SAP S/4HANA implementation.

New Implementation

In a new implementation scenario, you will be moving from some sort of legacy system to SAP S/4HANA, or you may be an existing SAP Business Suite customer who has decided to move to a clean SAP S/4HANA implementation. In this scenario, you will typically install the SAP NetWeaver Application Server ABAP 7.5 on SAP HANA, the SAP S/4HANA core, and SAP Fiori for SAP S/4HANA.

With all the core components in place, all that's left is migrating the master and transactional data from the legacy system using either SLT or SAP Data Services.

Regardless of which scenario you choose, SAP has best practice guides available to help with the move. Best practice information for both the on-premise edition and the cloud edition of SAP S/4HANA can be found at the SAP Service Marketplace at PRODUCTS • SAP BEST PRACTICES & SAP RAPID DEPLOYMENT SOLUTIONS • SAP S/4HANA.

6.6   SAP Business Warehouse on SAP HANA

SAP BW on SAP HANA is the most common form of SAP HANA implementation to date because SAP BW was the first application available for SAP HANA, and SAP BW is the most commonly used reporting system for SAP customers. As the most common reporting system, however, SAP BW was experiencing significant performance issues as data volumes at most companies grew to tens of terabytes. Traditional, relational, hard drive-based systems simply could not keep up with the required data reads and table inserts.

SAP BW version 7.4 was specifically written and redesigned to provide all the new capabilities of SAP HANA in a unified, flexible, and performance enhanced enterprise data warehouse. SAP BW 7.5 further extended the capabilities of SAP BW on SAP HANA by adding flexible planning features, better integration with Eclipse-based tools, performance optimization for SAP Fiori, improved lifecycle management, support for Hadoop and extended dynamic tiering, and simplified migrations and upgrades.

SAP rewrote several areas of the standard business content in the content release for SAP BW 7.47 SP 7 to simplify the data loads and data architecture and to create flexible data models. The new SAP HANA-optimized content included areas such as Accounts Payables (AP), Accounts Receivables (AR), Product Costs forecast and simulations, Profit Center Accounting (PCA), SAP General Ledger (G/L), sales overview, delivery services, billing conditions, backorders, purchasing overview, purchasing accounting, contract management, invoice verifications, and service levels. New content for other areas may be added in subsequent releases.

In addition, Core Data Services (CDS) was introduced with SAP NetWeaver 7.4 SPS 5 and provides the data layer for SAP S/4HANA and SAP Business Suite. CDS provides the framework for creating and consuming reusable data models at the database layer instead of on the ABAP server, which leverages the performance of the IMCE for reporting while avoiding the data redundancies common in previous versions of SAP BW.

There are two different versions of SAP BW 7.5, as follows:

▶ **SAP BW 7.5 SP 1 powered by SAP HANA**
SAP BW 7.5 SP 1 powered by SAP HANA simplified the SAP BW implementation while adding support for big data scenarios (see the comment above regarding support for Hadoop). This edition has all the old familiar objects from previous versions of SAP BW, while adding the enhanced features of SAP BW 7.5 on SAP HANA. This solution is best for companies with an established SAP BW implementation who want to migrate to SAP BW 7.5 for its new capabilities and optimizations for SAP HANA.

▶ **SAP BW 7.5, edition for SAP HANA**
SAP BW 7.5, edition for SAP HANA, is the preferred solution for companies that are implementing SAP BW from scratch, either because they've never used SAP BW or because they've chosen a greenfield migration approach. A greenfield approach is commonly undertaken to redesign an existing implementation to fully utilize the SAP HANA-based optimization in the latest version of SAP BW while leveraging the power of the LSA++ architecture. Figure 6.16 should clarify the difference between the two editions of SAP BW 7.5 on SAP HANA.

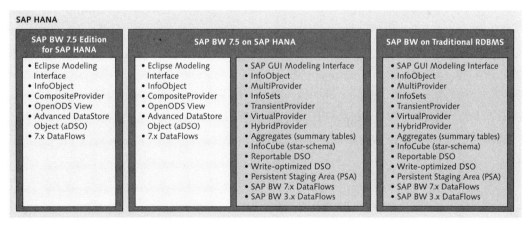

Figure 6.16 Comparing the Features of SAP BW 7.5 Versions and Traditional Databases

Both versions of SAP BW 7.5 provided enhancement for Advanced DataStore Objects (aDSOs) and Enhanced CompositeProviders (ECPs). In addition, a complete Query Designer and extended InfoObject maintenance were added for the Eclipse IDE. SAP HANA smart data integration (SDI) support was added for SAP BW, and nearline storage capabilities and SAP HANA dynamic tiering support were both extended.

In this section, we offer a high-level outline of what you need to consider when moving an SAP BW system to SAP HANA. The section is divided into several main steps: sizing, preparing for a migration, performing a migration, and optimizing a migration. We conclude the section with a discussion of the new features that were introduced in SAP BW 7.4 and those introduced in SAP BW 7.5.

6.6.1 Sizing

Two options are available for sizing an SAP BW on SAP HANA system: SAP Quick-Sizer (discussed in Section 6.4.3 for both SAP HANA as a data warehouse and SAP Business Suite on SAP HANA) and the SAP BW Migration Cockpit for SAP HANA. We'll discuss both next.

Sizing SAP BW Using SAP QuickSizer

The first sizing tool from SAP is the SAP QuickSizer, which is for those companies that don't yet have an SAP ERP or SAP BW system or for those that want to use Rapid Deployment Solutions. SAP QuickSizer should not be used for those who already have an SAP ERP or SAP BW solution. Instead, those customers with existing SAP BW implementations should use the SAP- and vendor-provided tools we covered in this chapter.

SAP HANA memory requirements for SAP BW caches and additional components are fixed at approximately 50 GB. (Additional memory requirements are driven by the size of the column and row stores.) The first step in using the SAP Quick-Sizer (see Figure 6.17) is to enter the project information: operating system, hardware, and database. After that, enter the SAP QuickSizer menus.

In the TABLE 1 area at the top of the screen, enter the planning information if you're using Integrated Planning (IP) in SAP BW. The fields marked with a red star are mandatory fields. For H-PLANN-1, enter the maximum concurrent users in the USERS field. The S.T. and E.T. fields are the start and end times for the processing. By entering this type of information, you'll also get estimates of loads on the SAP HANA system by time periods at the end of the sizing exercise.

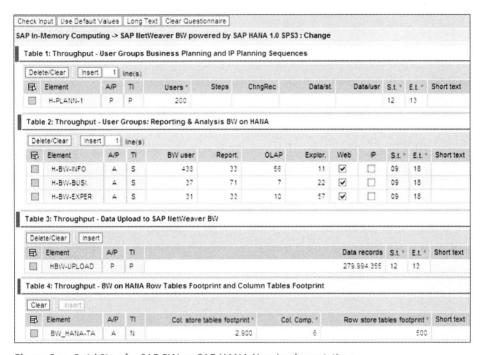

Figure 6.17 QuickSizer for SAP BW on SAP HANA New Implementations

In TABLE 2, enter the estimated number of information consumers (H-BW-INFO), business users (H-BW-BUSI.), and experts (H-BW-EXPER). SAP suggests a ratio of 71%, 26%, and 3%, respectively, for each user group, but you can enter your own mix if you have better estimates. It's important to note that the number of SAP BW users refers to *concurrent* users (not named users). You can get great estimates of this from your SAP EarlyWatch Alert report in SAP Solution Manager. Your SAP Basis team should be able to provide this information.

In the REPORT., OLAP, and EXPLOR. columns, enter the estimated percentage distribution of the users. In this example, we're estimating that, of the 438 information consumers, 33% will consume static preformatted reports, 56% will use online analytical processing (OLAP) tools such as SAP Business Explorer (BEx) Web Analyzer or SAP BusinessObjects Analysis, and the last 11% will be exploring data and have a high amount of navigation activity. These estimates help SAP QuickSizer estimate the size of the memory required.

In TABLE 3, you estimate how many records will be loaded to SAP BW periodically. In this example, we're estimating that 279,994,355 records will be loaded each day between noon and 1pm.

In TABLE 4, you estimate a 2.9 TB footprint in the column data store and a 500 GB footprint in the row data store in SAP HANA. This sizing number is database specific, and SAP provides a few programs to assist you in getting good estimates. SAP Note 1637145 (SAP BW on HANA: Sizing SAP HANA Database) lists programs you can run on SAP BW to get good sizing numbers. The shell script for each database type is located in the file *get_size.zip*, which should be extracted and executed along with the file called *load_RowStore_List.sql* for size input to TABLE 4. The exception to this approach is the IBM DB2 database on the z/OS for which you would use an ABAP program instead (see SAP Note 1736976). Also, we should note that only for DB2 is the inherent compression of the database included in the size estimate. For other databases with compressions turned on (i.e., Oracle), the sizing number has to be adjusted to account for this compression. Also, it's important to note that this program assumes that your SAP BW system is Unicode compliant. If your system is not compliant, you should add about 10% to your sizing output.

While actual compression rates and examples are frequently provided by SAP from real clients, in this example, we estimate a compression rate of 1:5. This compression rate will probably be higher or lower for your actual system but will ensure that we don't significantly undersize our hardware.

You're now ready to add the information of the actual SAP BW system. Most of the information required in TABLE 5 and TABLE 6 (Figure 6.18) is available in the Administrator Workbench (Transaction RSA1) in SAP BW; see reports such as SAP_ANALYZE_ALL_INFOCUBES, ANALYZE_RSZ_TABLES, and SAP_INFOCUBE_DESIGNS, all of which also provide information for each InfoProvider.

In TABLE 5, enter the InfoCube information. The max number of dimensions (DIM. field) you can enter is 13. The three fixed dimensions of an InfoCube are already included, so just enter the free dimensions. The field KEYF. refers to the number of key figures in the fact table of your InfoCube, while the field COM. is the estimated compression. If you don't have better estimates, a rate of 5 may serve for the initial sizing before you refine the estimates with your hardware vendor.

Table 5: Throughput - Definition of InfoCubes for HANA

Delete/Clear | Insert | 6 line(s) | Copy | 1 time(s)

	Element	A/P	TI	Dim. *	KeyF. *	Com. *	Initial load	Period. Upld *	Period *	Short text
☐	INFOCUBES	A		10	23	5	97.654.123	3.987	730	2 years
☐	INFOCUBES	A		11	5	5	103.398.762	26.893	208	3 years
☐	INFOCUBES	A		13	14	5	40.904.906	15.092	730	2 years
☐	INFOCUBES	A		13	7	5	67.986.407	67.094	730	2 years
☐	INFOCUBES	A		9	2	5	13.098.439	15.982	730	2 years
☐	INFOCUBES	A		12	10	5	10.502.483	29.722	730	2 years
☐	INFOCUBES	A		13	8	5	22.095.420	42.201	730	2 years
☐	INFOCUBES	A		13	6	5	14.609.589	72.558	208	3 years

Table 6: Throughput - Definition of DataStore Objects on HANA

Delete/Clear | Insert | 1 line(s) | Copy | 1 time(s)

	Element	A/P	TI	NumF. *	TxtFlds *	CharL. *	WO	Com. *	Initial load	Period. Upld *	Period *	Short text
☐	DS-OBJECT	A		23	42	11	☐	5	2.765.198	219.722	1.080	3 years
☐	DS-OBJECT	A		141	27	13	☐	5	42.984.222	45.882	1.080	3 years
☐	DS-OBJECT	A		11	33	8	☐	5	3.665.231	174.908	1.080	3 years
☐	DS-OBJECT	A		8	81	16	☐	5	20.986.137	45.114	1.080	3 years
☐	DS-OBJECT	A		8	17	22	☑	5	89.768.894	701.113	1.080	3 years
☐	DS-OBJECT	A		32	26	7	☐	5	1.882.290	1.042.775	1.080	3 years

Comment (max. 750 characters):

BW 7.3 on SAP HANA Sizing

Figure 6.18 SAP QuickSizer for SAP BW with SAP HANA: SAP BW Data

In the INITIAL LOAD field, enter the number of records in the existing InfoCube and, in the PERIOD. UPLD field, enter the number of records you estimate will be loaded periodically. This record number information is available in many ways in SAP BW. For example, you can find this information by going to each InfoCube in Transaction RSA1 and then right-clicking and selecting MANAGE in the CONTENT tab. From here, you select NUMBER OF ENTRIES to see the number of records of the fact table. The program ANALYZE_RSZ_TABLES will include all entries in the dimension tables as well. These numbers can be used for the initial load estimate. For the upload estimate, the data packages will tell you how many records are loaded daily. Because daily loads drive a significant portion of SAP HANA's size, it's important to spend some time getting these numbers as accurate as possible.

The last item in TABLE 5 is to estimate how many data loads will be kept in SAP BW. In this example, we're estimating daily loads for most InfoCubes and intend to keep 2 years of data. Thus, this estimate would be 2 × 365 = 730, but we've included scheduled downtime for upgrades, patches, and services planned for next year, so it will actually be somewhat lower. (Notice that the last InfoCube in the estimate is periodically loaded, so we only plan for 208 periods.)

In TABLE 6, the estimates for the DataStore Objects (DSOs) are added. The logic is quite similar to those in TABLE 5, but the fields NUMF., TXTFLDS, and CHARL. refer to the number of numeric fields in the DSO, the number of text fields, and the average length of character fields, respectively. These numbers are hard to estimate, so good design information from your SAP BW team is required.

The flag WO isn't required but allows you to identify whether the DSO is write optimized and therefore won't have as many log-file entries as a regular DSO. The remaining fields are the same as for the InfoCubes in TABLE 5.

After you've completed the entries, SAP QuickSizer will give you a good initial size estimate of the components required. Figure 6.19 shows the results of this example.

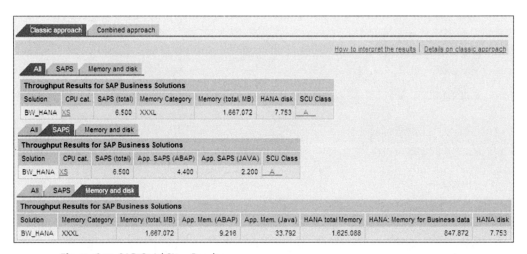

Figure 6.19 SAP QuickSizer Results

As you may have noted, this SAP HANA sizing example calls for 1.6 TB of memory. While this instance can easily be deployed on a single-node SAP HANA server (Silicon Graphics has certified SAP HANA appliances with 20 TB of memory!), for larger databases you may want to scale-out to a multinode system. In a multinode system, SAP BW on SAP HANA will deploy the master data, ABAP system tables, and row store data on the master node. The other connected server node(s) will contain the Persistent Staging Area (PSA), InfoCubes, and DSOs.

When adding many nodes, more processing on the master node (such as master data lookups) will be required, so it's important to work with your hardware vendor to add more memory to the master node beyond what the SAP QuickSizer estimated. Armed with this information, you can approach the hardware partner for quotes and cost estimates.

Sizing SAP Business Warehouse Using the SAP BW Migration Cockpit

For customers who already have an SAP BW system, much better alternatives are available for in-depth sizing results. In the SAP BW Migration Cockpit for SAP HANA, you will find a tool that takes into account your current operating system; the compression rates of the source database; and the fact that SAP BW 7.5 will "off-load" nonessential data, such as the PSA tables, from memory to disk when not needed (Figure 6.20).

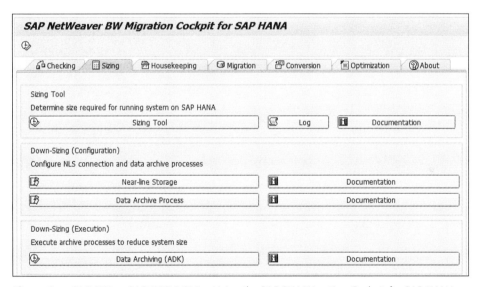

Figure 6.20 SAP BW on SAP HANA Sizing Using the SAP BW Migration Cockpit for SAP HANA

When you run this program on a production system, you will get quite accurate sizing information that includes sizing for RAM and dynamic runtime memory, log space, and disk space. The results even provide details on items such as data sizes with corresponding dynamic runtime memory for row stores and column stores, as well as the calculated size and the estimated size in SAP HANA memory.

The higher precision at which you run the estimate (selected by radio buttons in Figure 6.21), the longer the program is going to run. With 12 parallel processors and a 9 TB data warehouse, it isn't unusual to see 30–70 minutes of runtime. To increase speed, you can also suppress analysis tables that are smaller than 1 MB.

In addition, because timeouts are common when running this sizing program, you should temporarily change the parameter in rdisp/max_wprun_time to 0. You can do this in SAP BW Transaction RZ11. Finally, you estimate the growth for the system over a time period as a percentage or as absolute growth in gigabytes.

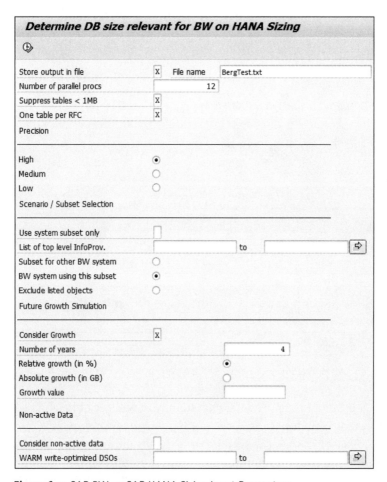

Figure 6.21 SAP BW on SAP HANA Sizing Input Parameters

The output (Figure 6.22) is also stored in the file you specified, and the file can now be emailed to hardware vendors for sizing input and hardware selection. For further references about sizing, we recommend the following SAP Notes:

▶ SAP Note 1514966: Sizing SAP HANA Database

▶ SAP Note 1637145: SAP BW on HANA: Sizing SAP HANA Database

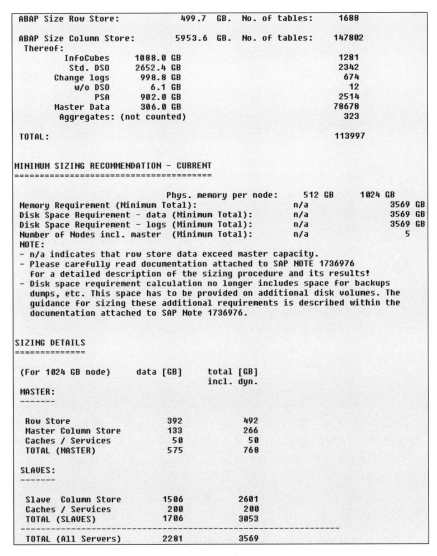

```
ABAP Size Row Store:              499.7  GB.  No. of tables:    1688

ABAP Size Column Store:          5953.6  GB.  No. of tables:  147802
  Thereof:
        InfoCubes    1088.0 GB                              1281
        Std. DSO     2652.4 GB                              2342
        Change logs   998.8 GB                               674
        w/o DSO         6.1 GB                                12
        PSA           902.0 GB                              2514
        Master Data   306.0 GB                             78678
        Aggregates: (not counted)                            323

TOTAL:                                                    113997


MINIMUM SIZING RECOMMENDATION - CURRENT
==========================================

                              Phys. memory per node:    512 GB    1024 GB
Memory Requirement (Minimum Total):                       n/a        3569 GB
Disk Space Requirement - data (Minimum Total):            n/a        3569 GB
Disk Space Requirement - logs (Minimum Total):            n/a        3569 GB
Number of Nodes incl. master  (Minimum Total):            n/a            5
NOTE:
- n/a indicates that row store data exceed master capacity.
- Please carefully read documentation attached to SAP NOTE 1736976
  for a detailed description of the sizing procedure and its results!
- Disk space requirement calculation no longer includes space for backups
  dumps, etc. This space has to be provided on additional disk volumes. The
  guidance for sizing these additional requirements is described within the
  documentation attached to SAP Note 1736976.


SIZING DETAILS
==============

(For 1024 GB node)    data [GB]     total [GB]
                                    incl. dyn.
MASTER:
-------

  Row Store            392           492
  Master Column Store  133           266
  Caches / Services     50            50
  TOTAL (MASTER)       575           768

SLAVES:
-------

  Slave  Column Store 1506          2601
  Caches / Services    200           200
  TOTAL (SLAVES)      1706          3053
  -------------------------------------------------------------------
  TOTAL (All Servers) 2281          3569
```

Figure 6.22 SAP BW on SAP HANA Sizing Results

As a best practice, we recommend that you work with your preferred vendor before ordering your hardware or finalizing your budgets.

6.6.2 Preparing for a Migration

Once you're ready to get started with your SAP BW to SAP HANA migration, you have to take a few preparation steps, as you will see in the following sections.

SAP BW System Housekeeping

SAP BW is a complex system with lots of redundancies and copied data in the database that can be cleaned up. Examples include log files, summary tables, temporary data staging areas, and interim data stores where data is kept before being pushed to higher-level data models. You can save significant amounts of work by completing a cleanup effort before you start your SAP HANA migration or an SAP BW upgrade project.

Cleanup efforts often reduce an SAP BW system size by 20%–30%. For example, a large oil and gas company had an SAP BW system with more than 108 TB. This system was reduced to less than 36 TB by moving more of the data to NLS prior to the SAP HANA migration, saving the company millions of dollars in hardware and licensing costs.

Because SAP HANA stores many of the system tables and master data (row store tables) on the master node, it is important to keep these tables as small as possible to fit on this node. The major items to pay attention to include the following:

▶ Clean the PSA for data already loaded to DSOs.

▶ Delete the aggregates (summary tables) because they won't be needed again.

▶ Compress the E and F tables in all InfoCubes to make InfoCubes much smaller. (F tables are fact tables including uncompressed data in the InfoCube as well as information about the requests which loaded the data. E tables contain compressed data for the InfoCubes, but information about the original data load requests is no longer included.)

▶ Remove data from the statistical cubes (they start with the technical name 0CTC_xxx). These contain performance information for the SAP BW system running on the relational database. You can do this using Transaction RSDDSTAT or the RSDDSTAT_DATA_DELETE program.

- Look at log files, bookmarks, and unused BEx queries and templates (Transaction RSZDELETE).

- Remove as much as possible of the data transfer process (DTP) temporary storage, DTP error logs, and temporary database objects. Help and programs to do this are available in SAP Notes1139396 and 1106393.

- For write-optimized DSOs that push data to reportable DSOs (LSA++ approach), remove data in the write-optimized DSOs, since that data is already available in higher-level objects.

- Migrate old data to NLS on a small server, which will still provide access to the data for the few users who infrequently need to see this old data. You'll also be able to query it when SAP BW is on SAP HANA, but it doesn't need to be in memory.

- Remove data in unused DSOs, InfoCubes, and files used for staging in the SAP BW system. This staging includes possible reorganization of master data text and attributes using process types in Transaction RSPC.

You may also want to clean up background information stored in table RSBATCH-DATA. This table can get very large if not managed. You should also consider archiving any IDocs and clean the tRFC (transactional remote function call) queues. All of this will reduce the size of the SAP HANA system and help you fit the system tables on the master node.

Furthermore, in SAP Note 706478, SAP provides some ideas on how to keep the SAP Basis tables from growing too fast in the future. If you are on SP 23 of SAP BW 7.0, or higher, you can also delete unwanted master data directly (see SAP Note 1370848).

Finally, you can use the program RSDDCVER_DIM_UNUSED to delete any unused dimension entries in your InfoCubes to reduce the overall system size. For many organizations, this SAP BW cleanup effort can be a mini-project in itself. Once completed, however, the next step is to start the preparation of the SAP BW system for SAP HANA.

While you can do these tasks manually, SAP has also provided several cleanup programs that can help you with some of these tasks. If you are on SAP BW 7.0 SP 32 or higher, you can generate a housekeeping task list and get automated help in cleaning the system (Figure 6.23). You first have to install the program from SAP Note 1829728 before you can generate the SAP_BW_HOUSEKEEPING task list using Transaction STC01.

Task List			SAP_BW_HOUSEKEEPING					
Task List Run			SAP_BW_HOUSEKEEPING_201401141578					
E	C	S	L	Autom. Phase	Comp.	Task Description	H	P
☐	✔	☐	⬛	Repair	BW	Repairs indices on InfoCube fact table(s) at the Data Dictionary level	📄	
☐	✔	☐	⬛	Repair	BW	Re-assign requests written into the incorrect PSA partition	📄	
☐	✔	☐	⬛	Repair	BW	Ensure request consistencies throughout the PSA landscape	📄	
☐	✔	☐	⬛	Repair	BW	Ensure partitioned tables are correctly indexed for the PSA	📄	
☐		📇		Repair	BW	Verify DataSource segments assignment to PSA	📄	
☐		📇		Repair	BW	Checks BW metadata with regard to the DDIC	📄	
☐		📇		Cleanup	BW	Deletes the entries that are no longer required in table RSIXW	📄	🗑
☐		📇		Cleanup	BW	Reorganize and delete bookmark IDs and view IDs	📄	🗑
☐		📇		Cleanup	BW	This program deletes RSTT traces	📄	🗑
☐		📇		Cleanup	BW	This program deletes BW statistical data	📄	🗑
☐		📇	⬛	Cleanup	BW	Delete Aggregate data via deactivation	📄	
☐		📇	⬛	Postprocessing	BW	Clear all OLAP Cache parameters	📄	

Figure 6.23 The SAP BW Housekeeping Task List for System Cleanup

SAP has also provided a cleanup list and automated support in version 3.0 of the SAP BW Migration Cockpit for SAP HANA (Figure 6.24). This list is a critical tool that you should be using before, throughout, and after your SAP BW to SAP HANA migration. The list provides a consolidated view of all major tasks that you will have to do as part of the SAP BW to SAP HANA migration.

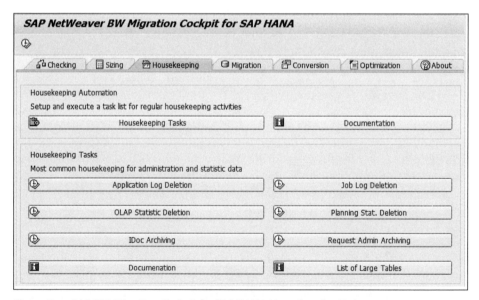

Figure 6.24 SAP BW Migration Cockpit for SAP HANA Housekeeping Tasks

Prechecks for SAP BW to SAP HANA Migration

After your system is cleaned up, you have to prepare to move the system to SAP HANA. For this to work, you have to be on SAP BW version 7.3, you need to have implemented Unicode, and the security conversion must be complete for the SAP BW 7.0 system (many organizations did not do Unicode or security conversions as part of their earlier SAP BW upgrade). Prior to the release of the DMO tool from SAP, companies would often begin their migration projects as quick technical upgrades to SAP BW 7.3. During this technical upgrade, the Unicode and security conversions would be completed in preparation for the migration.

However, the simplest way to do all these tasks is as a DMO. Using DMO, you can complete all the requisite tasks in a single step as part of the migration of SAP BW to SAP HANA. Since the initial release of DMO, the process has been further refined through successful migrations of the world's largest SAP BW systems, and DMO is now considered the best practice for migrating to SAP BW 7.5 on SAP HANA.

To plan for what should be done in the DMO migration option in SUM, SAP provides a checklist in version 3.0 of the SAP BW Migration Cockpit for SAP HANA. The checklist part of the cockpit and provides automatic check programs for both the 3.5 version and the 7.x version of SAP BW. You can find the latest version of the SAP BW Migration Cockpit for SAP HANA attached to SAP Note 1909597 (Figure 6.25).

In version 3.x of this tool, hundreds of checks are done automatically in the SAP BW system, including platform checks on database, application, and system information. SAP Basis checks are also included for support packs, ABAP/Java stacks, Unicode, SAP BW releases, and add-ons to your system.

The checklist from the SAP BW Migration Cockpit (Figure 6.25) is intended for use several times throughout the project: once before you start, periodically as you resolve issues and upgrade requirements, and then finally when the system has been migrated to SAP HANA. This last step is important because the checklist tool also has specific checks for the SAP HANA system that can help you identify any issues before turning over the system to end users. If the tool shows a red flag, you should resolve this issue before starting your SAP HANA migration, or if a new red flag shows up, fix it before completing the migration.

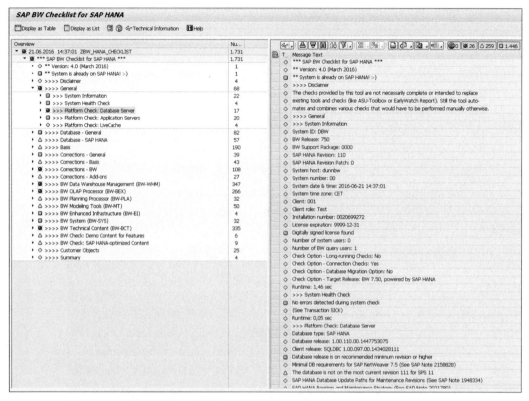

Figure 6.25 SAP BW Checklist for SAP HANA

If you have to upgrade the version of SAP BW to a higher release, SAP also provides a task list that you can complete before you start the upgrade in the DMO (Figure 6.26). If you are on SAP BW 7.0 SP 31 or higher, you can generate a before-the-upgrade task list and get help in preparing the system for the upgrade, as shown in Figure 6.26. The more of these tasks you complete, the faster the upgrade may proceed since you are reducing size and complexity, while assuring that your system is ready for the SAP BW 7.5 upgrade.

To get access to this task list, you have to install the program from SAP Note 1734333 and generate the SAP_BW_BEFORE_UPGRADE task list using Transaction STC01.

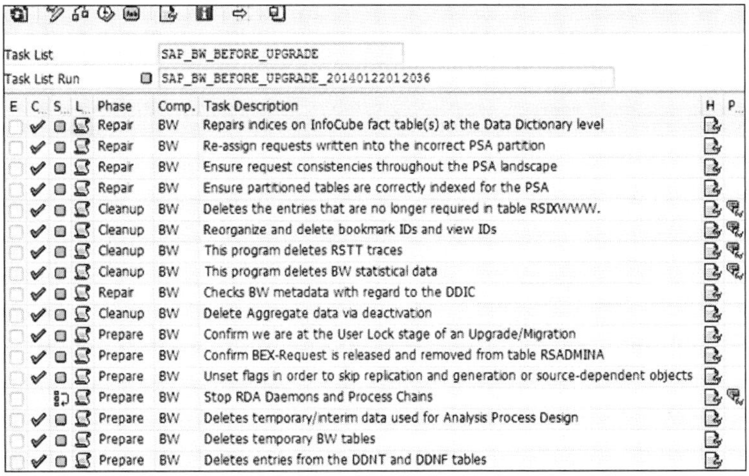

Task List SAP_BW_BEFORE_UPGRADE
Task List Run SAP_BW_BEFORE_UPGRADE_20140122012036

E	C	S	L	Phase	Comp.	Task Description	H	P
				Repair	BW	Repairs indices on InfoCube fact table(s) at the Data Dictionary level		
				Repair	BW	Re-assign requests written into the incorrect PSA partition		
				Repair	BW	Ensure request consistencies throughout the PSA landscape		
				Repair	BW	Ensure partitioned tables are correctly indexed for the PSA		
				Cleanup	BW	Deletes the entries that are no longer required in table RSIXWWW.		
				Cleanup	BW	Reorganize and delete bookmark IDs and view IDs		
				Cleanup	BW	This program deletes RSTT traces		
				Cleanup	BW	This program deletes BW statistical data		
				Repair	BW	Checks BW metadata with regard to the DDIC		
				Cleanup	BW	Delete Aggregate data via deactivation		
				Prepare	BW	Confirm we are at the User Lock stage of an Upgrade/Migration		
				Prepare	BW	Confirm BEX-Request is released and removed from table RSADMINA		
				Prepare	BW	Unset flags in order to skip replication and generation or source-dependent objects		
				Prepare	BW	Stop RDA Daemons and Process Chains		
				Prepare	BW	Deletes temporary/interim data used for Analysis Process Design		
				Prepare	BW	Deletes temporary BW tables		
				Prepare	BW	Deletes entries from the DDNT and DDNF tables		

Figure 6.26 SAP BW Before-the-Upgrade Task List

Many of the tasks in these three tools overlap somewhat, and some are not required. However, each tool provides useful guidance on how to get your system as clean and small as possible before the SAP BW upgrade and SAP HANA migration.

6.6.3 Performing a Migration

In Chapter 2, we introduced you to the three options for implementing an SAP BW on SAP HANA system:

- Migrate your entire SAP BW system to SAP HANA.
- Set up a new SAP BW system (with an SAP HANA database) alongside your existing SAP BW system and use that new SAP BW environment for particularly challenging or new requirements. Known as a *side-by-side* or *sidecar* installation, this approach often requires a partial migration of SAP BW transaction data and complete replication of most master data.
- Implement an SAP BW system for the first time and then run SAP HANA for it.

The first two of these three options both involve *migration*. In the first option—the standard migration—you are migrating your entire SAP BW system to SAP HANA. In the second option—the partial migration—you are setting up an additional instance of SAP BW and then migrating part of your transaction data into the new SAP BW system, on top of which you then run SAP HANA.

Each of these options has its own benefits and limitations, so you should decide early how much risk you can live with, what testing is required, what outage of the SAP BW system is acceptable, and what resources you can commit to the migration project. We'll discuss both options in more detail next.

Key SAP Notes for Migrating SAP BW to SAP HANA

▶ SAP Note 1909597: SAP BW Migration Cockpit for SAP HANA
▶ SAP Note 1729988: SAP BW powered by SAP HANA – Checklist Tool
▶ SAP Note 1799545: SAP BW Database Migration Option (DMO)

Standard Migration

In this approach, you simply treat your SAP BW move to SAP HANA as a database migration project. You start with the SAP BW system, complete the cleanup and preparations outlined earlier, and migrate the database over to SAP HANA. However, you would leave the application logic and data models the same.

In this scenario, you can again use the DMO tool (see Section 6.4.2). DMO is a key option in SUM, for those with older, out-of-date SAP BW systems that want to migrate to SAP HANA. You can use DMO if you are on at least SAP BW version 7.0 and have applied Service Pack 17 (see SAP Note 1799545) (Figure 6.27).

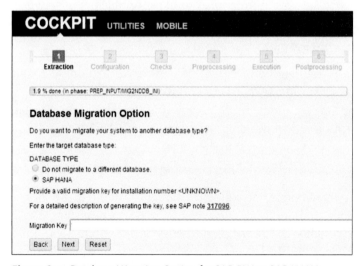

Figure 6.27 Database Migration Option for SAP BW to SAP HANA

The best way to approach the database migration with DMO is to start with the sandbox system and create a run book with step-by-step lists on how each problem and software task is created. At the end of this first migration, your run book could be a word document with 90–100 pages filled with screenshots and documentation, which would not be unusual. The run book is the key to a successful migration. You should build on the run book when you migrate to the development and then the quality assurance (QA) and the production systems.

If you are working with an SAP BW system that is not heavily used, or one that has lots of processing capacity, you can minimize the downtime by *extensively* using a *shadow system* during the upgrade. If you use a shadow system, the system will be copied (not the data), and many of the upgrade tasks will happen on this shadow system while the real system is still running. Only in the later stages is the system unavailable to the users while the configuration and data are moved to SAP HANA. Using a shadow system minimizes the downtime of the system.

By selecting the STANDARD option or the ADVANCED option in Figure 6.28, you can reduce the outage time for your migration, since the upgrade will all occur on the shadow instance and the outage is only required when the data is exported and imported to the SAP HANA instance.

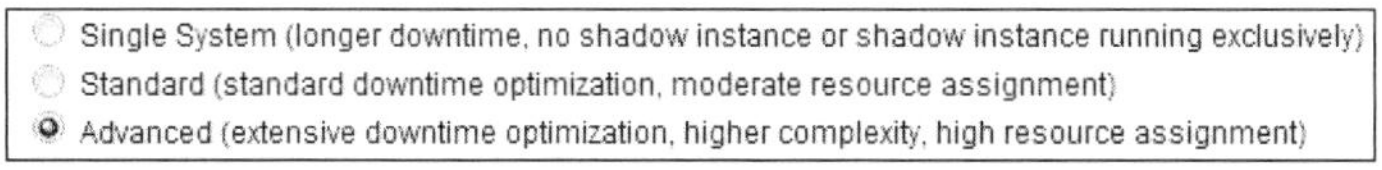

> ○ Single System (longer downtime, no shadow instance or shadow instance running exclusively)
> ○ Standard (standard downtime optimization, moderate resource assignment)
> ◉ Advanced (extensive downtime optimization, higher complexity, high resource assignment)

Figure 6.28 Minimizing System Outage for SAP BW Using DMO

Partial Migration

Many organizations have decided to perform the SAP BW to SAP HANA migration using the sidecar approach. This process involves setting up a new SAP BW system on SAP HANA parallel to the current SAP BW system running on a relational database. Then, for key areas, the InfoCubes and DSOs are transported to the SAP HANA system, and the data loads are switched over to the new system as part of smaller projects. (For more information about transports between different software releases, see SAP Note 1090842.) Meanwhile, other InfoCubes and DSOs continue running on the old SAP BW relational database management systems (RDBMS). Basically, you will be running two SAP BW systems at the same time, without duplicating the loads to InfoProviders in both systems.

While more costly, this approach allows you to keep the old system around and minimize risks of the SAP HANA migration. The outage required is also minimal and can be done over a weekend, functional area by functional area. Furthermore, this approach allows organizations to reimplement poorly designed SAP BW systems, which may have lots of customized code, nonstandard objects, and workarounds to achieve the query performance that SAP HANA provides without needing such tactics.

However, the trick to making this approach successful is to decommission the InfoProviders in the old system when switching over to SAP HANA. Loading to both systems is complex and also may place stress on the SAP ERP system. For example, master data may need to be duplicated in both the legacy SAP BW and the new SAP BW on SAP HANA system during the migration period. Therefore, you should plan to stop these jobs and migrate subject areas with shared master data as soon as possible. (For more information on loading SAP ERP data to two or more SAP BW systems, see SAP Notes 775568 and 844222.)

Migrate a Copy of SAP BW to SAP HANA

In either a standard migration or a partial migration, you can also start by migrating a copy of SAP BW to SAP HANA. This approach is common among organizations with low risk tolerance and lots of time to migrate SAP BW to SAP HANA. In this approach, you will be copying an existing SAP BW system, applying SAP Notes or SAP BW upgrades required to the copied version of the SAP BW production system, and then reconciling the old SAP BW and the new SAP BW on SAP HANA system from a functional standpoint. This reconciliation may include interfaces, open hubs, SAP BusinessObjects BI reports and analytics, security, broadcasted reports, queries, and data reconciliation.

After those tests are performed, the process chains are tested for functionality and runtimes, and the data is reconciled again. To make this approach work, you must plan carefully and will most likely run your duplicated process chains over the weekend to avoid impacts to the SAP ERP system. This approach also requires planning and some enhancements to your load programs to load the data to both the SAP BW and the SAP BW on SAP HANA system without impacting delta loads, but it can be done.

After the tests have been completed, you simply switch the users over to the new SAP BW on SAP HANA box and decommission the old SAP BW system on the relational database. You can even keep the old system inactive in the background for a few weeks as a risk-mitigation strategy during the cross-over. Additional helpful information is available in SAP Note 886102.

It is important to note that database migrations of SAP BW to SAP HANA are best done using the DMO tool covered in this chapter. While possible, migrating SAP BW to SAP HANA in a step-by-step fashion outside this tool is not recommended. DMO can be used either on the primary SAP BW system or on a copy.

Summary of Migration Approaches

For most organizations, the standard SAP BW to SAP HANA migration without significant optimization activities will be the simplest and most appropriate approach. So far, most organizations have planned their SAP BW migration projects this way, but the other approaches are also used. Table 6.7 summarizes the implementation options.

Approach	Effort	Risk	Benefits	Common
Standard migration without optimization	Low	Low	Medium	Yes
Standard migration with optimization	Medium	Medium	High	Yes

Table 6.7 Summary of Implementation Options

To complete your SAP BW to SAP HANA migration project quickly, you should seriously consider splitting the technical database migration effort from the SAP HANA optimization effort, since many of the optimization tasks can be done at a later date.

6.6.4 Optimizing a Migration

After you perform the DMO database migration, you can optimize your system. If you choose not to optimize, your database system will be SAP HANA, but there will be no model changes to your system and no impact on your queries, links to NLS, interfaces, or data loads, except for substantially faster performance and some internal changes regarding how SAP HANA processes at the database level (i.e., data activation and compression). Functionally, you have the same system, so this approach is therefore the fastest and most common.

If you do choose to optimize, you'll improve data structures to take advantage of the new capabilities in SAP HANA, which may include SAP HANA-optimized InfoCubes. Optimization may also include the addition of SAP HANA hints on your data transformations to make lookups go faster when loading data. This migration approach is basically a technical and functional upgrade at the same time. Although the impact on the queries is minimal, optimizing provides significant additional performance in data loads and query performance.

However, for very large SAP BW systems, this approach can be quite time consuming and may require substantially more testing. To reduce this, owners of large SAP BW systems can limit the functional upgrade to slow-performing areas that need this extra boost, or they can simply do the standard upgrade first and then optimize the system as part of future new development efforts, or when enhancements are made to existing InfoCubes.

You can also choose whether to migrate the data architecture from Layered Scalable Architecture (LSA) in the older SAP BW to a simplified LSA++ architecture with fewer layers and less partitions in SAP BW on SAP HANA. The new LSA++ data architecture simply accounts for the fact that much of the splitting up of tables and staging needed in a legacy SAP BW system to get load and query performance is often not needed when SAP BW is on SAP HANA. How much of the optimization effort you're willing to undertake depends on the resources available and how quickly you must complete the migration.

In the following sections, we'll talk about some of the possible optimization steps for SAP BW on SAP HANA.

Optimized DSOs

In early releases of SAP BW on SAP HANA, it was recommended that customers optimize their DSOs in SAP BW using Transaction RSMIGRHANADB or convert them manually in the Data Warehousing Workbench (DWB). Now, this recommendation is no longer valid. In 2014, SAP changed how the SAP BW DSOs work on SAP HANA in such a way that SAP HANA-optimized DSOs are no longer recommended. In fact, SAP now recommends that customers who converted their ODSs to SAP HANA-optimized versions reconvert them back to the older type and that new customers do not convert their DSOs when moving to SAP HANA. For more information, see SAP Note 1849498.

Optimizing Code

If not modified, some single-record lookups for data transformations during data loads into SAP BW on SAP HANA may actually run slower than on a relational database. While not required to be changed as part of the migration, to help identify these types of transformations, SAP has provided an ABAP Routine Analyzer program in the SAP BW Migration Cockpit for SAP HANA (Figure 6.29). This program helps you find suboptimal code and makes suggestions about how to improve upon it.

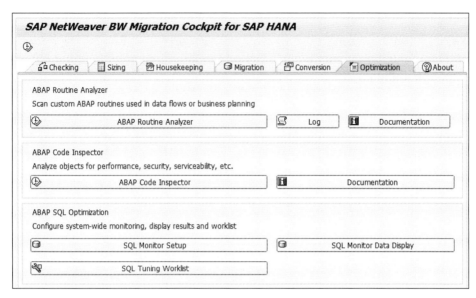

Figure 6.29 ABAP Routine Analyzer and Inspector in the SAP BW Migration Cockpit

This program can review SAP BW 7.x transformations, as well as SAP BW 3.5 update and transfer rules automatically, and flag any ABAP code that can benefit from further SAP HANA optimizations (Figure 6.30).

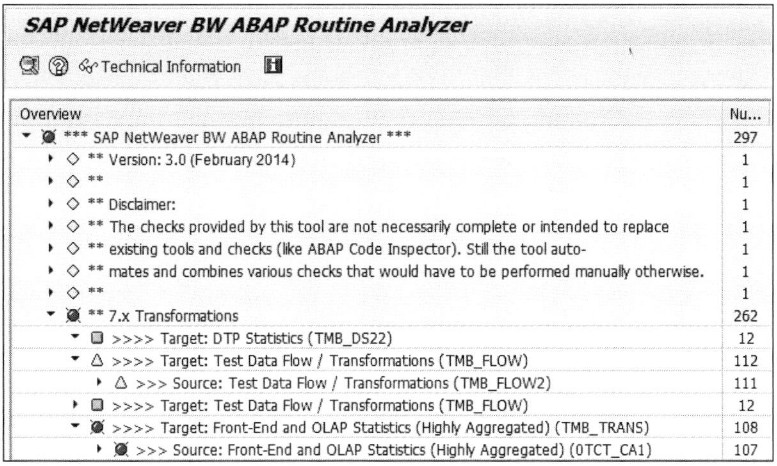

Figure 6.30 SAP BW ABAP Analyzer for SAP HANA Migrations

Optimized InfoCubes

You can continue using existing standard InfoCubes that don't have the SAP HANA-optimized property, or you can convert them. The core idea of the new SAP HANA-optimized InfoCube is that, when you assign characteristics and/or key figures to dimensions, the system doesn't create any dimension tables except for the package dimension. Instead, the master data identifiers (SIDs) are simply written in the fact table, and the dimensional keys (DIM IDs) are no longer used, resulting in faster data read execution and data loads. In short, dimensions become logical units instead of physical data tables. The logical concept of dimensions is used only to simplify the query development in the BEx Query Designer. The InfoCubes can be optimized from the standard SAP BW administration interface, as shown in Figure 6.32, or from a program delivered by SAP (RSDRI_CONVERT_CUBE_TO_INMEMORY).

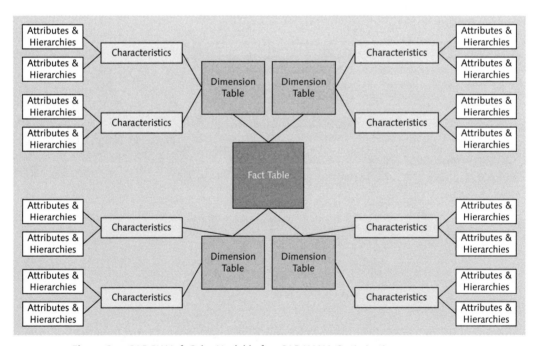

Figure 6.31 SAP BW InfoCube Model before SAP HANA Optimization

Figure 6.31 shows an example of an SAP BW InfoCube model before SAP HANA optimization. Because the physical star-schema table changes during the SAP HANA optimization, any custom-developed program that accesses InfoCubes directly instead of going through standard interfaces must be rewritten. However, because few companies have ventured into this area, the optional conversion will have little impact on most organizations except for providing faster InfoCube performance. Figure 6.33 shows an example of an SAP BW InfoCube model after SAP HANA optimization.

To convert existing InfoCubes, you can either do them one by one in the Administrator Workbench interface (Figure 6.32), or you can simply go to the program RSDRI_CONVERT_CUBE_TO_INMEMORY and select the InfoCubes you want to convert. The job is executed in the background as a store procedure and is extremely fast. Typically, you can expect the job to complete in 10–20 minutes even for very large InfoCubes with hundreds of millions of rows. During the conversion, users can even query the InfoCubes; however, data loads must be suspended. Currently, traditional InfoCubes with a maximum of 233 key figures and 248 characteristics can be converted to SAP HANA-optimized InfoCubes.

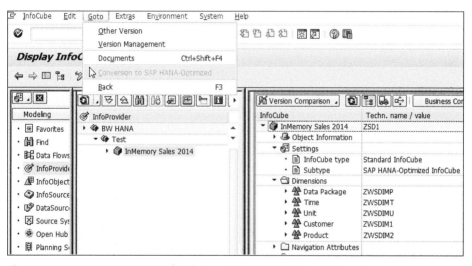

Figure 6.32 Converting SAP BW InfoCubes to SAP HANA-Optimized Infocubes

After the conversion to SAP HANA, optimized InfoCubes are maintained in column-based store of the SAP HANA database and are assigned a logical index (`CalculationScenario`). However, if the InfoCubes were stored only in SAP Business Warehouse Accelerator (SAP BW Accelerator) before the conversion, the InfoCubes are set to inactive during the conversion, and you'll need to reactivate them and reload the data if you want to use it.

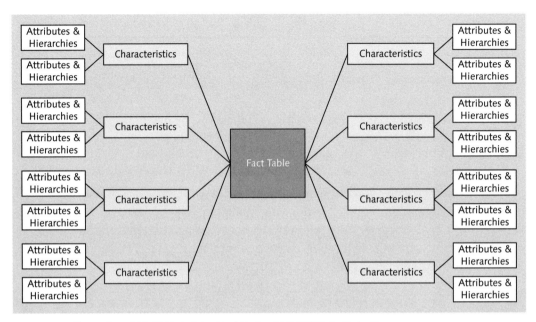

Figure 6.33 SAP BW InfoCube Model after SAP HANA Optimization

Although SAP HANA-optimized InfoCubes can't be remodeled, you can still delete and add InfoObjects using the InfoCube maintenance option, even if you've already loaded data into the InfoCube.

Other routine maintenance tasks in SAP BW have changed as well, including standard compression of fact tables and how you handle noncumulative key figures in SAP HANA, which we'll discuss in the following subsections.

Because SAP HANA-optimized InfoCubes have only one fact table, instead of the two fact tables of traditional InfoCubes (E tables with read-optimized partitioning and an F table with write-/delete-optimized partitioning), the star schema is significantly simpler and also more in line with classical logical data warehouse designs based on Ralph Kimball's dimensional modeling principles. This fact table simplification, combined with the removal of physical dimension tables, also results in two to three times faster data loads.

Some consideration has to be given to noncumulative key figures. Because SAP HANA loads the initial noncumulative, delta, and historical transactions separately, two DTPs are required for InfoCubes with noncumulative key figures (i.e., inventory cubes). In this case, one DTP is required to initialize the noncumulative data, and one is required to load data and historical transactions (for more details, see SAP Notes 1548125 and 1558791). Also, traditional InfoCubes with noncumulative key figures can only be converted to SAP HANA-optimized InfoCubes if they aren't included in a 3.x dataflow.

Because manual intervention and DTP changes are needed, inventory cubes and cubes with noncumulative key figures should always be tested in a sandbox, or development box, before being converted in production systems. Alternatively, these InfoCubes can be left in a nonconverted status.

Converting SAP BW 3.x Dataflows to 7.x DTPs for SAP HANA Migration

To help you convert your dataflows from SAP BW 3.x to the new data transformation process (DTP) of SAP BW 7.x systems, SAP has included a DATAFLOW CONVERSION tool in the SAP BW Migration Cockpit for SAP HANA (Figure 6.34).

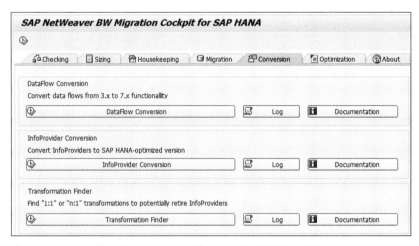

Figure 6.34 DataFlow Conversion Tool for 3.x to SAP BW 7.x DTPs

The DataFlow Conversion tool works by simply copying the 3.x dataflow and converting the copy. As a result, you'll still have the old 3.x version while you test the migration. Once the test is completed, you can delete the older version.

Partitioning of InfoCube Fact Tables and Compression

After optimizing SAP HANA InfoCubes, you can no longer partition the fact tables semantically, and you don't need to. However, four partitions still exist behind the scenes. The first partition is used for noncompressed requests, while the second contains the compressed requests. Another partition contains the reference points of the inventory data, and yet another is used for the historical inventory data movements. The last two partitions are empty if their noncumulative key figures aren't used. However, the first two partitions still require periodic compression to reduce the physical space used and increase the load times during merge processing (much like traditional SAP BW maintenance). This compression has only a minor impact on small InfoCubes (less than 100 million records) and InfoCubes without significant data reloads or many requests. Because the compression is also executed as a stored procedure inside SAP HANA, the compression is quite fast and should take no more than a few minutes even for very large InfoCubes.

> **The Future of InfoCubes**
>
> Currently, whether InfoCubes are needed with an SAP HANA system has been the subject of significant debate on blogs and Internet forums. However, for the interim period, InfoCubes are needed for several reasons.
>
> First, transactional InfoCubes are needed for SAP Integrated Business Planning (SAP IBP) and write-back options. InfoCubes are also needed to store and manage noncumulative key figures, and the direct write interface (SAP ABAP package RSDRI) only works for InfoCubes. In addition, the transition from SAP BW to SAP BW on SAP HANA is simplified by allowing customers move to the new platform without having to rewrite application logic, queries, MultiProviders, and data transformations from DSOs to InfoCubes.
>
> However, the continued use of InfoCubes has to be questioned. The introduction of star schemas, snowflakes, and other dimensional data modeling (DDM) techniques in the 1990s reduced costly table joins in relational databases, while avoiding the data redundancy of data stored in first normal form (1NF) in Operational Data Stores (ODSs).
>
> The removal of the relational database from SAP HANA's in-memory processing makes most of the benefits of DDM moot, and continued use of these structures is questionable. In the future, we may see multilayered DSOs with different data retention and granularity instead, and in fact, SAP BW 7.5 for SAP HANA has fully implemented SAP BW without the structures required for fast reporting in traditional relational databases. However, for now, InfoCubes will continue to serve as a transitional data storage method for many companies, especially those with SAP BW systems originally implemented before SAP HANA.

6.6.5 New Features in SAP BW 7.4

In the earlier releases of SAP BW on SAP HANA, you could not physically query data in native SAP HANA schemas with those in SAP BW. However, SAP BW version 7.4 provided two new functionalities for assisting with model integration, regardless of source:

- Enhanced CompositeProviders (ECPs)
- Open ODS view models

Using the enhanced CompositeProvider you can now consolidate SAP BW Multi-Providers, SAP HANA-based virtual providers and transient providers, and Info-Sets. The benefit is that you can query them from a single interface without having to move data between the various source systems or models (Figure 6.35).

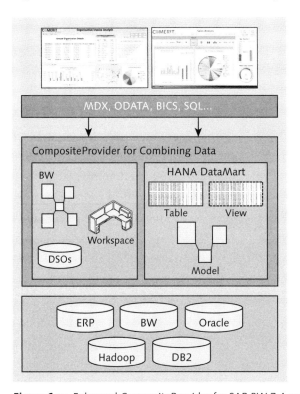

Figure 6.35 Enhanced CompositeProvider for SAP BW 7.4 on SAP HANA

You can also use the CompositeProvider join data from other SAP HANA data marts and applications. New support for noncumulative key figures (i.e., inventory numbers) is available in SAP BW 7.4 on SAP HANA. The modeling screen for creating CompositeProviders, based on the Eclipse platform, is shown in Figure 6.36.

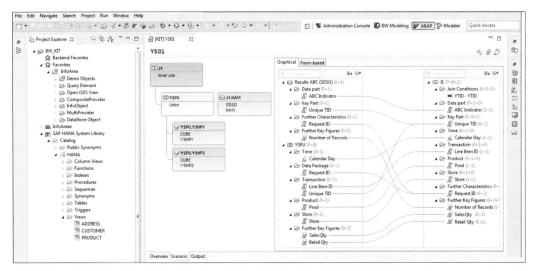

Figure 6.36 Eclipse Modeling for SAP BW 7.5 on SAP HANA

The new Open ODS feature of SAP BW 7.4 allows you to join SAP BW-based DSOs with tables that are created during native SAP HANA development. As a result, you can join SAP BW data with non-SAP BW data in ways not possible in earlier releases of SAP BW. The Open ODS modeling screen is shown in Figure 6.37.

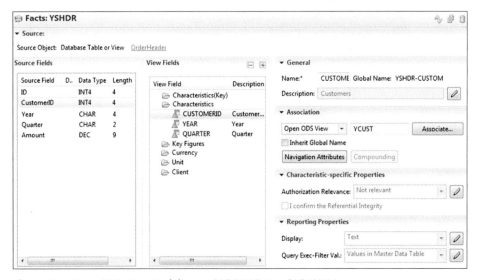

Figure 6.37 Open ODS View Modeling on SAP BW 7.4 on SAP HANA

Since many organizations are struggling with integration on SAP BW-based data warehouses with classical data marts on other platforms, this new tool enables moving non-SAP BW data marts to native SAP HANA while still having the ability to virtually merge the tables and query them both from a simple, unified BI interface. Non-SAP BW developers are now free to work inside SAP HANA without having to physically merge all their data into SAP BW.

6.6.6 New Features in SAP BW 7.5

The new features included in SAP BW 7.5 are quite extensive, so we'll only look at some of the most exciting features, as follows:

- **New modeling features**
  In order to simplify and unify the data modeling landscape in SAP BW, SAP has spent a great deal of time and effort to present a similar look and feel for data modeling. Regardless of whether you choose to create data models inside SAP BW or in SAP HANA Studio, the development environments are all based on the Eclipse platform. In spite of the transition to an Eclipse-based modeling environment, most experienced SAP BW developers should have little trouble navigating and modeling within the new interface. As an added bonus, most of the old transaction codes still work as well.

- **Enhancements to aDSOs and ECPs**
  Thanks to the integration of a new migration tool, older SAP BW InfoObjects can be easily migrated to Advanced DataStore Objects (aDSOs). In addition, aDSOs now support planning and NLS integration through dynamic tiering, which has also been extended with support for change logs and data activation. For those with inventory and headcount calculations, improvements have been made to delta calculations for noncumulative key figures.

  In addition to the improvements to aDSOs, ECPs have been optimized for faster execution thanks to performance improvements in SAP HANA SPS 10. You can also group similar output structures together for easier access, and you can even automatically convert old CompositeProviders and SAP BW Multi-Providers to ECPs.

- **New query designer and wizards**
  The Query Designer has also moved to Eclipse or SAP HANA Studio as part of the SAP BW modeling tools plug-in, and a new SAP BW Workspace Query Designer

is available for experienced business users. If you're already familiar with the BEx Query Designer, you should have little trouble learning the new interface. In our experience, most users have found the new interface easier to use with little need for retraining, thanks to intuitive integration with SAP's online help content. In fact, many of the development options that were obscured behind tabs in the old query designer are now much easier to find and update via the unified Eclipse interface, as shown in Figure 6.38.

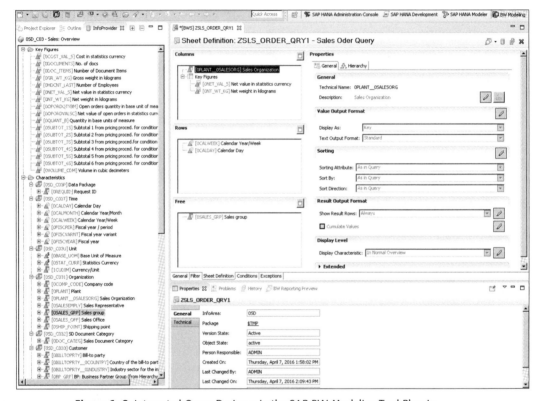

Figure 6.38 Integrated Query Designer in the SAP BW Modeling Tool Plug-In

In addition to all the old familiar query designer functions, the new integrated SAP BW Query Designer has a new editor for global key figures, structures and filters, calculated key figures, and restricted key figures. The formula editor has been enhanced with an if-then-else editor, and you can even easily generate SAP HANA views based on your new queries.

> **Note**
>
> Your older BEx queries will still work with SAP BW 7.5, and you're not required to migrate them to a newer version; however, you may want to consider migrating the older queries in order to simplify your landscape and fully leverage the benefits of the latest SAP HANA data modeling techniques.

SAP BW 7.5 even has several wizards to make your job easier. A simple right-click in the BWMT will allow you to SELECT A WIZARD that will walk you through the process of creating a new project, query, ECP, aDSO, or Open ODS view.

▶ **Enhanced planning integration**
For SAP BusinessObjects Planning and Consolidation (SAP BPC), a new SAP BW 7.5 add-on with embedded modeling for financial consolidation has been added. aDSOs can now be used with Integrated Planning (IP) for local planning scenarios and local hierarchies, and the SAP BW Workspace Query Designer for business users makes measures available to business users.

6.7   Summary

Planning an SAP HANA implementation is an effort that requires strong technical skills and also a solid understanding of the long-term architecture and system-deployment strategy of an organization. Implementing SAP HANA is not like upgrading servers, databases, and operating systems. Instead, organizations get an appliance that enables brand new functionality that fundamentally changes the way servers and databases work in the organization.

Companies should not underestimate the effort involved. The long-term benefits of simplifying application servers and database servers, while removing the performance limitations of relational databases, are so numerous that companies cannot ignore them. However, it's also important to involve skilled partners during the transition phase while committing serious resources for the training of existing support staff. Picking the right platform vendor and experienced partner is therefore crucial.

Numerous tools enable you to leverage SAP HANA's full power, especially in the area of business intelligence (BI). In this chapter, we'll take a look at each tool and how you can connect them to SAP HANA.

7   Reporting with SAP HANA

Companies that implement SAP HANA will also want to connect their data to a business intelligence solution. In this chapter, we'll offer a brief introduction to some of the SAP business intelligence tools that work with SAP HANA, including their connectivity options. We'll begin with an examination of the entire suite of SAP BusinessObjects reporting tools.

We'll cover well-established tools like SAP BusinessObjects Web Intelligence, SAP BusinessObjects Analysis for Microsoft Office, and SAP BusinessObjects Analysis for online analytical processing (OLAP), as well as the newest additions to the SAP BusinessObjects toolset: the SAP BusinessObjects Design Studio and SAP BusinessObjects Lumira. We'll finish up the chapter with an in-depth examination of SAP HANA Live, a powerful suite of well-defined views that are perfect for accelerating your business analysis efforts.

7.1   Overview of Tools

All of the tools in the SAP BusinessObjects Business Intelligence (SAP BusinessObjects BI) suite work with SAP HANA. In addition, SAP recently added SAP BusinessObjects Lumira to its business intelligence offerings, which can also run on SAP HANA. Let's introduce all of these tools next.

7.1.1   SAP BusinessObjects Dashboards

SAP BusinessObjects Dashboards (originally known as Xcelsius) is a visualization tool that allows interactive analysis with graphs, charts, maps, and other custom objects. Due to SAP's strategic direction and its new capabilities with dashboards,

SAP BusinessObjects Dashboards and SAP BusinessObjects Design Studio are the preferred alternatives to other legacy tools such as SAP Visual Composer and BEx Web Application Designer. Figure 7.1 shows an example of a report from SAP BusinessObjects Dashboards.

Upgrade to SAP BusinessObjects Design Studio

As SAP BusinessObjects Dashboards is still in wide use in the SAP community, we chose to include it in this section of the book; however, no further development or enhancement for SAP BusinessObjects Dashboards is planned. SAP BusinessObjects Design Studio is now the preferred tool for dashboard development, and new enhancements are being introduced for the SAP BusinessObjects Design Studio at a rapid pace. The latest version of SAP BusinessObjects Design Studio is version 1.6. Go to *http://scn.sap.com/docs/DOC-69824* for more information about SAP BusinessObjects Design Studio 1.6 and the software development kit (SDK).

For non-SAP HANA systems, SAP BusinessObjects Dashboards allow traditional data connectivity to the SAP Business Warehouse (BW) through Business Intelligence Consumer Services (BICS), to relational database connections through universes, and to other external data sources such as web services. In general, a universe is a semantic layer to access SAP HANA data; we'll discuss universes in much more detail in Section 7.2.

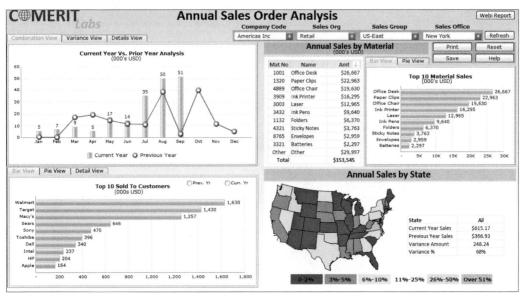

Figure 7.1 SAP BusinessObjects Dashboards

SAP BusinessObjects Dashboards allow developers to work in a rapid application design mode to quickly deliver stunning visualizations with minimal coding on standard objects. SAP BusinessObjects Dashboards also allows the developer to preview the final result before publishing to the working environment so that edits can be applied.

You can enhance the SAP BusinessObjects Dashboards experience using SAP HANA, which enables SAP BusinessObjects Dashboards to display more data faster than ever before. By running an SAP BW system on top of SAP HANA, SAP BusinessObjects Dashboards become more dynamic and interactive, providing more useful information to the end users without long wait times.

SAP BusinessObjects Dashboards is generally intended to be used by decision makers who need a quick view of their current business or area of responsibility. Decision makers can also perform "what-if" analyses to manage the next line of decisions. Prior to SAP HANA, SAP BusinessObjects Dashboards were built on top of summarized data to optimize performance. As performance becomes less of a concern, SAP HANA may change this design view and allow for more operational dashboards. In general, acceptable performance in the past was less than 20 seconds to launch any dashboard. However, SAP HANA is likely to change these expectation levels significantly to less than 5–8 seconds. (Some time is still required for security checks, networking, and image loading.)

7.1.2 SAP BusinessObjects Web Intelligence

SAP BusinessObjects Web Intelligence is a query tool that allows a deeper analysis to uncover hidden meaning in data. SAP BusinessObjects Web Intelligence allows users to easily add tables, charts, filters, and calculations to support a BI self-service model where users develop their own reports in an ad-hoc manner. Figure 7.2 shows an example of a report from SAP BusinessObjects Web Intelligence.

You can access SAP BusinessObjects Web Intelligence in three different interfaces: a rich client, which is installed onto a PC; a Java-based client, which is launched from the SAP BusinessObjects BI Launchpad; or the HTML web client, which can be executed by launching a report on the BI Launchpad.

SAP BusinessObjects Web Intelligence reports are intended to be used by business analysts or users who want to explore business questions. SAP BusinessObjects Web Intelligence can also deliver static reports that can't be edited by applying the "view only" security role to a user so that the queries can't be edited. Other business users may, however, easily modify existing reports or add new components with minimal IT development. These reports can also be shared on the BI Launchpad or exported into various static formats and sent by email to a wider audience.

Figure 7.2 SAP BusinessObjects Web Intelligence

Using SAP HANA with SAP BusinessObjects Web Intelligence allows for much faster query performance, decreasing the time required for data to be returned to the SAP BusinessObjects Web Intelligence report. As a result, the amount of interactivity and the drilldown capabilities in SAP BusinessObjects Web Intelligence increase, and the need to prerun the slow reports that users need periodically is removed.

7.1.3   SAP BusinessObjects Explorer

SAP BusinessObjects Explorer is intended for users who conduct unstructured analysis of data (Figure 7.3). The tool relies on *information spaces* that are exposed through a standard interface. Queries do not need to be defined, and graphics are built by the system intuitively without initial user input. The tool also allows you to navigate inside each information space, to create your own personalized views, and to download data into Microsoft Excel and CSV files, or as images. In addition, you can also create your own calculated key figures and use these in your on-screen analysis.

Although the tool doesn't provide as much flexibility as SAP BusinessObjects Web Intelligence or the stunning graphics of SAP BusinessObjects Dashboards, SAP BusinessObjects Explorer simplifies development and implementation and gives users significant control over data exploration. The tool has some basic capabilities to allow end users to modify their interface using personalized exploration views and facets. The ideal users of this tool are power users and, if the information space is simplified, sometimes even end users.

SAP BusinessObjects Explorer comes in two flavors. You can add it to any SAP BW system, SAP Business Suite, or legacy system and use it as a standalone platform with standard access, or you can use the accelerated version that relies on SAP HANA. You can even use the older SAP Business Warehouse Accelerator (SAP BW Accelerator) as a partial in-memory option.

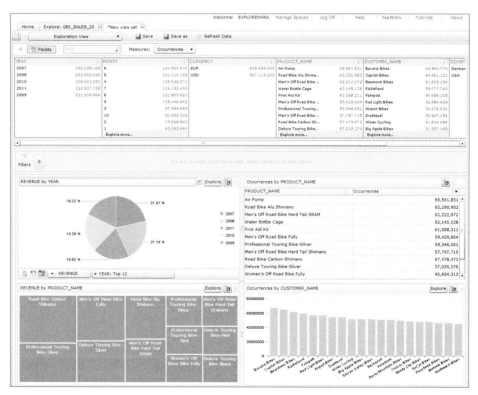

Figure 7.3 SAP BusinessObjects Explorer with a Customized Exploration View

For the SAP HANA-accelerated version, SAP BusinessObjects Explorer relies on the database structured query language (DBSQL) for direct access. Because the value proposition of this tool is that functionality is traded to gain speed, using SAP BusinessObjects Explorer in a nonaccelerated manner doesn't usually make sense. However, with SAP HANA, SAP BusinessObjects Explorer can become a key tool for analysis.

SAP BusinessObjects Explorer can access SAP HANA views through information spaces, which are quite easy to build. Simply log on to SAP BusinessObjects Explorer and click on MANAGE SPACES on the top-right side of the screen to list all views you have access to in SAP HANA. Click on the NEW button to create a new information space for users (Figure 7.4).

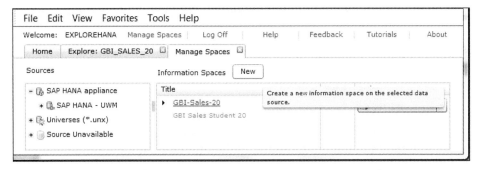

Figure 7.4 Creating New Information Spaces in SAP BusinessObjects Explorer for SAP HANA

All information spaces must have a name. This name should not be too technical because business users will see this as well as the description, so try to be as complete as possible. The description is also used for search within SAP BusinessObjects, so it should contain keywords to search on as well. While the term "Info-Cube" in the INFOCUBE NAME text field refers to SAP BW, if you're using SAP HANA, this field actually contains the name of the SAP HANA view which is the source for your InfoSpace. This field has nothing to do with SAP BW, since the view can be based on any data in SAP HANA (Figure 7.5).

In the OBJECTS tab, you can see all the fields available from the analytic view in SAP HANA (Figure 7.6). From these fields, you can select those you want to include in SAP BusinessObjects Explorer. You can also change the labels of the fields into something more meaningful and define measures as good when increasing (e.g., revenue) or decreasing (e.g., budget variance). These steps are helpful for navigation and if color codes are applied later. You can also exclude data that you don't want to be made public through filters.

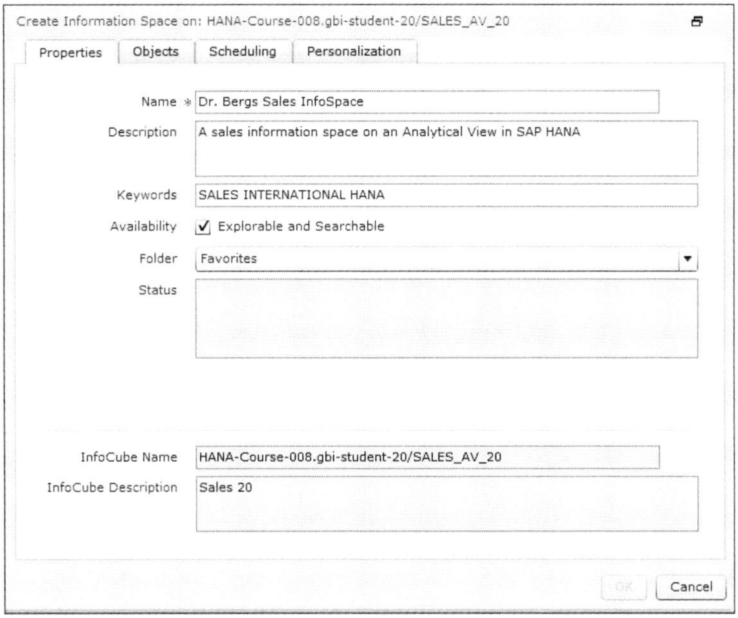

Figure 7.5 Defining an Information Space Based on an SAP HANA Analytic View

Figure 7.6 Selecting Fields from the SAP HANA Analytic View to Expose in SAP BusinessObjects Explorer

After you click SAVE, you'll see the information space on the front page in the SAP BusinessObjects BI platform and in the folder where you saved it. If you saved the information space to a public folder, everyone with access to this folder will instantly be able to use SAP BusinessObjects Explorer to analyze data in SAP HANA.

In Figure 7.7, we see that a result set of over 144 million rows was extracted from 1.2 billion rows and summarized by customer name, product name, year, month, and country—and graphed in less than 1.6 seconds. This speed is what makes SAP BusinessObjects Explorer really useful. Since SAP BusinessObjects Explorer also does not rely on flash objects, you can deploy it immediately to a mobile device of any kind.

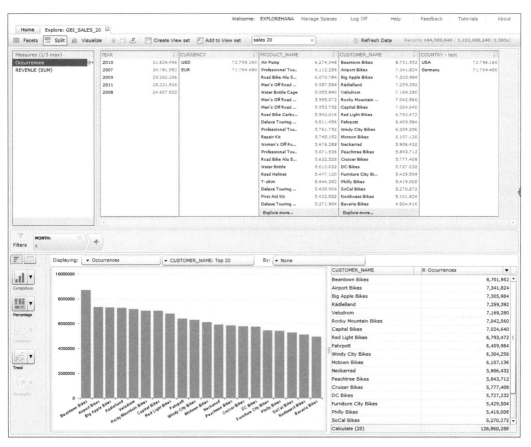

Figure 7.7 SAP BusinessObjects Explorer Accessing Data in SAP HANA

This speed, combined with extreme simplicity for end users, makes using SAP BusinessObjects Explorer and SAP HANA together a valuable combination. In addition, maintaining information spaces takes just a few minutes, and new, complex information spaces based on views in SAP HANA can be deployed to thousands of users in less than a day.

7.1.4   SAP BusinessObjects Analysis

SAP BusinessObjects Analysis is an online analytical processing (OLAP) tool that allows users to conduct in-depth interactive analysis. SAP BusinessObjects Analysis is available in two interfaces: the Microsoft edition (Figure 7.8), which is based on Excel and PowerPoint, and a web interface in the BI Launchpad (Figure 7.9). While the web-based interface has no prerequisite installs on a standard client PC, the Microsoft edition requires some prerequisites along with initial installations on each user's computer.

Both editions of SAP BusinessObjects Analysis are intended for use by power users who need to perform analysis on data. The tool also allows each user to have a saved view that can be refreshed with periodically updated data.

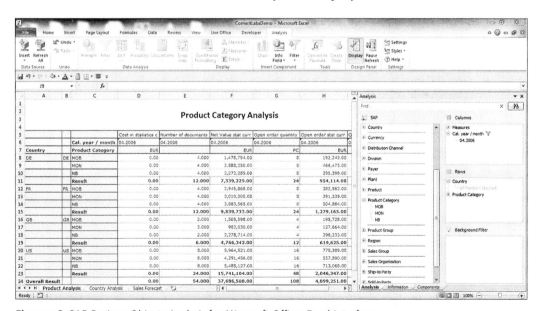

Figure 7.8 SAP BusinessObjects Analysis for Microsoft Office: Excel Interface

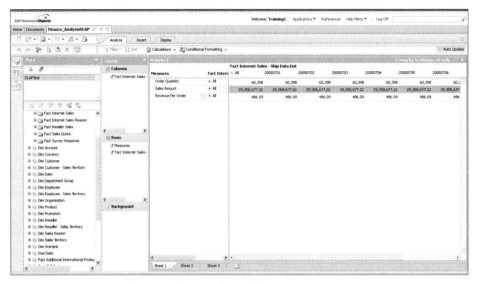

Figure 7.9 SAP BusinessObjects Analysis: Web Interface

To leverage the OLAP interfaces, the power user must have a good understanding of the available data, navigation, and filtering options. SAP BusinessObjects Analysis allows power users to share the work that they have created via the BI Launchpad or by exporting a static view of the report. You can also use SAP BusinessObjects Analysis as a data source, including for SAP BusinessObjects Web Intelligence, SAP BusinessObjects Explorer, or via SAP BusinessObjects Live Office as a sharing tool. SAP BusinessObjects Web Intelligence reports can be built on top of SAP BusinessObjects Analysis views that are saved after navigational steps have been performed. SAP BusinessObjects Analysis provides one of the most flexible forms of analysis and is frequently used by business and financial analysts.

With the combination of SAP BusinessObjects Analysis and SAP HANA, you get subsecond in-memory data retrieval as well as in-memory OLAP functions and calculations. This powerful combination of in-memory processing provides users with the ability to slice and dice data, drilldown to details, add new calculations, and interact with the data much faster than ever before.

7.1.5   SAP BusinessObjects Design Studio

SAP BusinessObjects Design Studio is a tool that gives application developers the ability to create mobile (iPad, Android, and Microsoft) and web-based dashboards and applications based on data in SAP BW, SAP Business Suite, third-party sources, and SAP HANA (Figure 7.10).

Figure 7.10 SAP BusinessObjects Design Studio

For SAP BW users, SAP BusinessObjects Design Studio replaces the older BEx Web Application Designer that has been available for more than twelve years. In addition, SAP BusinessObjects Design Studio is the go-forward solution for dashboard development, according to SAP's official statement available here: *http://cdn.blog-sap.com/analytics/files/2012/04/External-SAP-SOD-Dashboarding-2012.pdf*.

Right now, SAP BusinessObjects Design Studio is positioned as a tool for IT and developers with the technical capabilities necessary for building web applications. SAP BusinessObjects Dashboards is positioned as a pure dashboard development tool that requires fewer technical skills but does not have all of the functionalities and capabilities of SAP BusinessObjects Design Studio.

With the latest release, the SAP BusinessObjects Design Studio can use direct connectivity to SAP BW data sources, such as analysis views and query views, as well as to SAP HANA calculation and analytic views. To get access to SAP HANA data, simply click SELECT DATA SOURCE in the DATA CONNECTION panel of SAP Business-Objects Design Studio, and all the available SAP HANA data sources will be shown in a hierarchy node.

You can also search for any SAP HANA views (there could be thousands) by clicking DATA SOURCE VIEW in the DATA CONNECTION panel of the tool. It's important to emphasize that SAP BusinessObjects Design Studio is not an end-user or power-user tool; some IT experience is required to make industrial-strength applications and dashboards that can be consumed by thousands of users.

7.1.6 SAP Crystal Reports

SAP Crystal Reports is a tool with pixel-formatted reporting capabilities that allows developers full control to format reports. Two versions of SAP Crystal Reports come with the SAP BusinessObjects BI suite: SAP Crystal Reports 2013 and SAP Crystal Reports Enterprise. SAP Crystal Reports Enterprise allows connections with SAP HANA. Figure 7.11 shows an example of a report from SAP Crystal Reports Enterprise.

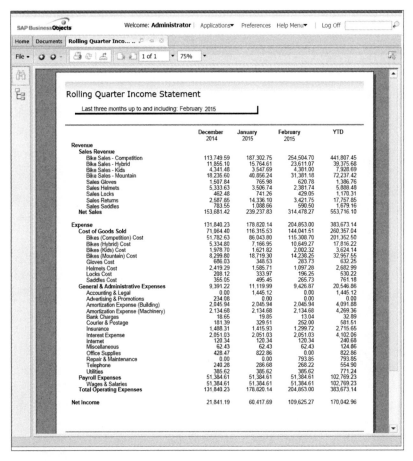

Figure 7.11 SAP Crystal Reports

SAP Crystal Reports Enterprise also allows users to choose from more than forty available charts as well as to add filters, cross-tabs, flash objects, and images to the reporting canvas. The BI Launchpad also allows users to enable email alerts from SAP Crystal Reports so that, if a condition is triggered, the user is quickly notified.

SAP Crystal Reports can have a large audience; for instance, a manager might need a summarized total for the end of a detailed report, employees on the shop floor may need a more detailed report to cross-check their production runs for the day, or a customer may need a printout of a utility bill. In general, SAP Crystal Reports can have many uses, especially for fixed-format reports or high-frequency batch reports. One benefit of SAP Crystal Reports is that a developer can create virtually any kind of fixed-format report easily because the tool allows developers to control each object at the pixel level.

SAP HANA supports SAP Crystal Reports with direct SQL connections through Java Database Connectivity (JDBC) and Open Database Connectivity (ODBC), as well as through universes built on top of SAP HANA data. As a result, you can generate high-volume batch reports in a shorter time frame, and your users can leverage SAP Crystal Reports in a more ad-hoc fashion than previously possible.

7.1.7 SAP BusinessObjects Lumira

SAP BusinessObjects Lumira is a tool to display and manipulate data to make it easier to understand in a graphical format (Figure 7.12). The tool is ideal for users who are exploring large data sets; looking for complex patterns; and seeking information on trends, concentrations, or abnormalities.

Because SAP BusinessObjects Lumira typically works with high-level, detailed data that is constantly changing to address "what-if" scenarios and changing displays, the tool greatly benefits from the inherent speed of SAP HANA. You no longer have to wait minutes to change graphs and displays or to drilldown to the data you want. Instead, seconds is the norm, even for hundreds of millions of rows.

With SAP BusinessObjects Lumira, you can build your own visualizations and then compose graphs into mini-dashboards with visualization and navigational controls while taking full advantage of SAP HANA's speed (Figure 7.13). You do not need any IT skills to accomplish this; the tool can be used by any business user with minimal technical experience. The final work product can be shared on any mobile, web page, or portal.

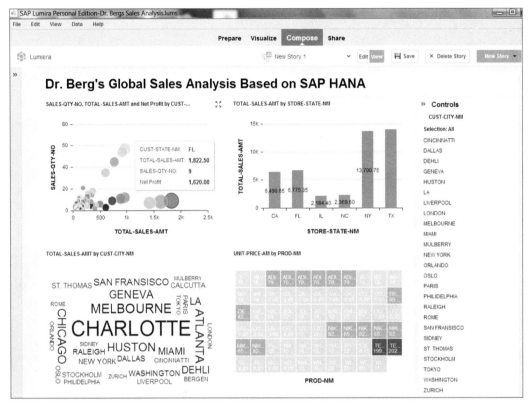

Figure 7.12 SAP BusinessObjects Lumira on SAP HANA Sales Analytic View

SAP BusinessObjects Lumira can be connected to SAP HANA using queries directly on standard universes in SAP BusinessObjects BI, as well as with views in SAP HANA (Figure 7.14). In addition to connecting to comma-delimited (CSV) files, SQL, universes, and Excel, you can create documents in SAP BusinessObjects Lumira based on SAP HANA views in offline or online mode. The offline mode allows you to keep your original data, while the online mode refreshes the information as new data is loaded to SAP HANA. For more information about connecting SAP BusinessObjects Lumira directly to SAP HANA views, see Section 7.2.1.

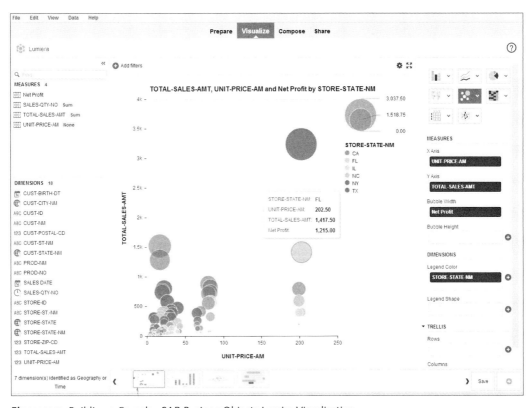

Figure 7.13 Building a Complex SAP BusinessObjects Lumira Visualization

Figure 7.14 Connecting to SAP HANA from SAP BusinessObjects Lumira

After the source is assigned, you can connect to the SAP HANA server using your logon credentials (Figure 7.15).

Figure 7.15 Entering Logon Credentials

You can now browse the available SAP HANA views (Figure 7.16).

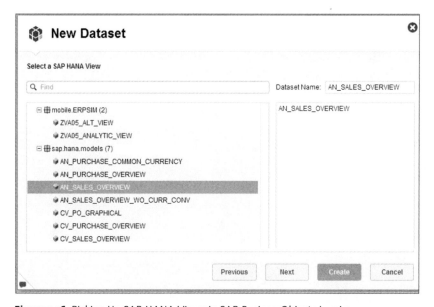

Figure 7.16 Picking Up SAP HANA Views in SAP BusinessObjects Lumira

In this case, the SALES OVERVIEW view is created in SAP HANA Studio (covered in more detail in Chapter 8). The view simply allows users to access data for visualization and graphing without further technical knowledge. The complexity is all nicely hidden from the user through the use of SAP HANA views that can contain cleaned, merged, and integrated data in a simple interface for SAP BusinessObjects Lumira to consume.

7.2 Connecting SAP BusinessObjects BI Tools to SAP HANA

In this section, we explore how the different SAP BusinessObjects BI tools connect to SAP HANA. We cover direct connections to SAP HANA views through the SAP BusinessObjects 4.2 platform and through ODBC and JDBC connections using the Information Design Tool (IDT) in SAP BusinessObjects BI as well as direct Excel access through multidimensional expressions (MDX) and open database objects (ODOs), Microsoft queries, and Business Intelligence Consumer Services (BICS) connections.

7.2.1 Direct Connection through the SAP BusinessObjects 4.2 Platform

When SAP released SAP BusinessObjects 4.2 in December 2015, they streamlined the entire process for connecting to SAP HANA views. In prior versions of the platform (SAP BusinessObjects 4.1 and XI 3.1), you had to connect to SAP HANA views through some rather complicated digital gymnastics, usually via ODBC or JDBC connections and universes built in the Information Design Tool (IDT) or Universe Design Tool. Since many of you may still be using those platforms, the steps for connecting through the legacy SAP BI platforms are covered in Section 7.2.2 and Section 7.2.3, but if you haven't already upgraded your platform, you should seriously consider upgrading to SAP BusinessObjects 4.2. To help you make the business case for upgrading, let's take a look at how simple it is to connect to SAP HANA views through SAP BusinessObjects 4.2.

First, go to the Central Management Console (CMC) for your SAP BusinessObjects platform. The console can be reached at *http://<server address>:<port>/BOE/CMC/*. Login to the console with your administrative user account and navigate to the OLAP CONNECTIONS screen from the dropdown menu or the list of configuration pages on the left of the console. Then, click the NEW CONNECTION icon.

We recommend creating an SAP HANA HTTP connection, although an SAP HANA connection will work in most cases. We recommend the HTTP connection because SAP BusinessObjects Analysis for Microsoft Office will currently not recognize the standard SAP HANA connection (although this may be fixed in future releases). Since Microsoft Excel is still one of the world's most preferred reporting tools, it's quite likely that your users will be most comfortable working with SAP BusinessObjects Analysis for Microsoft Office.

To create the connection, enter a NAME for the connection and select SAP HANA HTTP as the PROVIDER. Next to SERVER INFORMATION, enter the IP address and port for your SAP HANA server, usually *http://<HANA_server>:80<instance>*. Select your AUTHENTICATION type. We recommend PROMPT, which will require your user to authenticate to the server with their SAP HANA login, thus applying the appropriate analytic privileges to the connection. See Figure 7.17 for an example of how to create the OLAP connection to your SAP HANA server. When you're satisfied with the connection properties, just click SAVE to make the connection available from your SAP BusinessObjects 4.2 reporting tools.

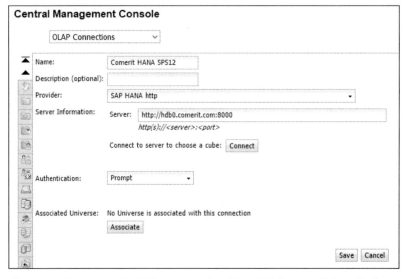

Figure 7.17 Creating an OLAP Connection from Your SAP BusinessObjects Platform to SAP HANA

Now that the OLAP connection has been created, connecting to SAP HANA views is simple. Launch SAP BusinessObjects Analysis for Microsoft Office from your START menu (on a Windows PC). When the application is open, go to the ANALYSIS tab and select Insert Data Source • Select Data Source from the ribbon. You'll be prompted to login to the SAP BusinessObjects platform. Enter your User and Password for your SAP BusinessObjects platform and the Web Service URL for the platform, usually *http://<BusinessObjects_server>:<port>/dswsbobje/services/Session*. Click OK to log on.

If you've followed the steps to this point, you should be prompted with the Select Data Source window. Choose the connection you created earlier and navigate to the content package where your views are activated (Figure 7.18).

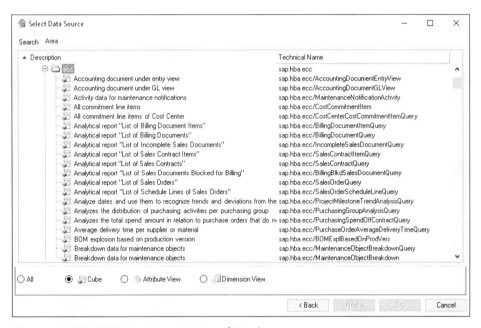

Figure 7.18 SAP HANA Live Views in Microsoft Excel

The process of connecting to your SAP HANA views is nearly identical for SAP BusinessObjects Web Intelligence and SAP BusinessObjects Analysis for OLAP. You'll be prompted to choose your SAP HANA connection and navigate to the desired view. However, please be aware that SAP does not plan to integrate SAP HANA native view connections for SAP BusinessObjects Dashboards, as further development for this tool is not expected. SAP BusinessObjects Dashboards has been replaced by the SAP BusinessObjects Design Studio, which uses a simple system DSN connection through ODBC or JDBC. The process for creating a system DSN on ODBC or JDBC is thoroughly explained in Section 7.2.2.

7.2.2 Universes with Open Database Connections and Java Database Connections

If you're on SAP BusinessObjects 4.2 or higher, you can connect directly to SAP HANA views, as we demonstrated in the previous section. However, if you're on an older version of the SAP BusinessObjects platform, you can still connect to data from SAP HANA. JDBC and ODBC connections are two possible methods to access SAP HANA data. Standard JDBC and ODBC connections can be used by third-party tools, by SAP Crystal Reports without a universe, by custom development tools, by SAP BusinessObjects Lumira, and by both the Universe Design Tool and the Information Design Tool (IDT).

A common way for legacy SAP BusinessObjects BI platforms to use ODBC and JDBC is as a connection method for universes. In general, a *universe* functions as a semantic layer to access SAP HANA data from tools such as SAP BusinessObjects Web Intelligence, SAP BusinessObjects Dashboards, SAP BusinessObjects Explorer, and even SAP Crystal Reports for Enterprise. (SAP Crystal Reports Enterprise can access SAP HANA via both universes and a direct ODBC or JDBC connection.)

In addition to accessing columnar tables in SAP HANA, you can use universes to access SAP HANA information models. These models are basically views on one or more tables. The models can filter data and exclude or provide added business logic in a virtual layer. SAP HANA supports three information model types: attribute views, analytic views, and calculation views. However, the latest guidance from SAP has shifted development away from attribute and analytical views (more on this in Chapter 8).

When choosing whether to access an information model using something other than a columnar table, remember that information models leverage the OLAP engine and also have aggregate awareness. Information models also support more complex calculations, so this access method is preferred in most cases instead of accessing the columnar tables in SAP HANA directly. You should also try to avoid reading row stores because column-based tables are much faster when filtering, aggregating, and reading.

When creating a connection, we recommend connecting the SAP BusinessObjects BI tools to SAP HANA using information models (views) or BEx queries, instead of adding the logic to the universe or the SAP BusinessObjects BI application. Because information models are executed on the database in memory instead of on the application server, using views or BEx queries is much faster.

The first step in making JDBC and ODBC connections is to install the SAP HANA middleware from SAP Marketplace using the wizard. After this middleware is installed, you can then go to your Control Panel and access data sources (Figure 7.19 and Figure 7.20).

Figure 7.19 Accessing the Control Panel

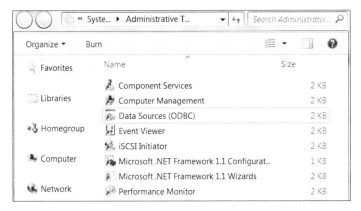

Figure 7.20 Accessing the ODBC Data Sources in the Administration Tools

Follow these steps:

1. Select ADMINISTRATIVE TOOLS.

2. Under the SYSTEM DSN (domain name server) tab, click ADD (Figure 7.21).

3. Select the SAP HANA driver from the middleware you installed and click FINISH (Figure 7.22).

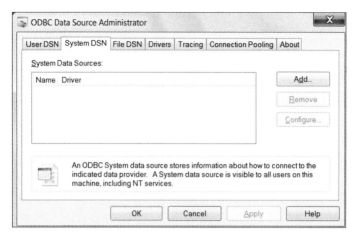

Figure 7.21 Adding a System Domain Name Server

Figure 7.22 Selecting the SAP HANA Database Driver for ODBC

4. Give the source a name, for example, "HANA," and a description. Enter the service port, which includes the server name and port. You'll also need a user name and password from your SAP HANA administrator to complete this task (Figure 7.23).

5. Enter your user name and password for access and authentication (Figure 7.24). After you've connected, you'll get a message stating whether the connection was successful.

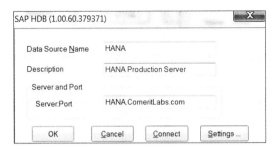

Figure 7.23 The Data Source and Server Port

Figure 7.24 Logging On with the New Connection

You can now go to the IDT and start creating the universe semantic layer for tool access. To do so, follow these steps:

1. Open the IDT.

2. Right-click on a resource in the REPOSITORY RESOURCE section of your SAP BusinessObjects BI environment.

3. Select OPEN SESSION.

4. Log on to the session with your user name and password (Figure 7.25).

5. From the FILE menu, create a new project by choosing NEW • PROJECT (Figure 7.26).

6. Give the project a name, and save it (for this example project, we used "HANA").

7. Now add a new relational connection to the project by going to the REPOSITORY RESOURCES in IDT and clicking INSERT RELATIONAL CONNECTION.

8. Give the resource a name (in our case, "HANA") and click NEXT (Figure 7.27).

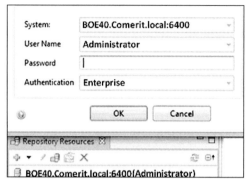

Figure 7.25 Open a Repository Resource Session in IDT

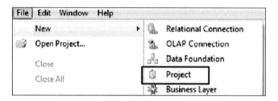

Figure 7.26 Create a New Project in IDT

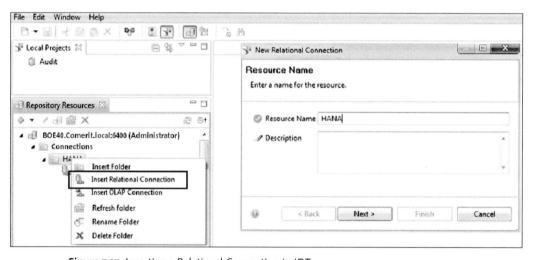

Figure 7.27 Inserting a Relational Connection in IDT

9. Navigate to the SAP drivers that are installed where you should find the SAP middleware. If you can't see the middleware in this list, you'll have to install it from

the SAP Marketplace. Select the middleware ODBC DRIVERS option (Figure 7.28). (You can also choose the JDBC DRIVERS option if you want a Java-based connection, but we'll focus on creating an ODBC connection in this example.)

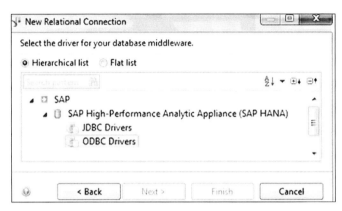

Figure 7.28 Selecting the ODBC Driver for SAP HANA in IDT

10. Select the connection (called "HANA" from earlier steps), enter your user name and password, and click NEXT (Figure 7.29).

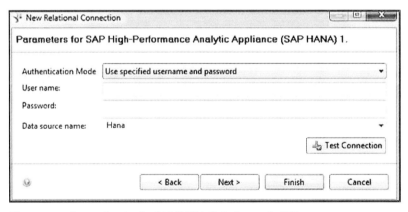

Figure 7.29 Connecting to the SAP HANA Data Source in IDT

11. You can now set timeout parameters for logons, pool parameters, and array parameters. Some companies will have login timeout rules, which you can implement here.

12. You'll have options to change custom parameters on the next screen, or you can simply accept the standard CONNECTINIT and click FINISH.

13. The new connection will now be displayed under the REPOSITORY RESOURCES, and you can create the required shortcut for your universe. Click on the connection and select CREATE RELATIONAL CONNECTION SHORTCUT (Figure 7.30).

Figure 7.30 Creating a Relational Shortcut in IDT

14. Select the HANA project and click OK. A message appears stating that the connection shortcut was created successfully.

15. Now the shortcut should appear under the project. From here, you can create a standard data foundation layer in IDT and use the standard universe functions that are leveraged by the SAP BusinessObjects BI tools (Figure 7.31).

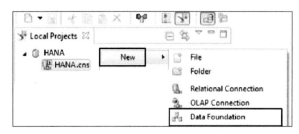

Figure 7.31 Using the Shortcut to Create the Universe Data Foundation

After these tasks are completed, standard functionality is leveraged, and you can attach tools such as SAP BusinessObjects Web Intelligence, SAP BusinessObjects Dashboards, SAP BusinessObjects Analysis, SAP Crystal Reports, SAP BusinessObjects Design Studio, SAP BusinessObjects Explorer, and SAP BusinessObjects Lumira to the universe.

16. Give the resource a name and click NEXT.

17. Select SINGLE SOURCE and click NEXT.

18. Select the HANA.CNS connection you created earlier and click FINISH.

19. The DFX file now shows up under the project, and you can start creating the business layer of the universe on all the tables and views to which the user has access.

These steps complete how to make connections to SAP HANA using ODBC. From this point, you can design the universe, add tables, add your own SQL logic, and make the universe available to the frontend tools like you normally would.

After the connections are completed, you can use the INFORMATION VIEWS option in SAP HANA to combine objects inside SAP HANA, create your own calculations, and access your results in SAP BusinessObjects BI tools. There are three types of information views:

▸ **Attribute view**
This view provides attribute-level details.

▸ **Analytic view**
This view forms the basis of an analysis (similar to an InfoCube in SAP BW).

▸ **Calculation view**
This view is basically a query that can be built on attribute views, database tables, and/or analytic views.

We'll cover each of these views in Chapter 8 and show you how to build calculation views. To access the views in IDT, you can connect to SAP HANA using an ODBC driver, and you'll see the views under the user called _SYS_BIC (Figure 7.32).

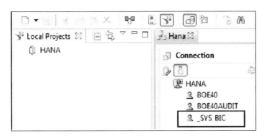

Figure 7.32 Accessing the SAP HANA Views in IDT

7.2.3 Connecting to Excel with Open Database Objects and MDX

An open database object (ODO) connection is a quick way to access data objects using a platform that supports this interface. In the implementation of SAP HANA as a data warehouse, SAP supports the Excel 2010 standard MDX. SAP does not support a complete set of MDXs; but does support a Microsoft version that allows for connections to Excel specifically.

To get started with the connections, you first need to go to the SAP Marketplace and download the client software for SAP In-Memory Database 1.0. Installation instructions are available in the *SAP HANA Master Guide* by SAP, which you can find on the SAP Marketplace. After SAP In-Memory Database 1.0 is installed, you need to create a connection to Excel by following these steps:

1. Go to the DATA tab in Excel.

2. Click FROM OTHER SOURCES • FROM DATA CONNECTION WIZARD, which will bring you to the screen shown in Figure 7.33.

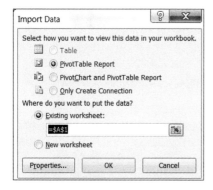

Figure 7.33 The Data Connection Wizard in Excel (Part 1)

3. Select the OTHER/ADVANCED option (Figure 7.34).

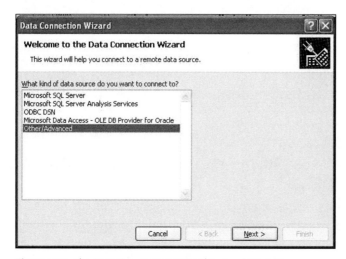

Figure 7.34 The Data Connection Wizard in Excel (Part 2)

4. In the screen shown in Figure 7.35, select SAP NEWDB MDX PROVIDER, which is the MDX-based Object Linking and Embedding Database (OLE DB) for SAP HANA, and click NEXT.

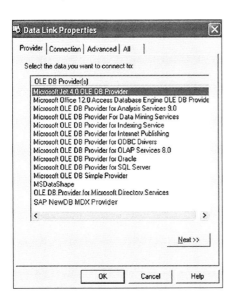

Figure 7.35 The OLE DB MDX Provider for SAP HANA

5. In the DATA LINK PROPERTIES, go to the CONNECTION tab.

6. Enter information for the DATA SOURCE, INSTANCE NUMBER, USER, and PASSWORD fields for your account on SAP HANA (Figure 7.36).

Figure 7.36 The Data Link Connection in Excel

7. Click the CONNECT TO A SPECIFIC CUBE checkbox.

8. Select from the list of cubes you have access to (Figure 7.37).

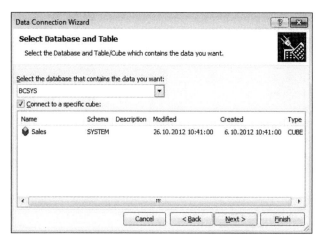

Figure 7.37 Selecting a Specific Cube in Excel

9. You can also save your password so that you don't have to enter it each time you use this connection (Figure 7.38).

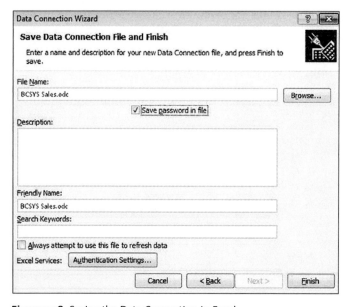

Figure 7.38 Saving the Data Connection in Excel

10. You can now import the data into your workbook as a pivot table report, a pivot chart and table, or only create the connection for future use. You can also assign the data to a new or existing worksheet (Figure 7.39).

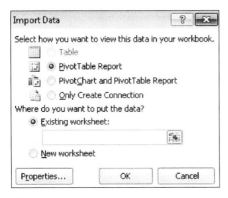

Figure 7.39 Importing Data into Excel

7.2.4 Building a Microsoft Query on SAP HANA

You can also consume raw data tables instead of cubes in Excel. To do so, your administrator will need to install an OBDC driver on SAP HANA and create a connection that you can consume (see the *SAP HANA Master Guide* for details). After this is completed, you can access the data from Excel (Figure 7.40).

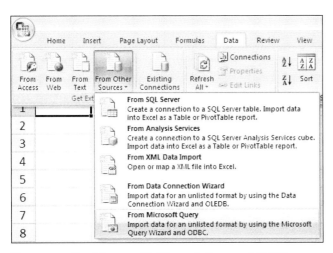

Figure 7.40 Excel Access with Microsoft Query and ODBC

The wizard now allows you to select the database and database connection, as well as see the tables you have access to. The Excel interface will also take you step by step through the process of building a Microsoft query through the query wizard.

After selecting the data and filters, you'll be prompted to select where you want to insert the Microsoft query data in the Excel spreadsheet (Figure 7.41).

Figure 7.41 Importing Data into Excel from Microsoft Query and ODBC

Make sure you select the MACHINE DATA SOURCE in the prompt. You'll also be asked to log on to the system to validate your security credentials before the data you requested is inserted into your spreadsheet.

7.2.5   BICS Connections

BICS connections are supported for SAP BusinessObjects Analysis for Microsoft Office and SAP BusinessObjects Design Studio. As a result, the tool can access SAP Business Explorer (BEx) queries and consume them directly. This interface is typically faster because it doesn't rely on the MDX interface. This connection type also allows you to use all of the features of the BEx Query Designer and take full advantage of the BI analytical engine in SAP BW.

7.3   SAP HANA Live

Any discussion of reporting with SAP HANA would be incomplete without a discussion of the excellent reporting content available in one of the many SAP

HANA Live content packages. SAP HANA Live content packages consist of private views, reuse views, and query views that have been developed to meet the needs of SAP ERP and SAP Business Suite clients. More information about SAP HANA Live can be found at *http://help.sap.com/hba*. The following SAP HANA Live content packages are available as of August of 2016:

- SAP HANA Live for EHP 4 for SAP ERP
- SAP HANA Live for EHP 7 for SAP ERP
- SAP HANA Live for Policy Management
- SAP HANA Live for Reinsurance Management
- SAP HANA Live for Commodity Management
- SAP HANA Live for Commercial Project Management
- SAP HANA Live for SAP CRM
- SAP HANA Live for Utilities, edition for SAP CRM
- SAP HANA Live for SAP CRM and SAP ERP cross-analytics
- SAP HANA Live for Event Management
- SAP HANA Live for Event Management and SAP Transportation Management 9.3 cross-analytics
- SAP HANA Live for SAP ERP
- SAP HANA Live for Extended Warehouse management
- SAP HANA Live for Financial Close
- SAP HANA Live for SAP Business Suite foundation component
- SAP HANA Live for SAP Global Batch Traceability
- SAP HANA Live for SAP solutions for GRC
- SAP HANA Live for SAP solutions for GRC 10.1
- SAP HANA Live for SAP GTS
- SAP HANA Live for Insurance
- SAP HANA Live for Utilities, edition for SAP ERP
- SAP HANA Live for SAP PLM
- SAP HANA Live for Production Revenue Accounting

- SAP HANA Live for Flexible Real Estate Management
- SAP HANA Live for Retail
- SAP HANA Live for Manufacturing
- SAP HANA Live for SAP SCM
- SAP HANA Live for SAP S/4HANA Finance
- SAP HANA Live for Transportation Management

As you can see, numerous prepackaged solutions are available through SAP HANA Live. For example, the base content package for SAP ERP currently includes more than a thousand views to meet many of your reporting needs. The views available just for SAP ERP Sales and Distribution (SD) are shown in Figure 7.42.

Favor...	View Name	View Description
☆	BillingBlkdSalesDocumentQuery	Analytical report "List of Sales Documents Blocked for Bil...
☆	CustomerSalesDocumentQuery	Query view for customer sales documents
☆	CustomerVolumeQuery	Query view for customer volume
☆	DeliveryBlkdSalesDocumentQuery	Query view for delivery blocked sales documents
☆	IncompleteSalesDocumentQuery	Analytical report "List of Incomplete Sales Documents"
☆	OpenSalesOrderQuery	Query view for open sales orders
☆	OpenSalesOrderSchedLineQuery	Query view for schedule lines of open sales orders
☆	RejectedSalesOrderQuery	Query view for rejected sales order items
☆	SalesContractItemQuery	Analytical report "List of Sales Contract Items"
☆	SalesContractQuery	Analytical report "List of Sales Contracts"
☆	SalesOfficeQuery	Query view for sales office
☆	SalesOrderItemNetAmountQuery	Query view for net amount of sales order items
☆	SalesOrderQuery	Analytical report "List of Sales Orders"
☆	SalesOrderScheduleLineQuery	Analytical report "List of Schedule Lines of Sales Orders"
☆	SalesOrderValueTrackingQuery	Query view for sales order value tracking per customer
☆	SlsOrdItmWithCustBscDataQuery	Query view for sales order items with customer basic data
☆	SlsQuotationValueTrackingQuery	Query view for quotation value tracking per customer

Figure 7.42 SAP HANA Live Views in SD

With so many reporting solutions already available, you should strongly consider locating a package that could meet many of your immediate business needs, especially since many of the prepackaged views can be extended and customized to meet your reporting needs.

In the following sections, we'll discuss how to install the SAP HANA Content Tools, how to install SAP HANA Live content delivery units, and the different types of views that are available in SAP HANA Live. Then, we'll take a look at extending and customizing SAP HANA Live views, and we'll examine some of the features of the SAP HANA Live browser.

7.3.1 Installing SAP HANA Live Content Tools and Content Delivery Units

To get started with SAP HANA Live, the first thing you should do is to download and install the SAP HANA Content Tools. You can find the SAP HANA Content Tools on the SAP Marketplace at *http://launchpad.support.sap.com*. Login to the marketplace with your ID and navigate to SOFTWARE DOWNLOADS • BY ALPHABET-ICAL INDEX (A-Z) • H • SAP HANA CONTENT TOOLS • SAP HANA CONTENT TOOLS 1.0 • INSTALLATION. Download the latest delivery unit and extract the files to your client PC.

Three components of the SAP HANA Content Tools need to be installed on your SAP HANA server. To install these components, just extract the ZIP files in the DATA_UNITS • SAP_HANA_CONTENT_TOOLS_1.0 directory. (See Figure 7.43 for an example of the required ZIP files.)

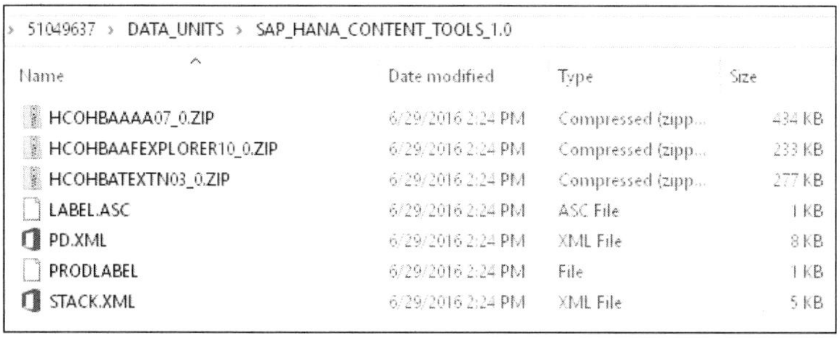

Name	Date modified	Type	Size
HCOHBAAAA07_0.ZIP	6/29/2016 2:24 PM	Compressed (zipp...	434 KB
HCOHBAAFEXPLORER10_0.ZIP	6/29/2016 2:24 PM	Compressed (zipp...	233 KB
HCOHBATEXTN03_0.ZIP	6/29/2016 2:24 PM	Compressed (zipp...	277 KB
LABEL.ASC	6/29/2016 2:24 PM	ASC File	1 KB
PD.XML	6/29/2016 2:24 PM	XML File	8 KB
PRODLABEL	6/29/2016 2:24 PM	File	1 KB
STACK.XML	6/29/2016 2:24 PM	XML File	5 KB

Figure 7.43 Compressed ZIP Files Needed for the SAP HANA Live Content Tools

Once these files have been extracted, the extracted TGZ files can be used to import the SAP HANA Live Content Tools into your SAP HANA installation through SAP HANA Studio. Go to the FILE menu, choose IMPORT • SAP HANA CONTENT • DELIVERY UNIT, and click NEXT. Select your target SAP HANA system and choose NEXT once more. Finally, you'll need to navigate to the directory where you extracted each TGZ file and select the file. If you've done things correctly up to this point, you should see a list of views to import in the OBJECT IMPORT SIMULATION panel at the bottom of the screen (see Figure 7.44). Just click FINISH to begin importing the SAP HANA Live Content Tools delivery unit.

> **Note**
>
> This process can be used for importing any delivery unit into SAP HANA, but you can also use Software Update Manager (SUM) to install new content. See Chapter 10, Section 10.4 for more information about updating with SUM.

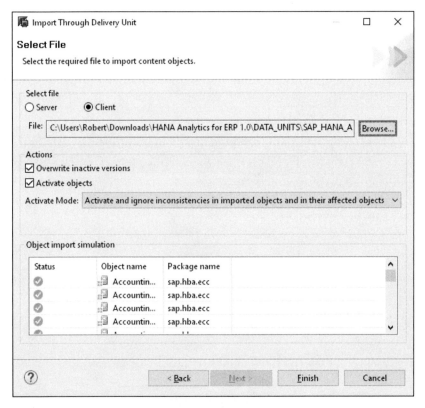

Figure 7.44 Importing an SAP HANA Live Delivery Unit

7.3.2 SAP HANA Live Browser

Once you have the SAP HANA Live Content Tools installed, you should be able to access the SAP HANA Live browser by navigating to *http://<your.HANA.in-stance.IP>:80<HANA Inst Number>/sap/hba/explorer/* in your web browser. Please be aware that your user will need to have the `sap.hba.explorer.roles::Business` or `sap.hba.explorer.roles::Developer` roles added to their GRANTED ROLES in order to access the SAP HANA Live browser, so make sure you have your system administrator provide those roles if you need access to the browser.

The business role is for users who want to view the available SAP HANA Live views and check the metadata for the views. The user with this role will only have access to the views that are permitted through his SAP HANA authorizations. The business user can also consume SAP HANA Live views in any SAP BusinessObjects tools that are capable of directly consuming SAP HANA views.

The developer role grants users the ability to examine all the views that are available in the SAP HANA system. You can personalize views by adding tags, generate SAP Landscape Transformation (SLT) file replication lists (for SAP HANA sidecar implementations), and examine the cross-references between views. As with the business role, the developer role will also allow you to consume SAP HANA Live views directly in SAP BusinessObjects, as long as your chosen tool supports a direct connection to SAP HANA views.

The SAP HANA Live browser is a powerful tool for helping your business users and developers understand the content that is available as well as understand how to leverage that content in your business landscape. When you navigate to the URL for the SAP HANA Live browser, you'll be prompted to login with your SAP HANA system credentials. After logging in, you'll be presented with an overview of the SAP HANA Live content that you've imported and activated within your landscape (Figure 7.45). The left side of the browser presents a hierarchical tree of your active content, broken down by SAP ERP functional modules.

The right side of browser window initially presents an overview of the VIEWS IN HANA. Each view has a VIEW DESCRIPTION, which will provide important information about the views that are available in your landscape. From the list of views, you can select a view and gather a lot of useful information about the view using the icons at the top of the screen. Let's take a closer look at each of those options.

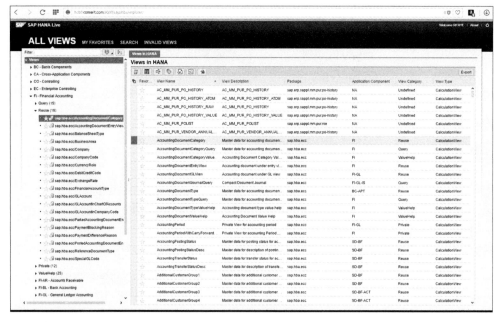

Figure 7.45 SAP HANA Live Browser

Open Definition

The OPEN DEFINITION button (top left) provides a detailed overview of the semantic layer in the selected view. The COLUMN NAME, POSITION, SQL DATA TYPE, DATA LENGTH, COLUMN STORE DATA TYPE, NULL VALUE STATUS, DEFAULT VALUE, COMPRESSION TYPE, INDEX TYPE, and COMMENTS are provided for each exposed field at the highest level of the view. The details for the selected view appear in a new tab in the right side of the browser window. You can close this internal tab when you're finished examining the details about the selected view.

Open Content

The OPEN CONTENT button (second from the left) provides a data preview for the selected view.

Open Cross Reference

The OPEN CROSS REFERENCE button (third from the left) provides an overview of the source tables that are used in the selected view. This cross-reference is initially visualized as a tree, but a graph view (Figure 7.46) is available to provide a useful visualization of the components of the view.

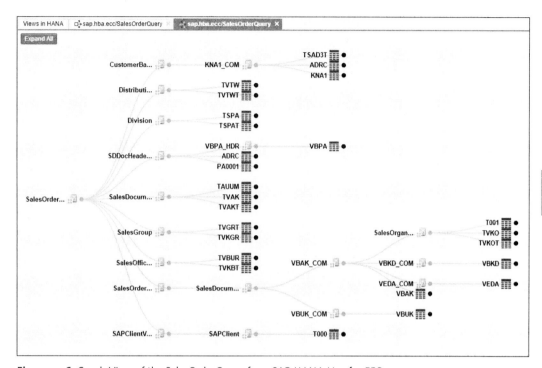

Figure 7.46 Graph View of the SalesOrderQuery from SAP HANA Live for ERP

Add

The ADD button (fourth button) allows you to create and save tags for specific views, which can make searching for relevant views much easier in the SAP HANA Live browser.

Generate SLT File

The GENERATE SLT FILE button (third from the right) is one of the most useful buttons in the SAP HANA Live browser, especially if you're implementing SAP HANA Live in a sidecar environment. In order to understand why this is useful, you must first understand what's needed to implement SAP HANA Live as a sidecar.

In a sidecar implementation, you will generally only replicate the tables to your sidecar system (using SAP Landscape Transformation) that are needed for the views you intend to use in reporting. As a result, you can limit the size of the SAP HANA sidecar to include only the tables that are necessary for reporting, instead of the entirety of your SAP ERP system. In order to identify those tables for SLT replication, you can spend a lot of valuable time searching the documentation for the content package that you intend to deploy, or you can use the GENERATE SLT FILE button to generate a CSV file with a complete list of the files and target schemas where the tables generally reside.

The target schema is important because you'll need to create a schema mapping in your sidecar environment to map the original schema to the actual schema where your tables have been replicated. The table names are also important, and this list can be copied to your buffer on your computer—for example, by pressing `Ctrl`+`C` in Windows—and inserted into the SLT replication table list on your SLT server.

Open View in SAP BusinessObjects Lumira

The OPEN VIEW IN SAP LUMIRA button (second from the right) will open SAP BusinessObjects Lumira and connect to the view you have selected to accelerate your reporting efforts.

Open View in Analysis Office

The OPEN VIEW IN ANALYSIS OFFICE button (upper right) will open SAP BusinessObjects Analysis for Microsoft Office and connect the view you have selected as the data source within Microsoft Excel.

7.3.3   SAP HANA Live VDMs

SAP HANA Live content packages include a wide selection of prepackaged virtual data models (VDMs), commonly referred to as SAP HANA views, designed to accelerate your reporting efforts on your SAP HANA system. For example, the SAP HANA Live for SAP ERP content package includes more than a thousand views, covering a broad range of SAP ERP modules, including the following functionalities:

- SAP Basis components
- Controlling
- Financial accounting
- Financial services
- Logistics
- Logistics execution
- Materials management
- Personnel management
- Plant maintenance
- Production planning
- Project systems
- Sales and distribution

Although more than a thousand views are available, all the views are not meant for consumption in your reporting tools. The prepackaged views fall into three general categories, namely, private views, reuse views, and query views, as follows:

- **Private views**

  Private views are generally views that have been created on top of raw tables from SAP ERP. These views are intended for internal use in other SAP HANA Live views and should not be modified in any way. Modifying the private views could cause any reuse or query views that depend on the private views to stop working properly, so you should never modify the private views. If for some reason you have a business case for modifying these views, use the right-click context menu for the view in question to make a copy of the private view and modify the copy only.

  In many cases, the apparent purpose of the private views is to simply apply a more user-friendly name to columns to make it easier for users and developers to work with the data. For example, the MANDT column is generally given a semantic mask of SAP CLIENT in the private, reuse, and query views. In other cases, the private views may filter the results from the tables to only the subset relevant for a particular reporting purpose.

▶ **Reuse views**

Reuse views are appropriately named. These views are designed to be reused within your own customized query views. For example, if you want to look at the total delivery status for your sales orders, the TotalDeliveryStatus reuse view will provide the overall status, and the TotalDeliveryStatusDesc reuse view will provide the text description for the master data status. These two views can easily be combined in a query view to provide a quick lookup of the sales order delivery status.

▶ **Query views**

Query views are the views that are designed for consumption in your developer and end-user reporting tools. These views are often highly specialized and may include prompts for currency selections, date ranges, order numbers, reporting periods, etc. Because these views often contain prompts for user filters, they are not appropriate to reuse as the source of other views; however, you may extend these views manually or by using the SAP HANA Live Extension Assistant.

7.3.4 SAP HANA Live Extension Assistant

If you followed the directions to install the SAP HANA Live Content Tools, you can add the SAP HANA Live Extension Assistant plug-in to your SAP HANA Studio or Eclipse IDE through the Help • Install New Software menu in the IDE. When the Install window opens, click the Add button and enter *http:// <your.HANA.instance.IP>:80<HANA Inst Number>/sap/hba/extn.* as the Location. Give the connection a user-friendly name and click OK. If you installed the SAP HANA Live Content Tools properly, you should have the option to install the SAP HANA Live Extension Assistant, as shown in Figure 7.47.

Once you've finished installing the extension assistant, you can use it to enhance the reuse or query views already provided. To do so, you'll need the `sap.hba.tools.extn.roles::ExtensibilityDeveloper` role to be added to your user in SAP HANA.

With the correct role for your user account, extending the reuse or query views with the SAP HANA Live Extension Assistant is a relatively simple task. Select Extend View from the right-click context menu of the view that you want to extend. The plug-in will open and guide you through the steps of extending the view.

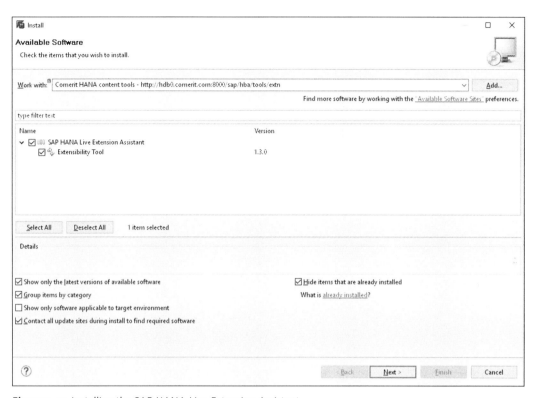

Figure 7.47 Installing the SAP HANA Live Extension Assistant

First, you will want to name the extended view and choose the package where it will be activated. Then, select the field that you want to add to the view from the list of source tables on the left and click the ADD button. You can either keep the original column name or change the semantic layer to something easier to identify. You can use the up and down arrows in the upper right to change the order of the columns. In our example (Figure 7.48), we're adding the BUTXT – COMPANY NAME field to our view, editing the semantic layer to COMPANYNAME, and changing the order to move the COMPANYNAME under the COMPANYCODE field.

On the next screen, you'll need to identify the join conditions for the new field. In our example (Figure 7.49), we'll join SAP CLIENT to MANDT and COMPANY CODE to BUKRS. To test whether the extended view is valid, you can click VALIDATE. When you're satisfied with the changes you've made to the view, just click ACTIVATE. The view will be activated and available for use in reporting from the package you specified.

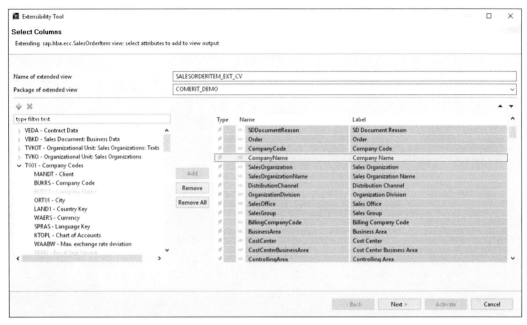

Figure 7.48 Adding CompanyName to the SalesOrderItem Reuse View

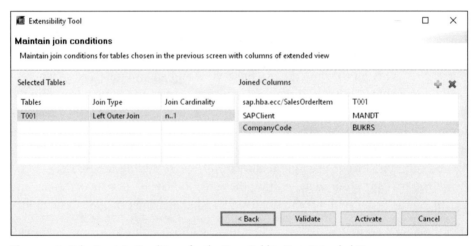

Figure 7.49 Selecting Join Conditions for the New Field in Your Extended View

7.4 Summary

In this chapter, we offered a high-level summary of some of the SAP tools that work with SAP HANA, with special focus on the SAP BusinessObjects BI platform as well as a detailed look at getting started with SAP HANA Live. Although not an exhaustive treatment of these topics, the information in this chapter should give you enough background information to understand your options and make choices about how to move forward.

The data modeling landscape has changed considerably with the latest support package stacks (SPSs) for SAP HANA, so in this chapter, we'll take a look at the newest guidance for creating views in both SAP HANA Studio and the SAP HANA Web-Based Development Workbench.

8   Data Modeling with SAP HANA

SAP HANA Studio and the SAP HANA Web-Based Development Workbench are the primary SAP HANA developer tools for defining the tables that will hold your data, for setting up data provisioning on SAP HANA, for importing and exporting data, for creating virtual data models (views), and much more. In this chapter, we'll focus on the modeling capabilities of SAP HANA Studio, the SAP Business Warehouse (SAP BW) modeling tools plug-in, and the SAP HANA Web-Based Development Workbench.

We'll take a practical, hands-on approach to modeling using real-life examples, and we'll follow a logical progression through the various data modeling tasks. We'll take a deep dive into both introductory and advanced modeling scenarios, starting with a detailed look at native SAP HANA development using SAP HANA Studio. You will learn how to create dimensional, cube, and star-join calculation views and how to migrate your older, deprecated attribute and analytical views to calculation views using the SAP HANA development perspective. You will also understand how to create joins, unions, and rank nodes as well as how to apply filters, perform currency conversions with user prompts for currency selections, and create calculated key figures.

When we've finished our discussion of traditional modeling through SAP HANA Studio, we'll then turn our attention to an overview of the SAP BW modeling tools plug-in for SAP HANA Studio. Next, we'll finish our discussion of data modeling in SAP HANA by learning about the SAP HANA Web-Based Development Workbench. We'll examine many of the same tasks that we covered in SAP HANA Studio, while also looking at some of the important differences between the development environments.

SAP HANA Studio and the SAP HANA Web-Based Development Workbench can both be used for native SAP HANA development. Some of the blogs and discussions you'll find online will refer to the SAP HANA Web-Based Development Workbench as the SAP Web IDE. This shorthand is confusing and inaccurate because the SAP Web IDE, formerly known as SAP River, is SAP's web-based application development experience based on SAPUI5 and does not allow for the creation of graphical data objects, like those available in SAP HANA Studio and the SAP HANA Web-Based Development Workbench.

SAP Web IDE for SAP HANA is the premier tool for creating SAP extended application services, advanced model (SAP XSA) applications, which we covered in Chapter 3.

8.1   Data Modeling with SAP HANA Studio

SAP HANA Studio is an integrated development environment (IDE) that is based on the Eclipse IDE. From SAP HANA Studio, you can create views; import and export data and table definitions; add, edit, and delete users; monitor the performance of your SAP HANA landscape; and much more. In this chapter, we'll focus on teaching you many of the native SAP HANA modeling tasks. We cover the administration and monitoring functions in SAP HANA Studio in detail in Chapter 10.

Note

Because SAP HANA Studio is based on Eclipse, you can install numerous development plug-ins, based on your company's specific development needs. Plug-ins are available for download from several locations, so check the installation guide for your specific modeling area for information on where to download your plug-in. See Section 8.4 for an example of installing the SAP BW Modeling Tool plug-in.

We begin this section with a review of the SAP HANA development perspective, and we'll also learn how to create tables, import data, and generate time data for use in our models. In addition, since SAP's current guidance and changes to the optimization engine favor calculation views, before we learn how to create calculation views, we'll learn how to migrate older views and objects to calculation views. Finally, we'll end this section with an examination of how to create packages and delivery units to better organize your development projects as well as to transport objects between systems.

8.1.1 SAP HANA Development Perspective

The preferred perspective for data modeling in SAP HANA Studio is the SAP HANA development perspective (Figure 8.1). This perspective in SAP HANA Studio allows you to create projects and share them with other users, create and modify data models and other objects, maintain version control for your objects, activate objects for consumption by your users, and many other tasks.

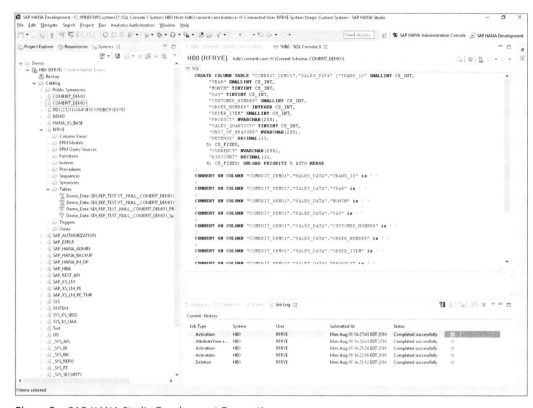

Figure 8.1 SAP HANA Studio Development Perspective

The development perspective is composed of two primary work areas. The browser pane on the left side allows you to navigate to tables, views, and other data modeling objects. The editing pane on the right is where most of your work will be completed. In the editor, you can run SAP HANA SQLScript in the SQL Console. You can also create calculation views, tables, analytic privileges, and many other objects, all of which comprise the comprehensive in-memory data appliance that is SAP HANA.

The browser pane is divided into three sections: the SYSTEMS, the REPOSITORIES, and the PROJECT EXPLORER views.

Systems View

The SYSTEMS view (Figure 8.2) presents an overview of your entire SAP HANA appliance. From the SYSTEMS view, you can perform administration and monitoring tasks (see Chapter 10) and explore and manage schemas, database tables, and other objects in the CATALOG section. You can manage both active and inactive database objects, views, procedures, and decision tables in the CONTENT section. The PROVISIONING section allows you to configure connections for SAP HANA smart data access (SDA) and SAP HANA smart data integration (SDI), provision your data, and to connect to other remote data sources. The SECURITY section allows you to manage the users and roles within your system landscape.

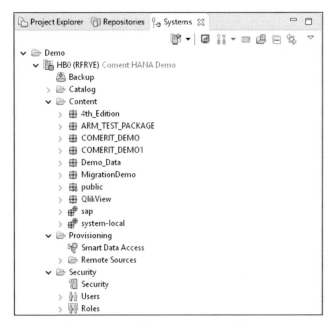

Figure 8.2 Systems View of the SAP HANA Development Perspective

Repositories View

To access the REPOSITORIES view, just click the tab at the top of the browser pane from the SAP HANA development perspective. From this view, you can browse the package hierarchies of the different SAP HANA systems to which you are connected. You can check out project files from a selected repository, which will download the files for the package to your local client, where you can edit the objects as required.

To begin our exploration of data modeling with SAP HANA, we'll create a repository workspace. Members of our team will use the workspace as a shared resource. To create the repository workspace, right-click in the REPOSITORIES view and click CREATE REPOSITORY WORKSPACE. A workspace creation wizard will open (Figure 8.3), and you'll need to select an SAP HANA system for the workspace. You can select the option USE DEFAULT WORKSPACE to use the default name, or you can uncheck the box and enter your own WORKSPACE NAME. You can also navigate to the WORKSPACE ROOT location on your local client where you'd like to save the local files when they're checked out of the repository. When you're satisfied with your selections, click FINISH to create the workspace.

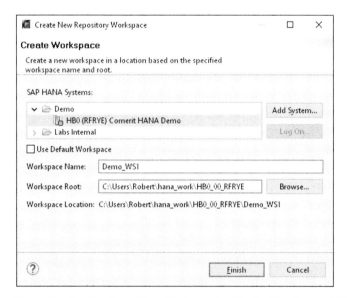

Figure 8.3 Creating Repository Workspace for Sharing Development Objects

Project Explorer View

The PROJECT EXPLORER view is accessed by clicking the tab at the top of the browser pane. Combined with the REPOSITORIES view, the PROJECT EXPLORER enables much of the same functionality as GitHub. By working primarily within the PROJECT EXPLORER, you can use the context menus for the objects in the explorer to save and activate objects directly to the repository. In fact, saving a file from the PROJECT EXPLORER automatically pushes the saved version to the repository, thus facilitating team project work and speeding up the overall development process.

In this chapter, we'll focus on database development objects, but you can see some examples of application development objects in Chapter 3. To create a new package for development in the project explorer, right-click in the explorer view and select NEW • PROJECT from the context menu (Figure 8.4).

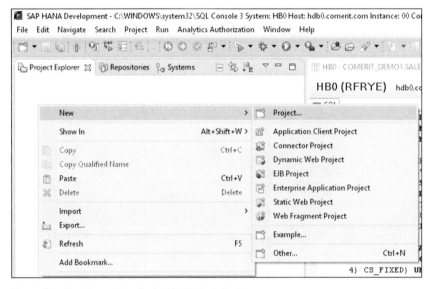

Figure 8.4 Creating a New Project in Project Explorer

A NEW window will open, and you'll be prompted to SELECT A WIZARD (Figure 8.5). You can either search for the wizard using the TYPE FILTER TEXT field to filter your options, or you can navigate to the wizard by opening the GENERAL folder, selecting PROJECT, and clicking NEXT.

Now, you'll need to fill out the PROJECT NAME and select a location to save the project files. Select USE DEFAULT LOCATION if you want to save the files to the working directory for SAP HANA Studio. You can also select ADD PROJECT TO WORKING SETS to add the project to work that's already in progress. For our first project, we'll just click NEXT.

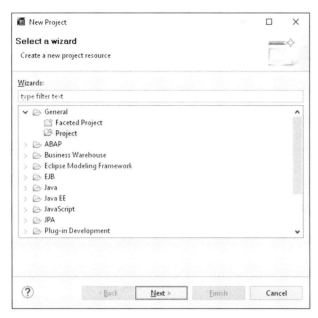

Figure 8.5 Using the Project Wizard to Create a New Project

On the PROJECT REFERENCES screen, select the repository workspace that we created earlier, and then click FINISH to create the project using that repository workspace (Figure 8.6). Your new project will appear in the PROJECT EXPLORER view and be available for saving development objects.

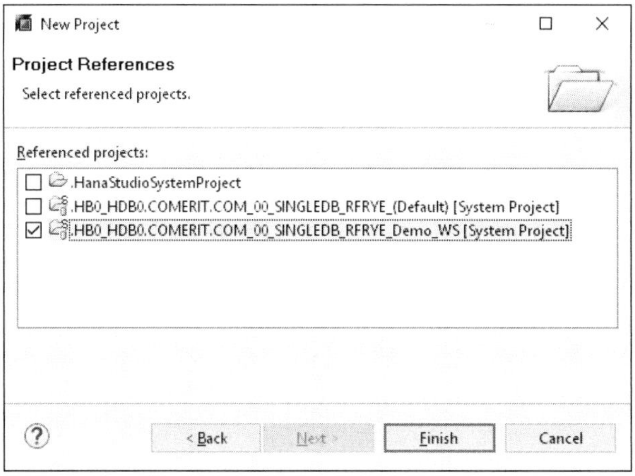

Figure 8.6 Referencing a Repository Workspace with a New Project

8.1.2 Creating and Importing Tables and Data

You can create tables in SAP HANA Studio in several ways. First, you can create a new table definition through the development perspective. To do so, simply select the SYSTEMS tab in the browser pane, expand the schema where you'd like to create a new table, and right-click the schema. From the context menu, select NEW TABLE, and the table definition screen will open in the editor (Figure 8.7). You can enter a NAME, SQL DATA TYPE, DIMENSION, COLUMN STORE DATA TYPE, and KEY for each column in your new table. You can also check the NOT NULL box to indicate whether null values are accepted in each column, set a DEFAULT value for the column, and even provide a COMMENT, which serves as a semantically friendly name for the column. To add another column to the table definition, just click the green + button.

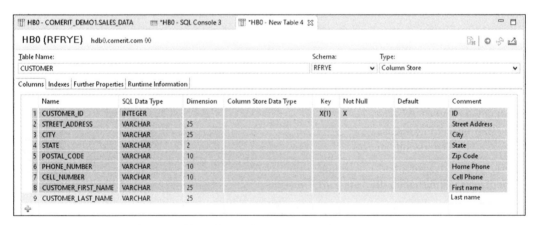

Figure 8.7 Defining a Table with the Editor in the Development Perspective

Before you attempt to save the table, make sure you enter a TABLE NAME and select the SCHEMA (which defaults to the one you right-clicked) and table TYPE.

The TYPE of table you choose will depend on how you intend to use it. Column store tables are optimized for reading, while row store tables are optimized for writing. Column store tables allow for much higher compression and allow for easy indexing and reading. Row store tables allow for faster insertion of new rows, but the access times are slower because they must be read as an entire line. When you're satisfied with your table definition, just click the green EXECUTE arrow in the upper right to create the table.

You can also create a table using SQL script in the SQL Console (Figure 8.8). Right-click the target schema and select OPEN SQL CONSOLE from the context menu to open the SQL Console. In the console, you can enter SQL script to define your table. Notice that you specify the table type just after the definition, and you can also add the semantically friendly comment for each column after the table has been defined. When you're satisfied with the SQL script for your table definition, click the green EXECUTE arrow in the upper right to run the script. The script will execute, and the results for your script will be shown in the execution window below the editor (Figure 8.9).

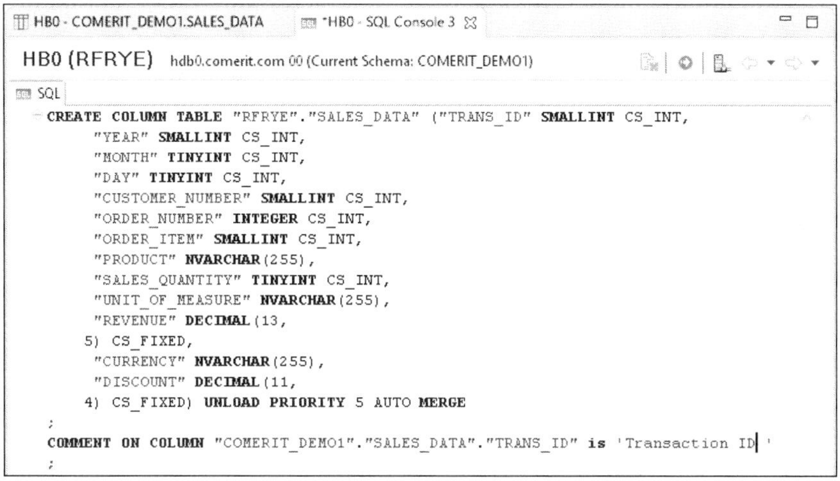

```
HB0 - COMERIT_DEMO1.SALES_DATA      *HB0 - SQL Console 3

HB0 (RFRYE)  hdb0.comerit.com 00 (Current Schema: COMERIT_DEMO1)

SQL
    CREATE COLUMN TABLE "RFRYE"."SALES_DATA" ("TRANS_ID" SMALLINT CS_INT,
        "YEAR" SMALLINT CS_INT,
        "MONTH" TINYINT CS_INT,
        "DAY" TINYINT CS_INT,
        "CUSTOMER_NUMBER" SMALLINT CS_INT,
        "ORDER_NUMBER" INTEGER CS_INT,
        "ORDER_ITEM" SMALLINT CS_INT,
        "PRODUCT" NVARCHAR(255),
        "SALES_QUANTITY" TINYINT CS_INT,
        "UNIT_OF_MEASURE" NVARCHAR(255),
        "REVENUE" DECIMAL(13,
        5) CS_FIXED,
        "CURRENCY" NVARCHAR(255),
        "DISCOUNT" DECIMAL(11,
        4) CS_FIXED) UNLOAD PRIORITY 5 AUTO MERGE
    ;
    COMMENT ON COLUMN "COMERIT_DEMO1"."SALES_DATA"."TRANS_ID" is 'Transaction ID'
    ;
```

Figure 8.8 Creating a Table with SQL Script from the SQL Console

> **Note**
>
> You can download the *SAP HANA SQLScript Reference Guide* for a complete description of the SQL scripts that may be used in SAP HANA.

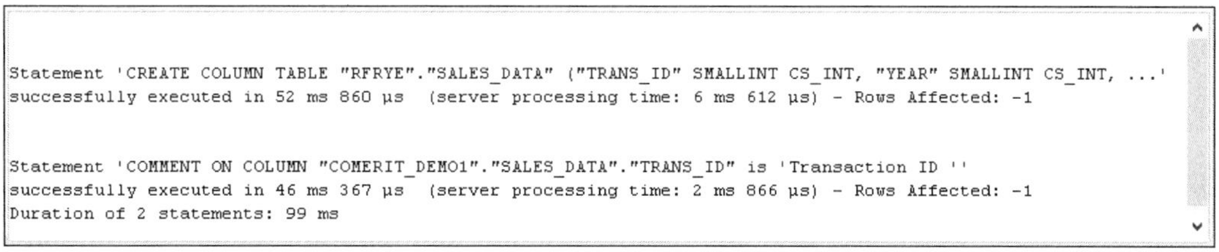

```
Statement 'CREATE COLUMN TABLE "RFRYE"."SALES_DATA" ("TRANS_ID" SMALLINT CS_INT, "YEAR" SMALLINT CS_INT, ...'
successfully executed in 52 ms 860 µs  (server processing time: 6 ms 612 µs) - Rows Affected: -1


Statement 'COMMENT ON COLUMN "COMERIT_DEMO1"."SALES_DATA"."TRANS_ID" is 'Transaction ID ''
successfully executed in 46 ms 367 µs  (server processing time: 2 ms 866 µs) - Rows Affected: -1
Duration of 2 statements: 99 ms
```

Figure 8.9 SQL Script Execution Log

You can also create tables by importing the table metadata or by importing both the table metadata and the data at once. To import the table metadata and data together, go to FILE • IMPORT. Then, expand the SAP HANA folder, select CATALOG OBJECTS, and click NEXT (Figure 8.10).

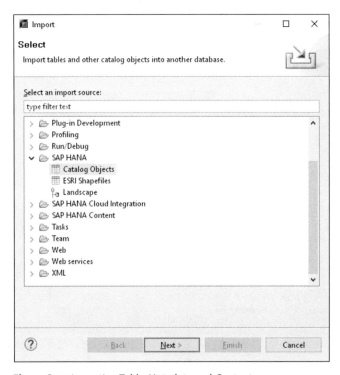

Figure 8.10 Importing Table Metadata and Content

Select the target system and click NEXT. On the SPECIFY LOCATION screen, select and navigate to the location where your source data is stored (Figure 8.11). Click NEXT to advance to the next screen in the IMPORT wizard.

On the next screen, select the CATALOG OBJECT that you want to import and click ADD. Select NEXT to progress to the OPTIONS FOR CATALOG OBJECT IMPORT window (Figure 8.12). In this window, you can choose INCLUDING DATA if you want to transport both the table metadata and the table. INCLUDING DEPENDENCIES will maintain the same dependencies from the original source object. If you want to overwrite any tables that are already in the target system, select REPLACE EXISTING CATALOG OBJECTS. The NUMBER OF PARALLEL THREADS textbox allows you to instantiate multiple processing threads to speed the import.

Figure 8.11 Select the Source Data for the Import

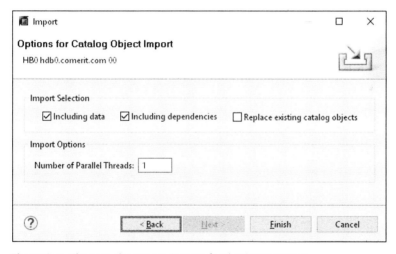

Figure 8.12 Choosing the Import Options for the Target System

Click FINISH to complete the import of the data into the target system. By default, the data will import to the same schema name where it was contained in the source system.

Schema Mapping

When transporting objects between systems, you may need to create a schema mapping from the original authoring schema to the physical schema in the target environment. A schema mapping is also useful if you intend to connect SAP HANA Live views to access data in an SAP HANA sidecar deployment between SAP ERP and SAP Business Warehouse (BW).

Creating a schema mapping is quite simple but can really be a lifesaver when you've transported objects between systems and you can't activate the views in the new environment. Select SCHEMA MAPPING from the QUICK VIEW window and then select the system where you want to create the schema mapping. On the NEXT screen (Figure 8.13), specify the AUTHORING SCHEMA (the schema from the original system) and the PHYSICAL SCHEMA (the schema where the source data currently resides). Now, when you try to activate the related view, the activation should be successful.

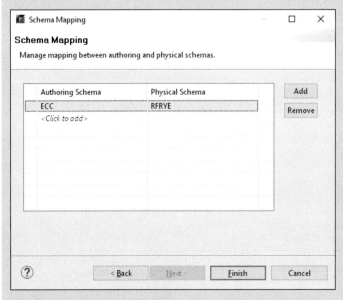

Figure 8.13 Creating a Schema Mapping

8.1.3   Generating Time Data

If you need to create data models with a time dimension, you will want to select the GENERATE TIME DATA option from the QUICK VIEW. This option will allow you to populate the default time-data tables in the _SYS_BI schema with data generated in a variety of ways, as shown in Figure 8.14.

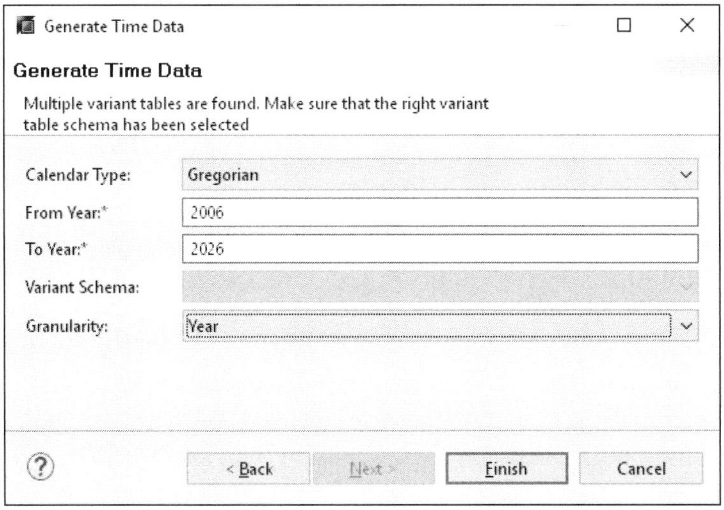

Figure 8.14 Generating Time Data in the Default Tables in _SYS_BI

For the CALENDAR TYPE, you can choose either GREGORIAN or FISCAL. The Gregorian calendar is the standard calendar. Choosing GREGORIAN will populate the M_TIME_DIMENSION_YEAR, M_TIME_DIMENSION_MONTH, M_TIME_DIMENSION_WEEK, and M_TIME_DIMENSION tables in the _SYS_BI schema, according to the GRANULARITY you select in the options.

The FISCAL calendar option is much more useful if you need to create data models for reports from SAP ERP or SAP BW, so make sure to choose this option if you're reporting on standard SAP systems. For the fiscal calendar, you'll need to specify the VARIANT SCHEMA used by your company (populated from tables T009 and T009B). The fiscal calendar data will populate in the M_FISCAL_CALENDAR table in the _SYS_BI schema.

You also need to specify the FROM YEAR and TO YEAR to limit the granularity of the generated data to only the range you specify. When you're satisfied with your selections, click FINISH to generate the data.

8.1.4 Migrating Attribute and Analytic Views

In previous editions of this book, we instructed you to create attribute and analytic views whenever possible to access your data. In order to unify the functionality and performance of all the SAP HANA views, SAP has changed their best-practice guidance to focus on developing graphical calculation views. For the foreseeable future, dimensional calculation views will replace attribute views, and cube or star-join calculation views will replace analytic views. Table functions will also replace scripted calculation views whenever possible. Furthermore, while you can still create attribute views and analytic views in SAP HANA Studio, the SAP HANA Web-Based Development Workbench will only support calculation views.

Beginning with SAP HANA SPS 11, SAP introduced a migration tool to assist users in moving their attribute and analytic views to calculation views. The migration tool is available from the QUICK VIEW pane within SAP HANA Studio (Figure 8.15).

Because of the numerous helpful links in the QUICK VIEW, we generally leave it open and minimize it to one side of the SAP HANA Studio IDE, but if your QUICK VIEW is no longer open, simply navigate to FILE • WINDOW • SHOW VIEW • OTHER. Then, expand SAP HANA, select QUICK VIEW, and click OK (Figure 8.16).

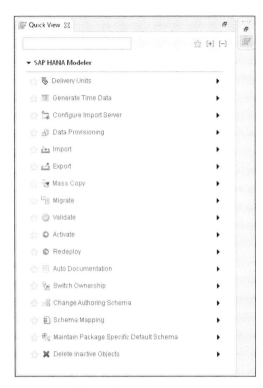

Figure 8.15 The Quick View Pane in SAP HANA Studio

Figure 8.16 Restoring the Quick View to the SAP HANA Studio IDE

To open the migration tool, just click MIGRATE from the QUICK VIEW. You'll be prompted to select the system with the objects to migrate, so select your system and click NEXT. On the next screen (Figure 8.17), you'll be prompted to select the type of migration. You can migrate the following types of objects:

▶ ATTRIBUTE VIEWS AND ANALYTIC VIEWS TO CALCULATION VIEWS.

▶ SCRIPT-BASED CALCULATION VIEWS TO GRAPHICAL CALCULATION VIEWS AND TABLE FUNCTIONS.

▶ CLASSICAL XML-BASED ANALYTIC PRIVILEGES TO SQL ANALYTIC PRIVILEGES.

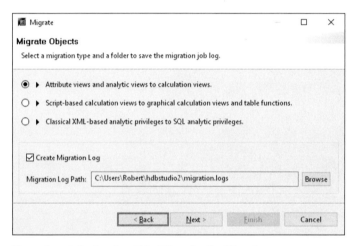

Figure 8.17 Selecting the Object Type for the Migration

You can select the CREATE MIGRATION LOG option to generate a log of the migration process. The migration log will be saved as an HTML file on your local system and will contain the following useful information:

▶ Objects that require user action in order to allow activation

▶ Total number of objects selected for migration

▶ Total number of objects successfully converted to the new object type

▶ Dependent objects whose references were automatically adjusted by the migration tool

▶ Dependent objects whose references could not be automatically adjusted, indicating that you need to convert those objects in another migration

▸ For XML-based analytic privilege conversion, the roles and users associated with the converted analytic privilege

With the correct options selected for the migration, click NEXT. Now you'll be prompted to select the objects for the migration (Figure 8.18). The easiest way to do this is to highlight the package that you want to migrate and click the ADD button, but you can also expand the list and select individual objects to migrate. If your package contains both views and analytic privileges, you should complete those as separate migrations, so you'll need to select the views individually or by folder.

Figure 8.18 Selecting Objects for Migration with the Migration Tool

In either case, your migration objects will be shown in the SELECTED panel. If you have hidden columns in your views, you should consider selecting the MAKE HIDDEN COLUMNS VISIBLE option. Choosing this option will avoid errors in activation due to columns being considered "missing" when they are simply hidden. You can always edit the migrated views to hide those columns after the migration has completed.

The COPY AND MIGRATE option will allow you to complete a simulation of the migration process by simply copying the views to a new target package. You can then activate the copied views and check for any errors. With this option selected, references to the migrated objects will not be updated within other objects, so you should rerun the migration without this option and delete the copied views, assuming you have no errors in activating the copied views.

> **Warning!**
>
> If you're very confident that the migration will work, you can select the ACTIVATE OBJECTS AFTER MIGRATION option. We don't really recommend this approach, which may prevent you from rolling the objects back to a state prior to the migration if problems occur during the migration.

You'll be presented with the IMPACTED OBJECTS window, which will summarize the objects to migrate as well as provide a summary of the impact for each object. Review the information and click the FINISH button if you're satisfied with the summary.

You should also make sure to adopt the following best practices during the migration process:

▶ **Start with a clean workspace**
Before the migration, make sure your workspace only has activated data models, which is a best practice because the migrated data models will be inactive after migration. If your workspace is clean, you can simply right-click on one of the inactive views and select ACTIVATE from the context menu. It's then a simple matter to select and ADD ALL of the inactive views for activation at once (Figure 8.19), which will streamline the activation process considerably, as the new calculation views, and the older versions of the objects will be added for activation and deletion, as appropriate. Then, simply click ACTIVATE to complete the migration process.

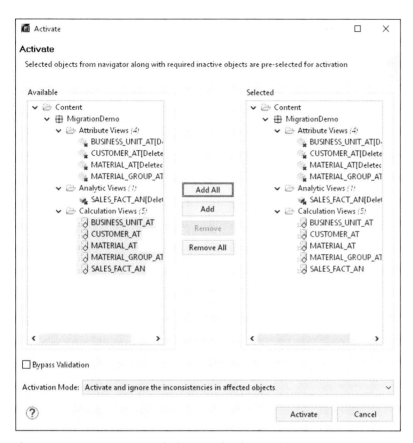

Figure 8.19 Activating Migrated Objects and Deleting Old Versions

▶ **Migrate views before privileges**

If you have both views and privileges to migrate, begin with the views as one migration, then migrate the privileges in the second migration. Using this approach should help the migration tool avoid errors in adjusting the references within the target objects.

▶ **Assign roles and privileges**

After migration, you'll need to assign your users and roles to the new privileges. The migration log will come in handy for this task. Consult the log to determine which users and roles were associated with the converted privilege and then assign those users and roles to the new privileges.

▶ **Don't activate before undoing the migration**
If you find that you need to roll back to a state before the migration, you can use the DELETE INACTIVE OBJECTS option in the QUICK VIEW to delete the newly migrated info objects. Objects will be rolled back to their previous versions and old objects that were marked for deletion will be restored. However, if you attempt to activate the new objects, you won't be able to roll back to the previous version of the objects.

▶ **Simulate before migration**
If you want to simulate the migration, you'll need to select the COPY AND MIGRATE option. This option will copy the impacted objects to the package you choose but will only copy the objects without updating any references. This simulation is useful if you simply want to test whether the migrated object will activate successfully, but you'll probably want to delete the copied object and perform a full migration without simulation after you verify that the migration will be successful.

▶ **Backup first**
As with any migration, you should back up all your modeler objects prior to the migration. Then, you can restore from the backup if a critical failure occurs during the migration.

8.1.5 Delivery Units and Packages

Next, we'll create a delivery unit for our database objects. The delivery unit is used in transporting objects automatically with the SAP HANA Lifecycle Manager or manually using the EXPORT and IMPORT functions in the FILE menu. However, before you can create the delivery unit, you may need to define a `content_vendor` for your SAP HANA system. To define the `content_vendor`, you'll need to open the administration console (double-click the system in the SYSTEMS view) then navigate to the CONFIGURATION tab. Type "content" in the filter text box, and you should be presented with the current `content_vendor` setting under the *indexserver.ini*. If it's "UNDEFINED," you'll need to add a value here. Just double-click the current setting and enter the new value for the `content_vendor` as shown in Figure 8.20. Click SAVE to update the setting. Now you can create a delivery unit.

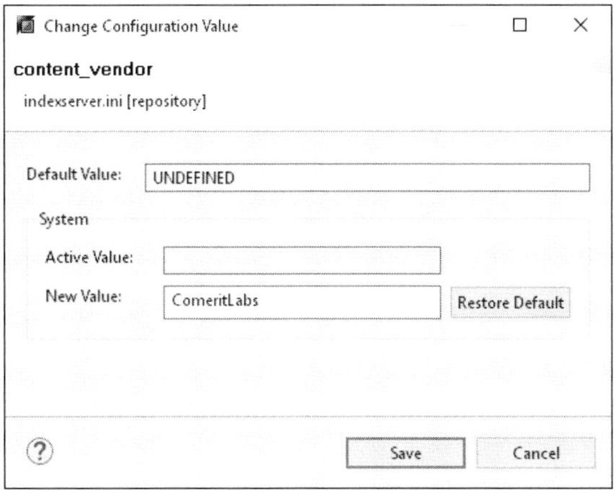

Figure 8.20 Adding a content_vendor to the System

To create a delivery unit, select DELIVERY UNITS from the QUICK VIEW menu. Select your SYSTEM and click NEXT. From the DELIVERY UNITS screen, click the CREATE button. The NEW DELIVERY UNIT window will open (Figure 8.21). Enter a NAME for the delivery unit, the person RESPONSIBLE, and the VERSION number. You can enter any of the supplemental information, such as SUPPORT PACKAGE VERSION and PATCH VERSION if you'd like, but these items are not required. Click OK to create the delivery unit.

Figure 8.21 Creating a New Delivery Unit for Your Content

Next, we'll create a new package for our database objects. To create a new package, right-click on the CONTENT folder from the SYSTEMS tab of the SAP HANA development perspective. From the context menu, click NEW • PACKAGE. The NEW PACKAGE window will open (Figure 8.22), and you'll need to specify the NAME and DESCRIPTION for your package. Select the DELIVERY UNIT that you created earlier and choose the ORIGINAL LANGUAGE and PERSON RESPONSIBLE. When you're satisfied with your selections, click OK to create the package.

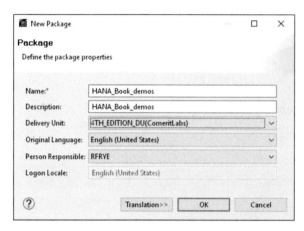

Figure 8.22 Creating a New Package for Your Database Objects

8.2   Calculation Views: Dimensional Views

As we discussed in Section 8.1.4, which covered migrating deprecated objects, calculation views should be your primary data model for the foreseeable future. Calculation views can contain all of the features that were found in attribute and analytic views, but they also allow for complex expressions (case statements, IF statements, counters), layered logical data modeling, joins, unions, aggregations, rankings, and more. SAP has also changed the in-memory computing engine (IMCE) query optimization to favor calculation views.

> **Note**
>
> We covered the process to migrate the deprecated objects, including attribute views, analytic views, and analytical privileges, to their corresponding new object types in Section 8.1.4. If you have an older system and need to learn about deprecated objects, the *SAP HANA Academy* content on YouTube has detailed examples about their creation and use.

Because many new features have been added, calculation views have many areas to cover, and previous editions of this book focused primarily on attribute and analytic views. We'll start with the most basic concepts and then move on to more advanced concepts as we build on the things we've already learned.

8.2.1 Dimensional Views

Dimensional calculation views should be your choice for making data available when no measures are required. As such, they should be used to model and extend master data tables, and you may consider the dimensional calculation views as the replacement for attribute views.

To create a dimensional calculation view, from the Systems view of the SAP HANA development perspective, right-click on the content package you created earlier and navigate to New • Calculation View from the context menu. The New Information View window will open.

In our example (Figure 8.23), we're creating a dimensional calculation view and extending the base customer master data to add a customer level stored in a supplemental data table.

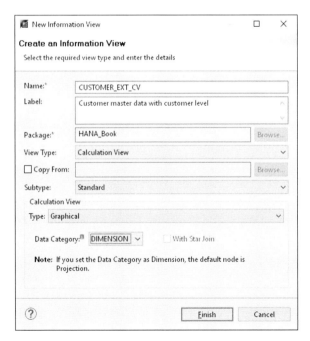

Figure 8.23 Creating a Dimensional Calculation View

First, we assigned the NAME to the view (the extension "CV" is our convention for naming calculation views) and added a LABEL to explain the purpose of the view. By creating the calculation view from the context menu, the PACKAGE is automatically assigned, as is the VIEW TYPE. We could select COPY FROM if we wanted to use an existing view as the basis for this view, but we're creating a new view from scratch, so we'll leave that unchecked in this example.

The view SUBTYPE can be either STANDARD or TIME, but we'll simply select STANDARD for our dimensional calculation view. To create a dimensional view, we also need to change the DATA CATEGORY from CUBE (the default) to DIMENSION, which will change the top-level node in the view to a PROJECTION node. Since we'll have no measures in this view, we don't need an AGGREGATION node. When you're satisfied with your selections, click FINISH to create the new dimensional calculation view. The new view will be available in the editor pane of the SAP HANA development perspective.

> **Note**
>
> You may also select the blank (empty) field for the DATA CATEGORY, which will create the view but make it unavailable for use in reporting tools. You can still use the view in other calculation objects, so leaving the DATA CATEGORY blank will essentially create a private view for reuse with other data modeling objects.

Before we continue building the dimensional calculation view, let's take a moment to examine the DETAILS pane in the editor. When the new view is first created, the VIEW PROPERTIES tab (Figure 8.24) will open by default. Numerous properties can be configured, so let's take a look at our options.

The DATA CATEGORY and TYPE were discussed in the previous section, so we won't revisit those. If you select SESSION CLIENT as the DEFAULT CLIENT, it can be both a blessing and a curse. Some SAP systems are configured with multiple clients, with the different clients designated as development or testing environments. Your company's strategy for dealing with clients will dictate the setting you select here. If you set this to SESSION CLIENT, the view will attempt to limit your results based on the SESSION CLIENT, which is configured for your user or role properties in the SECURITY section of the SYSTEMS tab. If you choose not to set a SESSION CLIENT for your user or role, and you don't set one for in your views, then you may have problems when you attempt to configure currency and unit of measure conversions in your views. Check with your implementation partner or your company

IT department to determine which strategy is most appropriate for your system landscape.

If you want to add comments to the view, you can click the small yellow icon to the right of the VIEW DESCRIPTION text box. A small window will open much like a Post-It note for developer comments to be added to the view.

On the other hand, if you specify a client in your view and then transport the view to another system, you'll have to make sure the target client in the new environment is the same as the one where the view was developed. If the client is not the same in the new environment, you'll have to edit your views in the new environment before you can activate them, which can lead to a lot of tedious view editing and activation. Again, make sure you confirm which client assignment strategy is right for your company before you begin development.

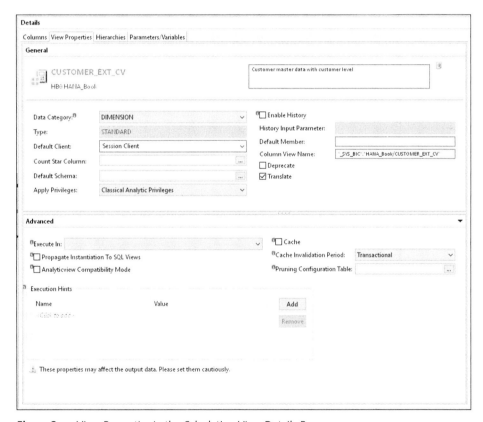

Figure 8.24 View Properties in the Calculation View Details Pane

The DEFAULT SCHEMA field is used to select the schema that will be used by default and is relevant for currency and unit of measure conversions. If the target schema is different between environments, you'll need to create a schema mapping when you transport the objects to the new environment. See Section 8.1.2 for more details about schema mapping.

Selecting the ENABLE HISTORY checkbox will allow you to retrieve historical data from a specific time for the view. Selecting this option will enable time travel queries using the AS OF TIMESTAMP <timestamp> SQL script. Enabling the history also means that the SAP HANA will create a history table to track changes made to the database tables. You'll also need to create a HISTORY INPUT PARAMETER (available after output columns have been added to the view) to request the timestamp for the view from the user upon execution of the view.

The DEFAULT MEMBER selection allows the modeler to select the default member for any hierarchies created in the calculation view.

The DEPRECATE checkbox is selected if you want to indicate that the view is no longer the preferred virtual data model and should not be used.

The TRANSLATE checkbox is tied to the developer language texts in the repository text tables, so be very careful about unchecking this box. Doing so will delete the existing language texts from the repository text tables.

With the APPLY PRIVILEGES selection, you can choose to apply CLASSICAL ANALYTIC PRIVILEGES, SQL ANALYTIC PRIVILEGES, or no privileges at all. You will generally want some sort of analytic privilege to enable role-based authorizations based on your user and role, so consider this selection carefully and make a selection based on your company's security and authorizations policies.

You can choose to push as much of the calculation logic down to the SQL ENGINE as possible, by selecting this option in the EXECUTE IN dropdown.

The PROPAGATE INSTANTIATION TO SQL VIEWS checkbox will prevent the calculation engine from considering any attributes not requested in SQL views on top of the calculation view from being considered.

The ANALYTICVIEW COMPATIBILITY MODE checkbox instructs the calculation engine to ignore N:M cardinality when no fields are requested from left or right outer joins.

The CACHE option allows the user to enable caching for the view, and the CACHE INVALIDATION PERIOD may be set to TRANSACTIONAL, HOURLY, or DAILY.

A PRUNING CONFIGURATION TABLE may be selected to allow query optimization processing of union nodes through the use of pruning tables.

EXECUTION HINTS are advanced features, so we won't cover those in any detail, but these hints may influence the execution optimization for the calculation view. For more information, consult the *SAP HANA Modeling Guide*.

8.2.2 Adding Projection Nodes

All new calculation views begin with two nodes in the graphical editor. The top node is the SEMANTIC layer and contains the COLUMNS, VIEW PROPERTIES, HIERARCHIES, and PARAMETERS/VARIABLES tabs. We'll take a closer look at the COLUMNS, HIERARCHIES, and PARAMETERS/VARIABLES tabs later. For now, you should focus on the SCENARIOS pane where you can add additional nodes.

In most cases, the first step you'll take when creating a new calculation view is to add a projection node for each table used in the view. While it's possible to add a table directly to a join, doing so is not a best practice. By adding the table to a projection node first, you have the ability to filter the table data before connecting the table to other objects. On the other hand, if you add a table directly to a join, your options are limited. You won't be able to add a filter to the table, create calculated columns, or add input parameters to the table.

In our example (Figure 8.25), we've added two projection nodes to the SCENARIOS canvas, and we've added a table to each projection node. We added the projection nodes by dragging and dropping them from the node picker on the left.

We also clicked on the node name and edited the name to describe the contents of the node. For this example, we named the nodes "Customer" and "Customer_ NEW", respectively. User-friendly names are useful when you're troubleshooting complex calculation views and you need to remember what each node does without opening the comments for the node or consulting your development documentation (if it even exists).

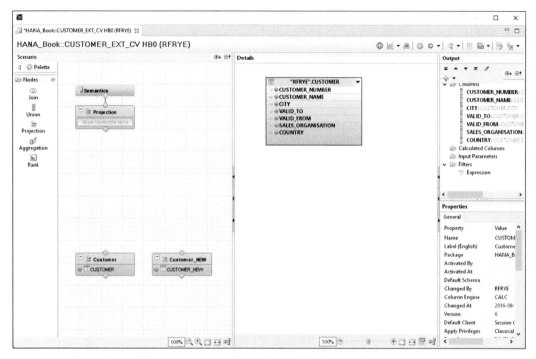

Figure 8.25 Adding Projection Nodes to the Graphical View Editor

You can add comments to each node as well. Either right-click on the node and click MAINTAIN COMMENT or mouse-over the node and select the yellow comment icon. A comment window will open (Figure 8.26) where you can enter your comments about the node.

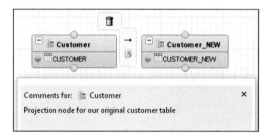

Figure 8.26 Adding Comments to the Projection Node

To add tables to the projection nodes, you can either right-click on the projection node and select ADD OBJECTS from the context menu or you can mouse-over the node and click the green + sign. You can also drag and drop the table from the SYSTEMS view in the browser pane, but entering the table name in the search window and selecting it from the list (Figure 8.27) is usually faster and easier. When you've located the table, click the OK button to add it to the projection node.

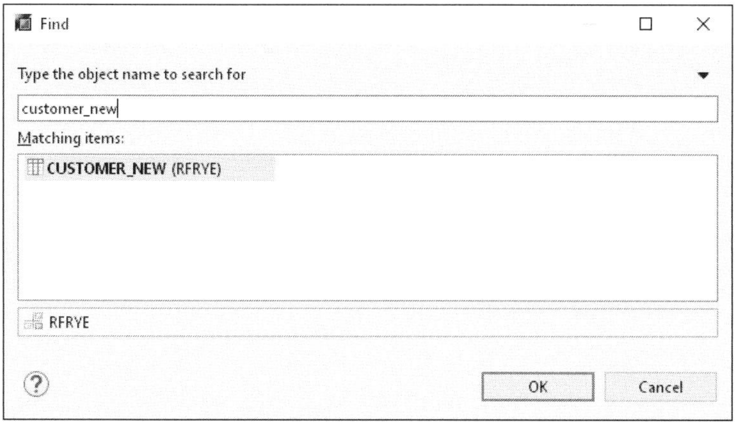

Figure 8.27 Searching for a Table from the Add Objects Window

Now that you've added the table to the node, you need to select the columns that you want to add as output to the next node in the view. To add a column to the output, you can simply click the grey orb to the left of the column name, and the orb will turn orange to indicate that the column has been added to the output. However, this process is slow and tedious, so we use either hold `Shift` or `Control` while clicking to select the columns that we want and then right-click on the node to open the context menu. From the context menu, click ADD TO OBJECTS to add the selected columns as output to the next node.

> **Note**
>
> If the node you're working with is already connected all the way to the semantic layer, you can also select PROPAGATE TO SEMANTICS to add the columns to the output for the view. Please note that the PROPAGATE TO SEMANTICS option will always add the columns to the bottom of the output column list, so you'll need to edit the order of the output columns to reflect the order you want.

If you want to remove a column from the output, you'll have to click the orange orb beside the column you want to remove and confirm the removal of the column from the output in the dialogue box that appears. If you have a large number of nodes to remove, it's often easier to simply remove the object from the node (and remove all columns in the object by doing so) and then add it again, as the process of deactivating the orb and confirming the removal is quite tedious and also, sadly, unavoidable. Also, bear in mind that removing a column from the output cascades upwards through the view to the semantic layer, and any calculation or input parameters that are dependent upon that column will need to be edited in order to work again.

> **Warning!**
>
> When you begin learning to create graphical calculation views, we recommend checking the output of every layer as you progress through the logic of the calculation view. Don't rush ahead because doing so will likely result in some unexpected output from your view, which in turn will lead to a round of troubleshooting. Per Murphy's Law, during troubleshooting, you'll probably end up removing a column with a dependent calculation or a filter higher in the view, and you'll have to redo some tedious and time-consuming work that you've already done. This extra work is especially onerous if you've created a view with numerous currency conversions, so consider this fair warning that rushing to build a complex view nearly always leads to rework that could have been avoided through meticulous testing of the output for every layer.
>
> To test this way, simply connect your node to the top projection or aggregation node, activate the output to the semantic layer, and activate the view. Then, you can run a data preview for the view to make sure your output is expected.

Returning to the task at hand, we've now added the CUSTOMER_NUMBER, CUSTOMER_NAME, CITY, and COUNTRY columns to the output for the projection node. Notice that these columns also now appear in the OUTPUT pane of the view editor. Let's now take a look at applying filters to our node.

8.2.3 Applying Filters

We can add a filter to the node by selecting a column to filter and right-clicking the column. Select APPLY FILTER from the context menu (Figure 8.28).

Let's assume we want to create a view that combines all of our original customers (from the customer projection node) with only our new customer from London. In this case, we could simply set our filter value EQUAL to "London" in the APPLY FILTER dialogue for the CUSTOMER_NEW node (Figure 8.29). Click OK to add the filter to the projection node. You'll see a yellow filter icon to the right side of the filter column, and the filter icon will also be added to the end of the name for the projection node. If you want to remove the filter, you can simply right-click the column and select REMOVE FILTER from the context menu.

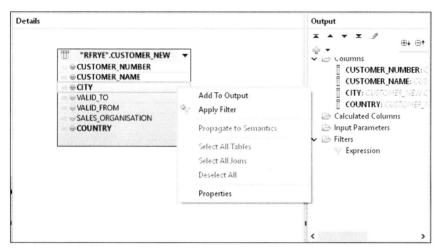

Figure 8.28 Adding Output and Applying a Filter to the Projection Node

Figure 8.29 Applying a Filter to a Column in the Calculation View

You can also apply filters as expressions. To use a filter expression, expand the FILTERS folder in the OUTPUT pane and double-click EXPRESSION. The FILTER EXPRESSION editor opens and allows you to apply more complex filters, such as compound filters on more than one column. See Table 8.1 for a detailed list of the possible filter operators and a description each operator's function.

327

Filter Operators	Functional Description
EQUAL	Show any rows with data corresponding to the value in the filter
NOT EQUAL	Show any rows with data not corresponding to the value in the filter
BETWEEN	Show any rows where the column value matches a range of values between a FROM and TO value
LIST OF VALUES	Show any rows where the column value matches one of the values in a range of comma-separated values
NOT IN LIST	Show any rows where the column value does not match one of the values in a range of comma-separated values
IS NULL	Show any rows where the column value of the filter column is NULL
IS NOT NULL	Show any rows where the column value of the filter column is NOT NULL
LESS THAN	Show any rows where the column value is lower than the specified filter value
LESS THAN OR EQUAL TO	Show any rows where the column value is lower than or equivalent to the specified filter value
GREATER THAN	Show any rows where the column value is higher than the specified filter value
GREATER THAN OR EQUAL TO	Show any rows where the column value is higher than or equivalent to the specified filter value
CONTAINS PATTERN	Show any rows where the filter column value matches the pattern specified within the filter, which is equivalent to `match("CITY",'Lond*')`

Table 8.1 Filter Operators Available in Calculation Views

8.2.4 Union Nodes

Union nodes are used to combine the data in two or more tables into one unified result set. In our example, we're combining our original customer table with another table containing new customers. To add a union node to our dimensional calculation view, click the UNION icon in the NODES picker and click the location on the SCENARIO canvas where you want to add the node. Then, you need to click the orb at the top of the projection node, hold the mouse button, drag a connection to the union node, and release the mouse button, as shown in Figure 8.30. A connection from the projection node to the union node is created, and the nodes will be listed in the DETAILS pane.

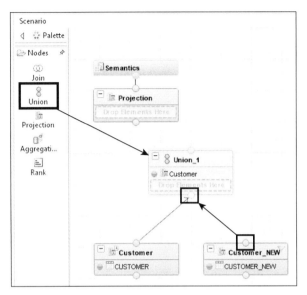

Figure 8.30 Adding a Union Node to a Calculation View

In the DETAILS pane, you'll still need to map your columns in the union. To map the columns, you can expand the nodes, right-click the column that needs to be added or mapped, and choose ADD TO TARGET or MAP TO TARGET from the context menu. Then, you just pick the column(s) for the mapping from a dropdown box and click OK. This method is useful when you have numerous columns to map in a union with multiple sources.

If the column names match between the sources, the easiest way to complete the mapping is to click the AUTO MAP BY NAME button, as shown in Figure 8.31. The columns from both sources will automatically be added to the TARGET section, and the mappings will be visible as converging lines from the SOURCE columns.

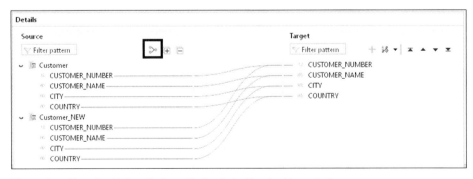

Figure 8.31 Mapping Union Nodes with the Auto Map by Name Button

329

You can also drag columns from the SOURCE to the TARGET sections of the DETAILS pane. If the column does not yet exist in the TARGET, it will simply be added to the bottom of the list. If the column does exist, just drop the additional SOURCE column onto the correct TARGET column to create the mapping, represented by converging lines from both sources, as explained earlier. Be careful when using this mapping method because the drag-and-drop method makes it easy to map columns incorrectly. If you make a mistake in the mapping, you can simply click the line for the incorrect mapping to select it and press Delete to remove the mapping.

Let's examine another useful element of the DETAILS pane. We already know about the AUTO MAP BY NAME button, but the FILTER PATTERN box is also quite useful, especially when you're working with larger data sources. Do not confuse the FILTER PATTERN box with creating a filter. This text box allows you to enter partial column names to search for columns and limit their display in the DETAILS pane. Please be aware that using the FILTER PATTERN box will make the mapping lines disappear in the TARGET, but the mappings will still exist. Just delete any characters from the FILTER PATTERN box to restore the full view of the SOURCE or TARGET columns, as well as the mapping lines.

You can also use the SORT DIRECTION button to sort the columns in the TARGET pane in ascending or descending alphabetical order. You can reorder the target columns using the arrow buttons in the upper right of the TARGET pane, and the columns will be ordered to match when connected to the next node in the view. Finally, you can add a new target column independent of any source columns using the green + button. See Figure 8.32 for the location of the toolbar buttons.

Figure 8.32 Useful Design and Navigation Controls in the Details Pane

When you're satisfied with the union node details, drag a connection between the top of the union node and the bottom of the top-level projection node to create a connection.

8.2.5 Scenarios Pane Controls

Before we configure the final projection node in our dimensional calculation view, let's take a moment to examine some useful layout tools in the SCENARIOS pane. While these tools are mostly cosmetic in nature, get used to working with them, as you will definitely need them in more complex data models.

First, you can zoom in and out using the magnifying glass icons, and you can even enter a zoom level manually in the text box. These zoom options useful when you have large, complex views to edit, as complex views may have more than ten levels of nodes within the view. You can select RESET ZOOM to reset the zoom level to 100%, and you can select FIT TO WINDOW to have the view centered and adjusted to fit the size of the SCENARIOS canvas.

The AUTO LAYOUT button can be used periodically throughout the design process to rearrange the nodes into a well-aligned layout. This button is especially useful when you've finished designing the view and just want to tidy up the workspace. Context menus for nodes allow for exporting diagrams for the nodes in picture formats, such as PNG and BMP. Right-click any given node to access their context menus.

In our example (Figure 8.33), we've manually zoomed to 120% of the original size and used the AUTO LAYOUT button to rearrange the nodes as suggested by the tool. You can click the top PROJECTION node and add all the columns to the output (remember to hold Shift while clicking and to use the right-click context menu to make this process easier). You can then click the SEMANTICS node to verify that the CUSTOMER_NUMBER, CUSTOMER_NAME, CITY, and COUNTRY columns are all available as output.

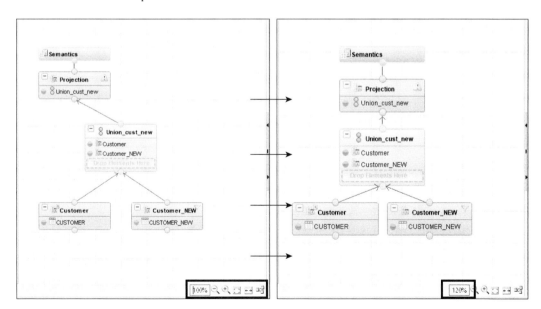

Figure 8.33 Scenarios Pane Layout Tools

8.2.6   String Functions

When creating calculation views, performing string functions on your text columns is common, so let's take a look at creating a calculated column with a concatenation of text columns and characters. Let's suppose, for example, that we need produce a shipping bin designation from a simple concatenation of the data in the COUNTRY and CITY columns, divided by a dash (-) and with all characters in uppercase. To create the calculated column, we can right-click the CALCULATED COLUMN folder in the OUTPUT pane and then select NEW from the context menu.

The CALCULATED COLUMN window will open (Figure 8.34). You'll need to enter a NAME and LABEL for the new column, and you'll also need to select the DATA TYPE and LENGTH for the new column. Since we're concatenating strings, we've selected VARCHAR as the data type and entered "50" for the length. You could select the HIDDEN checkbox if you wanted to create a HIDDEN column (for example, if you wanted to use the calculated column in another calculation), and you could even assign semantics to the column (if you wanted to designate the column as a unit of measure, a currency code, quantity, date, or geolocation).

In our example (Figure 8.34), you're simply concatenating the string values from the selected columns and adding a delimiter between them. First, you'll need to cast each of your columns to uppercase. To do so, you'll navigate to the STRING FUNCTIONS folder in the FUNCTIONS section of the window and double-click the UPPER() function. The expression `upper(stringarg)`, which will transform the text to uppercase, will be added to the EXPRESSION EDITOR. Next, you'll double-click `stringarg` to highlight it in the editor; then you'll expand the COLUMNS folder in the ELEMENTS section of the window. Next, double-click the COUNTRY column to replace `stringarg` with "COUNTRY".

> **Note**
>
> You'll find the syntax of the EXPRESSION EDITOR in SAP HANA Studio to be somewhat different than the syntax used in similar expression editing tools. In the SAP HANA Studio EXPRESSION EDITOR, columns are indicated by enclosing the column name with double quotation marks (""), whereas string literals are indicated with single quotation marks (' ') enclosing the string value. Integers and decimals, on the other hand, generally do not need any special characters.

Next, we need to add the delimiting dash to the expression. To concatenate two string values in the EXPRESSION EDITOR, you'll need to click the + button under OPERATORS or simply enter the plus sign using your keyboard. To tell the editor that you're about to enter a string literal, you'll need to type in " ' - ' ". To test the work you've done so far, click the VALIDATE SYNTAX button above the text entry field for the expression editor. You should receive a popup notification indicating that you've entered a valid expression, but if not, check your syntax.

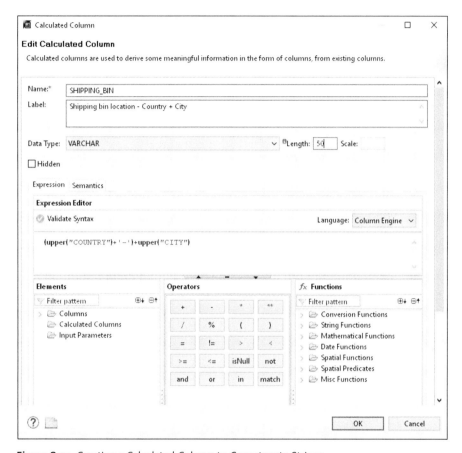

Figure 8.34 Creating a Calculated Column to Concatenate Strings

Now in a perfect world, we could simply enter another + sign to concatenate the CITY column with the rest of the expression, and we'd be done. Unfortunately, as of July 2016, the EXPRESSION EDITOR will not allow concatenation of multiple strings in one expression, but there's an easy workaround for this. As you can see in our example (Figure 8.34), the expression editor will parse the expression properly if you nest one expression within another. To do so, simply place parentheses before and after the original expression, add the + operator and the upper(stringarg) function, and then add the column to the expression. Click VALIDATE SYNTAX again, and you should be notified that the expression is valid once more. Click OK to finish creating the calculated column.

You'll now see the SHIPPING_BIN calculated column added to the OUTPUT pane, and if you click the SEMANTICS node, you'll find SHIPPING_BIN at the bottom of the output. To test that our calculated column is working as expected, we can activate the view, then right-click the SEMANTICS node and select DATA PREVIEW from the context menu. If you've followed the steps from our example properly, your concatenated column should look like the SHIPPING_BIN column in Figure 8.35.

CUSTOMER_NUMBER	CUSTOMER_NAME	CITY	COUNTRY	SHIPPING_BIN
1,000	Rocky Mountain Bikes	Denver	US	US-DENVER
2,000	Big Apple Bikes	New York ...	US	US-NEW YORK CITY
3,000	Philly Bikes	Philadelphia	US	US-PHILADELPHIA
4,000	Peachtree Bikes	Atlanta	US	US-ATLANTA
5,000	Beantown Bikes	Boston	US	US-BOSTON
6,000	Windy City Bikes	Chicago	US	US-CHICAGO
7,000	Furniture City Bikes	Grand Rap...	US	US-GRAND RAPIDS
8,000	Motown Bikes	Detroit	US	US-DETROIT
9,000	SoCal Bikes	Irvine	US	US-IRVINE
10,000	Silicon Valley Bikes	Palo Alto	US	US-PALO ALTO
11,000	DC Bikes	Washingto...	US	US-WASHINGTON DC

Figure 8.35 Previewing the Data to Validate Our String Function Calculation

8.2.7 Input Parameters

What if we wanted to let our users limit the results of the queries to some subset of the data? In this case, we can create an input parameter to prompt the user to make a selection. Then we simply create a filter in a projection node to limit the data according to the user's selection in the input parameter.

To add an input parameter to our example, you'll first need to delete the connection between the union node and the top projection node. Just click the link to select it and then press Delete to delete it. Next, you need to add another projection node between the union node and the top projection node. The additional node is needed because you can't create a filter expression in the top-level projection node, so you'll add one to enable you to create the filter expression in the lower projection node.

As you're just using this node to add a filter expression, now is the perfect time to propagate the columns all the way to the semantic layer. First, make sure you've connected the union node to the new projection node and that you've connected the new projection node to the top-level projection node. Click the AUTO LAYOUT button in the bottom right of the SCENARIOS pane, and your view should be similar to the one shown in Figure 8.36. Next, to highlight all of the columns, select the first column and then hold the [Shift] key while clicking the last column. Right-click the highlighted columns and select PROPAGATE TO SEMANTICS to add the selected columns to the output of the top-level projection node as well as the SEMANTICS node.

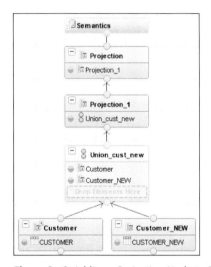

Figure 8.36 Adding a Projection Node to Filter by Input Parameter

To create the input parameter, select the new projection node, right-click the INPUT PARAMETERS folder and click NEW. The EDIT INPUT PARAMETER window will open (Figure 8.37), where you can enter a NAME and LABEL for your new input parameter.

Input parameters may be one of several types. See Table 8.2 for a description of each input parameter type. In our example (Figure 8.37), we selected COLUMN as the PARAMETER TYPE, and then we selected the COUNTRY column from the current view REFERENCE COLUMN. If you want the user to have the ability to select multiple values (e.g., more than one country), select the MULTIPLE ENTRIES checkbox. To require selection of an input parameter, select the IS MANDATORY checkbox.

Note

If you enable the Is MANDATORY option, make sure you also set a DEFAULT VALUE. This default setting will automatically populate a value for the input parameter and improve the user experience. For example, if you intend to use an input parameter in a currency conversion, failing to set a default will cause the query execution to fail if a user fails to select a value and simply clicks OK to run the query, because the currency conversion function will not be able to determine which currency is the target currency for the conversion.

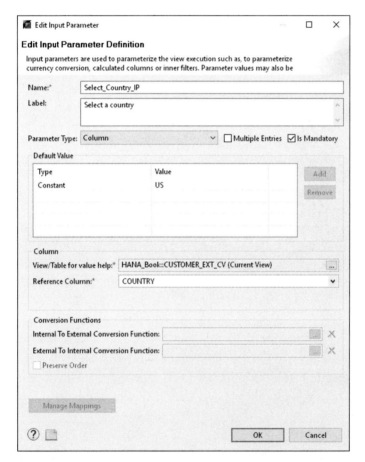

Figure 8.37 Creating an Input Parameter for User-Selected Filtering

When entering a DEFAULT VALUE, you can choose to ADD a CONSTANT or an EXPRESSION. We selected CONSTANT as the TYPE and entered "US" as the value to force our query to default to customers in the United States.

Parameter Type	Description
DIRECT	Allows you to specify the data type, length, and scale of the input parameter. You can also set the semantic type for a direct parameter to currency, unit of measure, or date.
COLUMN	Accesses the specified REFERENCE COLUMN to provide a list of values from which the user can select (acts as a SELECT DISTINCT statement for the reference column).
DERIVED FROM TABLE	Typically used for runtime calculations based on values from a table. For example, you could access a table of discounts and apply a discount based on the customer ID.
STATIC LIST	Allows you to specify the data type, length, and scale of the input parameter and then declare a list of values. The values are provided to the user for selection and the results are filtered accordingly.
DERIVED FROM PROCEDURE OR SCALAR FUNCTION	The modeler calls a procedure or scalar function at runtime to determine the input parameter value.

Table 8.2 Input Parameter Types

The CONVERSION FUNCTIONS allow you to apply conversion functions from your SAP system to perform conversions between internal and external formats. For example, if the input parameter is a date, you could call a conversion function to format the date into the standard SAP date format or into a friendlier calendar format. CONVERSION FUNCTIONS were added to input parameters in SAP HANA SPS 11, so you make sure your documentation is more recent than SAP HANA SPS 11 for more information about these functions.

MANAGE MAPPINGS is useful if you need to use views with input parameters in a node within your calculation view. If you don't map the input parameters from the original view to the input parameters in the new view, the original view will not give you the results you're expecting.

Finally, to add a comment to your input parameter, click the yellow note icon in the bottom left of the EDIT INPUT PARAMETER window. As the process of creating input parameters can be somewhat complex, you should make sure to add comments explaining the logic you're using in the input parameter in case you have to revisit the view months after you created it. Adding a comment will also help other developers on your team to easily understand your logic for the input parameter. When you're satisfied with your selections, click OK to add the input parameter to the view.

Next, you'll need to create a filter that will use the input parameter as a user-specified filter. To create the filter using the input parameter, expand the FILTERS folder in the OUTPUT pane and double-click EXPRESSION to open the FILTER EXPRESSION editor (Figure 8.38). Expand the COLUMNS folder and double-click the column that needs to be filtered by the input parameter (COUNTRY in our example).

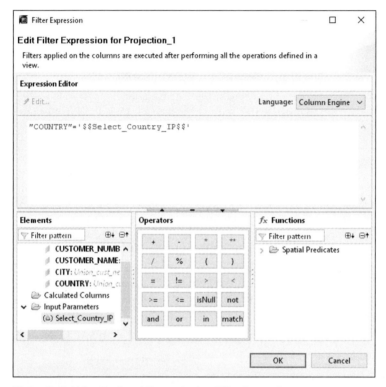

Figure 8.38 Using the Input Parameter in a Filter Expression

Next, add the operator for your filter expression (= in our example). Expand the INPUT PARAMETERS folder and double-click the input parameter that you created earlier. When you've finished editing the expression, click OK to create the filter. Next, activate the view and use the context menu for the SEMANTICS node to open a data preview for the view.

You'll now be prompted to select the country in the VARIABLES AND INPUT PARAMETERS window before the preview opens. Enter your desired country in the FROM column and click OK to preview the data. In our example (Figure 8.39), we selected GB (Great Britain) as the input parameter.

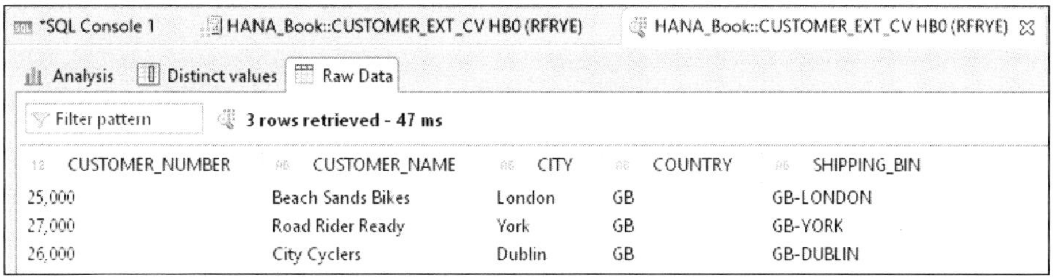

Figure 8.39 Data Preview with GB as the Input Parameter

8.2.8 Semantics Node

The SEMANTICS node is the highest node in a calculation view. We already examined the VIEW PROPERTIES tab from the SEMANTICS node in Section 8.2.1, so now let's take a closer look at the COLUMNS tab in the DETAILS section (Figure 8.40).

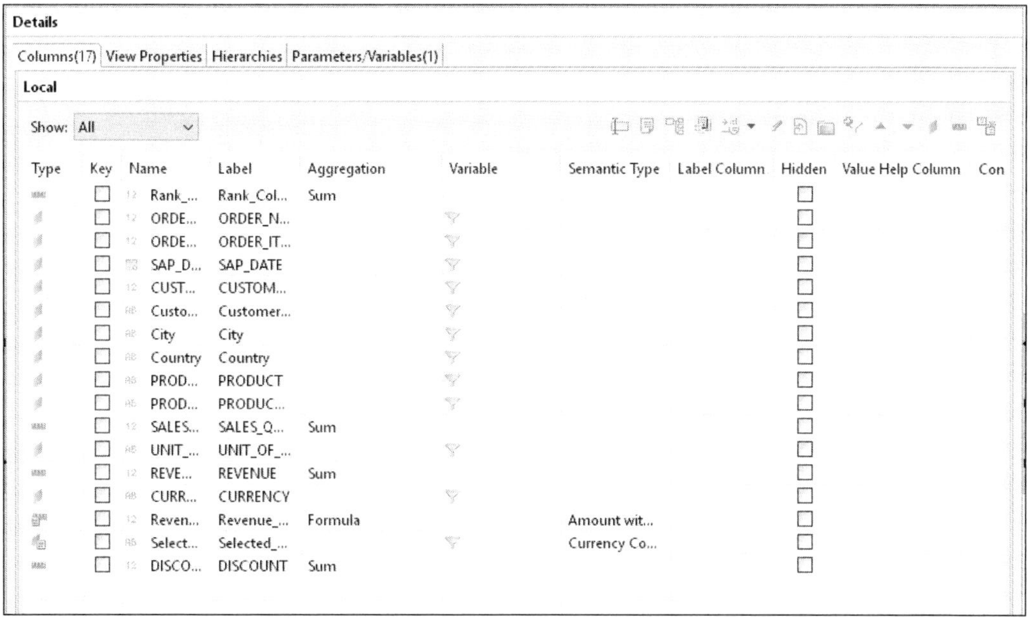

Figure 8.40 Semantic Node Details in the Calculation View

If you're working with a calculation view cube, you'll be able to edit the TYPE, so we'll discuss this in more detail when we create a calculation view cube in Section 8.3. You can designate a column as a key by selecting the checkbox under KEY for that column.

In the Name column, you may change the column name to a friendlier, mixed-case name; however, we don't recommend changing the column name here. The Rename and Adjust References button on the toolbar will change column names throughout the view and, as such, is a much more effective means of adjusting column names. Also, the Label column serves the same purpose and may ultimately cause less confusion when you begin troubleshooting problems.

The Aggregation column is not used for dimensional calculation views, so we'll discuss aggregation when we create calculation view cubes. The Variable column will show any variables you create (using the New Variable button in the toolbar above the column headings). We'll discuss variables in detail when we examine the toolbar buttons later in this section.

You can assign Semantic Types from the Semantics node if you'd like, but one general best practice is to assign semantic types in the top-level Projection node or at a lower node where the column was first added to the view. The Label Column field can be used to assign a text column from your SAP system to the selected column.

If you want to hide a column from your reporting tools, select the checkbox for the column under Hidden. We'll discuss the Value Help Column in detail when we discuss the toolbar buttons later in this section.

The Conversion Functions column offers another chance to assign a system conversion function to a column (for example, for converting between the SAP and standard date formats).

The Semantics toolbar (Figure 8.41) has seen significant improvements when compared to the earliest versions of SAP HANA Studio, so let's examine the buttons on the toolbar in detail. We'll start from the left and work our way to the right end of the toolbar.

Figure 8.41 The Toolbar for the Semantics Node

The RENAME AND ADJUST REFERENCES button is at the far left of the toolbar (the button that looks like a text cursor over a text box). Use this button to rename columns and have the name change cascade throughout the entire view. Click the button, and the RENAME AND ADJUST REFERENCES window (Figure 8.42) will open. In our example, we've changed the column names to mixed case instead of uppercase with delimiters. Enter the NEW NAME for any columns you want to change and click NEXT.

Figure 8.42 Cascade Name Changes Throughout the View with the Rename and Adjust References Button

After you click NEXT, you'll be provided with a list of objects that reference the columns with the changing names (Figure 8.43). Click FINISH, and the tool will update the column names in any objects that depend on the view. As a result, if you edit the name of a column in one of your base views, as long as you use the RENAME AND ADJUST REFERENCES button, the change will cascade out to all the dependent objects. Perhaps more importantly, the dependent object's semantic layer does not change, so you do not have to worry that changing a column name in one of your first views will force you to rework all your other objects.

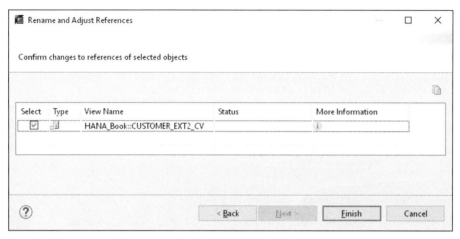

Figure 8.43 Dependent Objects Detected and Updated

After you click FINISH, you'll still need to activate the original view and any objects that depended on the original view, but as we learned earlier in the chapter, you can simply click ACTIVATE from the context menu for the affected views.

> **Note**
>
> The option to RENAME AND ADJUST REFERENCES is a very cool addition to SAP HANA Studio for SAP HANA SPS 12. In previous iterations of SAP HANA Studio, you had to manually work your way through the view to rename a column in each node, and then you had to make the same change in every node of every dependent object.

The next button (the yellow button, second from the left) is the MAINTAIN COMMENT button, which allows you to create a comment for each column in the view output. Make sure to use the comment feature as documentation whenever practical to do so, since you never know when team members may join or leave the team.

The SHOW LINEAGE button (third from the left) is another useful addition to SAP HANA Studio. This button allows you to highlight a column in the SEMANTICS node and trace it back to its point of origin in the view. Every node in which the column appears is highlighted, and the name used for the column in that node is also displayed (Figure 8.44). To close the lineage trace, click the x button on the left of the LINEAGE FOR COLUMN <SELECTED COLUMN> bar.

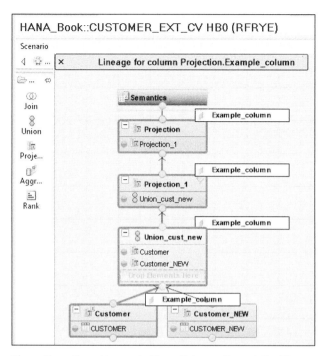

Figure 8.44 Show Lineage to Trace Columns through the View

The EXTRACT SEMANTICS button (fourth button from the left in the toolbar) allows you access the underlying data sources for your columns and hierarchies in order to extract and copy the semantic definitions for those columns. This speeds the development process as you need to only define the semantic definition (labels and texts) for your columns in the source view on the original database object. As we described in Section 8.1.2, you can add comments for each column in your tables when you create them, so the base table can provide the semantics for a column wherever it's used.

Click the EXTRACT SEMANTICS button to make use of this feature. The EXTRACT SEMANTICS window will open (Figure 8.45), and you can simply place a checkmark beside each column for which you need semantic definitions. The OVERWRITE SEMANTICS ALREADY DEFINED checkbox is selected by default, and you could lose any custom semantics already defined if you're not careful. Click OK to extract the semantics when you're satisfied with your selections.

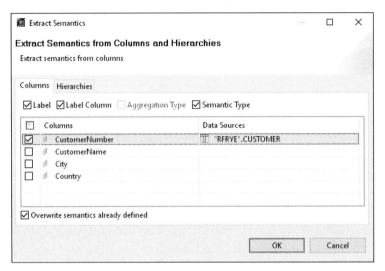

Figure 8.45 Extracting Semantic Definitions from the Source Table

The ASSIGN SEMANTICS button (fifth from the left, with a dropdown menu) functions exactly as described earlier in this book, but we still recommend assigning semantics in the underlying nodes whenever possible.

The REFERENCES button (seventh from the left) helps you locate calculated columns and conversions that depend on the selected column. The DISPLAY FOLDER button allows you to create folders where you can group related measures (this button is not available in our dimensional calculation view).

The CREATE VARIABLE – APPLY FILTER button (yellow filter icon, sixth from right) is another way to create user-selected input parameters (as discussed in Section 8.2.7), and in many ways, this method is easier. You simply select the column for the input parameter and click the button to create the filter, and then the NEW VARIABLE window (Figure 8.46), which is quite similar to the FILTER EXPRESSION window, will open. The filter column will already be selected, and you can just click OK to create a user input variable, which will prompt the user to select from the distinct values for the column. You can also tie the input parameter to a hierarchy.

However, this method is limited: This type of input parameter can't be used to pass a value to a currency conversion. Standard input parameters can be used in other calculated columns and currency conversions.

Figure 8.46 New Variable as a Filter for a Calculation View

8.3 Calculation Views: Cube Views

Next, we're going to take a look at creating calculation view cubes. Calculation view cubes offer many of the same capabilities as analytic views but are much more flexible in design because they allow layers of logic to be applied instead of being limited to a data foundation, a star-join node, or the semantics layer.

Cube-based calculation views are created using the graphical view editor and are similar in design to dimensional calculation views; however, since calculation view cubes have measures, you can perform numerical calculations, rank your data based on numerical values using rank nodes, and aggregate calculated values with aggregation nodes.

To create a calculation view as a cube, you follow many of the same steps you used when creating a dimensional cube. In the Systems view, right-click the package where you want to create the view and select New • Calculation View from the context menu. The New Information View window will open, and you'll be prompted to enter the Name and Label for the view. For a complete description of the fields in this window, see Section 8.2.1.

To specify that this view will be cube-based, you need to select Cube as the Data Category, as shown in Figure 8.47. You may also create the view using a traditional star join by selecting the With Star Join checkbox, but if you select the star join, you'll lose the ability to create layers of nodes and apply logic at each layer. Select Cube and click Finish to create the new view.

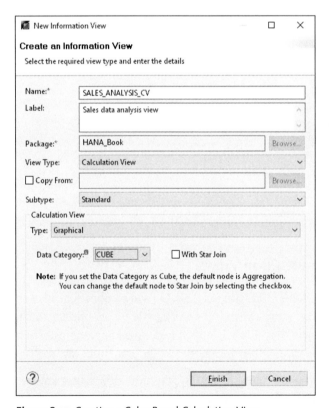

Figure 8.47 Creating a Cube-Based Calculation View

For calculation view cubes, all of the same development principles apply as those used with dimensional views (as described in Section 8.2). You can add projection and union nodes to the view, apply filters, create calculated columns, define input parameters, and so on. You can also use aggregation nodes, rank nodes, and join nodes with calculation views.

> **Note**
>
> Joins may also be used in dimensional views, but we're going to take a look at them as part of cube-based views. The same principles apply whether they're used in dimensional or calculation views.

Since calculation view cubes are built with many of the same techniques that we used with dimensional views, in the following discussion, we're going to focus on the types of nodes and modeling techniques that we have not yet used. In this section, you'll learn about:

- Join nodes
- Temporal and spatial joins
- Aggregation nodes
- Rank nodes
- Currency conversions

8.3.1 Join Nodes

Join nodes are used to join or limit data from two data sources. A join node is limited to two data sources as input, and in calculation views, the data sources should generally be provided by projection nodes. While you can use two tables or other views as the data sources for a join, we generally recommend adding data sources to projection nodes and then connecting the nodes to the join.

We prefer to connect projection nodes to join nodes instead of adding the original data sources to the join node because the projection node can be used to limit the data provided to the join, by applying filters and limiting the output of each projection node. As a result, the join node will have fewer columns and rows to process, which in turn increases the performance for the join node. Take a look at Figure 8.48 to better understand this concept. In this example, we've connected PROJECTION_3 (sales facts) and PROJECTION_2 (product master data) to JOIN_1. In fact, we even passed our SALES_DATA through PROJECTION_3 from PROJECTION_1, in order to resolve some format issues for our date fields in our SALES_DATA.

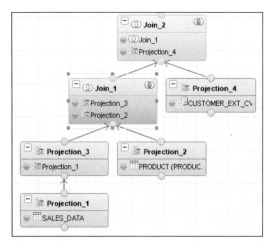

Figure 8.48 Connecting Projection Nodes to Join Nodes

To add a join node to a view, you can simply click the join node from the SCENARIOS editor and click the canvas to add the join node to the view. Then, if you've followed our recommendation to use projection nodes for your data sources, you will simply drag and drop a link from the top of each projection node to the bottom of the join node.

When connecting the projection nodes, you should remember that the first node connected to the join is generally considered, in the node logic, to be the left table for the join, although this can be switched by right-clicking the table in the DETAILS pane and choosing the SWAP AS <OPPOSITE> TABLE option from the context menu, as shown in Figure 8.49.

To join the two data sources, you can simply drag a connection from the join column of one table to the target column in the other data source, or you can use the CREATE JOIN option in the context menu for either column to open the NEW JOIN window.

We prefer to use the NEW JOIN window, as you're prompted to select the options for the join as part of the dialogue. In this window, simply drag the join column from one side and drop it on the other to create the join (Figure 8.50).

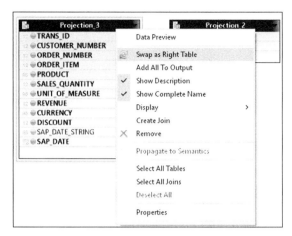

Figure 8.49 Swapping the Logical Left/Right of the Join Data Source

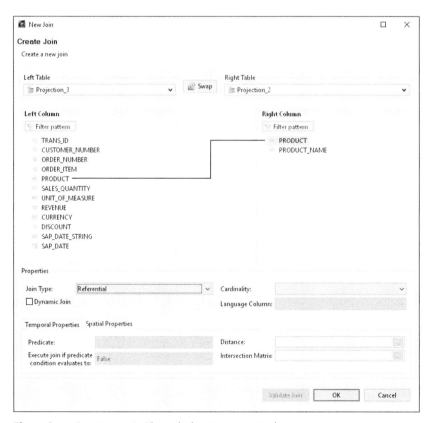

Figure 8.50 Creating a Join Through the New Join Window

You'll need to select the JOIN TYPE and CARDINALITY for the join. See Table 8.3 for a summary of all the supported join types in a join node, as well as a summary of the results and use cases for each join type. If you're using a TEXT join, you'll need to specify the LANGUAGE COLUMN to add the join as well.

If you're joining on more than one column in the data sources, you can select the DYNAMIC JOIN checkbox. Selecting the DYNAMIC JOIN tells the modeler to define the join condition columns based on the columns requested by the runtime query. As long as one of the join elements is requested by the query at runtime, the execution processing time will be improved. Dynamic joins execute data aggregations before executing the join, whereas static joins aggregate after the join.

> **Warning!**
>
> If your client query does not request one of the columns in a dynamic join, you'll receive a runtime error for that query, so use this feature carefully.

When you're finished selecting the join properties, just click OK to finish creating the join. To test the output of the join node, you can activate the view then click DATA PREVIEW from the right-click context menu of the join node. If your join is working properly, you should see results like the ones in Figure 8.51. Notice that our sales transaction data has now been joined to the product table by the product identifier to add the product name to the data.

TRANS_ID	CUSTOMER_NUMBER	ORDER_NUMBER	ORDER_ITEM	PRODUCT	PRODUCT_NAME	SALES_QUANTITY
260	21,000	100,133	10	DXTR2100	Deluxe Touring Bike-Sil...	1
271	21,000	100,133	20	PRTR2100	Professional Touring Bi...	1
280	24,000	100,082	10	DXTR2100	Deluxe Touring Bike-Sil...	1
289	24,000	100,082	20	ORMN1100	Men's Off Road Bike Fu...	1
298	24,000	100,082	30	ORHT1110	Men's Off Road Bike Ha...	1
307	24,000	100,082	40	ORHT1120	Men's Off Road Bike Ha...	1
315	18,000	100,107	10	ORMN1100	Men's Off Road Bike Fu...	1
323	18,000	100,107	20	ORHT1110	Men's Off Road Bike Ha...	1
331	18,000	100,107	30	RACA1110	Road Bike Carbon Shim...	1

Figure 8.51 Joining the Product Table to the Sales Data

Join Type	Result	Use	Comments
Inner	Rows where there is at least one match in *both* tables—if left unspecified, a join is executed as an inner join.	Dimensional and cube-based calculation views.	In the specific case where there is a filter on a field in the right table, but no field from the right table is requested, the filter isn't taken into account. The reason is that, if no field of the right table is requested, the join engine skips this table for performance reasons.
Referential	An inner join where referential integrity is assumed. (The default join type in the graphical interface for view definitions)	Same as for inner join. For example, for joins between item and header data for documents (a header record always exists for any item record) or for joins between different levels of the same master data, such as plant/material and material general data.	Can be faster than an inner join because the right table isn't checked when no column from the right table is requested. In that specific case, note that the join engine doesn't check the right table, and even if an entry in the right table is missing, the row from the left table is still returned. In this case, this join type behaves more like a left outer join. If the join *must* always be executed as inner, use the type INNER JOIN instead. (See the "Referential Join Types" box following this table.)
Left outer	All rows from the left table, even if there is no match in the right table.	Analytic views, to join fact table as left table to attribute views as right table. Cardinality in that case should be set to N:1.	This is the join type used between the fact table and dimensions in a basic star schema (e.g., "Even if no entry exists for product *x* in the product dimension, show all the facts in the output").

Table 8.3 Summary of Supported Join Types

Join Type	Result	Use	Comments
Right outer	All rows from the right table, even if there is no match in the left table.	Rarely used. Potential use is in calculation views to display all master data values even if there are no facts in the fact table for them.	For example, when joining customer master data (right table) with sales documents (left table), this join would display all customers, even the ones who did *not* buy anything. Typically used in the type of scenario, "Give me all customers/products/ ... with no sales last period" and so on.
Full	All rows from both tables, regardless of whether they match.	Rarely used. Potential use is to check master data relationships.	For example, when joining customers with customer account managers, this join gives all customers (even if no account manager is assigned) and all account managers (even if they have no customers assigned). May be useful to verify the accuracy of master data relationships.
Text	Retrieves descriptions for codes, for example, material descriptions, and so on.	To join text tables, especially if they are language dependent. Can retrieve descriptions based on the language the user is logged in with.	Text joins can only be used in dimensional calculation views; they are not supported in cube-based calculation views.

Table 8.3 Summary of Supported Join Types (Cont.)

Referential Join Types

An exception to the exception mentioned in Table 8.1 is when a referential join is executed outside of an analytic view—in which case the OLAP engine is bypassed, and only the join engine is used. In this case, this join will always execute as an inner join.

8.3.2 Temporal and Spatial Joins

Temporal joins are a recent addition to SAP HANA, in SPS 11. Temporal joins enable the joining of master data to fact tables based on the time data from the transaction and a specified validity time from the master data. For example, consider the case where a product's master data contains validity dates. If our sales data contains the product identifier, the date of the transaction, and the revenue for the transaction, we can use a temporal join to join the transaction to the product masterdata that was valid on a given date.

Spatial joins are also a recent addition to SAP HANA, in SPS 11. Spatial joins may be used with the following data types:

▶ **Geometries**
This includes points, linestrings, and polygons. Geometries are the super type for all spatial data types.

▶ **Points**
This is a single location in space, without length or area. Points always consist of X and Y coordinates. Points are generally used for addresses or geographic features.

▶ **Multipoints**
This is a collection of individual points, generally used to specify a set of locations.

Spatial joins allow the implementation of numerous methods that are useful in geospatial applications. The complete list of supported spatial methods is provided in Table 8.4.

Spatial Method	Description
ST_WithinDistance	Determines if two geometries are within a specific distance of one another.
ST_Within	Determines if one geometry is within the spatial area covered by another geometry.
ST_Touches	Determines if a geometry touches the area of another geometry.
ST_Relate	Uses an intersection matrix to determine if one geometry value is related to another. Uses a 9-character string from the DE-9IM to describe the relationship between two specific spatial terms.

Table 8.4 Spatial Methods Supported for Analyzing Spatial Geometries

Spatial Method	Description
ST_Intersects	Determines if one geometry value has a spatial intersection with another.
ST_Overlaps	Determines if a geometry value overlaps with another.
ST_Equals	Determines if the spatial value of one geometry is equal to another.
ST_Disjoint	Determines if a geometry value is disjoint with another.
ST_Covers	Determines if one geometry value spatially covers another.
ST_Crosses	Determines if one geometry value crosses another.
ST_CoveredBy	Determines if a geometry value is spatially covered by another.
ST_Contains	Determines if one geometry value spatially contains another.

Table 8.4 Spatial Methods Supported for Analyzing Spatial Geometries (Cont.)

8.3.3 Aggregation Nodes

Aggregation nodes are used to summarize the data in a column for a given group of row values. For example, consider the problem of calculating the total sales for a store within a month. Before the release of SAP HANA, you had to store aggregate tables with this data precalculated to enable fast reporting. Now, by passing the values through an aggregation node, the totals for the month for a given store can be calculated on the fly in the SAP HANA in-memory computing engine (IMCE).

When you use a calculation view with an aggregation node in your reporting layer, you'll only need to connect to the view and filter the report values to the selected store and time period. The aggregation node will deliver aggregated values to the reporting layer, based on the granularity you specified in your report and the aggregation type you selected in your cube-based calculation view.

In early releases of SAP HANA, you were limited to sum, min, and max aggregation types; however, SAP HANA SPS 11 and higher supports the following types of aggregation, as shown in Figure 8.52:

▸ SUM
Summarizes the values for the column, based on the granularity selected in the reporting layer.

▸ MIN
The minimum value for the column, based on the granularity selected in the reporting layer.

► MAX

The maximum value for the column, based on the granularity selected in the reporting layer.

► AVG

The average of the values in the column, based on the granularity selected in the reporting layer.

► COUNT

The number of rows in the column, based on the granularity selected in the reporting layer.

► STDDEV

The standard deviation from the norm of the values in the column, based on the granularity selected in the reporting layer.

► VAR

The variance from the norm for the values in the column, based on the granularity selected in the reporting layer.

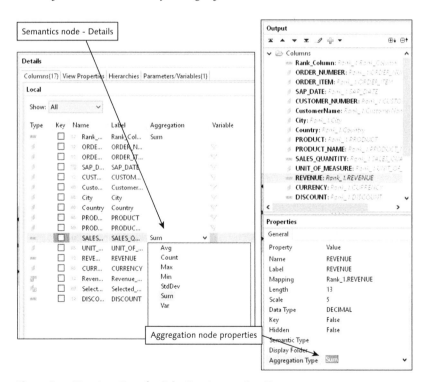

Figure 8.52 Two Locations for Selecting Aggregation Type

You can select the type of aggregation in one of two locations, either in the column PROPERTIES of the aggregation node (usually located below the OUTPUT pane), or in the AGGREGATION column of the semantics node (Figure 8.52). In either location, you simply need to click the dropdown arrow and select the aggregation type for the measure from the types listed earlier.

You can add aggregation nodes to your view in the same way as projection nodes, joins, or unions. Like projection nodes, aggregation nodes only accept one input. You can also create calculated key figures, filters, input parameters, and restricted columns in aggregation nodes.

8.3.4 Rank Nodes

Rank nodes are another recent addition to SAP HANA data modeling, added in SAP HANA SPS 10. With rank nodes, you can do things like returning the top five stores for a region based on sales. You can partition the data based on one column or a set of columns and also order the results based on a column.

Rank nodes are added to views in the same way that projection nodes, joins, and unions are added. You simply select the RANK node from the PALETTE in the SCENARIOS pane and drop it in the view. Like aggregation nodes and calculation nodes, rank nodes accept only one input.

Next, you'll need to select your input for the node, either by connecting a lower node or by adding an object through the context menu for the rank node. With the input added to the node, you'll need to select SORT DIRECTION from the RANK NODE configuration pane. You can choose DESCENDING(TOP N) to rank the columns by the top values or ASCENDING(BOTTOM N) to rank the columns by the lowest values.

Now, enter a THRESHOLD value for the rank node. This threshold will limit the results to the number of results you specify by partition. You'll also need to select an ORDER BY column. We chose REVENUE in our example (Figure 8.53). You may partition by one or more columns, so we chose to partition by PRODUCT_CATEGORY and PRODUCT. You can choose the DYNAMIC PARTITION ELEMENTS checkbox to limit the partitioning to only the columns that are requested in a query for this view. If you do not make this selection, the query will partition the ranking by all the columns selected in the RANK NODE properties, regardless of whether or not the column is actually requested in the query. Finally, you may want to select the GENERATE RANK COLUMN checkbox in order to add a column displaying the rank for a given row.

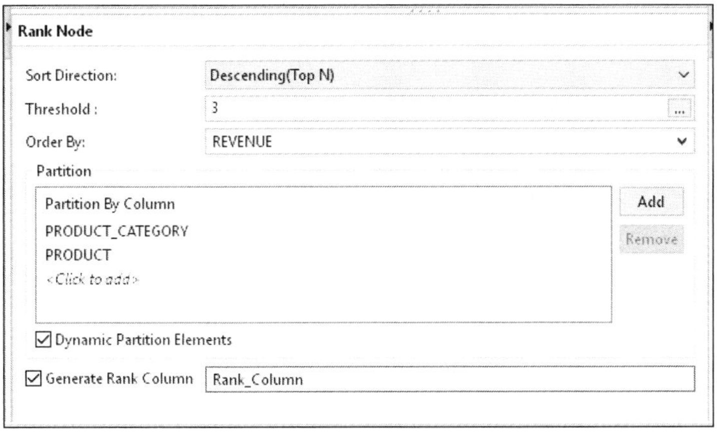

Figure 8.53 Configuring a Rank Node in a Calculation View

8.3.5   Currency Conversions

Most of the amounts in any given fact table are expressed in one specific currency. For example, in SAP ERP tables, links between any monetary amount field and its currency are mandatory and explicit. Converting currencies is a necessary function for many reporting scenarios, and SAP HANA offers the ability to do this as part of the modeling of the cube-based calculation views.

In general, to convert an amount to a different currency, you must specify the following:

► Source currency

► Target currency, either fixed or with the use of an input parameter

► Date you want to use as the exchange rate between the two currencies

Additionally, you must of course have the necessary tables in the system to store the exchange rates. For an SAP ERP system, the following tables must be replicated to SAP HANA:

► TCURR
  Exchange rates

► TCURV
  Exchange rate types

► TCURF
  Conversion factors

- ▶ TCURN

  Quotations

- ▶ TCURX

  Currency decimal settings

In order to use the conversion tables, you need to specify the DEFAULT SCHEMA for the view in the VIEW PROPERTIES. The best place to perform currency conversions in SAP HANA is in the cube-based calculation view, where the conversion can be done using the graphical interface.

Measures in SAP HANA have their own type. By default, all measures are defined by the system as SIMPLE and can be used as standalone fields, without a currency or unit attached to them, which is different from the SAP ERP concept of measure definition. However, you can establish the same link between the amount field and its associated currency field as exists in SAP ERP by changing the measure type to AMOUNT WITH CURRENCY, which is a necessary step in enabling currency conversion for the measure.

To perform currency conversions for a measure, follow these steps:

1. Ensure you're in the SYSTEMS tab of the SAP HANA development perspective.

2. Open the calculation view that contains the measure.

3. Click on the measure in the OUTPUT section of the screen.

4. Select the SEMANTIC TYPE field property by clicking in the PROPERTIES PANE of this entry and then clicking on the small ellipsis button at the right.

5. When the SEMANTICS FOR <COLUMN_NAME> window opens, change the semantic type to AMOUNT WITH CURRENCY CODE. A new section of the window will open (Figure 8.54) called CURRENCY, along with four checkboxes: DECIMAL SHIFT, CONVERSION, ROUNDING, and DECIMAL SHIFT BACK.

6. Check the CONVERSION checkbox, which will make the fields needed to specify the conversion parameters editable.

7. Specify the SCHEMA FOR CURRENCY CONVERSION, if you didn't set the default schema when you created the view.

8. Specify the CLIENT FOR CURRENCY CONVERSION, unless your company sets a session client for the users as part of their account creation policy. If session clients are already set for the user, then you can leave this set to SESSION CLIENT.

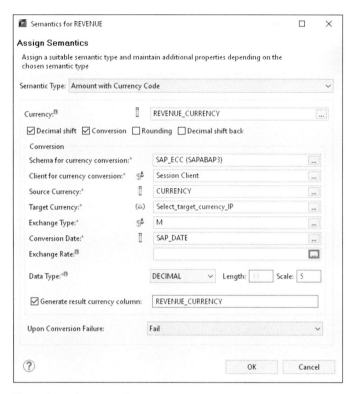

Figure 8.54 Creating a Currency Conversion

9. Specify the SOURCE CURRENCY in one of the following two ways:

   ‣ As a FIXED source currency, for example, EUR.

   ‣ As a COLUMN from the view, for example, VBAP.WAERK for a sales document currency.

10. Specify the TARGET CURRENCY in one of following three ways:

    ‣ As a FIXED target currency, for example, USD.

    ‣ As a COLUMN from the view, for example, T001.WAERS for company code currency.

    ‣ As an INPUT PARAMETER, which prompts the user to choose the target currency. (See later in this section for how to create such a parameter.)

11. Specify the EXCHANGE TYPE. Many types of exchange rates exist, for example, M for mean daily rate or G for bank buying rate, and so on.

12. Specify the DATE in one of the following three ways:

    ▶ As a FIXED DATE, for example, "12/31/2012."

    ▶ As a COLUMN from the view, for example, VBAK.ERDAT for the sales document creation date.

    ▶ As an INPUT PARAMETER or variable which prompts the user to choose the date, or the value is specified at runtime using a procedure that runs in the background.

13. The system automatically checks the option DECIMAL SHIFT to shift the decimal point to the correct position for specific exchange rate configurations from SAP ERP. Shifting the decimal may be necessary, for example, for specific combinations of from–to currencies among the Japanese yen, the New Taiwan dollar, the Hungarian forint, and the Ukrainian hryvnia, to name a few. Be sure to consult an expert in the configuration of the TCUR* tables in SAP ERP if you use some of the less common currencies.

14. Set the UPON CONVERSION FAILURE option to tell the system how to respond to requests where no exchange rate can be found. Three choices are available:

    ▶ FAIL

    ▶ SET TO NULL

    ▶ IGNORE

15. Set the EXCHANGE RATE to reference one of the columns in the view, if relevant to your conversion scenario. If you're planning to use the conversion tables in the SAP environment, you can be skip this step.

16. Finally, click OK. The currency conversion for the measure has now been defined.

As an example, let's say you need to perform a simple conversion from the document currency to USD, so that aggregation works easily across all reporting levels and so that all reports have an apples-to-apples view of sales amounts. To create a currency variable for the target currency in currency translation, follow these steps:

1. Navigate to and open the calculation view in which you want to define an input parameter variable.

2. In the OUTPUT section, right-click on the folder INPUT PARAMETERS and choose NEW.

3. When the INPUT PARAMETERS dialog box opens, choose the DATA TYPE to be VARCHAR with LENGTH "5." This step is how currency fields are defined in the TCUR* tables.

4. Choose the TYPE to be CURRENCY.

5. Choose the IS MANDATORY option.

6. Specify a DEFAULT VALUE.

7. Click OK to create the variable.

> **Note**
>
> When you use an input parameter in currency conversion, you must set the parameter as mandatory because the system can't calculate the result of the output measure without it.

The variable is now available in the dialog boxes for currency conversion to use as needed. To use the input parameter for target currency in a measure, select the input parameter as the TARGET CURRENCY when you define the measure type in the measure properties (Figure 8.55).

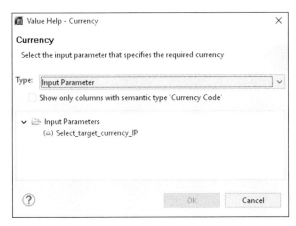

Figure 8.55 Using an Input Parameter as the Target Currency

> **Note**
>
> Before you begin, the DEFAULT SESSION CLIENT must be set for the user master record, which is necessary because the TCUR* tables are client-dependent in SAP ERP.

> ### Linking Measures with Currencies without Using Conversion
>
> The measure type AMOUNT WITH CURRENCY can be used even if you don't want to perform any currency conversion. In such a case, the amount displays with its currency.
>
> Note that, in this case, you set the CURRENCY in the dialog box to the currency the amount is expressed in, but you don't check the CONVERSION option. For example, to always display the sales amount in the document currency, set the CURRENCY to the attribute value VBAP.WAERK, which will automatically set the target currency to VBAP.WAERK as well.
>
> Note that performing a conversion is a different scenario. If you do want conversion, for example, from the document currency to the company code currency, you specify the document currency VBAP.WAERK as the *source* currency and the company code currency T001.WAERS as the target currency using the CURRENCY field.
>
> In other words, whichever currency is specified in the CURRENCY field in the dialog box is always the output currency for the measure. If you want to output the amount in its original currency, specify the source currency in the SOURCE CURRENCY field and leave the CONVERSION checkbox blank. The source currency will also become the target currency for output. If you want to output the amount in any other currency, check the CONVERSION checkbox, specify the target currency in the TARGET CURRENCY field, and specify the original currency as the SOURCE CURRENCY.

You should now have enough information to get started with native SAP HANA data modeling, but make sure you check the SAP Community Network forums often for more information, as the Eclipse-based interface of SAP HANA Studio is being extended and enhanced to provide a more flexible and powerful development environment. Next, we'll take a look at building cross-platform data consumption models to combine SAP BW and non-SAP BW data with the SAP BW Modeling Tool.

8.4   SAP BW Modeling Tool for SAP HANA Studio

To facilitate the integration of traditional SAP BW InfoObjects with native SAP HANA data models, SAP created a plug-in for SAP HANA Studio called the SAP BW modeling tools. The SAP BW modeling tools are used to create cross-platform data consumption models, including:

- Open Operational Data Store (ODS) views
- CompositeProviders
- Advanced DataStore Objects (aDSOs)

▸ SAP BW queries

▸ InfoObjects

Please note that the SAP BW modeling tools were first available for use with SAP BW 7.40 SP 5 or higher, but you'll need SAP BW 7.5 on SAP HANA in order to create InfoObjects in SAP HANA Studio.

When you're ready to install the SAP BW modeling tools plug-in for SAP HANA Studio, navigate to FILE • HELP • INSTALL NEW SOFTWARE. You'll need to enter the URL or folder location for the plug-in, and then you'll be presented with a list of plug-ins available for download. See the *Installation Guide for Modeling Tools for SAP BW powered by SAP HANA – SAP BW Modeling Tools 1.14* for a complete guide on installing the SAP BW modeling tools.

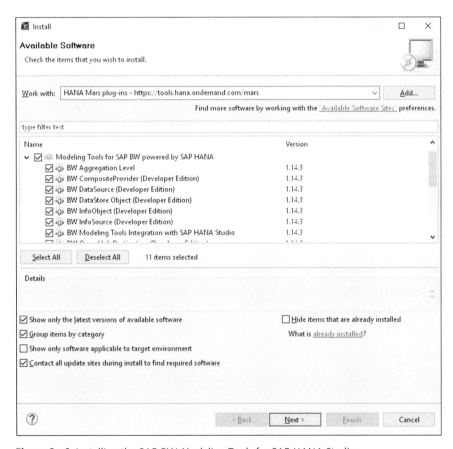

Figure 8.56 Installing the SAP BW Modeling Tools for SAP HANA Studio

To download the latest version of the SAP BW modeling tools, as of August 2016, go to *https://tools.hana.ondemand.com/mars*. Select MODELING TOOLS FOR SAP BW POWERED BY SAP HANA from the list of available plug-ins (Figure 8.56). Click NEXT, and you'll see the INSTALL DETAILS window (Figure 8.57) with a list of all the components that will be installed. Click NEXT on this screen, and you'll be prompted to accept the license agreement(s) for any plug-ins. Accept the conditions and click FINISH to install the plug-in components.

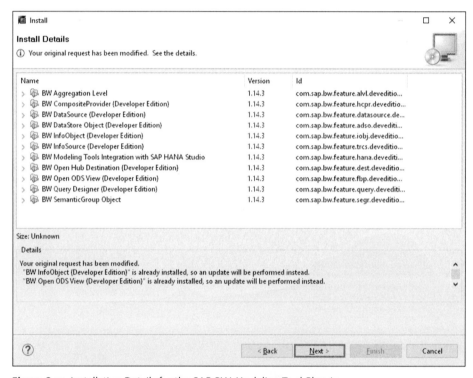

Figure 8.57 Installation Details for the SAP BW Modeling Tool Plug-In

With the SAP BW modeling tools installed, you can switch to the perspective by navigating to WINDOW • PERSPECTIVE • OPEN PERSPECTIVE • OTHER in the SAP HANA Studio FILE menu. Select BW MODELING from the OPEN PERSPECTIVE window and click OK to switch to the SAP BW modeling perspective.

To create a new SAP BW project, select NEW • PROJECT from the right-click context menu of the PROJECT EXPLORER tab. Select BW PROJECT from the BUSINESS WAREHOUSE folder in the NEW PROJECT window and click NEXT. You'll be presented with the same list of SYSTEM CONNECTIONS that you have configured in your SAP logon application for the SAP Graphical User Interface (SAP GUI). Select a connection from the list and click NEXT. Confirm your connection settings are configured correctly and click NEXT again.

Next, specify the CLIENT, USER, PASSWORD, and LANGUAGE for the connection and click NEXT. Enter a PROJECT NAME for the connection and click FINISH to create a new project connected to the system you selected. The project will be available in the PROJECT EXPLORER tab.

When you expand the project folder, you should see a list of FAVORITES as well as the BW REPOSITORY. When you expand the repository, you should see a list of the current InfoObjects in your SAP BW system (Figure 8.58).

Figure 8.58 InfoObjects in the SAP BW Repository in the SAP BW Modeling Tool

A comprehensive exploration of SAP BW modeling is beyond the scope of this book; however, we'll provide a brief overview of how to create CompositeProviders, aDSOs, and Open ODS views in the following sections. These three object types were specifically created to allow the integration of SAP BW data with external data sources, such as SAP ERP and external data marts. SAP offers the BW310H course, a comprehensive 5-day training course covering enterprise data warehousing on SAP HANA.

8.4.1 CompositeProviders

To create a new CompositeProvider, expand the InfoArea where you want to create the new object. Right-click the COMPOSITEPROVIDER folder and select NEW • COMPOSITEPROVIDER from the context menu. If you used the context menu for your new project and InfoArea, the BW PROJECT and INFOAREA should be selected by default. For convenience, you may consider selecting the ADD TO FAVORITES checkbox to make the new object easy to find in your FAVORITES in both SAP HANA Studio and the Developer Workbench in SAP BW.

Enter a NAME and DESCRIPTION for your new CompositeProvider. You can also COPY FROM existing objects, if you want to make a copy of an existing object and modify the copy. When you're satisfied with your selections, you can click FINISH to create the CompositeProvider, or you can click NEXT to advance to the SELECT PARTPROVIDER OBJECTS window.

If you click NEXT, you can select data providers to join or union in your new object. You can add, remove, and reorder objects using the ADD, REMOVE, UP, and DOWN buttons. Click FINISH to create the CompositeProvider.

The new object will open in the editor of the SAP HANA BW modeling perspective (Figure 8.59). From here, you can configure general object settings in the GENERAL tab. You can use the SCENARIO tab to select your join or union conditions and map your data as a target for the CompositeProvider. You can select navigational attributes and configure the presentation layer for your new object in the OUTPUT tab.

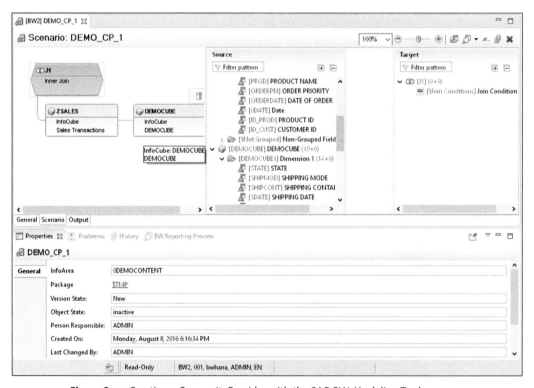

Figure 8.59 Creating a CompositeProvider with the SAP BW Modeling Tool

> **Note**
>
> Make sure you enable the option to create the object as an EXTERNAL SAP HANA VIEW if you want to create a view for consumption in your reporting tools as a native SAP HANA data model. For example, this scenario is often used to enable consumption of data from an external data mart, either virtually using SDA, SDI, SAP HANA smart data streaming (SDS), or physically with a sidecar schema or multitenant database.

When you've finished configuring the output for the CompositeProvider, click the ACTIVATE BW OBJECT icon in the toolbar to activate the object and make it available for use in SAP BW queries.

8.4.2 Advanced DataStore Objects

To create an aDSO, right-click the DATASTORE OBJECTED (ADVANCED) folder for your selected INFOAREA and select NEW DATASTORE OBJECT (ADVANCED) from the context menu. The NEW DATASTORE OBJECT (ADVANCED) window will open (Figure 8.60), and the BW PROJECT and INFOAREA should be selected by default. You can select the ADD TO FAVORITES checkbox to add the new object to your favorites in both SAP BW and in the SAP BW modeling tools in SAP HANA Studio.

Enter a NAME and DESCRIPTION for the new aDSO, in accordance with your company's established naming conventions. You can COPY FROM another aDSO if you want to copy and modify an existing object.

You'll also have the option to select from several template choices, including:

▶ NONE
No template is used.

▶ DATASOURCE
The template uses an existing data source as a template by selecting the SOURCE SYSTEM and DATASOURCE.

▶ INFOPROVIDER
The template is based on an existing InfoProvider.

When you're satisfied with your selections, click FINISH to create the new aDSO, which will be opened in the editor

Figure 8.60 Creating a New aDSO with the SAP BW Modeling Tool

From the GENERAL tab, you can select EXTERNAL SAP HANA VIEW to automatically create a calculation view based on the new object when the object is activated. You can configure the ACTIVATION options and SPECIAL TYPES characteristics, and you can even select a MODEL TEMPLATE for the aDSO. If you have a dynamic tiering server running for your SAP HANA system, you can enable the SAP HANA DYNAMIC TIERING checkbox. From the DETAILS tab, you can add and delete fields, InfoObjects, and groups to the output for the aDSO. You can also MANAGE KEYS and MAINTAIN PROPERTIES for the objects. From the SETTINGS tab, you can configure the partitioning and indexing for the aDSO, and you can even specify the HASH PARTITION CRITERIA to use.

When you've finished configuring the output for the aDSO, click the ACTIVATE BW OBJECT icon in the toolbar to activate the object and make it available for use in SAP BW queries.

8.4.3 Open ODS Views

Open ODS views allow you to create SAP BW data models for tables, views and SAP BW DataSources. Using Open ODS Views, you can integrate external data sources with SAP BW data without the need to stage or load the external data to the SAP BW system. As a result, cross-platform data consumption is possible, which is typically used for integrating supplemental data from external data marts or SAP HANA sidecar scenarios.

> **Note**
>
> Open ODS views are available as long as the SAP BW system is on SAP HANA but cannot be defined for hierarchies.

To create an Open ODS view, right-click your selected InfoArea and select New Open ODS View from the context menu. The New Open ODS View window will open, and the BW Project and InfoArea should be selected by default. You can also select the Add to Favorites button to add the new object to your Favorites in SAP BW and in SAP HANA Studio.

Next, you'll need to enter a Name and Description for the new open ODS view, in accordance with your company's established naming conventions. If you select the Create with Proposal checkbox, the field definitions for the view will be created based upon the structure of the underlying data source. You can use the Copy From dialogue to select an existing open ODS view to copy and modify.

You can choose from the following Semantics types for the open ODS view:

▶ Facts

▶ Master Data

▶ Texts

You can also specify the Source Type as one of the following:

▶ Database Table or View

▶ DataSource (BW)

▶ Transformation

▶ DataStore Object (advanced)

After you select the SOURCE TYPE, you'll need to select the DATASOURCE from the NEXT screen. When you're satisfied with your selections, click FINISH to create the open ODS view and open it in the editor.

8.5   SAP HANA Web-Based Development Workbench

The SAP HANA Web-Based Development Workbench offers a browser-based alternative to SAP HANA Studio. One of the advantages to developing with the workbench is that developers and administrators can complete many of the same development tasks that are possible through SAP HANA Studio, without the need to download and install a separate application. Instead, developers and administrators can login to the workbench to complete their tasks, and the SAP HANA Cockpit will provide any of the remaining administrative functionality that has traditionally been handled through SAP HANA Studio. While the SAP HANA Web-Based Development Workbench has been improved and extended in recent revisions of SAP HANA, and in some areas even improves on the functionality of SAP HANA Studio, some features are still in development, so you should consider the workbench and SAP HANA Studio as useful complements to one another. You'll need at least SAP HANA SPS 7 to take advantage of the SAP HANA Web-Based Development Workbench.

The SAP HANA Web-Based Development Workbench can be accessed through your web browser at *http://<HANA_server>:80<instance>/sap/hana/ide/editor/*. Navigate to this page in your web browser, and you'll be required to login. Please be aware that your user account will need to have some prerequisite roles assigned to it in order to access the workbench. See Table 8.5 for a listing of the required roles for using relevant sections of the workbench.

Required Role	Workbench Section	Description
sap.hana.ide.roles:: EditorDeveloper	Editor	Create, change, delete, activate, and view SAP HANA data objects.
sap.hana.xs.debugger:: Debugger		Debug server-side JavaScript.

Table 8.5 Required Roles for the SAP HANA Web-Based Development Workbench

Required Role	Workbench Section	Description
`sap.hana.ide.roles:: CatalogDeveloper`	Catalog	Create, execute, edit, and manage SQL artifacts in the SAP HANA database catalog.
`Sap.hana.ide.roles:: SecurityAdmin`	Security	Create and modify users and user roles.
`Sap.hana.ide.roles:: TraceViewer`	Traces	View and save SAP HANA trace files. Configure trace levels.

Table 8.5 Required Roles for the SAP HANA Web-Based Development Workbench (Cont.)

As shown in Figure 8.61, the workbench consists of the following sections:

▶ EDITOR

This section is roughly analogous to the old SAP HANA modeler perspective and allow you to create and edit packages, calculation views, analytic privileges, flow graphs, replication tasks, and procedures.

▶ CATALOG

This section is used for managing catalog objects and provisioning connections to data sources.

▶ SECURITY

This section is like the SECURITY folder of the SYSTEMS tab in the SAP HANA development perspective and allows you to create and manage users and roles.

▶ TRACES

This section is analogous to the DIAGNOSIS FILES and PERFORMANCE tracing sections of the SAP HANA Administration Console and allows you to view, download, and modify traces in the SAP HANA system.

▶ LIFECYCLE MANAGEMENT

This section allows you to comprehensively manage many SAP HANA systems features including product instances, delivery units, and transport management.

To help you become familiar with the SAP HANA Web-Based Development Workbench, we'll take a brief look at the CATALOG, SECURITY, and TRACES sections of the workbench before finishing the chapter with a detailed look at the EDITOR. The LIFECYCLE MANAGEMENT section of the SAP HANA Web-Based Development Workbench is covered in Chapter 10.

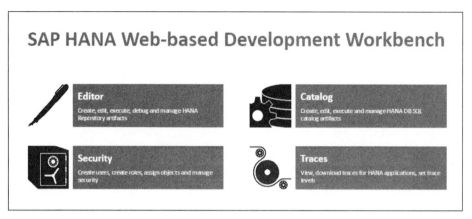

Figure 8.61 The SAP HANA Web-Based Development Workbench

> **Note**
>
> As you may recall from our discussion of migrating attribute and analytic views Section 8.1.4, the latest guidance from SAP recommends not developing those views and recommends instead migrating your existing attribute and analytic views to calculation views. In service of this objective, the EDITOR in the SAP HANA Web-Based Development Workbench does not offer the ability to create analytic or attribute views.
>
> Be aware that calculation views with rank nodes are supported in the SAP HANA Web-Based Development Workbench; however, rank output columns are not currently supported in the graphical editor, so if your calculation view has a rank node and an automatically generated rank output column, you'll need to edit the view in SAP HANA Studio or using the text editor for the view's XML.

8.5.1   Catalog

The CATALOG section of the workbench (Figure 8.62) is quite flexible and allows you to manage catalog objects in your SAP HANA system. From the CATALOG, you can create new schemas, sequences, and connections to remote sources. You can use the SQL Console to execute SQL scripts, just like in the SQL Console in SAP HANA Studio. You can even use the context menu for a catalog object to generate the creation, insertion, and selection SQL for that object.

The toolbar at the top of the CATALOG window will change to offer different options according to the type of object you select in the navigation pane. If you select a table, you can use the OPEN CONTENT button on the toolbar to view a data preview of the contents for a data source, and the EDIT SQL STATEMENT WITH SQL

CONSOLE can be used to generate the SQL script for the data preview and edit it to refine your query. You can also use the WHERE-USED BROWSER to locate any objects that are dependent on the catalog object you've selected.

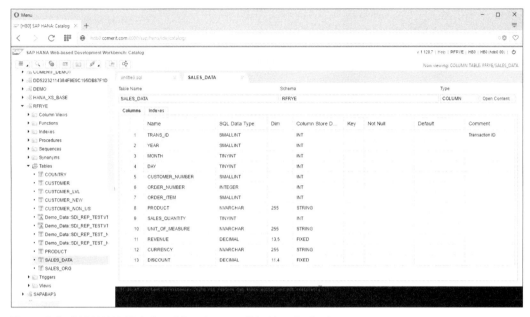

Figure 8.62 SAP HANA Web-Based Development Workbench: Catalog

From the SQL Console, you can use the RUN button to execute the SQL you've written, and you can also SAVE the script to be used later. You can apply formatting to your SQL script with the FORMAT CODE button and download a .SQL file to your local machine with the DOWNLOAD button.

To summarize, many of the functions available in the CATALOG window are nearly identical to their counterparts in SAP HANA Studio, so if you're already familiar with SAP HANA Studio, using this section of the workbench will be easy.

8.5.2 Security

The SECURITY section of the workbench (Figure 8.63) is used for creating users and roles within the system. You can edit existing users and roles, and you can use the OPEN SECURITY CONSOLE button to configure the auditing and password policies for the system.

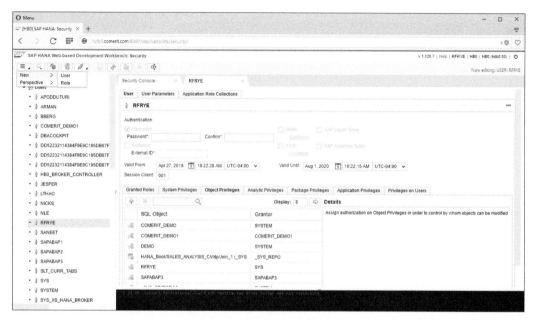

Figure 8.63 SAP HANA Web-Based Development Workbench: Security

The screen for creating and editing users is nearly identical to the same screen in SAP HANA Studio. You can add, modify, and delete the GRANTED ROLES, SYSTEM PRIVILEGES, OBJECT PRIVILEGES, ANALYTIC PRIVILEGES, PACKAGE PRIVILEGES, and APPLICATION PRIVILEGES and attach a debugger to a user with PRIVILEGES ON USERS. You can also perform password maintenance for users, including password changes, activating and deactivating user accounts, and configuring single sign-on (SSO) parameters.

In short, if you're familiar with maintaining the security settings for your SAP HANA system through SAP HANA Studio, the SECURITY section of the workbench will be familiar and easy to use.

8.5.3 Traces

The TRACE section of the SAP HANA Web-Based Development Workbench is simple and intuitive—in some ways more convenient—to use for tracing problems than SAP HANA Studio. When you click the TRACES link on the workbench, the TRACE window will open (Figure 8.64), and you'll be presented with a comprehensive list of the trace files that are available for your SAP HANA system.

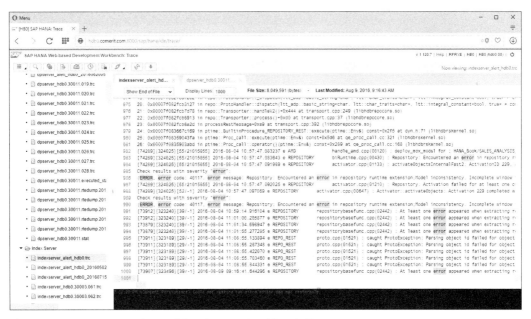

Figure 8.64 SAP HANA Web-Based Development Workbench: Traces

Clicking the trace file will open the file in the DETAILS pane of the browser window, where the convenient addition of keyword highlighting greatly simplifies the process of identifying problems within the system. Errors are highlighted in pink, and failed messages are highlighted in yellow.

> **Note**
>
> The TRACES section of the workbench is one of the simplest and most useful additions to the SAP HANA landscape. This feature allows you to quickly and easily identify problems within any log file, so bookmark the workbench URL (*http://<hana_server>:80<instance>/sap/hana/ide/*) for your system and use the TRACES section as your default solution for viewing trace files.

You can also use the CONFIGURATION button to modify the system traces within your SAP HANA environment. You can use the CONFIGURATION button to modify the following traces:

▶ XS APPLICATION TRACE

▶ DATABASE TRACE

▶ EXPENSIVE STATEMENTS TRACE

► SQL TRACE

► PLAN TRACE

To summarize, the TRACES section of the workbench is a powerful addition to the SAP HANA landscape, as it makes configuring the system traces and locating and analyzing problems much easier.

8.5.4 Editor

If you're a developer, the editor in the SAP HANA Web-Based Development Workbench is a good alternative to developing data models and other content in SAP HANA Studio. As this chapter is devoted to modeling in SAP HANA, we'll take a close look at some examples data modeling examples in this section. You'll see much that is familiar, although these items may look a bit different, and the methods for getting things done may differ in some ways.

The process for creating objects using the workbench editor is quite similar to the process used in SAP HANA Studio. Open the editor by clicking the EDITOR link from the SAP HANA WEB-BASED DEVELOPMENT WORKBENCH (Figure 8.61). The editor will open with a list of content packages available for editing (Figure 8.65).

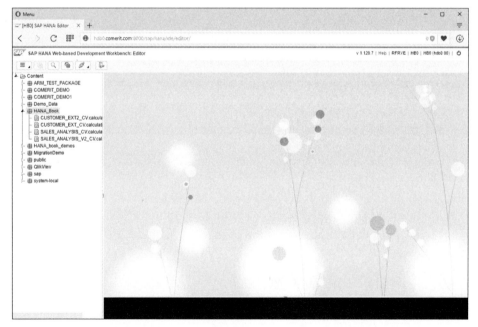

Figure 8.65 SAP HANA Web-Based Development Workbench: Editor

To create a new package, right-click the CONTENT folder and select NEW • PACK-AGE. As an alternative, you can use ⟨Ctrl⟩+⟨Alt⟩+⟨Shift⟩+⟨N⟩ to create a new package. The CREATE PACKAGE dialogue will open in the browser window (Figure 8.66). Enter a PACKAGE NAME and DESCRIPTION in accordance with your company's naming standards. You can also designate the person RESPONSIBLE for the package and the ORIGINAL LANGUAGE for the content. Click CREATE to create the new package.

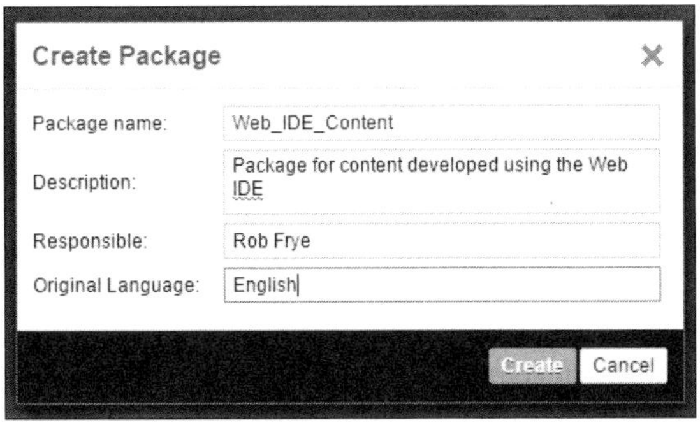

Figure 8.66 Creating a New Package with the SAP HANA Web-Based Development Workbench

Follow these steps to create a new calculation view in the editor:

1. Right-click the package where you want to create the view in the navigation pane and select NEW • CALCULATION VIEW from the context menu.

2. Enter a NAME and LABEL (description) for the view, in accordance with your company's naming standards for calculation views.

3. Select the TYPE of view that you want to create from the following options:

   ▹ STANDARD

   ▹ TIME

4. Select either the GRAPHICAL or SCRIPT radio button to determine which editor is required for creating the view.

5. Select the DATA CATEGORY for the view from the following choices:

   ▹ NONE (Leave this blank to create a private or reuse view)

   ▹ CUBE

   ▹ DIMENSION

For a detailed explanation of the settings for views, including data categories, view types, node types, and which choices are appropriate for your modeling scenarios, see Section 8.2 and Section 8.3 in this chapter.

6. (Optional) Select WITH STAR JOIN to create a view with a star-schema design.

7. Click CREATE to open the view (Figure 8.67).

New Calculation View

Name *	Sales_Analysis_CV
Label	Sales analysis calculation view - Web
Type	STANDARD
	⦿ Graphical ○ Script
Data Category	CUBE
	☐ With Star Join

Create   Cancel

Figure 8.67 Creating a Calculation View with the Workbench

The new calculation view will be opened in the DETAILS pane of the browser. The layout for creating a calculation view is similar to the layout from SAP HANA Studio, so if you're familiar with SAP HANA Studio, learning to use the SAP HANA Web-Based Development Workbench will cause you little trouble; however, a few differences are worth noting, so let's take a look at some of the similarities and differences.

The default inactivity timeout for the SAP HANA Web-Based Development Workbench is rather low. We recommend changing your settings in the editor to enable periodic autosaving on the local client to prevent losing work in the event of an unexpected timeout.

Compare the layout for a calculation view in the SAP HANA Web-Based Development Workbench (Figure 8.68) to the layout for SAP HANA Studio (Figure 8.69). In the web-based editor, the node types are displayed across the top of the scenarios pane, as are the controls for expanding and collapsing the nodes, deleting nodes, and automatically arranging the layout. In SAP HANA Studio, the node palette is arranged vertically along the left side of the SCENARIOS pane, and the other controls are in the bottom right of the pane.

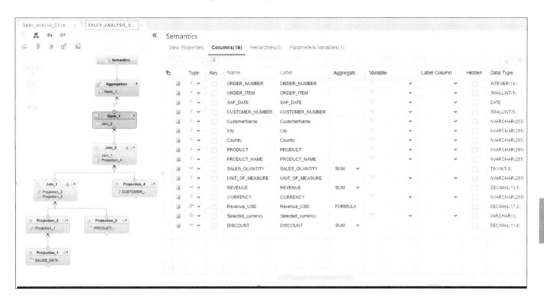

Figure 8.68 SAP HANA Web-Based Development Workbench: Calculation View

Figure 8.69 SAP HANA Studio: Calculation View

On the other hand, the DETAILS pane in SAP HANA Studio aligns rather closely with the details in the SAP HANA Web-Based Development Workbench. The order of tabs is different, but the modeling options are quite similar. In the VIEW PROPERTIES tab, SAP HANA Studio offers more options than the SAP HANA Web-Based Development Workbench, so if you need to deprecate a view, in the current landscape, you'll need to do so through SAP HANA Studio.

In the PARAMETERS/VARIABLES tab, the SAP HANA Web-Based Development Workbench offers more functionality when compared to the same tab in SAP HANA Studio. In SAP HANA Studio, only the name, label, value help column, and conversion function are available, but in the SAP HANA Web-Based Development Workbench, the details for the input parameters are available for review and editing.

> **Note**
>
> When comparing the SAP HANA Studio to the SAP HANA Web-Based Development Workbench, the bottom line is that both compare favorably to one another. You'll need to experiment with each to see which you prefer, and in the end, you're likely to find that the answer is a mix of the two.

The process of adding nodes through the workbench editor is quite similar to the process in SAP HANA Studio; however, the context menu for the nodes is currently rather limited. In SAP HANA Studio, once you've added a node to the view, you can add a table or view to the node through the right-click context menu, but you'll need to select the node and click the green + button to add an object to a node in the SAP HANA Web-Based Development Workbench (Figure 8.70). If you try to use the context menu for an empty node, the only option you'll have is to REMOVE the node.

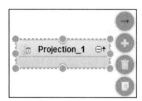

Figure 8.70 SAP HANA Web-Based Development Workbench: Node Controls

You can delete a selected object in the view with the delete icon (the trashcan) in the upper left or in the selection toolbar. You can also add comments to the nodes using the note icon. These actions are explained in Section 8.2.1 in detail, so we won't review them here.

The method for connecting nodes is a bit different in the SAP HANA Web-Based Development Workbench. To connect nodes or join columns, you'll need to select the source to highlight it, which will cause the selection toolbar to display the connection icon (an arrow). Next, click and hold the arrow button to activate the connection tool. Finally, drag a connection to the target and release the mouse button to create the connection. This process is the same for both node and join connections.

> **Note**
>
> We've found that the choice of browser can affect the functionality of the SAP HANA Web-Based Development Workbench, so if you're having trouble with some of the controls, try a different browser or a different version of the same browser. For example, using drag and drop to add columns to the OUTPUT columns for a projection node worked much better in Internet Explorer than in Opera.

The process for adding output columns is also changed in the SAP HANA Web-Based Development Workbench. Whereas SAP HANA Studio uses the selection orb or the context menu to add a column to the output for a node, you'll need to use the MAPPING tab to select your output columns in the SAP HANA Web-Based Development Workbench. You can either drag a connection from the DATA SOURCES on the left to the OUTPUT COLUMNS on the right, or you can use the context menu for the selected column and select ADD TO OUPUT. You can also select multiple columns by holding either Ctrl or Shift while clicking and then use the ADD TO OUTPUT button at the top of the DATA SOURCES pane to add all of the highlighted columns to the output at once (Figure 8.71).

When you're finished editing the view, click the SAVE icon from the toolbar in the upper left of the editor or simply use the Ctrl+S hotkeys to save and activate the view in SAP HANA. For a data preview of the view, you can click the RUN CALCULATION VIEW icon (the green play button) or press F8 to execute the view and see the raw results as a table in the editor (Figure 8.72).

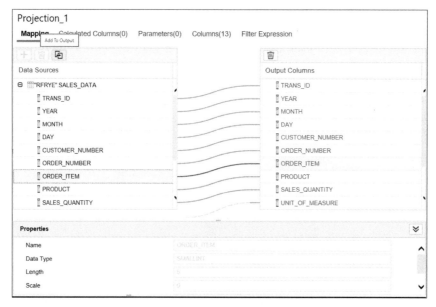

Figure 8.71 Adding Columns to Output with the Mapping Tab

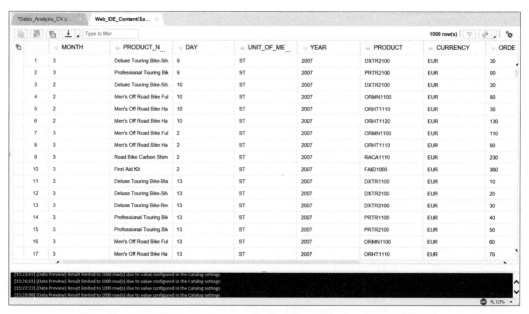

Figure 8.72 SAP HANA Web-Based Development Workbench: Data Preview

8.6   Summary

SAP HANA continues to evolve and adapt into a solution for all your data management needs, and the selection of tools for data modeling with SAP HANA continues to grow and evolve as well. In order to be successful in your endeavors, make sure you pick the tool that is best suited for your project goals. Since the first release of SAP HANA, SAP HANA Studio has been the tool of choice for data modeling, administration, and security, with good reason. SAP HANA Studio is currently the most comprehensive solution for native SAP HANA development, and the addition of plug-ins like the SAP BW Modeling Tool further extend the capabilities of SAP HANA Studio.

On the other hand, SAP is also working to expand your options. The SAP HANA Web-Based Development Workbench provides much of the same functionality that had been traditionally provided by SAP HANA Studio in a convenient, robust, browser-based environment. When coupled with the SAP HANA Cockpit, you can complete most of your SAP HANA modeling and administration tasks without ever opening SAP HANA Studio, so the choice is yours. Give each tool a try to see which best suits your needs, while keeping a close eye on the SAP Community Network forums and the *What's New in SAP HANA* blogs for more information about the next round of exciting changes to SAP HANA waiting just around the corner.

Getting data into your SAP HANA system requires some forethought.
In this chapter, learn what your data provisioning options are and how
to work with them.

9   Data Provisioning

Propagating data in SAP HANA can be done in many ways. In this chapter, we'll go over the main data provisioning tools, including the different options, how they compare, and their installation effort and features. Several fundamental options are as follows:

▶ SAP Landscape Transformation (SLT), also called *trigger-based replication*

▶ SAP Data Services, also called *extract, transform, and load (ETL)-based replication*

▶ SAP (Sybase) Replication Server (RS), also called *log-based replication*

▶ SAP HANA smart data access (SDA)

Any of these options can be used independently, or they can be used in various combinations. Depending on the technical characteristics of the source system and on the desired data provisioning strategy, you can implement the appropriate mechanism for each source of data.

In this chapter, we'll discuss all of these data provisioning mechanisms. In the first section, we'll give you some information that will help you choose which data provisioning model is most appropriate for your business scenario. In the subsequent sections, we'll explain how to perform each of the different methods.

9.1   Choosing a Data Provisioning Method

In the following sections, we will provide a brief overview of the available data provisioning methods before we briefly discuss the strategic and technical considerations that will influence your choice of data provisioning model.

9.1.1   Data Provisioning Methods at a Glance

Each of the main data provisioning mechanisms (Figure 9.1) is fundamentally different from the others. Before we go into the details of each, let's compare and contrast the four options.

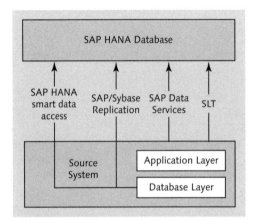

Figure 9.1 Main SAP HANA Data Provisioning Mechanisms

SLT or trigger-based replication is the primary data provisioning mechanism for SAP source systems, such as SAP ERP. When considering SLT replication, here are some key facts to keep in mind:

▸ SLT requires the installation of an SLT Replication Server.

▸ Both data and metadata from tables can be replicated to SAP HANA with this technology.

▸ The SLT Replication Server records any changes to a set of designated tables inside the source system and makes them available to be pulled into the SAP HANA database.

▸ The SLT Replication Server intercepts changes to the tables in the application layer when transactions are executed in SAP ERP by detecting the triggers that are sent to the database to update tables. As a result, this solution is database independent on the SAP ERP side.

▸ The replication of data to SAP HANA can be set up according to a schedule or as a continuous, nearly real-time feed.

▸ You can filter data within a table; for example, when replicating the accounting tables, you can specify which company codes you want the data for and which fields should come across to SAP HANA.

▶ You can also perform limited transformations during the data export from the source system using the SLT Replication Server. More complex transformations are technically possible, but pay special attention to performance with this functionality to avoid impacting replication performance, especially for continuous data feeds that you want to use for operational reporting.

▶ The SLT Replication Server is an ABAP-based technology that leverages several proven system landscape optimization technologies from SAP, which have been updated to work for SAP HANA and thoroughly tested through multiple projects.

▶ The SLT Replication Server can also be used for non-SAP sources that meet some basic database criteria, enabling the SLT Replication Server to capture the changes in the source system.

SAP Data Services/ETL-based replication uses the SAP Data Services technology that is already in place in many implementations. When considering SAP Data Services replication, here are some key facts to keep in mind:

▶ You will have to install the SAP Data Services software component.

▶ The replication can leverage existing extractors, function modules, and programs in the source system.

▶ Both data and metadata can be replicated to SAP HANA with this technology.

▶ Replication of data typically runs on a more traditional batch job schedule, for example, every few hours or once per day.

▶ SAP Data Services is often used to integrate non-SAP source systems into the reporting landscape.

▶ Highly complex transformations and data-cleansing capabilities are possible.

▶ SAP Data Services is a proven, highly stable technology for which many companies already have the necessary tools and skill sets in house.

SAP (Sybase) Replication Server (RS)/log-based replication is a database-specific technology that is available only for specific database systems, namely, the Sybase and IBM DB2 for LUW (Linux, UNIX, and Windows) systems. When considering SAP (Sybase) Replication Server (RS) replication, here are some key facts to keep in mind:

▶ RS starts from the database level, using database log tables to identify any changes to tables in the source system.

- RS is a high-performing, real-time replication technology that bypasses the application layer.

- Because the application layer is bypassed, no opportunities for filtering or transforming data are available; the mapping is one-to-one and at the table level.

- The data is copied to SAP HANA exactly as it had been entered into database tables in the source system. The database commits are essentially replayed on the SAP HANA database.

> **Note**
>
> Although IBM calls its product DB2 for Linux, UNIX, and Windows, in SAP speak, this product is more often than not referred to as DB6. The two are synonymous. SAP uses the name DB6 to distinguish this version of the DB2 database from other versions, such as the version that runs on mainframes.

SAP HANA smart data access (SDA) represents a new paradigm in data provisioning with SAP HANA. Instead of the risk and effort involved in moving data between systems, you can now connect directly to external databases, including Teradata, Netezza, Hadoop, other SAP HANA systems, and many more (see Table 9.7 for a complete list of systems). SDA allows you to embrace the concepts of data federation and virtualization in your data management approach. With SDA, keep the following ideas in mind:

- Data is not copied to the SAP HANA server from external systems.

- Virtual tables are created through SDA connections, which can then be used in native SAP HANA views.

- The relevant Open Database Connectivity (ODBC) drivers must be configured on the SAP HANA server before the connection to the external data source can be created.

- With SDA, you can virtually consolidate your data sources without moving or replicating any data.

From these highlights of the available replication mechanisms, you can see how each differs fundamentally in both technical and functional terms. How do you then decide which scenario you should implement? In general, no precise decision tree exists for this, so we recommend that you spend some time evaluating your data provisioning strategy based on your specific needs.

9.1.2 Strategic Considerations

Strategically, you should always keep in mind both your operational and corporate requirements. Operational requirements are typically granular, real-time or near real-time data provided in (usually) small data sets at a time. Corporate requirements refer to what is typically served by a data warehouse solution. These requirements are typically for higher-level, often cross-process, views of the data and accept (or even demand) some degree of data latency.

You must also consider that you have many different potential sources of data, such as:

▶ SAP systems

▶ Non-SAP systems that run on SAP-supported databases compatible with SLT

▶ Legacy systems on other databases

▶ External data feeds, often provided as files (e.g., comma-delimited files)

▶ Unstructured data

The overall goal is to find the best path from each of the sources to the final delivery of information to end users. For example, for operational reporting requirements, you'll need to identify the sources that are required and then choose the data replication method and system that can satisfy the requirements.

As an exercise and instead of the usual very high-level diagrams that only map the main flows, we'll construct an example diagram with a large number of data flows that cover many of the functional and technical requirements listed previously. The system-level diagram will incorporate many different sources of data and different requirements:

▶ An SAP ERP source system

▶ A non-SAP system with an SLT-compatible database

▶ External data feeds

▶ Unstructured data for use in reporting

▶ A legacy system on an older database version

▶ A requirement to build custom hierarchies for reporting based on multiple sources of data

▶ A requirement to perform complex transformations and data cleansing on some sources

389

The objectives are to maximize the availability of real-time or near real-time data for end users, to provide a consistent presentation of the data in the reporting tools, to maintain internal consistency and coherence of all data used in reporting tools regardless of source, and finally to leverage available technology and connections as much as possible.

In this specific example, you'll make use of SLT and SAP Data Services to get data into the appropriate target systems, but you aren't incorporating SAP/Sybase replication. You can begin with the data flow for operational data from the applicable sources, which is the area where you primarily deploy SAP HANA as a solution. Figure 9.2 shows the necessary flows, labeled **01** through **06**.

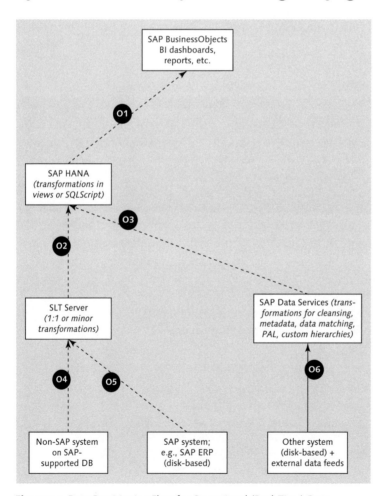

Figure 9.2 Data Provisioning Flow for Operational (Real-Time) Data

The data flow has the following characteristics at this point:

- The use of SLT to provide up-to-the-minute operational data from all source systems compatible with SLT, maximizing the availability of this data for users.

- The use of SAP Data Services for all other sources of data. SAP Data Services would likely run on a scheduled-load basis, although there are some limited capabilities in SAP Data Services to provide near real-time data as well, if absolutely needed.

- The collection of all operational data is in one SAP HANA system, most likely be in different schemas in SAP HANA.

- As a result, the system enables a consistent approach to data transformations: transformations specific to the source systems can take place in SLT or SAP Data Services, while SAP HANA will combine the sources and perform any extra transformations.

- SAP HANA becomes the one central source of operational data for SAP Business-Objects BI reporting tools. In SAP BusinessObjects BI, transformations are no longer needed.

Next, consider the data flow for corporate reporting and other requirements that are served from the data warehouse. In this example, you have an SAP Business Warehouse (BW) on SAP HANA system as the data warehouse. For a disk-based or SAP Business Warehouse Accelerator (SAP BW Accelerator)-enabled SAP BW system, however, the changes to the diagram are small (the data connections from SLT to SAP BW fall away and can be left out or be replaced by connections through SAP Data Services). These requirements don't need real-time data; however, they are typified by much more complex transformations and a higher degree of integration of data across separate source systems.

Figure 9.3 adds the necessary flows to get corporate data to the target systems in the connections labeled **C1** to **C6**.

Note the following in Figure 9.3:

- The SLT server is leveraged for the non-SAP system.

- However, for the SAP ERP source, the existing implementation of SAP BW extractors is leveraged. For SAP HANA as a data warehouse, this is simply the existing data sources. Alternatively, you can use the SLT server for this as well.

▶ The necessary data cleansing and complex transformations for the legacy source system can be accomplished in SAP Data Services, which also leverages the connection from the legacy system to SAP Data Services that already existed in the operational data flow.

▶ Several connections and configurations already used for the operational data flow are leveraged here for corporate data.

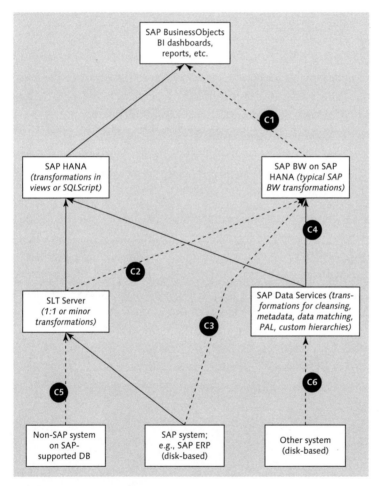

Figure 9.3 Adding the Data Provisioning Flow for Corporate Data (Higher-Level, Not Necessarily Real-Time Data)

Finally, the flows are added for supplemental data such as hierarchies and other highly transformed data sets that are needed in reporting, as well as the flows for external data feeds. A few possible paths for unstructured data are also included.

Figure 9.4 adds the additional flows in the connections labeled **S1** through **S5** and 🄤 through 🄥.

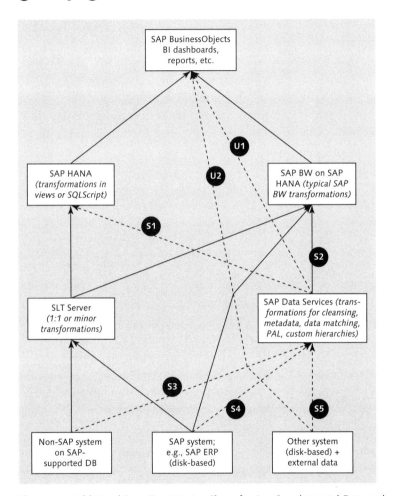

Figure 9.4 Additional Data Provisioning Flows for Any Supplemental Data and External and Unstructured Data

Remember that the tables underlying hierarchies in SAP HANA must be built explicitly with a certain structure. To accomplish this, you can route the data through SAP Data Services, for example. In general, data of this type can be fed to SAP Data Services from any source and distributed from there to all SAP HANA and data warehousing systems that require it or even to SAP BusinessObjects BI tools directly.

For this small-volume but important data set, the following occur in the flow:

▶ All target systems and reporting tools use the same data coming from a single source in SAP Data Services.

▶ The only exception is nonsystem information, such as Microsoft Word documents and other written documents provided in the SAP BusinessObjects BI Launchpad as additional information. Because this information has no application in SAP HANA or SAP BW, it can consequently be incorporated directly in the SAP BusinessObjects BI layer. The same applies to unstructured data that is only needed as a supplement in reporting but doesn't need to be incorporated into system data in SAP HANA.

▶ Again, several existing connections are leveraged.

The total diagram with all connections for all data source systems now looks like Figure 9.5.

Our example has taken a fairly wide scope in terms of both the sources of data and the required actions on them. We've considered both operational reporting using SAP HANA and the existence of a data warehouse. We haven't made use of all possible data provisioning methods all at once because your own strategy will probably not need them all. More likely, in its first incarnation, the flows you establish for an SAP HANA system will be much simpler than the example you've just seen because they will contain fewer elements, but the task remains the same. As you construct your own flows, remember to leverage both existing and new technologies, consider where you want to deploy SAP HANA and when, and decide the initial scope and the longer-term direction of your landscape. Deciding which source systems are in scope now and which will become part of scope in the future is important in drawing up a roadmap for which replication technologies you should adopt. Additionally, consider the point at which you anticipate moving your SAP BW and SAP ERP systems to run on the in-memory database as a primary database and how to ease the transition. Depending on these scope decisions, you may wind up with a very different decision on which replication technologies you'll implement.

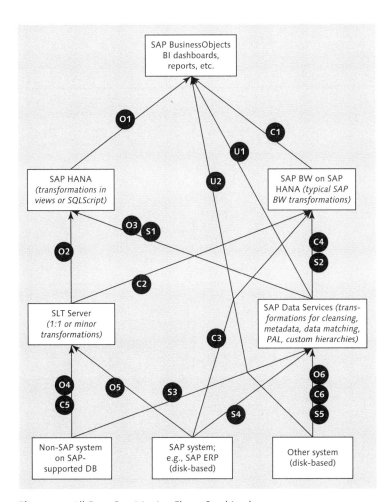

Figure 9.5 All Data-Provisioning Flows Combined

9.1.3 Technical Considerations

Aside from the more strategic considerations, you need to keep in mind a few technical constraints when you devise a data provisioning setup. The most important of these are summarized from Table 9.1 to Table 9.4, along with the overall technical characteristics of each replication method. SAP HANA capabilities are still expanding with every major and minor release, so make sure to check in detail with SAP before you embark on an implementation. Consult the Product Availability Matrix (PAM) and the latest info pages and installation guides.

	SAP Landscape Transformation (SLT)	SAP Data Services	SAP (Sybase) Replication Server (RS)	SAP HANA Smart Data Access
Installation Requirements	SLT server must be installed either on a separate machine or on an SAP ERP application server. SLT server is based on SAP NetWeaver 7.02, kernel release 7.20 EXT.	At least SAP Data Services 4.0 SP 2 must be installed. As a regular SAP Data Services implementation, no special components need be installed on SAP Data Services to work with SAP HANA.	SAP (Sybase) Replication Server (RS) must be installed on the SAP HANA server. SAP (Sybase) Replication Agent (RA) must be installed on the source system server.	The SDA add-on must either be installed during the initial SAP HANA installation or as an update to an existing SAP HANA system.
Number of Source Systems	Multiple source systems to any number of SAP HANA systems.	Multiple source systems to any number of SAP HANA systems.	One source system per SAP HANA instance.	Multiple source systems connected to an SAP HANA instance.

Table 9.1 Comparing the High-Level Architectures

	SAP Landscape Transformation (SLT)	SAP Data Services	SAP (Sybase) Replication Server (RS)	SAP HANA Smart Data Access
Data Movement	Real-time and scheduled replication.	Scheduled replication.	Real-time replication.	No data movement is required.
Data Replication Approach	Replication set up on the table level.	Replication according to SAP Data Services configuration.	Replication by logical unit of work.	No replication needed. Data available as virtual tables.
Presence of Load Balancing	Load balancing (parallelization).	Load balancing (parallelization).	No load balancing.	No load balancing.

Table 9.2 Comparing Data Replication Capabilities

	SAP Landscape Transformation (SLT)	SAP Data Services	SAP (Sybase) Replication Server (RS)	SAP HANA Smart Data Access
Data Transformation	Limited data transformations and filtering are possible.	Complete ETL toolset for data transformations.	No transformation of data.	Data transformation available through virtual table integration to SAP HANA views.
Supported Tables	Transparent, pool, and cluster tables can be replicated.	Transparent, pool, and cluster tables can be replicated.	Transparent tables can be replicated. No support for pool and cluster tables, but consult SAP Notes.	Very few limitations. Update, insert, and delete to remote databases supported as of SAP HANA SPS 7.
Support of Compressed Tables	Compressed tables are supported.	Compressed tables are supported.	Tables with compressed values are supported for DB2 9.1, 9.5, and 9.7. Row-compressed tables are only supported for DB2 9.7.	Compressed tables are supported, including ORC file compression with Hadoop Hive.

Table 9.2 Comparing Data Replication Capabilities (Cont.)

	SLT	SAP Data Services	SAP (Sybase) Replication Server (RS)	SAP HANA Smart Data Access
SAP Systems	SAP ERP systems from 4.6C, other ABAP-based systems from SAP Basis 4.6C. For SAP systems, the connection to SLT goes over an RFC (remote function call).	SAP ERP systems from 4.6C; other ABAP-based systems from SAP Basis 4.6C.	SAP ERP 6.0.	SAP HANA SPS 6 or higher.

Table 9.3 Comparing Source System Compatibility Aspects

	SLT	SAP Data Services	SAP (Sybase) Replication Server (RS)	SAP HANA Smart Data Access
Non-SAP Systems	Any system on SAP-supported database (note: DB2 for iSeries and SAP (Sybase) ASE as of SAP HANA 1.0 SPS 4 only). For non-SAP systems, the connection to SLT is a database connection.	Any.	Feasible in RS, but currently not in scope for SAP HANA.	See Table 9.7 for a full list of supported systems.
Unicode	Unicode or non-Unicode source systems.	Unicode or non-Unicode source systems.	Unicode source systems only.	Unicode or non-Unicode source systems.
Database Source Support	Source system can be on any SAP-supported database.	Source system can be on any SAP-supported database.	IBM DB2 for LUW only.	See Table 9.7 for a full list of supported systems.

Table 9.3 Comparing Source System Compatibility Aspects (Cont.)

	SAP Landscape Transformation (SLT)	SAP Data Services	SAP (Sybase) Replication Server (RS)	SAP HANA Smart Data Access
Administration	Administration in SAP HANA Studio.	Administration via regular SAP Data Services Management Console, or through SAP Solution Manager.	Administration in SAP HANA Studio using the SAP Load Controller (LC) component.	Administration in SAP HANA Studio.

Table 9.4 Comparing Administration and Configuration Aspects

	SAP Landscape Transformation (SLT)	SAP Data Services	SAP (Sybase) Replication Server (RS)	SAP HANA Smart Data Access
Configuration	Some configuration in SLT server, especially with first setup of new replication scenarios.	Configuration in SAP Data Services.	Configuration in RS.	Configuration in SAP HANA Studio.
Transformations	Transformations are configured and processed on SLT server.	Transformations are configured and processed in SAP Data Services.	No transformations possible.	Virtual transformations available through native SAP HANA views.

Table 9.4 Comparing Administration and Configuration Aspects (Cont.)

9.2 Trigger-Based Replication: SAP Landscape Transformation

For SAP source systems such as SAP ERP, SLT is the premier replication method. SLT offers filtering and some transformation capabilities while still achieving near real-time replication and can be administered from within the existing SAP HANA Studio application. Because of this combination of flexibility, functional capabilities, and ease of administration, SLT is considered the default choice in many cases. In this section, we'll walk through what you need to know about trigger-based replication.

9.2.1 How SLT Works

Always keep the following three general rules in mind for connecting a source system to SAP HANA:

- Each *source system* can connect to only one SLT system.
- Each *SLT system* can connect to multiple SAP HANA systems.
- Each *SAP HANA system* can get data, through SLT, from multiple source systems.

The steps in the data replication are always the same, regardless of which installation scenario you choose:

1. The SLT software detects database triggers on the source system.
2. The data is written to special log tables for SLT, which are created in the source system during the SLT installation.
3. Read modules poll the log tables for new data and pass the data along when requested by the controller modules.
4. Controller modules then pass the data to write modules.
5. Write modules perform any operations required and pass the data to the SAP HANA database.
6. Data is written to the application tables in SAP HANA.

Note that, while the steps in the data transfer process (DTP) are always the same, the precise location of some components differs depending on your installation scenario. Of course, if SLT is installed on the SAP source system directly, all the components reside there (Figure 9.6).

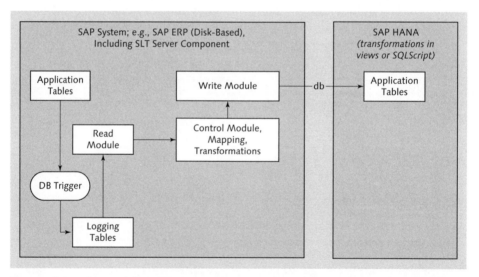

Figure 9.6 Installation of the SLT Server Component on the SAP Source System Application Server

However, you should keep in mind one difference between SAP and non-SAP sources, even if you install SLT as a separate SAP system. For an SAP source system, the read modules are placed on the source system, and the connection to SLT goes over a remote function call (RFC) (Figure 9.7).

However, if the source system is non-SAP, the read modules are installed on the SLT system, and the connection to SLT is a database connection (Figure 9.8).

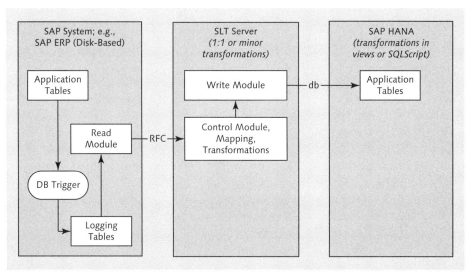

Figure 9.7 Installation of a Separate SLT Server for an SAP Source System

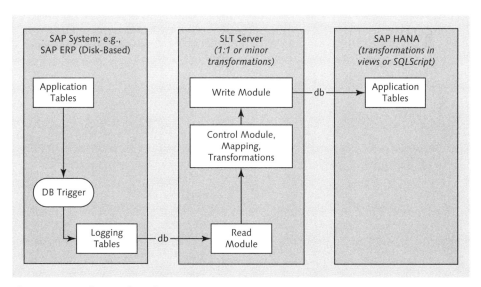

Figure 9.8 Installation of SLT for a Non-SAP Source System

9.2.2 Installation

SLT software can be installed in different ways. You need to consider the use cases for SLT to determine the best installation method, that is, whether you intend to use SLT only for SAP source systems, or if non-SAP source systems are also in scope. The installation may be done differently in both cases.

Installation for SAP Source Systems

For use with an SAP source system, two options exist for where you place SLT in your system landscape:

▶ Installation as a separate SAP system

▶ Installation on the SAP source system itself

For production source systems, we recommend installing SLT as its own, separate system, which has some very important benefits, including:

▶ Software updates, support packages, and so on can be applied to the source system and to SLT separately, reducing risk and regression testing effort and avoiding any impact from software changes on the SLT system to the source system.

▶ The impact of data replication on system resources of the source system is avoided. Apart from recording the changes and sending them over to the SLT server, no activity occurs on the source system for replication purposes. Filtering, transformations, and control processing of the replication all occur on the SLT system.

▶ A standalone SLT server can remain operational for non-SAP sources when SAP ERP gets moved to an SAP HANA database without further impact.

In general, if the SLT system is administered on its own, the cost of maintaining another server and instance may result in significant benefits in terms of reliability and lower maintenance costs elsewhere as well.

As of July 2016, SLT Replication Server 2.0 is available. If you want to run the latest version of SLT, you will need SAP Basis Release 7.31 or higher. For a complete list of the product requirements for your selected version of SLT, check the PAM from *http://launchpad.support.sap.com*.

A full deployment of the SLT software requires two add-ons, SHC_CONT 2011 and DMIS 2011 SP 5. In order to manage an SAP Landscape Transformation project, you will need to install SLT on the SAP Solution Manager system. SAP Solution Manager 7.1 with SP 15 is a prerequisite for this type of installation. On the other hand, if you don't intend to integrate SLT with SAP Solution Manager, you can install DMIS 2011 on your chosen server and then install the required service packs to upgrade to the latest version. For more information about installing SLT, see Table 9.5.

SAP Note	Contents
1577441	Installation and delta upgrade of DMIS 2011_5
1577503	Upgrade to DMIS 2011_5 in the System Switch Upgrade
1618947	Installation or upgrade of SHC_CONT 2011_1_700

Table 9.5 SAP Landscape Transformation 2.0 Installation Notes

When you do this, remember to provide enough processing power on the application server on which SLT is installed. Replication is done using background processes, so enough processes and memory must be available. The connection between the SAP source system and the SLT system is made via RFC.

Installation for Non-SAP Source Systems

To use SLT for non-SAP source systems, the SLT Replication Server must be installed as a standalone system. The source systems for which you can use SLT must satisfy the following criteria:

- Source system must be on an SAP-supported database.
- The database must be on a version compatible with SAP NetWeaver 7.02 or higher as defined in the PAM.
- The database operating system must be on a version compatible with SAP NetWeaver 7.02 or higher as defined in the PAM.

The SLT server in this case is installed somewhat differently. The communication between the source and SLT systems takes place over a permanent database connection (instead of via RFC).

9.2.3 SLT Configuration

To establish the data transfer to SAP HANA using SLT, some configuration is required. The Configuration and Monitoring Dashboard is accessed in SLT using Transaction LTR. From this dashboard, you can define the data transfers individually as pairs of a source system and a target schema. Each pair is saved as a replication configuration and is assigned a unique mass transfer ID.

For each such combination of source system and target schema, you must do the following:

1. Define the incoming connection from the source system (SAP or other).

2. Define the outgoing connection to SAP HANA. You'll need the host name and instance number of the SAP HANA system, as well as the user ID and password that should be used for the connection. Have your SAP HANA administrator set up a dedicated user ID for this purpose in SAP HANA.

3. Specify a target schema.

4. Specify the number of background jobs to be used for data replication.

5. Specify the replication frequency:

   ▸ REAL TIME will establish a continuous stream.

   ▸ SCHEDULE BY INTERVAL enables a load at specific intervals (e.g., every 15 minutes or every 8 hours).

   ▸ SCHEDULE BY TIME enables a load at a specific time of day.

6. Assign tablespaces for the logging tables on the source system. We recommend placing the logging tables in separate tablespaces for easier monitoring of table sizes.

7. Specify if you want to allow this source system to map to multiple target schemas.

8. Specify if you want this configuration to only read data from a single client for an SAP source system.

If you do not need to filter or transform data, you've done everything you need to enable data replication to SAP HANA. From this point, you can go to SAP HANA Studio and start loading data with a 1:1 mapping.

Note that activating a data transfer configuration does more than just save configuration settings; it also does the following:

► Creates the database schema on the SAP HANA system (if it doesn't exist already)

► Creates the necessary logging tables on the source system to capture changes

► Copies over the table metadata from the source system

► Creates authorization roles and grant/revoke procedures on the SAP HANA system for the target schema

► Registers the replication parameters in SAP HANA

► Creates the control and job log tables in SAP HANA that will keep track of the replication jobs and allow you to see the status within SAP HANA Studio

Each source–target configuration is assigned a mass transfer ID, which is used elsewhere in SLT—for example, when creating transformation rules—to identify the configuration to which the extra settings should be applied.

SAP Landscape Transformation 2.0

The latest version of SLT has moved the Configuration and Monitoring Dashboard to the web browser, using either standard HTML or SAP Business Client on HTML. Use Transaction LTR to access the dashboard.

Please be aware that the configuration for this feature can be a bit tricky, so make sure you consult the *SAP Landscape Transformation Replication Server for SAP HANA Platform SPS 12* guide for information on configuring the HTML connection. As of July 2016, the guide can be downloaded from *https://help.sap.com/hana/SAP_Landscape_Transformation_for_SAP_HANA_Operations_Guide_en.pdf*. Make sure you get the latest version of this guide and follow the instructions for setting up and troubleshooting the Web Dynpro connection. If for some reason you're unable to get the dashboard working, the same functionality is available through Transaction LTRC in the SAP GUI.

9.2.4 SLT Administration

The administration of the data replication itself isn't done on the SLT server but inside SAP HANA Studio. In the MODELER perspective, you can choose DATA PROVISIONING, from which you're able to start and stop loading data to SAP HANA.

There are five functions to choose from for the data loading:

► LOAD drops the target table and starts a new one-time load of the current data.

► REPLICATE performs a load (if none has taken place yet) and starts the replication based on the parameters defined in SLT (i.e., REALTIME, SCHEDULE BY INTERVAL, SCHEDULE BY TIME, or ON DEMAND).

- STOP halts any future data loads and deletes the logging tables from the source system; data integrity is no longer ensured when you do this, and to load again, you'll have to choose LOAD or REPLICATE again.

- SUSPEND pauses data loads temporarily, meaning the logging tables in the source system remain intact, and changes are still being tracked on the source system. At any point, the replication can be resumed again without loss of data and without compromising data integrity. Suspending loads for a long period is not recommended because the logging tables may grow large, and the system may automatically move to a stop operation.

- RESUME is used after a suspend operation to begin loading data where the loads left off on the SUSPEND function.

You can monitor all data loading, table by table, in the DATA LOAD MANAGEMENT screen in SAP HANA Studio where the current job status is displayed along with the exact timestamp of the last replication.

> **Advanced SLT administration**
>
> While many of the features of SLT can be administered through SAP HANA Studio, the advanced functions for managing your replication configurations require the use of the SLT replication console in the SAP GUI, available with Transaction LTRC.

Although we focused on monitoring capabilities in SAP HANA Studio, SLT also offers monitoring and troubleshooting capabilities. In SLT, you can start and stop what is called the *master job* for each configuration (which effectively toggles the configuration from an active state to an inactive state and back). More important for day-to-day operation are the statistics that SLT offers: you can find—by individual table—the last, minimum, median, and maximum data latency times of the replication and how many records were inserted, updated, and deleted.

The capabilities of the technology in terms of monitoring and troubleshooting are still expanding, and new ways to monitor the replication are just now making it to market, such as integration with SAP Solution Manager (including alerts) and the availability of the Configuration and Monitoring Dashboard in the web browser and SAP Business Client on HTML.

9.2.5 Extended Features

During the data replication, you can make use of a number of features to specify the data replication more fully, as follows:

▸ Select specific tables to replicate.

▸ Apply filters for certain field values to replicate only certain records of a table.

▸ Apply transformations to the data, such as:

  ▹ Transform individual fields.

  ▹ Extend the replicated table structure with extra fields.

  ▹ Reduce the replicated table structure by leaving out certain columns.

Be aware that every filter or transformation defined in SLT relates to one specific mass transfer ID.

Selecting Specific Tables

Specific tables are selected in SAP HANA Studio when you start data loading. Both the LOAD and REPLICATE functions will allow you to choose the specific tables in a dialog screen before you begin the data transfer itself.

> **Note**
>
> SAP developers and administrators will be familiar with the special table type of cluster tables and the specific challenges it sometimes poses. SLT can replicate cluster tables to SAP HANA. The process has been described in SAP Notes, listed under the application area BC-HAN-LTR, for your reference. Please review the latest SAP Notes if you want to replicate cluster tables using SLT.

Applying Filters

You can apply filters for certain field values in a few different ways to replicate only certain records of a table. Filtering records by using event-based or parameter-based rules takes place within SLT; in other words, all changed records are still tracked in the logging tables on the source system and then transferred to the SLT server. Once there, the filter is applied, and only the remaining chosen records are sent on to SAP HANA. This type of filter is applied during both the load and the replicate operations.

For an event-based filter, you specify exactly at which point in the processing logic the filter is to be applied in the rule configuration. Event-based rules consequently offer the most flexibility in implementing filters and transformations, but you'll have to familiarize yourself with the different events available in this type of rule.

Parameter-based filters don't require you to specify this event because they occur at a predefined point in the processing where the incoming record is available.

Within SLT, the way records are processed resembles the mechanism used in SAP ERP data sources or in SAP BW update rules/transformations. Every replication cycle breaks up the data it receives into portions (by default, 5,000 records per portion in a replication cycle) and loops through the portions. Within each such loop, any rules are applied (filters or transformations), and the data is then transferred by the Write module to the SAP HANA target.

Figure 9.9 displays the flow of the processing logic in SLT with regard to transformations. This default flow logic applies to parameter-based rules and event-based rules where the event `Begin Of Record` (BOR) is chosen. Other events are available that allow you to execute a rule elsewhere, for example, at the start and end of each portion (similar to start and end routines in SAP BW).

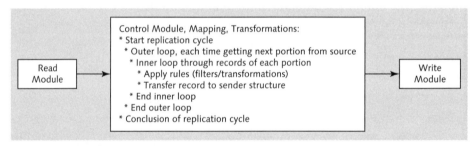

Figure 9.9 Internal Data Processing Login in SLT for Parameter-Based Rules and BOR Event-Based Rules

The following are the essential activities to create rules of this type:

► Create an entry in a configuration table in SLT with the appropriate values using a standard SAP program in SLT.

► Maintain an ABAP program of the INCLUDE type with the desired filter.

The coding of the filters themselves is usually fairly easy because a simple IF/ENDIF statement will suffice for the condition, and SAP has provided a small macro called SKIP_RECORD. Using this macro, the filters are specified from a negative condition (the condition specifies which records to skip, not which to retain).

A sample filter is shown here in which we're selecting only specific company codes to transfer to SAP HANA by skipping the ones we don't want loaded:

```
IF e_bukrs = '1000' OR e_bukrs = '1100'.
SKIP_RECORD.
ENDIF.
```

Another way to filter records is to modify the trigger on the source system itself, which would apply the filter on the source even before any data is transferred to the SLT server and thus will perform better. This filter works on the source system on the database level, however, so the syntax of the rule itself is database specific.

This type of filter is applied by making entries in a configuration table, where you can specify the mass transfer ID to which the rule should be applied, the type of the source system database, the specific table to which it relates, and, of course, the rule itself. The filter conditions are specified with positive conditions in this case, meaning records that satisfy the condition will be transferred to SLT for further processing.

An important note here is that trigger-based filter conditions are only applied during the replication cycles and not during the initial load because they are applied during the tracking of changes in the SLT logging tables by use of the database triggers. If you use this method to filter data and also want to have a filter during the initial load into SAP HANA, you need to specify a second event-based or parameter-based filter in SLT.

Applying Transformations by Transforming Individual Fields

Value transformations happen on the SLT server after receiving the data from the source system and before sending it to SAP HANA. The SLT system is an ABAP system, so code for transformations is written in ABAP.

To implement value transformations, two things are needed:

▶ An entry is made in a configuration table on SLT to tell the system to call the transformation code.

▶ The code itself is inside an ABAP program of the INCLUDE type.

As with filters, value transformations can be event based or parameter based.

The code you place in the transformations has an impact on the throughput performance of the replication, so be careful how much code you place here. Especially if you want to get real-time data into SAP HANA (latencies of just a few seconds), we recommend avoiding transformations. However, in some cases, transforming the data at this stage (before it's forwarded to the SAP HANA system) makes sense. Examples include unit or currency conversions to fixed target units/currencies or filling in initial fields—such as a source system or client identifier if the target table in SAP HANA is fed from more than one source table, system, or client.

Applying Transformations by Altering the Replicated Table Structure

When you extend a structure with extra fields, you have to add transformation routines, as described in the previous section, to populate these fields. With the additional complexity of this type of enhancement, you now have to change metadata as well or, to be more precise, you have to provide new metadata for use in the output of data.

To implement this type of transformation, the following needs to happen:

▶ An entry is made in a configuration table on SLT to tell the system to use a different structure as the sender structure, that is, different from the table definition in the source system.

▶ A table with the desired target structure must be created in the system—a regular, transparent table created in the ABAP Dictionary. The table can be created either in the source system or in the SLT system; you specify where in the entry made in the configuration table.

▶ An entry is made in a configuration table on SLT to tell the system to call the transformation code that will populate the new field (event-based or parameter-based rule).

▶ The code itself is inside an ABAP program of the INCLUDE type.

Reducing the number of fields in the sender structure requires the first two of these steps but not the last two because, in this case, the value of any field does not need to be determined.

Special Filter Rule for Client in SAP Source Systems

Because SAP HANA has no client concept in its tables, by default, data from all clients in client-dependent tables is read from a source SAP system into SAP HANA. However, this result is rarely what you want. Even when you want to load data from more than one client, we still recommend maintaining control over which clients get loaded where and when into SAP HANA, instead of leaving it wide open.

Loading data from multiple clients can be useful in development, testing, or training systems, depending on your SAP client landscape. In many cases, however, only data from one client is to be replicated to SAP HANA, for example, for all production systems but often also for other systems.

You could add a filter rule on the MANDT field for this purpose, but because of the special role the field plays in so many source system tables, SAP has also provided a way to specify only one client while configuring the data replication itself. You specify if you want this configuration to only read data from a single client. The value for the client in that case is taken from the configuration of the RFC connection. The main advantage of this approach is performance: the configuration setting will incorporate this specification as a trigger-based filter at the very beginning of the data logging and replication process.

9.2.6 Setting Up a New Replication Configuration in SAP HANA

After SLT is installed, you can add new tables to load into SAP HANA from within SAP HANA Studio or from within the SLT system itself. Before adding new tables is possible, however, SLT replication must be configured, and even then, some activities can only be performed on the SLT server, such as transformations within SLT, and so on. We'll illustrate the ways in which you set up the SLT data transfer to SAP HANA with an example. Because this example involves setting up a data replication for the first time, the activities described are all performed on the SLT server. This example is split into two parts. This section deals with setting up a new configuration for the first time. In the next section, we'll then show you how to add the desired tables to the configuration for immediate replication of data into SAP HANA.

A number of transactions are important on the SLT server, but first and foremost, you'll need to use Transaction LTR. In this transaction, the data replication is first configured and can be monitored when it's running.

The initial screen of the LTR transaction will look like Figure 9.10. The system presents a list of the AVAILABLE CONFIGURATIONS with a summary traffic light status (red, yellow, or green).

Each configuration has one unique MASS TRANSFER ID for easy reference and represents the following:

▶ A single combination of one source and one target system

▶ A set of tables that is being replicated

▶ A specific replication frequency (real time or not)

If you want to extract different tables with a different frequency from a single source system, you have to create at least two configurations in SLT.

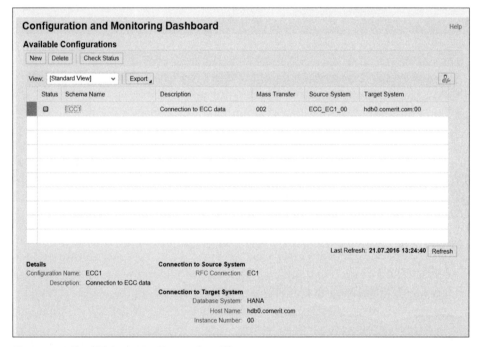

Figure 9.10 The SLT Overview: Transaction LTR

To create a new configuration, click the NEW button on the initial screen of Transaction LTR. In the popup window that appears, shown in Figure 9.11, you need to perform the following tasks:

1. Provide a CONFIGURATION NAME and DESCRIPTION for the configuration, then click NEXT.

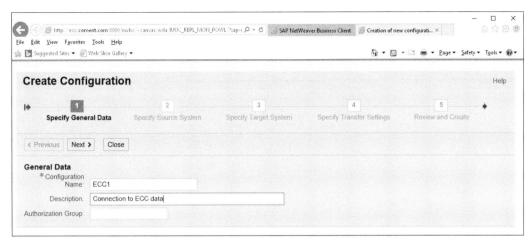

Figure 9.11 Creating a New Configuration for SLT Replication

2. Select the connection details for the source system. For an SAP source system, the connection is made over RFC. For SAP source systems, two additional settings are also available:

   ▸ ALLOW MULTIPLE USAGE
   Enables you to replicate the data retrieved for the tables to more than one target SAP HANA system. If you anticipate having more than one target SAP HANA server, we recommend checking this box. The setting is no longer editable after the data replication has started.

   ▸ READ FROM SINGLE CLIENT
   Restricts the data replication to the client specified in the connection. Checking this box makes sense for production systems that often have only one client.

3. For a non-SAP source, the connection is established as a database connection. In this case, choose the type of database first and then supply the necessary database user logon credentials. Click NEXT to advance to the SPECIFY TARGET SYSTEM screen.

4. Now, you'll need to specify information about the target system. In our example (Figure 9.12), we're specifying an SAP HANA system as a sidecar replication environment. Enter the credentials for your target database and click NEXT.

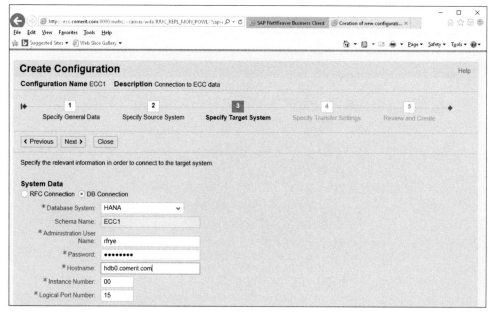

Figure 9.12 Specifying the Target System for SLT Replication

5. On the SPECIFY TRANSFER SETTINGS screen (Figure 9.13), you'll need to make several selections.

- The INITIAL LOAD MODE can be set to RESOURCE OPTIMIZED (the default) or PERFORMANCE OPTIMIZED. If you want to accelerate the data load, especially if real-time replication is your goal, you can choose the PERFORMANCE OPTIMIZED method.

- DATA CLASS OF TABLESPACE allows you to choose a tablespace for the logging tables in the source system.

- The NO. OF DATA TRANSFER JOBS the system can use. This selection effectively tells the system how many job processes may be taken up (maximum) by the data replication process running on the source system.

- NO. OF INITIAL LOAD JOBS allows you to choose how many jobs may be used during initial table loads to the target system.

- NO. OF CALCULATION JOBS allows you to choose how many jobs may be used to calculate the data transfer portions used for the initial load.

- REPLICATION OPTIONS is where you specify the frequency. For this example, we'll use the default REAL TIME setting. Other options include SCHEDULE BY

INTERVAL (specify the time between replication triggers); SCHEDULE BY TIME (specify the hour, minute, and second for the replication job; and ON DEMAND (trigger replication whenever the data changes).

▷ ACTIVATE REPLICATION LOGGING will allow you to save the replicated data to tables in the SLT system for a specific period of time. As a result, you can view and replicate the data in the event of a point-in-time recovery of the target system.

6. Once you've configured the transfer settings, click NEXT to review the settings for the configuration. When you're satisfied with the settings, click CREATE CONFIGURATION to finish creating the SLT connection between the source and target systems.

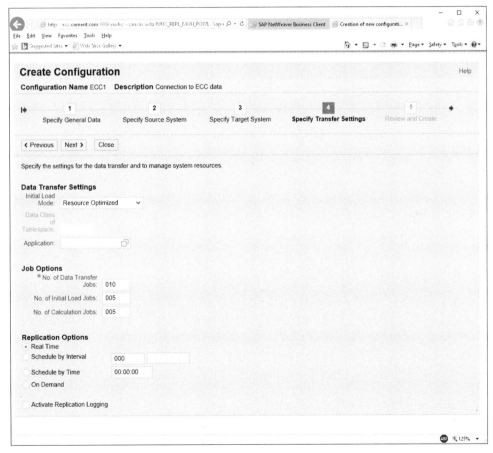

Figure 9.13 Specifying the Transfer Settings for SLT

When the replication configuration has been created, the configuration appears on the home screen of Transaction LTR, as shown in Figure 9.10.

In this screen, you can now monitor the data replication, start and stop the replication, and so on. However, before we move on, you should verify one more configuration setting: INITIAL LOAD JOBS. To check this setting, go to Transaction LTRC to open the SLT Replication Server Cockpit. Click on CONFIGURATION NAME for your replication configuration, and the cockpit for that specific configuration will open. Navigate to the ADMINISTRATION DATA tab where you can click the CHANGE NO. OF JOBS button to adjust the INITIAL LOAD JOBS to an appropriate value. This number represents job processes that will be used during the initial load, so depending on how many tables you want to add (at the same time) and how much data they contain, you may increase this number (Figure 9.14).

From the ADMINISTRATION DATA tab, you can also ACTIVATE or DEACTIVATE the configuration (useful for troubleshooting), CHANGE AUTHORIZATION GROUP, and CHANGE JOB SETTINGS.

You're now ready to start replicating any other tables you require. By default, SLT always transfers data for the basic dictionary tables—necessary to create the correct table definitions in SAP HANA—from an SAP source system, so even without adding tables explicitly first, you can already test the configuration to see if the system connections can be made and everything is working fine with SLT.

Next, let's take a look at the status of the configuration you created. To do this, click the TABLE OVERVIEW tab, where you'll get a very detailed overview of what is happening with all of the tables included in the configuration. Figure 9.15 shows the initial state of the replication configuration you created.

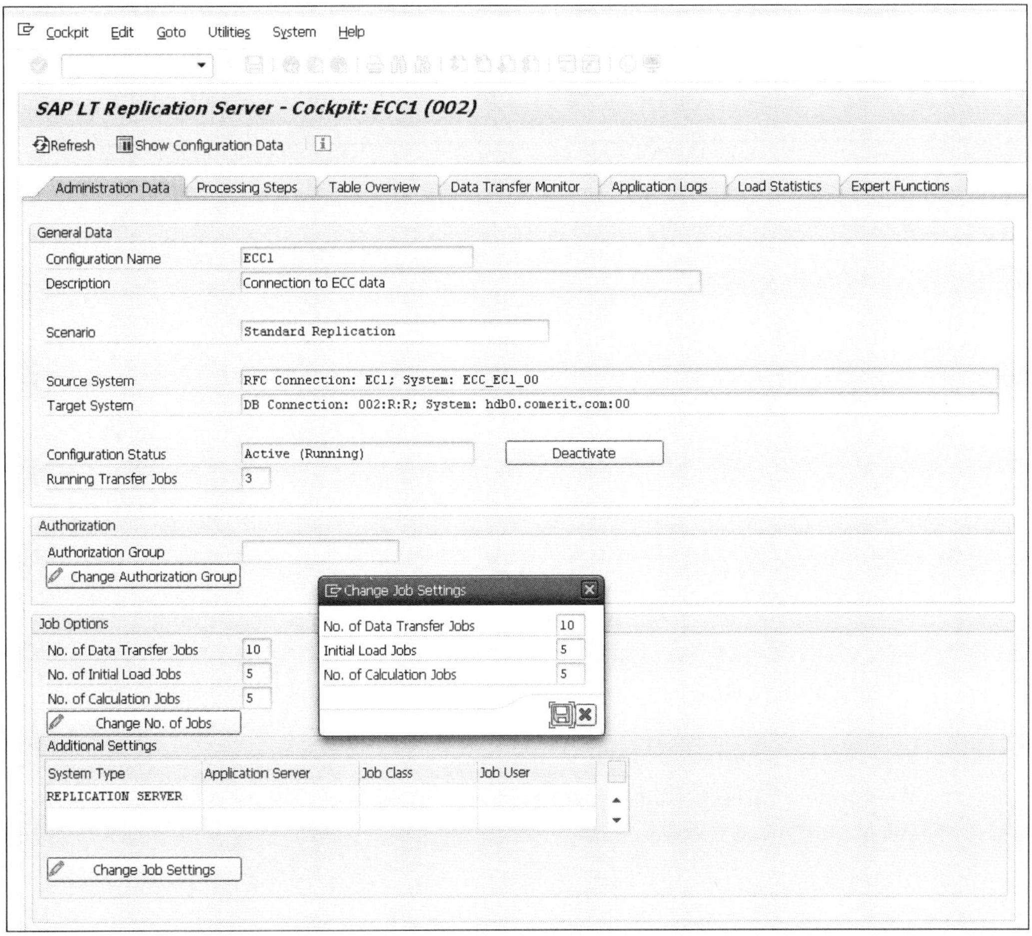

Figure 9.14 Adjusting the Number of Jobs from the Configuration Cockpit

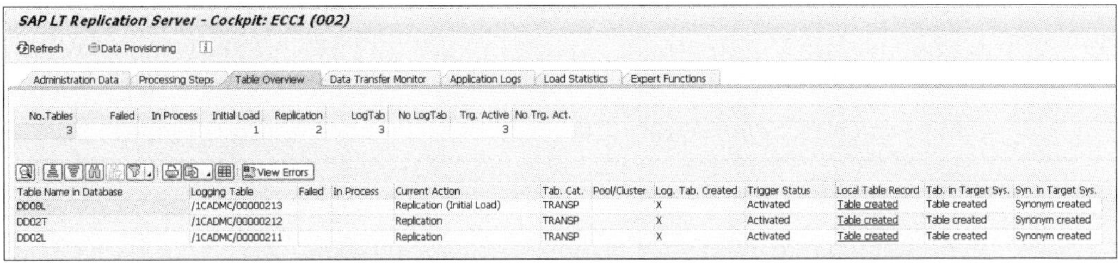

Figure 9.15 Table Overview from the SLT Replication Server Cockpit

At the top of the screen, the number of tables is listed. The number of tables given in the columns NO LOGTAB and NO TRG. ACT. indicates that there have been no logging tables or database triggers created on the source system yet. The detail section below also lists the TRIGGER STATUS as ACTIVATED, and the tables will all be fully loaded as soon as the replication completes (the value in the IN PROCESS column is empty).

You can use the TABLE OVERVIEW and DATA TRANSFER MONITOR (Figure 9.16) for detailed monitoring of the load and replication jobs. As the initial load starts, you'll see entries change as the job progresses. During real-time replication, this overview transaction checks the pulse of the SLT system, providing real-time monitoring details.

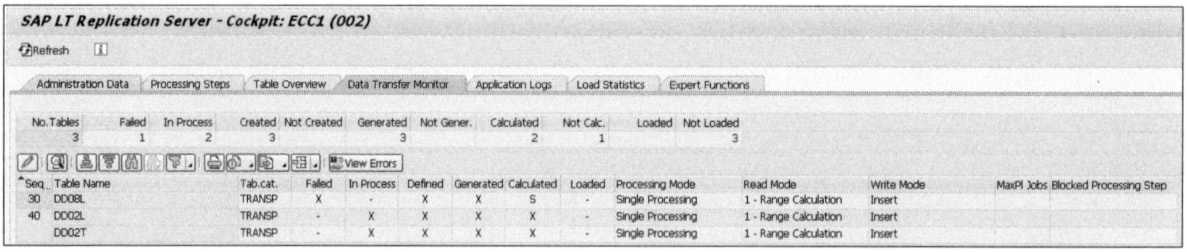

Figure 9.16 Monitoring Data Transfers for Each Table in the Replication Server Cockpit

The LOAD STATISTICS tab, finally, provides an overview of how well the replication is running, with median, minimum, and maximum values of the data latency between the source system and SAP HANA.

9.2.7 Adding Tables to an Existing Replication Configuration

After an SLT configuration has been created, you can start adding the tables you want to replicate to SAP HANA in two ways:

▶ **From within SAP HANA Studio**
This method only works for the simplest replication scenarios. You won't be able to start the replication at the time of your choosing, and you can't configure any transformations of filters, among other limitations.

▶ **From within the SLT system**
This method offers the full range of SLT functionality.

We'll use the SLT server approach in this example to show you more about how SLT works.

Go to Transaction LTRC and select the CONFIGURATION NAME corresponding to your replication configuration. If necessary, click on the TABLE OVERVIEW tab. The DATA PROVISIONING button becomes available at the top of the screen, as shown in Figure 9.17.

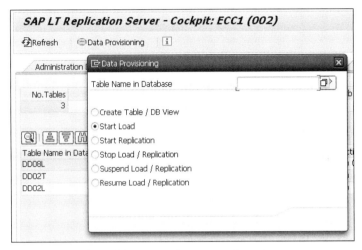

Figure 9.17 Adding Tables to a Replication Configuration

Click the DATA PROVISIONING button and provide the name of the table you want to replicate to SAP HANA. Next, select whether you want to START LOAD or START REPLICATION. START LOAD will perform a one-time load of the table. START REPLICATION will perform an initial load of the selected table and replicate changes based on the replication settings you selected when you created the configuration. You can either enter the table name directly, or you can click the MULTIPLE SELECTION button (to the right of TABLE NAME IN DATABASE field) to open a helpful dialog window.

So what makes this dialog window so helpful? If you've been reading this book in order, you may remember the discussion about SLT in the SAP HANA Live in Chapter 7, Section 7.3. We discussed how you could use the SAP HANA Live browser to generate a list of tables needed for SLT in an SAP HANA Live sidecar implementation. If you've generated an SLT file (either from the SAP HANA Live browser or manually), you can open the CSV file with Microsoft Excel and select all the table names in the TABLE NAME column. Copy these table names to the memory buffer in your computer—for Microsoft Windows either use the right-click context menu or Ctrl+C —then click the COPY FROM CLIPBOARD button in the MULTIPLE SELECTION FOR TABLE NAME IN DATABASE window (the helpful dialog window mentioned earlier) or just press Shift + F12 . All of the table names will then be pasted into the SINGLE VALUE list, and you can click EXECUTE to add all the tables to the selection (Figure 9.18). Without the option to copy from the memory buffer or load from text or CSV files, the process to select multiple tables would be quite tedious.

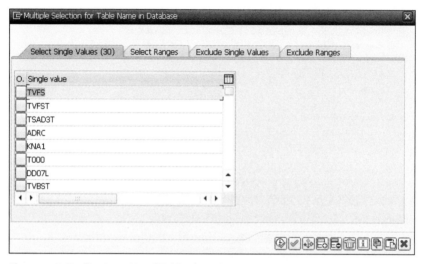

Figure 9.18 Replicating a List of Tables from CSV

Thanks to the helpful features in the MULTIPLE SELECTION FOR TABLE NAME IN DATABASE window, the configuration has been updated with the new table to load or replicate. The SLT system will automatically begin the process of loading or replicating the table. See Figure 9.19 and Figure 9.20 for examples of a table being processed by SLT.

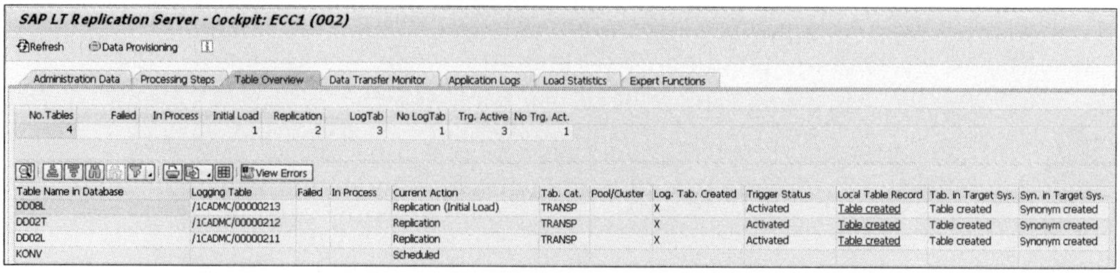

Figure 9.19 Table KONV Scheduled for Replication

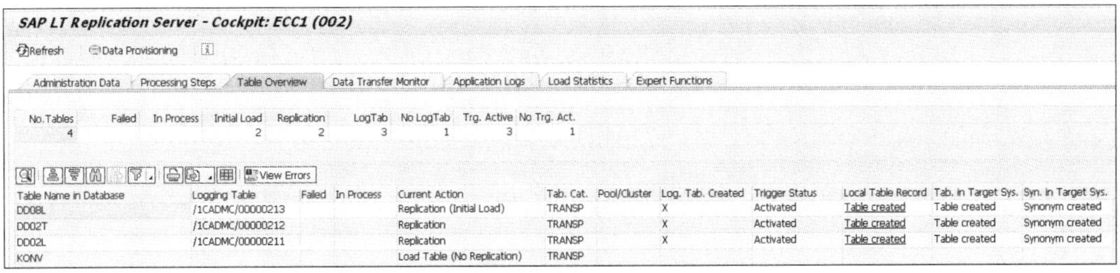

Figure 9.20 Table KONV Being Loaded to the Target System

You can now add as many tables as you like. Pay attention to the number of processes that may be used for initial data loading, as specified in the replication configuration; if you add too many tables at one time, you may want to increase this setting, as too few processes may cause the replication process to grind to a halt. With a large number of tables and too few processes to handle them, the last tables may not be finished replicating before the next trigger event occurs.

The same options you find in SAP HANA Studio will be presented here: LOAD, REPLICATE, STOP, SUSPEND, RESUME. Remember that the LOAD option only does a one-time load to SAP HANA. To perform continuous replication of data, you need to choose the START REPLICATION option, which will trigger a number of events:

1. If the table doesn't exist yet in SAP HANA, it will be created there. If it does exist already, the table will be truncated and adjusted (altered), if necessary.

2. SLT will perform the creation of the database trigger and logging tables on the source SAP system. Because the trigger is created before any data is transferred, changes are already being recorded, making SLT effectively a zero-downtime process.

3. An initial load of data will be performed.

4. SLT will automatically switch to the regular, continuous replication of data after the initial load.

As we explained earlier, you can monitor the data replication from the web browser in the Configuration and Monitoring Console using Transaction LTR, or you can monitor the data replication from Transaction LTRC on the DATA TRANSFER MONITOR tab.

After the initial load has finished, all systems will automatically reflect the delta mode in which the replication is then running, with the following results:

- ▸ Transaction LTR will now reflect the CURRENT ACTION as REPLICATION, and the trigger status, as active.

- ▸ Transaction LTRC now has the name of the logging table, and the PROCESSING MODE has changed to SINGLE PROCESSING (Figure 9.21).

- ▸ In the SAP HANA system in SAP HANA Studio, the table shows up in the monitor with the ACTION as LOAD and the STATUS as SCHEDULED (Figure 9.22).

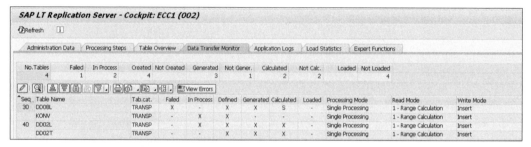

Figure 9.21 The Table Replication Status in Transaction LTRC

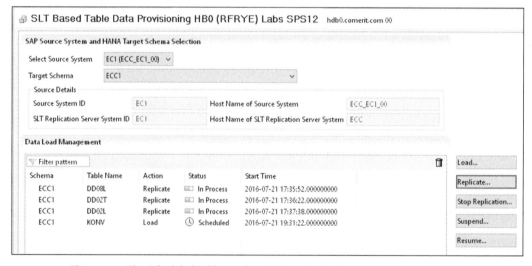

Figure 9.22 The Scheduled Table Load in SAP HANA Studio

As a final check, you can find data in the table in SAP HANA, for example, by looking at the table definition. Figure 9.23 shows that nearly a million records are in the table now.

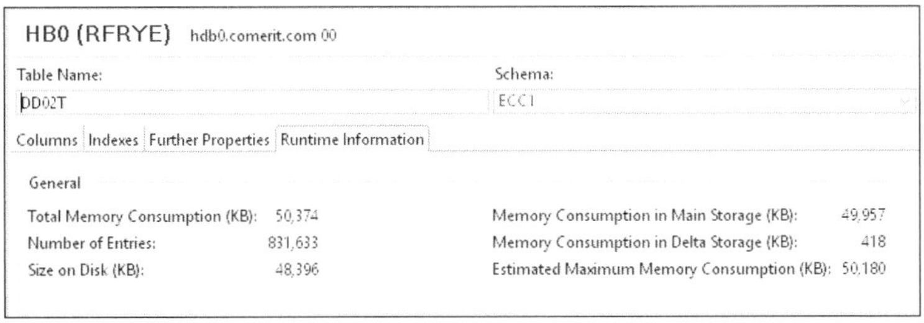

Figure 9.23 Checking the Number of Table Entries in SAP HANA

9.3 ETL-Based Replication: SAP Data Services

If you require a high degree of data transformation prior to putting the data in SAP HANA, and a scheduled data feed is sufficient for your needs, you should consider SAP Data Services. If you need to include non-SAP sources, consider combining a real-time mechanism with SAP Data Services. Even some data provisioning from SAP ERP may be better suited to SAP Data Services while the bulk of SAP feeds flow through SLT or SAP/Sybase.

In this section, we'll go over the capabilities, the sequence of activities needed, and the positioning of SAP Data Services in terms of data provisioning to SAP HANA systems. The internal processes within SAP Data Services aren't discussed in great detail; because these processes are firmly established, SAP Data Services itself works and doesn't need to be changed.

SAP Data Services is designed to work primarily as a batch processing application; that is, the loads through SAP Data Services generally take place at regular times of day instead of in real time. Although having some limited capability for real-time processing, the tool isn't capable of performing the real-time feeds of large volumes of data that an operational reporting scope for an SAP HANA implementation typically requires.

But don't assume that SAP Data Services offers fewer capabilities than, for example, SLT. In fact, SAP Data Services has a more robust assortment of ETL functionality available for loading data to SAP HANA, when compared to SLT, as well as the following benefits:

▶ For SAP source systems, extraction can be done from tables (as in SLT or SAP/Sybase) but also from data sources, enabling you to leverage existing extraction

423

codes for a quicker implementation and reducing the required modeling effort in SAP HANA.

▸ Metadata can also be transferred to SAP HANA using SAP Data Services.

▸ The delta capabilities of SAP Data Services are available as usual.

SAP Data Services 4.2

With release 4.2, SAP Data Services was optimized to work better with SAP HANA in several ways worth noting, such as:

▸ **Data flow**
Previously, SAP Data Services would perform data flows by executing simple SQL statements; the workload would be shared with SAP Data Services. In release 4.2, queries are no longer necessary. Instead, SAP Data Services creates a calculation view that retrieves the data and also performs the transformation. This results in two significant performance benefits:

  ▸ The push down of data transformation to the SAP HANA database for more efficient and rapid processing.

  ▸ Faster loading with parallel data extraction, partitioned data load, and multinode data load.

▸ **Parallel reading and loading using physical and logical partitions**
Because SAP HANA now supports partition support for column store tables, SAP Data Services now also supports the SAP HANA partition feature for parallel reading and loading using physical and logical partitions.

▸ **SAP's Rapid Deployment Solutions (RDS)**
SAP Data Services provides an SAP HANA on SUSE Linux Enterprise Server (SLES) rapid deployment solution (SUSE 11 only), a customized preinstallation package for speeding up first-time installation and configuration of SAP Data Services on the SAP HANA landscape. As a prerequisite, you will need at least SAP HANA 1.0 SPS 6.

To take advantage of the new SAP Data Services capabilities for SAP HANA, we recommend upgrading to SAP Data Services 4.2 or higher as soon as possible.

9.3.1 Configuration Requirements

To transfer data to SAP HANA, SAP Data Services 4.1 SP 1 or higher is required, at a minimum. The components of the software that must be installed to be able to transfer metadata to SAP HANA are the Metadata Service and the Viewdata Service.

> **Note**
>
> While SAP Data Services 4.1 SP 1 is the minimum version required for loading data to SAP HANA, the exact version of SAP Data Services you need is determined by the version of SAP HANA you're using. SAP Note 1600140 provides a comprehensive compatibility list comparing versions of SAP Data Services and versions of SAP HANA, so make sure you check this note in order to correctly match your version of SAP Data Services to your SAP HANA installation.

In terms of configuration, you must turn off the session security for the `IMPORT_REPO_OBJECT` Web Service in SAP Data Services to enable the metadata transfer to SAP HANA. The SAP HANA system itself has no specific configuration requirements.

9.3.2   Preparing SAP HANA to Receive Data from SAP Data Services

Before data can be loaded to SAP HANA, the necessary tables must exist in a schema in SAP HANA to receive the data. Creating target tables in the SAP HANA system can technically be done by SAP Data Services during the data load; however, this method doesn't allow you to review the table definitions or the field typing before data is populated into the table. After data is populated, the definitions can no longer be changed, for example, to switch a field from being non-Unicode (type `VARCHAR`) to Unicode (type `NVARCHAR`). The best solution is that you create the tables beforehand.

Of course, the internal functionality of SAP HANA can be used to create tables through the MODELER perspective or with the use of the SQL Editor. For SAP source systems, an easier way is to get the metadata definitions from SAP Data Services and have SAP HANA create the tables automatically.

In summary, you can create the target tables in SAP HANA in four ways:

▶ Using SAP HANA Studio, through the graphical interface

▶ Using SAP HANA Studio, through the SQL Editor

▶ Automatically with a mass metadata import, for SAP source systems only

▶ Automatically during the SAP Data Services load job execution, table by table

To create tables for SAP source systems automatically in a mass operation, do the following:

1. If the connection doesn't exist yet (e.g., the connection between SAP Data Services and the SAP source system is brand new), create a data store of the type SAP APPLICATIONS in SAP Data Services. This data store will be the source of the metadata for SAP HANA.

2. Establish the connection between the SAP Data Services data store and the SAP HANA system.

   ▶ In SAP HANA, start QUICK LAUNCH.

   ▶ In the SETUP section, click the entry CONFIGURE IMPORT SERVER.

   ▶ In the dialog box that appears, provide the host name of the SAP Data Services system as the SERVER ADDRESS and provide the name of the SAP Data Services repository where the data store was created. Don't specify a value for the ODBC DATA SOURCE field.

   ▶ Click OK to finish the configuration. The source of the metadata import is now known to SAP HANA.

3. Import the metadata into SAP HANA.

   ▶ In SAP HANA, in the CONTENT section of the QUICK LAUNCH screen, click the entry IMPORT.

   ▶ A dialog screen appears asking you to select an import source. Under the heading INFORMATION MODELER, click the entry SOURCE OBJECTS.

   ▶ Specify a target system. Remember that one SAP HANA Studio installation can be connected to any number of SAP HANA systems simultaneously. Click on the desired target SAP HANA system.

   ▶ Select the specific SAP Data Services source system as the connection to be used. Select the SAP source system name that was created with the data store earlier.

   ▶ On the same dialog screen, select whether you want to import metadata for tables or for extractors. If you want both, choose one now, and simply repeat the whole process for the other later.

   ▶ Select for which individual tables or extractors you want to import metadata definitions. Add the objects you want. Don't forget to specify the desired schema in SAP HANA in which target tables for the objects should be created.

   ▶ Review the metadata definitions. You can make corrections or desired changes here for data type, length, nullability of the fields, and so on.

   ▶ At the completion of this step, the metadata import is fully specified. Click NEXT to get a short summary of the proposed import.

▷ Click FINISH to perform the import itself and create a target table in SAP HANA for each of the objects selected for import.

This method allows you to create tables in SAP HANA based on the source table definitions in a quick way, handling many tables or extractors at once. Unfortunately, this method is currently not supported for non-SAP source systems.

The second way to create tables in SAP HANA automatically, based on the metadata provided by SAP Data Services, is through batch job definition. You'll need one data store for the source system tables and a second data store for the SAP HANA table definitions, both created in SAP Data Services. You can then create a batch job that makes use of the template table functionality to export the metadata to SAP HANA.

Your batch job definition will look like Figure 9.24. Without going into great detail, in the definition, the following occurs:

▶ The source table becomes the individual table from the source system data store that you want to load to SAP HANA.

▶ The template table contains the definition of the target table in the SAP HANA data store: table name and target schema in the SAP HANA system. (The schema name is placed in the OWNER NAME field of the template definition.)

▶ The fields that will be part of the target table to be created in SAP HANA are specified in Query 2.

▶ In Query 1, you map the fields you want to load to SAP HANA (which would normally be the same list as in Query 2).

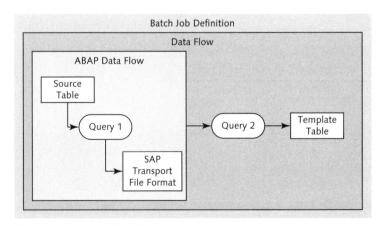

Figure 9.24 Batch Job Definition for a Metadata Import

When you execute this batch job in SAP Data Services, the target table will be created in the SAP HANA system.

9.3.3 Data Update Methods

In a discussion of the different ways to load data into SAP HANA through SAP Data Services, we must take into account different possible sources and different delta mechanisms, called *change data capture* (CDC) mechanisms in SAP Data Services.

The main characteristics of the different data update modes are as follows:

▶ *Full refresh* performs a complete drop and reload of the data.

▶ *Timestamp-based CDC* is based on timestamps that must be available in the table on the source system. Depending on the timestamps available, slightly different implementation scenarios exist.

▶ *Target-based CDC* loads all data from the source system but sends only new and changed records on to SAP HANA.

▶ *Source-based CDC* extracts only new and changed records from the source, which is the functional equivalent of a timestamp-based extraction but for Business Content data sources instead of for tables. Only extractors that support delta recognition can perform this type of CDC.

Table 9.6 summarizes the different options for updating data by the type of source you want to use.

		Full Refresh	Timestamp-Based CDC	Target-Based CDC	Source-Based CDC
Table	Inserts only	✓	✓	✓	
	Updates possible	✓	✓	✓	
Data Source	With ODP and delta recognition	✓		✓	✓
	Without ODP or without delta recognition	✓		✓	

Table 9.6 Update Types by Type of Source Data

You'll notice in Table 9.6 that the extraction scenarios for data sources are considered separately for ODP (Operational Data Provisioning) or non-ODP compatible data sources. For the purpose of data replication, the ODP interface mainly enables the use of data sources with delta queues for those extractors that support a delta. Not all data sources delivered by SAP are ODP-compatible, so you'll need to check the individual data sources to see if the ones you want to use with SAP Data Services are in the list. For those that are ODP-compatible and have delta recognition, an efficient delta extraction is available to SAP Data Services. An additional benefit for ODP-compatible data sources is that they don't require the use of an ABAP data flow in SAP Data Services (regardless of whether they support delta capabilities or not).

A full refresh of all of the data in a table is the simplest way to load data. For a full refresh, setting up the batch job in SAP Data Services looks the same as for any other target system (Figure 9.25).

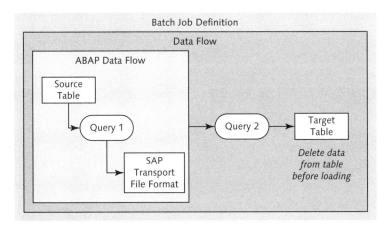

Figure 9.25 Batch Job Definition for Full Refresh of Data (from a Table)

The batch job definition just shown is for tables. For data source extractors, the definition is basically the same, except that, for ODP-compatible data sources, no ABAP data flow is required, as illustrated in Figure 9.26. We won't present the ODP-compatible data source batch job definitions for the other scenarios in this section. To modify a scenario for these data sources, the principle is always exactly the same.

In the target-based CDC mechanism, all data is loaded from the source, and a full table comparison is done in SAP Data Services to generate the delta records. This type of batch job will look almost the same as a full refresh; the only difference is the addition of a table comparison (Figure 9.27).

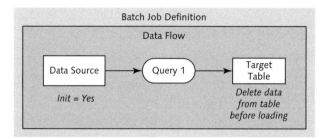

Figure 9.26 Batch Job Definition for Full Refresh of Data (ODP-Compatible Data Source)

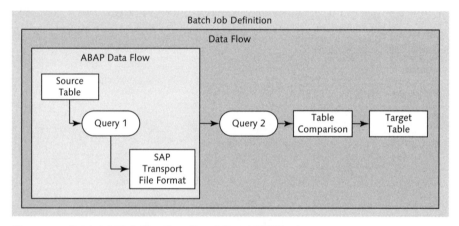

Figure 9.27 Batch Job Definition for a Target-Based CDC Feed

The other CDC mechanisms deserve some special consideration when you want to use them to feed an SAP HANA system. Remember that you're populating simple tables in SAP HANA; there is no data activation mechanism, for example, like there is for DataStore Objects (DSOs) in SAP BW. Depending on the available change dates and so on for the records—and, for extractors, the delta mechanism of the extractor itself—you may need to adjust the batch job definitions specifically for use with SAP HANA. The logic for generating the correct delta and mapping the correct insert, update, and delete operations needs to be implemented in SAP Data Services.

Using a timestamp-based CDC method for generating the delta to send to SAP HANA, for example, might look Figure 9.28.

Depending on exactly which timestamps are available in the source data, the design may vary. The preceding example is for a source that has separate timestamps for new and changed records and for tables with both inserts and updates in the source system. If the source table only gets new records (inserts only), the second data flow (Data Flow 2) would simply be omitted.

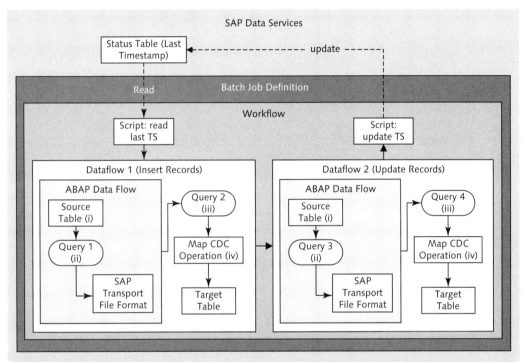

Figure 9.28 Batch Job Definition for a Common Timestamp-Based CDC Data Feed

A source-based CDC method is the fastest way to load data using data source extractors because, in this case, only the new and changed records are loaded from the source system to SAP Data Services. All that is required to prepare the delta for SAP HANA is to map the correct CDC operations (insert, update, delete). For an ODP-compatible extractor with delta recognition capability, the batch job definition would look like Figure 9.29.

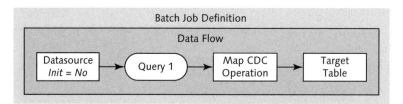

Figure 9.29 Batch Job Definition for an Extractor with Delta Recognition (Source-Based CDC Mechanism)

You will work with these basic batch job definitions for the different update scenarios to SAP HANA. Of course, you can enhance these with transformations as needed.

9.3.4 Loading Data

We'll illustrate the use of SAP Data Services to load data into SAP HANA with a walkthrough of the process for loading flat files. This example loads a flat file (a comma-delimited file, to be precise) into an existing table in an SAP HANA system. The process is largely the same if the target table doesn't exist yet in SAP HANA or if you're loading from a database instead of from a flat file, and we provide notes on how exactly the process differs and what to do in such cases.

A data flow is designed by using the SAP Data Services Designer tool. You'll need the following before you begin:

▶ SAP Data Services Designer installed on your client computer.

▶ Credentials to log on to the tool.

▶ The name of the SAP Data Services server on which you'll be working.

▶ Repository name. All work is done in a specific repository. Repositories are typically created by your SAP Data Services administrators, so you'll need to get the name of the repository that you need to use from them.

▶ The name(s) of the *data stores* inside the repository that you need to use. In this example, you'll create the data store required to illustrate how this works, but creating a data store only needs to be done once for each connected system (whether source database or target SAP HANA system). In most cases, the required data stores will already exist.

▶ The name of the *project* in which you need to create the load jobs. All data load jobs that are configured in SAP Data Services must belong to a project; the projects help organize the development work in the system. Depending on your organization's preferences, projects may have already been set up for you by the SAP Data Services administrators, or you may be directed to create your own.

With this information handy, you can now log on to the SAP Data Services Designer.

Setting Up the Necessary Data Stores

Log on directly from the START menu in Windows. A popup screen appears in which you can fill in the SAP Data Services server name and your credentials, as shown in Figure 9.30. Clicking LOG ON will bring up the list of repositories to which you have access. Simply click on the name of the desired repository, and click OK to complete the logon procedure.

Figure 9.30 Logging On to the Correct Repository in Data Services Designer

You'll arrive at the initial screen shown in Figure 9.31. The screen opens with a START PAGE where some common activities are listed for easy access. Notice that the START PAGE is a tab. In this same pane, any other screens you open to see table definitions, create batch jobs, and so on will open as new tabs later.

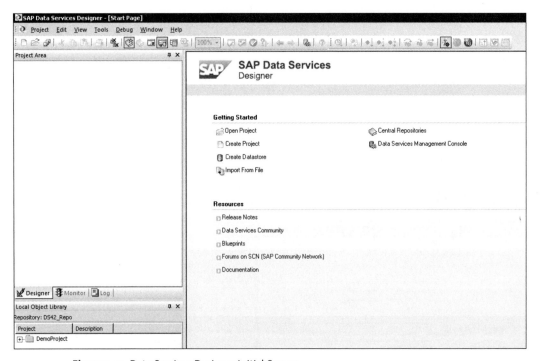

Figure 9.31 Data Services Designer Initial Screen

The other screen elements of the most importance to this discussion are on the left:

▶ The PROJECT AREA lists all projects. Each one can be expanded to see the objects within it in a tree structure. A project consists of a collection of real-time jobs and/or batch jobs. Each job then has any number of other objects in it, chosen from the LOCAL OBJECT LIBRARY.

▶ The LOCAL OBJECT LIBRARY lists all objects in the repository. Of primary interest to this discussion are the DATASTORES, which hold the definitions of tables and, possibly, functions. Using the tabs at the bottom of this pane, you can also find other objects in the system; each tab is essentially a major category of objects (see Figure 9.32).

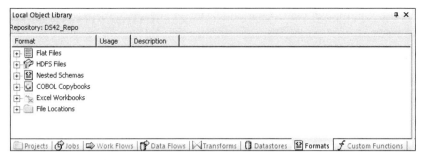

Figure 9.32 Types of Objects in the Local Object Library

If the target SAP HANA system for the desired data load has already been added to the SAP Data Services repository, navigate to it in the LOCAL OBJECT LIBRARY. In this example, the target system hasn't been defined in SAP Data Services yet, so you need set it up now.

To add a new target SAP HANA system to your repository, follow these steps:

1. Ensure you are in the DATASTORES tab in the LOCAL OBJECT LIBRARY pane.

2. Right-click in a blank portion of the pane and choose NEW as in Figure 9.33.

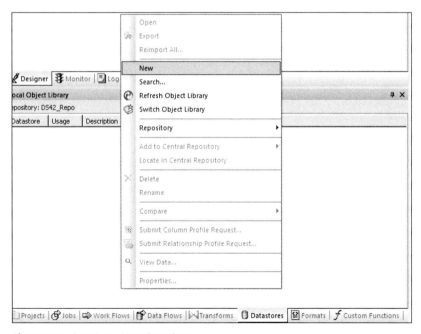

Figure 9.33 Creating a New Data Store

3. In the popup window, enter a name for the new data store and your logon credentials to the SAP HANA system. Choose the other settings as shown in Figure 9.34, and click OK to create the connection to SAP HANA.

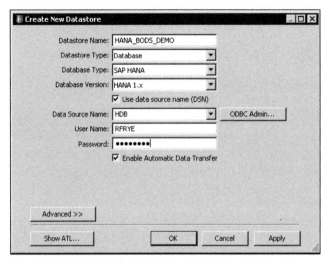

Figure 9.34 Defining SAP HANA Target System as a Data Store

The SAP HANA system is now connected, but no metadata or data has been exchanged, for example, on table definitions. The connection shows up as a data store, and if you expand it, no tables will be listed yet (Figure 9.35).

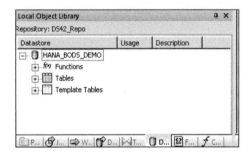

Figure 9.35 Objects Available in the SAP HANA Data Store

Before you can create a job to load data, SAP Data Services first needs to know exactly what the structures of the tables and/or files are that you want to use. The next step is then to either define or import this metadata into the repository.

Importing Metadata into SAP Data Services from a Database

The table definitions from a database can be imported in a few easy steps. This process applies both to any database you want to use as a source of data and to the target SAP HANA database itself; the steps are identical.

In this example, you'll import the table definition of the target SAP HANA table. If the table you want to load data into doesn't yet exist in SAP HANA, simply skip this activity.

As shown in Figure 9.36, in the LOCAL OBJECT LIBRARY, navigate to the DATA-STORES tab. Expand the data store you want to import metadata into. Right-click on the node TABLES and choose one of two options:

▶ IMPORT ALL (or REIMPORT ALL, if this is not the first time)

▶ IMPORT BY NAME

Be careful with the IMPORT ALL function, which may bring a very large number of table definitions across and take a while to complete. Unless your SAP HANA system is still very small, importing individual table definitions as needed is a better approach. Figure 9.36 shows the choice to import metadata from a single table.

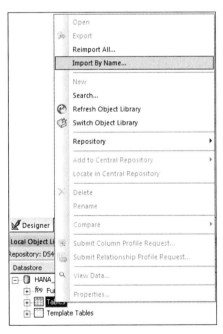

Figure 9.36 Importing Metadata from SAP HANA into SAP Data Services

Only a few parameters are required to complete the process. In the NAME field on the popup that appears (Figure 9.37), fill in the name of the table. In the OWNER field, you need to provide the database schema in which the table resides on the connected database. Our example uses an SAP HANA schema. Clicking IMPORT will establish a connection to the database that is represented by this data store, obtain the table metadata, and create a corresponding table definition in SAP Data Services.

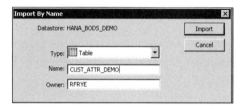

Figure 9.37 Specifying the SAP HANA Table for Metadata Import

Defining Metadata in SAP Data Services for Flat Files

By definition, no data dictionary in a connected database exists here, so you'll have a little more work to establish the metadata. The following activities serve as a general guide:

1. Navigate to the FORMATS tab in the LOCAL OBJECT LIBRARY.

2. Right-click the top node called FLAT FILES and choose NEW, as shown in Figure 9.38.

3. The FILE FORMAT EDITOR window opens as shown in Figure 9.39. You'll define all of the properties of the file here:

   ▶ TYPE
   For this example, DELIMITED is used.

   ▶ NAME
   The name that you want this file format to be known as in SAP Data Services is used here. The format itself will be stored as a metadata definition in SAP Data Services and can be reused later, for example, for other files with the same structure.

   ▶ LOCATION
   This field shows where the file can be found.

   ▶ DELIMITERS, DEFAULT FORMAT, INPUT/OUTPUT
   The technical properties of the file, such as which delimiters are used, which date format, whether or not there is a column header row, and so on.

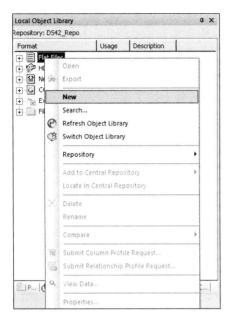

Figure 9.38 Creating Metadata for a Flat File

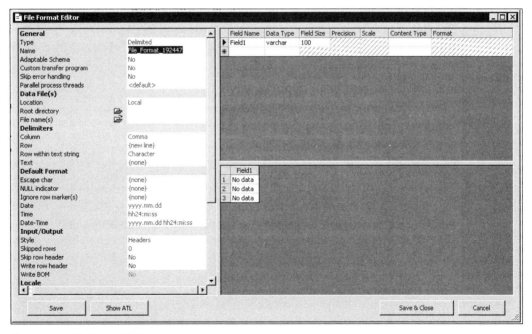

Figure 9.39 File Format Editor

4. Fill in the information and click SAVE.

5. In the top-right section of the FILE FORMAT EDITOR screen, make sure the field types and lengths are correct. The bottom-right section shows you a data preview. Figure 9.40 shows the necessary information filled in for the example file. The field typing is verified, and the data preview looks good.

6. Click SAVE & CLOSE to finish.

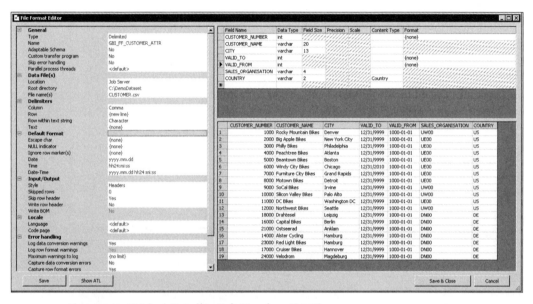

Figure 9.40 Finished Metadata Definition for a Flat File

Creating the Batch Job

With both the source and target structures known to SAP Data Services, you're now ready to create a job that will link these definitions together and allow you to move data between them.

To create a new job, navigate to the appropriate project in the PROJECT AREA pane. Right-click the project name and choose NEW BATCH JOB as shown in Figure 9.41. A new tab in the main window pane will open in SAP Data Services.

A batch job consists of one or more data flows. Consider carefully how many data flows you combine into one job. On the one hand, including more data flows allows you to group several loads into one, reducing the overall number of jobs that need to be scheduled in the system, and thus simplifying the job schedule. On the other hand, loads are performed at the job level, and you'll no longer have the flexibility to run only one data flow. To increase flexibility, include only one or a few data flows in each job and allow the job schedule to handle the start times and frequency of each data flow—especially if you have a scheduling tool that allows for resource-based scheduling, which will optimize the total load time for all loads.

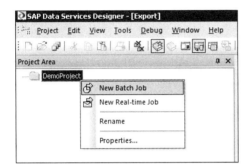

Figure 9.41 Creating a New Batch Job

To add a new data flow to the job, either right-click on the job name in the PROJECT AREA and choose ADD NEW DATA FLOW or, alternatively, drag the DATA FLOW icon—on the right side of the screen—onto the central pane. Figure 9.42 shows the recently added data flow, which will be the only data flow in the job for this example.

Double-clicking on the data flow will open its definition in yet another tab in the central pane. Inside the data flow is where you'll place the objects you need to move data between the source and target system, link them together in the proper order, and define any custom transformations you want to apply in the data load process.

You add the table definitions by locating the definitions in the LOCAL OBJECT LIBRARY and then dragging them into the central pane to the DATA FLOW tab (see Figure 9.43). Once the definitions are dragged into the pane, the system automatically asks you if this is to be a source or target table. Make the flat file definition into a source, and the SAP HANA table, into a target in for this example.

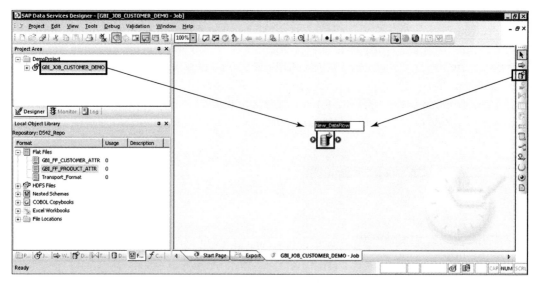

Figure 9.42 Adding a Data Flow to the Batch Job

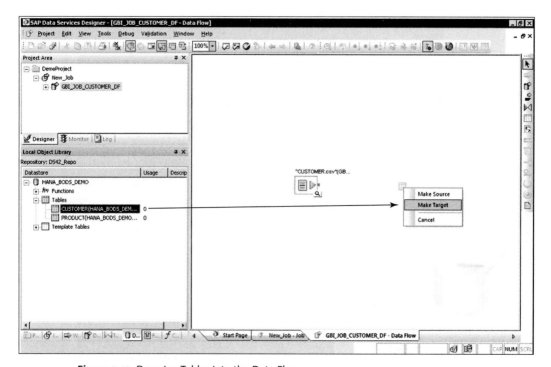

Figure 9.43 Dragging Tables into the Data Flow

With the required structures in place, the last step is to connect them to each other so data can be moved between them. This connection is created using a *query*. Place a new query in the data flow by dragging the TRANSFORM icon from the right side of the screen onto the DATA FLOW canvas. Then, you can connect the source with the query simply by drawing the connection on the canvas. Link the query's output to the target SAP HANA table definition in the same way. The result is reflected in Figure 9.44.

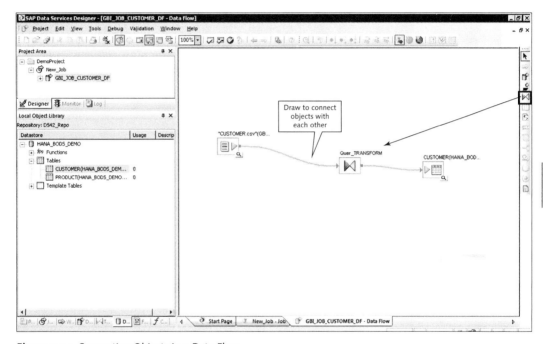

Figure 9.44 Connecting Objects in a Data Flow

The following lists a few important points concerning how SAP Data Services works with the objects you define:

▶ The flat file object you created in the LOCAL OBJECT LIBRARY has all of the information needed to find the file, decipher it with the proper delimiters, and present the data inside SAP Data Services as a runtime table with a fully defined structure (field sequence, field typing, etc.).

▶ Likewise, the SAP HANA table object in the library has all of the required information to either read from or write to the table in the connected SAP HANA database; that is, the SAP HANA table object has the connection information, the correct table definition, and the schema to which it belongs in SAP HANA.

▶ Both of these objects can now simply be "called" within any data flow in SAP Data Services by a query. The query acts as the following:

  ▶ As a trigger to read from and/or write to the source and target databases simply by being connected to these objects.

  ▶ As a mapping tool between the ingoing and outgoing structures from the query itself, that is, between the structure of the object serving as source and the structure of the object serving as target in the data flow.

This concept is also clearly visible in the query definition. Click on the query in the data flow to view its definition, and you'll see three panes in this tab as shown in Figure 9.45.

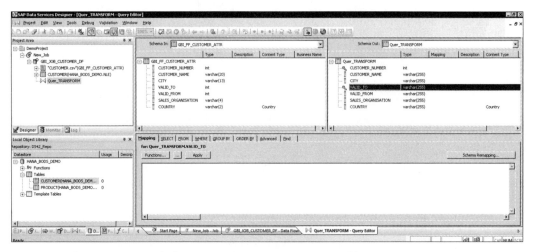

Figure 9.45 Query Definition: Mapping Source to Target Fields

The SCHEMA IN and SCHEMA OUT panes are the structures of the source and target objects, respectively; in this example, the structures are the flat file and the SAP HANA table. The bottom pane holds the mapping between them, with the potential to add to the different ways in which the SQL statement in the data flow can further affect how the data is presented by the query, such as the WHERE and GROUP BY clauses of the SQL statement that reads the source object's data to name a few.

For a simple one-to-one mapping, you only need to drag the source fields from the SCHEMA IN structure to the desired field in the SCHEMA OUT structure. Such a mapping is reflected in the bottom pane as shown in Figure 9.46. You can now enhance this mapping in many ways. The SELECT clauses can be manipulated, as well as the mapping itself—you can type the required SQL commands for the field into the MAPPING tab for this.

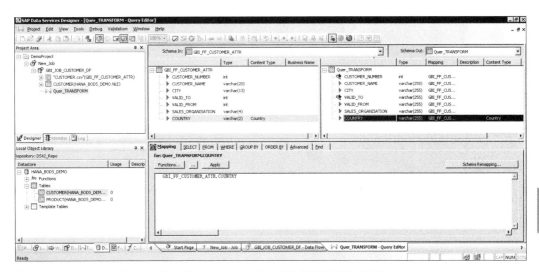

Figure 9.46 Query Definition: Flat File Now Mapped to SAP HANA Table Fields

The batch job is now defined. Save the objects you've created (the easiest way is to use the SAVE ALL button on the main taskbar). The example project now contains an executable batch job.

Executing the Batch Job

Automated batch job execution of SAP Data Services jobs can be done in a number of different ways. Whether or not an SAP HANA database is involved in the jobs has no bearing on how the jobs get automated so we'll leave that (extensive) discussion out of this chapter. However, you do need to test the job now that it's fully defined. Fortunately, you can execute it manually from within SAP Data Services Designer to check the results.

To execute a job once, right-click on the batch job name in the PROJECT AREA and choose EXECUTE (see Figure 9.47).

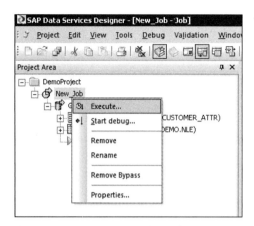

Figure 9.47 Executing a Batch Job from SAP Data Services Designer

A window pops up where you must set the desired EXECUTION PROPERTIES (see Figure 9.48). On the whole, you can go with the defaults on this screen. If you've used global variables or substitution parameters in your query mappings, you can provide those values for executing this one job here. To troubleshoot a particular job, you can set the trace level to BRIEF, VERBOSE, or FULL. Higher trace levels provide very detailed information about the problem in the job execution; however, you should be careful when selecting the trace level because some settings slow down the load by an order of magnitude and create very large log files in the system.

> **Note**
>
> For more information on troubleshooting data services jobs, you can download the *SAP Data Services Management Console Guide* from the SAP Marketplace.

Click OK to run the job. The system automatically switches the screen to show you the job log as the job progresses, as shown in Figure 9.49. You can always consult the log later by going to the PROJECT AREA and choosing the LOG tab, where the job execution logs are organized in a tree structure and can be called up anytime.

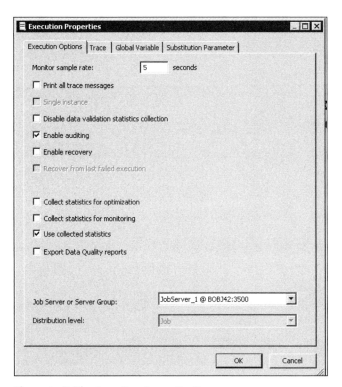

Figure 9.48 The Execution Properties Screen

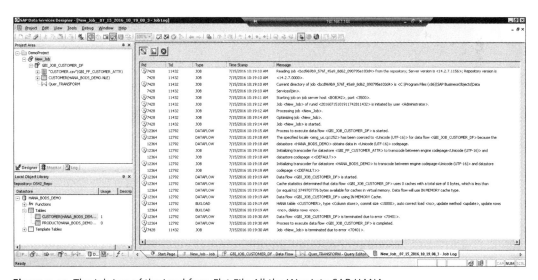

Figure 9.49 The Job Log of the Load from Flat File All the Way into SAP HANA

9.4 Log-Based Replication: SAP (Sybase) Replication Server (RS) and SAP HANA Load Controller (LC)

If your source system is on IBM DB2 for LUW as a database, log-based replication is an option. Remember that, when you use this replication method, the mapping is a purely one-to-one affair. You must have confidence in your source system's data quality, and the data must be usable as is in the target SAP HANA system.

If these criteria are met, this replication method offers you high-performance, real-time replication. Given the combination of a pure 1:1 mapping and real-time replication, this method is most often used to satisfy detailed operation reporting requirements.

Figure 9.50 illustrates the software components required to use SAP/Sybase replication to SAP HANA.

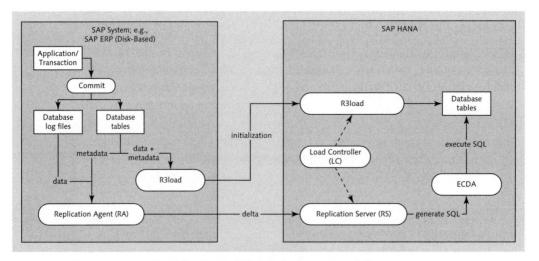

Figure 9.50 Log-Based Replication Software Components and Flows

The following are the components on the source system:

▶ **SAP (Sybase) Replication Agent (RA)**

  ▷ RA gets data from the database logs in raw format and combines it with metadata from the database tables to construct meaningful records to send to the target system.

- ▷ RA runs on the accompanying Embedded Replication Agent System Database (ERASD), which is installed implicitly with RA.

- ▷ Reading from the database logs satisfies the delta data feed requirements; any changes are captured and forwarded.

- ▶ **R3load**
R3load is an SAP component that is used for the initial loads to SAP HANA.

The following are the components on SAP HANA:

- ▶ **SAP (Sybase) Replication Server (RS)**

  - ▷ RS is the target component where records sent by RA are received. Once received, RS generates the appropriate SQL statements needed to insert the data into the target tables on SAP HANA.

  - ▷ RS runs on the accompanying Embedded Replication Server System Database (ERSSD), again implicitly installed with RS.

- ▶ **Enterprise Connect Data Access (ECDA)**
ECDA is the second SAP/Sybase software component that needs to be installed on SAP HANA. ECDA takes generated SQL statements from RS and executes them on SAP HANA, inserting and updating records in the data tables as needed.

  - ▷ ECDA connects to the SAP HANA database to update data by using an Open Database Connectivity (ODBC) connection.

  - ▷ RS and ECDA together handle the delta records sent by RA.

- ▶ **R3load on the SAP HANA side**
R3load receives the initial loads from the corresponding R3load component on the source system and propagates the data to the SAP HANA database tables.

- ▶ **Load Controller (LC)**
This component pulls all of the functionality together. When a load is started from within SAP HANA Studio using this replication method, LC invokes both R3load (for the initial data transfer) and RA (to start capturing changes). After the initial load has finished, LC switches to a continuous data stream from RA instead, first catching up on changes made since the start of the initial load and then running on a continuous, real-time basis.

- ▶ **SAP Host Agent**
This prerequisite is required for communication between the systems.

We'll now take a quick look at the steps necessary to install and run SAP/Sybase replication to SAP HANA.

9.4.1 Installation

Installing these components is straightforward, and installation scripts are provided with the software to make the process easy. The following are the high-level steps:

1. **SAP HANA**
   Verify that SAP Host Agent is installed and running, which should be the case because SAP Host Agent is automatically installed with the initial SAP HANA database install.

2. **Source system**
   Verify that the SAP Host Agent is installed, which, again, should already be the case, but depending on your release, you may need to upgrade the SAP Host Agent component to version 7.20, which is the minimum required to work with this replication method.

3. **SAP HANA**
   Install RS and ECDA. The software will arrive in an archive file format. After unpacking it, you will need to configure a few small items and run the installation script.

4. **Source system**
   Install RA, which will also arrive in an archive file format. After unpacking it, you need to configure a few small items and run the installation script.

5. **SAP HANA**
   Install LC by unpacking the software and running the installation script.

6. **Source system**
   Create a new directory to be used for the data export, and patch R3load to the latest level if required.

After the installation, you need to run several configuration scripts to set up the connections between the systems. The scripts are provided by SAP and are as follows:

1. Configure RS by entering the pertinent system information (SAP HANA host name, instance number, etc.) into a configuration file and then running the RS configuration script.

2. Create a user in the source system that can be used by RA to log on to DB2 so that the user can monitor the logs and capture changes.

3. Configure RA by entering the required system information into a text file and running the RA configuration script.

4. In SAP HANA, set up a password for LC's communication with the SAP Host Agent.

5. In SAP HANA, create a target schema to hold the tables that will be replicated by SAP/Sybase.

6. Configure LC by entering parameters in a configuration file and running the LC configuration script. Because it's LC that ties together all of the parts, you'll need to enter quite a few parameters, covering information from hosts and ports, RS and RA, both the SAP HANA and source database systems, and the target schema in SAP HANA, to name the most important ones.

7. Finally, start running LC on the SAP HANA server with the provided script.

9.4.2 Running SAP (Sybase) Replication Server (RS)

Running RS is a straightforward task. Remember that, by definition, RS is a pure 1:1 replication that is a continuous stream. Ensure that you have the required metadata (table definitions) in SAP HANA to receive data.

All you need to do to get RS running is to log on to SAP HANA Studio, go to the ADMINISTRATOR perspective, and choose DATA PROVISIONING. Using the LOAD function, select the schema and tables you want to start loading, and kick off the initial load. From here on out, LC takes the process over by both starting and completing the initial data transfer and then starting the subsequent real-time replication stream.

9.5 SAP HANA Smart Data Access for Data Federation and Virtualization

Before we can discuss SAP HANA smart data access (SDA) in detail, let's define a couple of terms: data federation and data virtualization. To avoid the expense and avoid introducing potential errors involved in the extraction, transformation, and loading (ETL) of data from one database to another, many companies are moving towards the related ideas of data federation and data virtualization.

Data federation means that multiple, independent databases have been mapped into a single, integrated database system. The independent databases may or may not be located in the same geographic location. In either case, a combination of network connectivity and database drivers are used to create a connection to the original source databases.

When we discuss *data virtualization*, we mean that each source database continues to reside in its original location, and an abstraction layer is created to provide users with a uniform interface for accessing the data, regardless of its physical location. Applications are allowed to retrieve and manipulate data, without concern for where the data is located, which type of database is being used, whether the database resides on disk or in memory, the drivers and hardware used, or how the data is formatted.

With SAP HANA smart data access, you can create a connection to a source system, and the source table will be available as a virtual table within SAP HANA. Because virtual tables and physical tables are treated alike, no special effort is required to access the data. The data in the virtual table will still reside on the source system, and SDA will allow you to access that data in real time.

For a listing of the currently supported source system connections with SAP HANA smart data access, see Table 9.7.

Remote Data Source	Supported Hardware Platform
SAP HANA	Any
SAP IQ	Any
SAP Adaptive Server Enterprise	Any
SAP Event Stream Processor	Intel-based hardware only
SAP MaxDB	Intel-based hardware only
Apache Hadoop	Intel-based hardware only
Teradata	Intel-based hardware only
Microsoft SQL Server 2012	Intel-based hardware only
Oracle Database 12C	Any
IBM DB2	Intel-based hardware only

Table 9.7 Supported SDA Data Sources

Remote Data Source	Supported Hardware Platform
IBM Netezza Appliance	Intel-based hardware only
Apache Spark	Any

Table 9.7 Supported SDA Data Sources (Cont.)

In the following sections, we will walk you through setting up database drivers on SAP HANA to connect to SDA, connecting Hadoop to SDA, and consuming data from SDA.

9.5.1 Setting up Database Drivers

The first step in connecting any data source through SDA is to set up the correct ODBC database drivers on the SAP HANA server that will connect to the data source. We'll discuss the general steps for completing this setup in this section, but the specific details for your connection are available in the *SAP HANA Administration Guide*, available for download from *http://help.sap.com/hana/SAP_HANA_Administration_Guide_en.pdf*.

SDA requires a file named *.odbc.ini* to be present in the home directory of the SAP HANA server's administrator. Please note that *.odbc.ini* is a hidden file, so you'll need to view hidden files within your Linux installation to see this file. Once the file has been created, you usually need to add an entry in the file for each remote source.

You'll need to either install the ODBC driver library files to a location that is already searched by the SAP HANA server, or you'll need to update the LD_LIBRARY_PATH environment variable in Linux to include the directory where the ODBC driver for your data source is deployed. To install to a path that is already searched, you can use the SAP HANA EXE directory. Otherwise, you'll need to add the following code to your *.customer.sh* file in the home directory of the SAP HANA user:

```
export LD_LIBRARY_PATH=$LD_LIBRARY_PATH:/<path_to_driver>
```

With the driver deployed and the LD_LIBRARY_PATH updated, you will typically be required to define a DSN entry in the *.odbc.ini* file and create the remote source from the Linux command line. As each of the data sources in Table 9.7 has a different process for installing the drivers and creating the DSN, you should refer to

Section 9 of the *SAP HANA Administration Guide* for the exact details relevant to your selected data source.

9.5.2   Connecting Hadoop to SDA

SDA can also be used to combine the in-memory processing of SAP HANA with Hadoop's capacity to process large quantities of unstructured data. Hadoop uses the Hadoop Distributed File System (HDFS) to break large files into numerous blocks and replicate these blocks across data nodes. The MapReduce (MR) programming paradigm is used to process the HDFS blocks. MR includes native support for Java, but C++, Python, and other programming languages may be used with MR as well.

When combining SAP HANA and Hadoop, you will need to:

1. Set up the Hadoop Hive ODBC driver.
2. Set up the SAP HANA Spark controller (using Ambari or through manual configuration).
3. Add a Hadoop system as a remote source.
4. Add a MapReduce program to SAP HANA.
5. Create a virtual function.

Once you've completed these steps, you can add an Ambari URL to the SAP HANA Cockpit (for more about the SAP HANA Cockpit, see Chapter 10), use the SAP HANA Data Warehousing Foundation (DWF) Lifecycle Manager to move data between SAP HANA and Hadoop and even run SAP HANA Vora on a Hadoop cluster.

As with other data sources, we recommend referring to the *SAP HANA Administration Guide* for the exact details on configuring the SDA connection to Hadoop. The process for connecting and configuring Hadoop can be quite complex, depending on the options you choose for your installation. As such, a detailed examination of this topic is beyond the scope of this introduction to SDA and Hadoop.

9.5.3   Consuming Data with SDA

To consume data from a remote source, you'll first need to create a connection to the external data source. To do so, navigate to the PROVISIONING folder from your

SAP HANA source system in SAP HANA Studio. Expand the PROVISIONING folder and right-click on the REMOTE SOURCES folder to open the context menu. Then click NEW REMOTE SOURCE to open the window to create a new connection.

In the connection window, you'll need to specify a SOURCE NAME and choose the ADAPTER NAME that matches the type of external data source to which you're connecting. In our example (Figure 9.51), we're connecting to another SAP HANA server, so we've selected the HANA (ODBC) adapter. Next, we entered the SERVER and PORT for the connection, as well as the USER NAME and PASSWORD for the server. When all the settings are correct, click the green activation arrow in the upper right to create the connection.

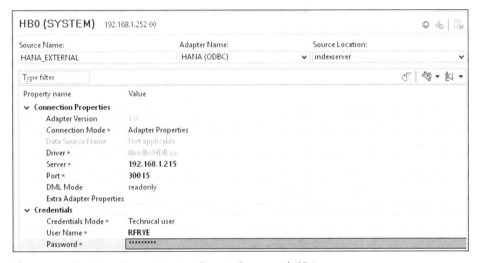

Figure 9.51 Creating a Connection to a Remote Source with SDA

Now that you have a connection to your remote source, you need to create a virtual table from the connection. To create the virtual table, expand the connection you just created (double-click or use the arrow icon to the left of the connection) and navigate to the table that you want to access through your SAP HANA server. Right-click the table and select ADD AS VIRTUAL TABLE from the context menu. In the CREATE VIRTUAL TABLE WINDOW (Figure 9.52), specify a unique TABLE NAME and select the SCHEMA where you want the virtual table to be located, then click CREATE. Now that the virtual table has been created, you can use it as an object within an SAP HANA view. The data will be consumed directly through the SDA connection without requiring it to be moved to the original SAP HANA server.

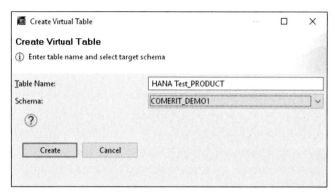

Figure 9.52 Creating a Virtual Table from an External Data Source with SDA

Since SDA allows us to create virtual data models (views) on virtual tables, we've satisfied our goal of data virtualization and avoided the risk and effort involved in a full ETL of the data. Furthermore, since we can connect to numerous external data sources in the same way, we've also created a federated data source for our varied data landscape. As you can see, SAP HANA smart data access makes the process of data federation and virtualization quite simple.

9.6 Summary

You can provision your SAP HANA system with data in several ways. Each method has its own technological components and its own strengths and limitations. With a wide field to choose from, you should learn about all of the options and consider both your short-term and long-term scope for data provisioning. Devise a strategy that allows you to leverage existing development and at the same time steers you toward the desired long-term layout of your system landscape.

We've given a short comparison of the different data provisioning options available to you. SAP Landscape Transformation (SLT) is a real-time data provisioning method that can be implemented quickly and is often the default choice for SAP source systems; on the other hand, SLT offers only limited transformation capabilities. SAP Data Services works with SAP HANA but doesn't offer real-time feeds in general. However, for data that doesn't need to be in real time or for data that requires extensive cleansing or other transformations, SLT is the best solution. SAP (Sybase) Replication Server (RS) is a highly specific solution that works with IBM DB2 for LUW sources to deliver simple 1:1 data replication in real time. SAP HANA smart data access is a great solution for data federation and virtualization, while avoiding the need to move data between systems.

SAP HANA is, at its heart, a technical component. The general support concepts are similar to—and just as essential as—the management of other SAP environments. In this chapter, we'll look at the major administration tasks involved in maintaining, monitoring, and updating SAP HANA.

10   SAP HANA Administration

SAP HANA administration involves most of the regular administration tasks with which you're probably already familiar. You'll have to apply periodic software updates, add new users, maintain security roles for authorizations and authentications, and keep the environments in sync as other software and hardware updates are applied.

Before we dive into the details, you should first know that you can get an overview of your system by going to the Navigator pane in SAP HANA Studio and opening the System Information tab (Figure 10.1). Some of the information in the System Information tab is only available here, but much of the information in these tables can also be found in the editors and options that we cover in this chapter.

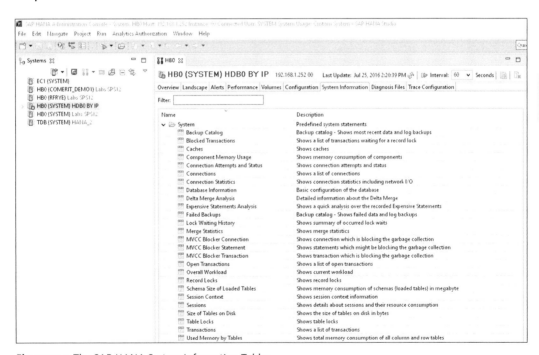

Figure 10.1 The SAP HANA System Information Tables

In this chapter, we'll introduce you to the ADMINISTRATION CONSOLE, an important tool for SAP HANA administration. We'll also take a look at the SAP HANA Cockpit, introduced in SAP HANA SPS 10 and extensively updated with new functionality in SPS 12.

Then we'll move on to high-level explanations of some of the most important SAP HANA administrative tasks: system monitoring, updating, security, license keys, and backup and recovery.

We'll then discuss new capabilities in the latest SAP HANA support package stacks (SPS), including multitenant database containers, dynamic tiering, Multiple Components in One Database (MCOD) and Multiple Components in One System (MCOS) deployments, and virtualized SAP HANA implementations. Finally, we'll conclude the chapter with a brief look at two other administration tools that can be used for SAP HANA implementations: SAP Solution Manager and the Database Administrator (DBA) Cockpit.

10.1 Using the SAP HANA Administration Console

You'll remember SAP HANA Studio from our data modeling content in Chapter 8. In this section, we'll give you a different view of SAP HANA Studio by focusing on the way it can help you perform specific administrative tasks via the ADMINISTRATION CONSOLE. You can access the ADMINISTRATION CONSOLE in several ways. The three that are most frequently used are as follows:

▶ Go to WINDOW, select OPEN PERSPECTIVE, and then select the ADMINISTRATION CONSOLE (Figure 10.2).

▶ Select the OPEN ADMINISTRATION CONSOLE option from the WELCOME screen when you open SAP HANA Studio (Figure 10.3).

▶ Type "administration console" in the QUICK ACCESS text box, then select the SAP HANA ADMINISTRATION CONSOLE perspective from the dropdown list (Figure 10.4).

Figure 10.2 Accessing the SAP HANA Administration Perspective

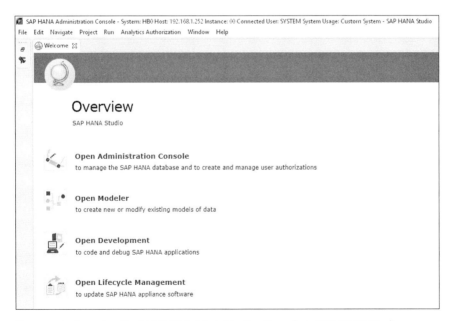

Figure 10.3 Accessing the SAP HANA Administration Console in SAP HANA Studio

Figure 10.4 Quick Access to the SAP HANA Administration Console

Each option will take you to the administration functions of SAP HANA Studio. In this section, we'll explain the most important administration activities that you'll perform using the ADMINISTRATION CONSOLE and the administration functions of SAP HANA.

10.1.1 Adding Systems

Systems can be added from the ADMINISTRATION CONSOLE. Right-click in the SYSTEMS pane and click ADD SYSTEM from the context menu that appears. First, you'll need to type in the HOST NAME of the system you want to add and the INSTANCE NUMBER. In our example, we entered "hdb0.comerit.com" as the host and "00" as the instance.

As of SAP HANA SPS 11, SAP added support for multitenancy and multitenant database containers in SAP HANA. We'll discuss multitenancy more in Section 10.10, but for our example, we'll be creating a connection to a single container system. Give your new connection a logical description, so that you'll recognize it in the future. You can also organize your SAP HANA system connections into folders in the SYSTEMS pane. If you do so, you'll need to select the folder where you want to save your new connection. Next, enter your locale and click NEXT (Figure 10.5).

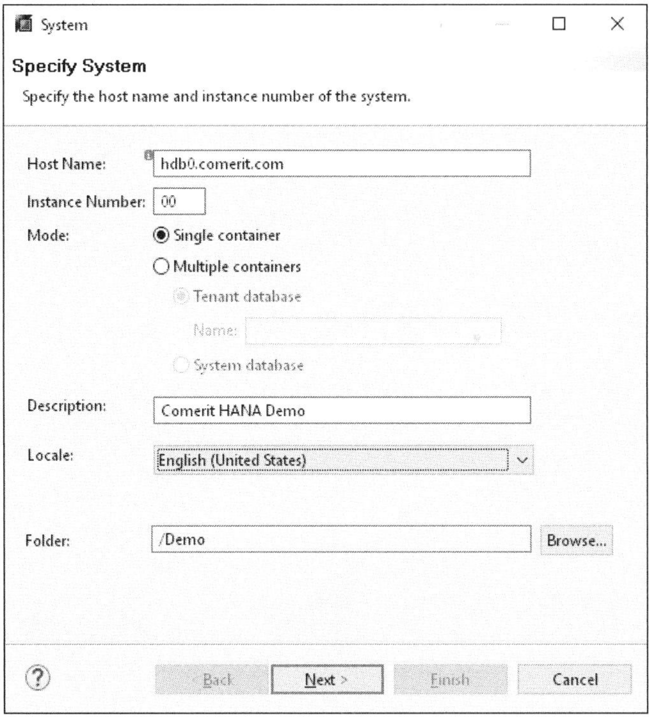

Figure 10.5 Specifying Connection Parameters for Your New SAP HANA System

On the next screen, you'll have a few options: You may choose to authenticate as a user from your operating system, or you can enter the USER NAME and PASSWORD of a database user, as we've done in our example (Figure 10.6). For convenience, you can select STORE USER NAME AND PASSWORD IN SECURE STORAGE.

> **Warning!**
>
> If you choose to save the user name and password in secure storage, you won't be prompted for the login information again. For greater security, you should consider entering the user name and password each time you connect to the system.

If Secure Sockets Layer (SSL) encryption is configured on your SAP HANA appliance, you can select CONNECT USING SSL for a secure connection (your data will be encrypted when transmitted from the system). The option to ENABLE SAP START SERVICE CONNECTION is selected by default. You can disable this option if you like, but if you do so, you should be aware that any administrative actions that require operating system access will not be possible through the connection in SAP HANA Studio. You can also select Use HTTPS to communicate with the SAP start service through a secure connection. When you're satisfied with the Connection Properties, click Next (Figure 10.6).

Figure 10.6 Security Settings When Adding a New System

From the Additional Properties screen (optional, not pictured), you can choose to Auto-Reconnect in the event that SAP HANA Studio detects a broken connection or the SAP HANA system is rebooted. You can also add database connection parameters in the URL if applicable.

For SSL connections, you can test if the connection is secure by validating the SSL certificate. Select Validate SSL Certificate. You can override the system hostname if needed (i.e., with a valid certificate). Finally, you can select the Use user key store as trust store option if you're using certificates from trusted issuers such as VeriSign and others. When you're satisfied with your connection properties, click Finish. If you've entered all your connection parameters correctly, you should see the new system in the Systems pane.

10.1.2 Exporting and Importing Systems

The administration functions also allow you to export a list of systems and connection settings from one SAP HANA system to another. This list reduces the chance for manual errors and also makes the systems much easier to manage.

To export the systems, or folders, go to the main menu and select FILE • EXPORT. Look in the SAP HANA folder structure for LANDSCAPE and click NEXT. You can then select the systems from which you want to export connections and select the target file location to which you want to save the file with the system definitions. Pay attention to the location on the network where you saved it because you'll need this information again when you import the system definitions.

To import the systems, go to the main menu and select FILE • IMPORT. Look in the SAP HANA folder structure for LANDSCAPE and click NEXT. Now you'll have to find the folder where you stored the export file in the preceding steps and select the file. All system definitions that you exported previously will be imported, and any connections that are working in one system should also work across multiple SAP HANA platforms.

10.1.3 Viewing System Installation Details

To view the system installation details, you can click HELP • ABOUT SAP HANA STUDIO in the ADMINISTRATION CONSOLE in SAP HANA Studio (Figure 10.7).

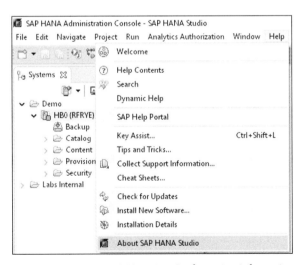

Figure 10.7 Accessing SAP HANA Configuration Information

From the ABOUT SAP HANA STUDIO screen, select INSTALLATION DETAILS (Figure 10.8).

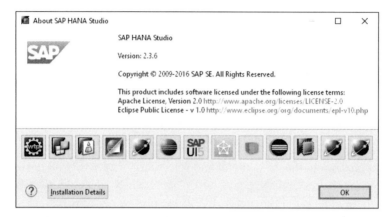

Figure 10.8 Getting Installation Details

In the resulting set of tabs, go to the CONFIGURATION tab (Figure 10.9), which will provide you with all of the technical details of your SAP HANA system in a textual format.

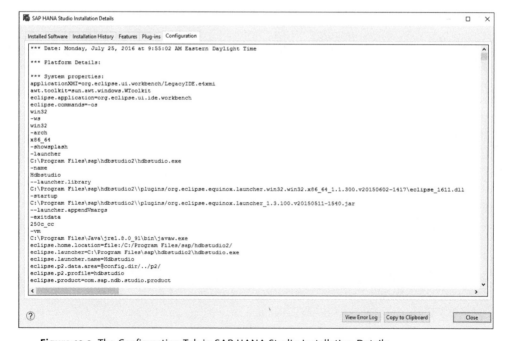

Figure 10.9 The Configuration Tab in SAP HANA Studio Installation Details

You can also download technical information about your system if your hardware vendor or SAP requests it. Just click on HELP at the top of your menu and COLLECT SUPPORT INFORMATION... to download all support details in a ZIP file that you can then mail to your support group (Figure 10.10).

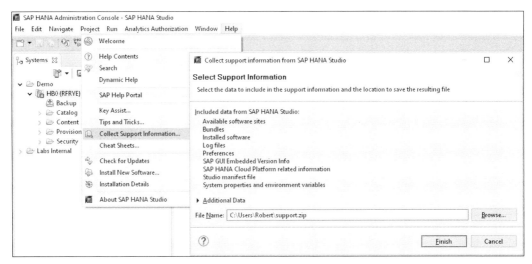

Figure 10.10 Collecting Information for Support Tickets

10.1.4 Administration Editor and Diagnosis Mode

If a system isn't running, you can open the ADMINISTRATION EDITOR, which opens by default in diagnostic mode. This editor allows you to see the SQL statements that attempted to execute while the system was being started or stopped (information collected by the `sapstartsrv` connection).

You can read these files in the ADMINISTRATION EDITOR even when the general system isn't available. An administrator can access the ADMINISTRATION EDITOR at any time by selecting the ADMIN button on the main menu and then selecting OPEN DIAGNOSIS MODE from the dropdown list.

10.1.5 Changing File Locations

Although not required, you can change the default locations of files such as log files and configuration files, which are maintained in the System Landscape Directory (SLD).

You can change default file locations under the CONFIGURATION tab in the ADMINISTRATION EDITOR. Select the NAME SERVER.INI configuration file and then select ADD SECTION to add a new section called SLD. You may now add or change parameters in the name server configuration file that keeps track of your system directories. (For more information about this topic, see SAP Note 1018839.)

10.1.6 Changing Configurations

The configuration of your SAP HANA system is contained in configuration files. You can change some of the parameters in this file in the ADMINISTRATION EDITOR. To see the file, you should select the CONFIGURATION tab and then select the file you want to edit (Figure 10.11).

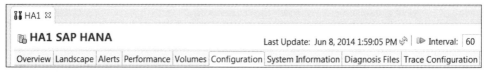

Figure 10.11 SAP HANA Configuration Tab

For each row, you can select the CHANGE option in the context menu and make modifications. If you modify a value, you'll see a green mark next to the value that was changed. You can't modify the values in columns that are marked with a minus sign. These values are set by the system and can't be changed.

To change the global allocation of memory, open the *GLOBAL.INI* file, and look in the MEMORYMANAGER area. Using the context menu, you can change the GLOBAL_ALLOCATION_LIMIT for both hosts and the overall system.

You can always reset the configuration values you changed back to default values by selecting the file and choosing DELETE in the context menu for the parameter. This will restore the default parameter value.

10.1.7 Modifying the Administration Console

You can also change the ADMINISTRATION CONSOLE to fit your needs by going to SAP HANA Studio and selecting WINDOW • PREFERENCES. Under SAP HANA • RUNTIME, you can now make your changes (Figure 10.12).

Modifications may include changing how many screens are displayed and their default values for new development, restricting database display to the user logged on, and controlling how many catalog objects are retrieved initially. You can also control settings such as how frequently background saves are executed (i.e., to reduce loss of work in case of a failure), how to display null values, and how many tables are initially opened in the VIEW TABLE DISTRIBUTION options.

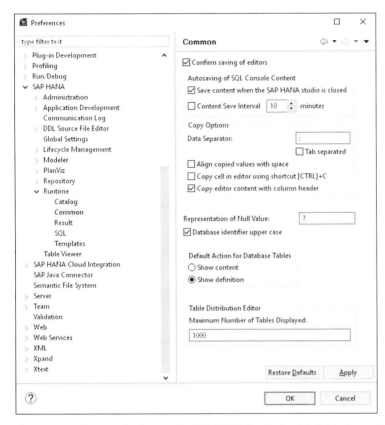

Figure 10.12 Changing Preferences in SAP HANA Studio for Administrators and Developers

You also get access to global settings to control default dialog settings for opening diagnosis files for error analysis. Settings include whether confirmation is required and whether the information dialog is displayed after deleting files or viewing trace files.

In the RESULT area, you can control how many bytes are returned to the results editor for a column, how many bytes are available for line of business (LOB) solutions, and country-specific formatting of values. You can even control whether the system appends values to a file, instead of overwriting the file, when exporting the data.

469

In the SQL area, you'll get detailed controls over how SQL statements are executed. These controls shouldn't be changed by anyone except experts in SQL execution. Controls include cancelling batch SQL statements if errors occur, log handling, and parameters for how and what data is displayed in the SQL Editor in SAP HANA Studio (e.g., start times, durations of SQL statements, and command separator characters).

You can also set system preferences for displaying data in the table viewer and for templates based on the editor you currently have open. For example, in the SQL Editor, you can use autofill for template(s) by pressing Ctrl + Space . Autofill allows you to rapidly select from a set of templates you frequently use in the SQL Editor.

10.2 SAP HANA Cockpit

As of SAP HANA SPS 10, the SAP HANA Cockpit (Figure 10.13) has been installed by default as part of the SAP HANA platform. The cockpit has core system administrative features deployed by default, and other applications, such as dynamic tiering, are available for installation as required for your SAP HANA implementation.

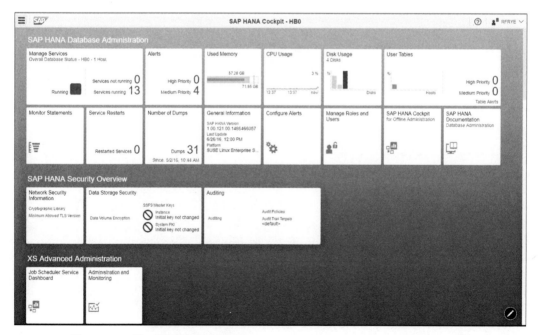

Figure 10.13 The SAP HANA Cockpit

The SAP HANA Cockpit can be accessed through the SAP Fiori launchpad, which is similar in form and function to the SAP Marketplace, now located at *http://launchpad.support.sap.com*.

The recommended (secure) access for the SAP HANA Cockpit is available at *https://<HANA_address>:43<instance>/sap/hana/admin/cockpit*, or you can use *http://<HANA_address>:80<instance>/sap/hana/admin/cockpit* if you don't have SSL configured on your SAP HANA server. You can also reach the SAP HANA Cockpit through SAP HANA Studio. Just right-click the selected system to open the context menu and select CONFIGURATION AND MONITORING • OPEN SAP HANA COCKPIT.

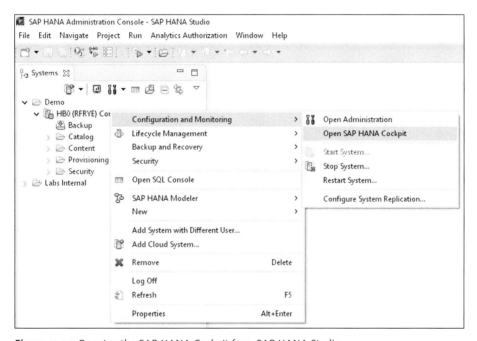

Figure 10.14 Opening the SAP HANA Cockpit from SAP HANA Studio

Please be aware that you'll need the `sap.hana.admin.roles::Monitoring` and `sap.hana.admin.roles::Administrator` roles in order to access the SAP HANA Cockpit and the database administration tiles. Additionally, if you're connecting to the primary system database from a multitenant system, you'll need the `sap.hana.admin.cockpit.roles::SysDBAdmin` role. Without this role, you won't be able to access the system administration tile catalog.

If your system is configured for single sign-on (SSO), you'll need to configure your user authentication through the SAP HANA XS Administration Tool. For detailed information about configuring the SAP HANA Cockpit for SSO, see the *Maintaining the SAP HANA XS Classic Model Run Time* section of the *SAP HANA Administration Guide*. You can download the guide from *http://help.sap.com/hana/ SAP_HANA_Administration_Guide_en.pdf*.

In the following sections, we'll look at customizing the SAP HANA Cockpit, some of the most important user roles, and offline administration with the SAP HANA Cockpit.

10.2.1 Customizing

The SAP HANA Cockpit home page has certain tiles available by default when you first access the cockpit. You can make changes to the default selections as needed, including adding and removing tiles, adding and removing groups, and rearranging the layout of the tiles on the home page.

Customizing the SAP HANA Cockpit to fit your needs is quite simple. In Figure 10.13, click the PERSONALIZE HOME PAGE icon (pencil icon) in the bottom-right of the cockpit, which will give you option to either add a new group of tiles to the page or to add a new tile to an existing group (Figure 10.15).

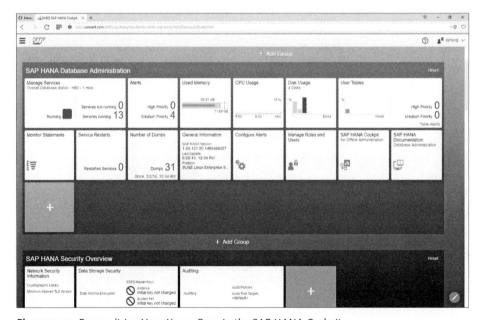

Figure 10.15 Personalizing Your Home Page in the SAP HANA Cockpit

SAP has provided numerous tile catalogs for use with the SAP HANA Cockpit. Table 10.1 has a comprehensive list of the tile catalogs that are available to use.

Functional Area	Available Tile Catalogs
Administration and Monitoring	System Administration
	Database Administration
	Backup
	System Replication
	Smart Data Access Administration
	Performance Management
Security Administration	Security Overview
	User Management
	Certificate Management
Platform Lifecycle Management	Platform Lifecycle Management

Table 10.1 Tile Catalogs Available for Use in the SAP HANA Cockpit

If you want to add a new group of tiles, just click the + ADD GROUP icon. You'll be prompted to enter a name for the new group. In our example (Figure 10.16), we added a new group called SAP HANA XS ADMINISTRATION.

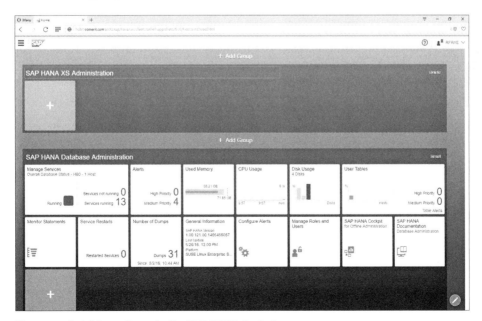

Figure 10.16 Adding a Group to the SAP HANA Cockpit

To add tiles to an existing group, just click the + icon from within the group. The
TILE CATALOG will open, and you can use the text box to search for the tiles you
want to add. In our example (Figure 10.17), we searched for "xs" tiles so we can
add them to the group we created. When you've found a tile you want to add,
click the + button under the tab and select the group for the new tile. Click OK,
and you'll be notified that the tile was added to the group you selected. Now, you
can just click the back arrow in the upper left of the cockpit to see the tile added
to your group.

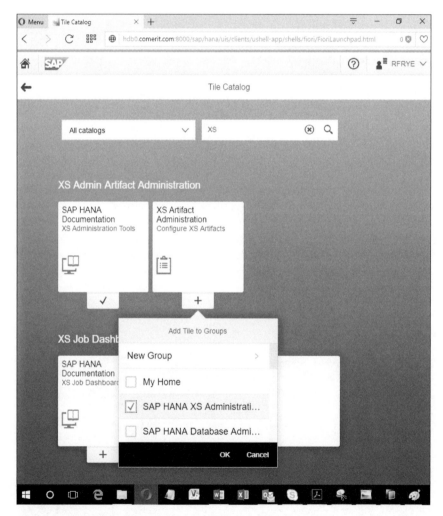

Figure 10.17 Searching for New Tiles in the Tile Catalog

Removing tiles and groups is also quite simple. To remove a group, from the personalization page, just click DELETE in the upper-right corner of the group. To remove a tile from within a group, click the tile and select REMOVE from the context menu.

Finally, if you want to rearrange groups or icons, simply click on and drag the tile or group to the location of your choice. Drop the item in the new location and then navigate back to the home page with the left arrow in the upper left of the screen to verify that your changes have been saved.

10.2.2 Roles for Users and Catalogs

Each tile catalog has specific requirements in order for users to be able to make use of the tiles in the catalog. Table 10.2 has a list of the available catalogs and the roles that must be assigned in order for a user to access the catalog. Please be aware that a catalog with multiple roles does not require the user to have all the roles listed. Instead, the proper role will depend on the user's role within the organization (e.g. administrator versus operator).

Tile Catalog	Required Roles
System Administration	`sap.hana.admin.cockpit.sysdb.roles::SysDBAdmin`
Database Administration	`sap.hana.admin.roles::Monitoring` `sap.hana.admin.roles::Administrator`
Platform Lifecycle Management	`sap.hana.admin.roles::Monitoring` `sap.hana.admin.roles::Administrator`
Backup	`sap.hana.admin.roles::Operator` `sap.hana.admin.roles::Administrator`
System Replication	`sap.hana.admin.cockpit.sysrep.roles::SysRepAdmin`
Security Overview	`sap.hana.security.cockpit.roles::DisplaySecurityDashboard`
User Management	`sap.hana.security.cockpit.roles::DisplayAssignedRoles` `sap.hana.security.cockpit.roles::EditAssignedRoles`

Table 10.2 Required Roles for Each Tile Catalog in the SAP HANA Cockpit

Tile Catalog	Required Roles

Certificate Management	`sap.hana.security.cockpit.roles::`
	`DisplayCertificateStore`
	
	`sap.hana.security.cockpit.roles::`
	`MaintainCertificates`
	
	`sap.hana.security.cockpit.roles::`
	`MaintainCertificateCollections`
	
	`sap.hana.security.cockpit.roles::`
	`EditCertificateStore`

Performance Management	`sap.hana.replay.roles::Capture`
	`sap.hana.replay.roles::Replay`
	`sap.hana.workloadanalyzer.roles::`
	`Administrator`
	`sap.hana.workloadanalyzer.roles::`
	`Operator`

Table 10.2 Required Roles for Each Tile Catalog in the SAP HANA Cockpit (Cont.)

10.2.3 Offline Administration

Sometimes, you may need to access the SAP HANA Cockpit with the database offline. For example, if you're just starting the SAP HANA database or need to troubleshoot a performance problem that is keeping database services from starting, you can use the SAP HANA Cockpit for offline administration.

You can navigate directly to the offline administration version of the cockpit at *https://<HANA_server>:1129/lmsl/hdbcockpit/<sid>/index.html*. Please note that the https connection is created and configured during the initial setup of the SAP HANA system, so this should always be your preferred method for opening the administration cockpit offline. You can also access the offline administration cockpit with via an unsecured http connection; however, http transmits your password in plain text, so using the unsecured connection may unnecessarily expose your password.

You will need the credentials for the <sid>adm user in order to use this version of the cockpit, so make sure you have these credentials available before you attempt to connect. You'll also need to make sure that network communication via port 1129 is allowed through your firewall. The SAP Host Agent uses port 1129 for the https connection in your web browser, so if the port is not open, you won't be able to connect via a secured connection.

10.3   System Monitoring

Let's return to SAP HANA Studio, where you'll find the system monitoring tool. To access this tool, just open the administration console using one of the processes we described in Section 10.1. In the system monitoring tool, you'll find overview information to help diagnose the state of the SAP HANA environment (Figure 10.18).

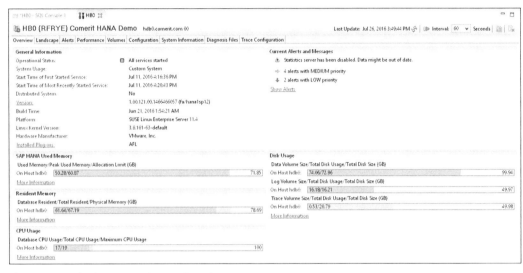

Figure 10.18 The SAP HANA System Overview

First, in the GENERAL INFORMATION section of the OVERVIEW tab, let's look at the OPERATIONAL STATUS of the system(s), which is indicated in green, yellow, or red. Green means that all services were started correctly, whereas yellow indicates that the `sapstartsrv` service did not start or that one of the other services is still in the process of starting. A red operational state for a system means that either a Java Database Connection (JDBC) can't be executed or one of the services has stopped.

In the DISK USAGE section, the disk space used and available on the disk holding the data files is also displayed. Data disk utilization is measured in gigabytes. You can see how much space is used in the gray area of the bar displayed and the free space in the white area. You can also create thresholds and color code the area based on your own parameters such as "if less than 500 GB, make yellow." Setting thresholds will help you quickly see available space on systems.

This type of space monitoring is also available for disks holding log files and trace files, as well as for physical memory and virtual memory, all measured in gigabytes. More than 150%–200% utilization of memory may indicate serious performance issues. SAP has stated that physical memory is the actual physical RAM on the host machine, whereas virtual memory includes swap-space on disk, and SAP HANA should always execute out of physical memory. A virtual memory size that is much larger than physical memory size may be an indicator that more memory is required.

In the CPU USAGE section, you'll also see the CPU utilization of the system as a percent of the maximum available. From the monitor, administrators can investigate when services were started, ended, first executed, and last executed as well as see the hostname and operating system version of the SAP HANA system and the software release version currently being used by the system.

Now that we've explored an overview of our system, in the next sections, we'll introduce you to some of the main monitoring activities for SAP HANA.

10.3.1 Monitoring Disk Usage

SAP HANA copies the data in memory to disks on a periodic basis to ensure that there is limited loss of data in case of a system failure. The data is stored in one volume per index server. If you run out of disk space, this feature can no longer be performed, so you need to make sure you always have enough disk space available. To help you, SAP HANA provides a disk space monitoring feature. To access this feature, go to the ADMINISTRATION OVERVIEW and the VOLUMES tab (Figure 10.19).

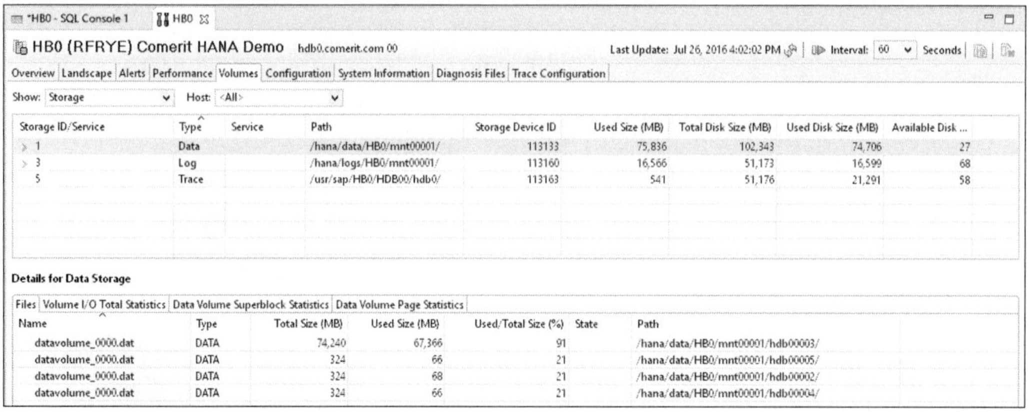

Storage ID/Service	Type	Service	Path	Storage Device ID	Used Size (MB)	Total Disk Size (MB)	Used Disk Size (MB)	Available Disk ...
1	Data		/hana/data/HB0/mnt00001/	113133	75,836	102,343	74,706	27
3	Log		/hana/logs/HB0/mnt00001/	113160	16,566	51,173	16,599	68
5	Trace		/usr/sap/HB0/HDB00/hdb0/	113163	541	51,176	21,291	58

Name	Type	Total Size (MB)	Used Size (MB)	Used/Total Size (%)	State	Path
datavolume_0000.dat	DATA	74,240	67,366	91		/hana/data/HB0/mnt00001/hdb00003/
datavolume_0000.dat	DATA	324	66	21		/hana/data/HB0/mnt00001/hdb00005/
datavolume_0000.dat	DATA	324	68	21		/hana/data/HB0/mnt00001/hdb00002/
datavolume_0000.dat	DATA	324	66	21		/hana/data/HB0/mnt00001/hdb00004/

Figure 10.19 The Disk Volumes of SAP HANA

Here you'll find information about disk usage, free space, and log stores on the disks. All measures are in megabytes. To diagnose the disk volume usage and performance in detail, file and volume level details are found under the DETAILS FOR DATA STORAGE area (Figure 10.20). This area displays I/O, buffer performance, sizes, and disk performance statistics.

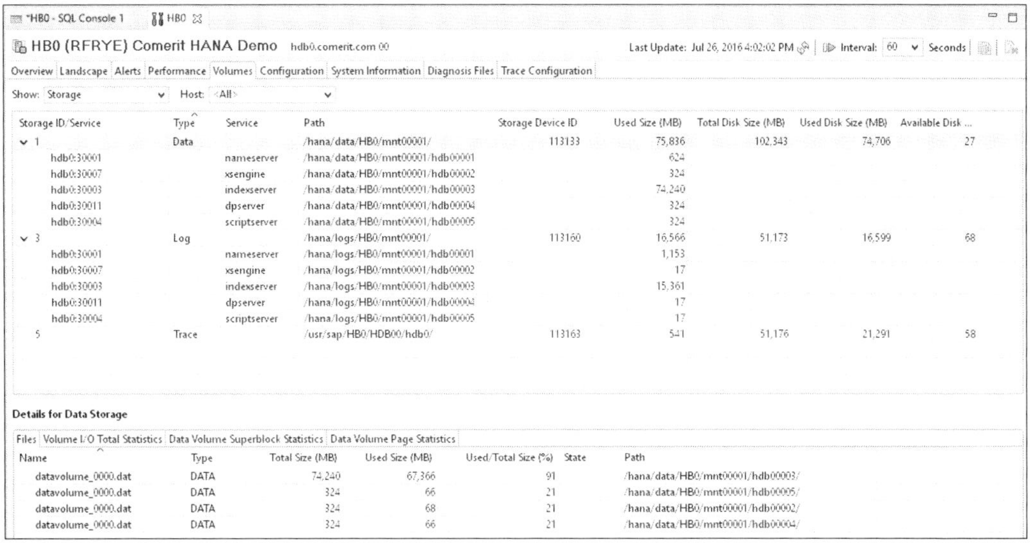

Figure 10.20 Details of Disk Storage Areas

10.3.2 Performance Monitoring

In the PERFORMANCE tab in the ADMINISTRATION OVERVIEW, you can find information on thread performance, runtimes, blocked threads, and which SQL statements are causing the most stress on the system (Figure 10.21).

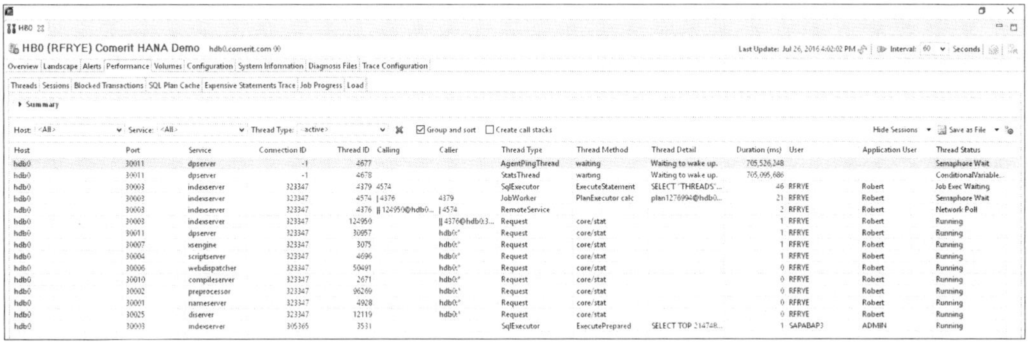

Figure 10.21 The Performance Tab of SAP HANA

In addition, you find query performance statistics for all compiled queries in the SQL plan cache, which you can use to decide which queries are candidates for elimination or which should be revisited for better design (e.g., nested SQL selects that can be costly). You also get information on resources consumed by tasks such as compression, merges of deltas (new records), logs, and more.

For Service Level Agreements (SLAs), you may consider using the system load history for key performance indicator (KPI) metrics. Here you find historical performance, loads, up-times, and memory usage. You can also compare the performance of one system against another.

10.3.3 Monitoring with Alerts

Alerts are a great way to keep track of your current and historical system performance. You can create your own alerts and have them emailed to you when triggered. You can set up alerts for when servers stop, disks are reaching critical capacity, or the system is experiencing high stress such as CPU bottlenecks.

Behind the scenes, the statistics server is collecting information about the system status and events and storing it inside SAP HANA. You can access key alert information in the ADMINISTRATION OVERVIEW under the OVERVIEW tab, while the details are found under the ALERTS tab (Figure 10.22).

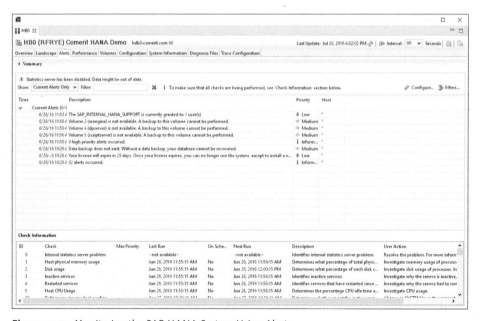

Figure 10.22 Monitoring the SAP HANA System Using Alerts

You can display all of the alerts grouped under different time periods, or you can select only Current Alerts. If you do this, you'll only see recent alerts that haven't been resolved. To get the latest data, you'll have to click Refresh periodically if you're keeping this screen open.

10.3.4 Configuring Alerts

You can create your own alerts to help in monitoring the system performance in the Administration Overview under the Alerts tab. To add a new alert, click Configure Check Settings, and enter the email information where you want the alert sent. It may be a good idea to create an email account called *HANA_Administrator@your_company.com,* and send all emails to this address to enable future administrators to monitor the system separately from an individual email account. The SMTP port is normally 25, and the mail server must be added as well as the email address.

You can also click Modify Recipients and add email addresses for those who should receive alert notifications instead of targeting different alerts to specific email addresses. This is an optional step. If, instead, you want to target specific types of alerts to different emails, you can click Configure Recipients for Specific Checks and add emails to each of the specific checks available in the list displayed.

Each alert has three specific thresholds for when the alert can be executed: high, medium, and low. You can define the value for each of these thresholds. For example, 80% for the alert "check disk space" can be coded as "high," and automatic emails can be sent to the administrator if the disk utilization exceeds 80%. To define or change the thresholds, click on Configure Check Settings under the Alerts tab, and select the subtab called Configure Check Thresholds. You may now make any changes, and the color-coded alerts on the main Alerts tab will reflect your changes as well as trigger emails.

10.3.5 Monitoring Services and Distributed Systems

The Landscape tab includes the Services subtab (Figure 10.23).

This tab provides in-depth details about services, memory utilization, and system configurations. In the Services subtab, you'll find the information listed in Table 10.3.

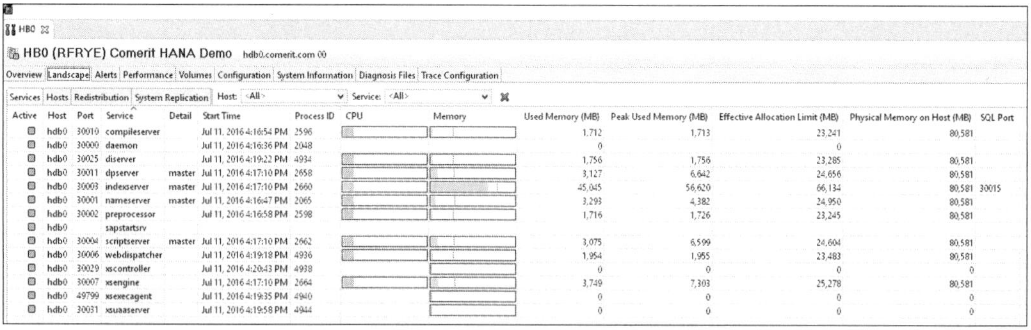

Figure 10.23 System Landscape Services

Detail	Description
HOST	The hostname(s) where the services are running.
DETAIL	Master and normal hosts for distributed systems.
PORT	Communication port between services.
SERVICE	For the host(s), shows the daemon, index server, name server, statistics server, preprocessor, and `sapstartsrv`.
PROCESS ID	The operating system ID for the process.
START TIME	Start time of each service.
ACTIVE	Red: The service isn't running. Yellow: The service is stopping or starting. Green: The service is started.
MEMORY	The memory usage of individual services and total for the server. Performance problems may occur if more than 150% of the physical memory is used (the system will start to use slower virtual memory). The maximum physical memory is shown as a mark in the middle of the graph.
EFFECTIVE ALLOCATION LIMIT	Reserved memory for a service from the operating system.
USED MEMORY	Used memory for a service (actual).
PHYSICAL MEMORY ON HOST	The total amount of physical memory on the current SAP HANA system.
PEAK USED MEMORY	The most memory used for a service (actual) during the active database cycle.

Table 10.3 Components of the Services Subtab

Detail	Description
CPU	Shows the CPU usage for a service and the overall CPU usage in bar form and details.
SQL PORT	The SQL connection port for a service.

Table 10.3 Components of the Services Subtab (Cont.)

You also get information about your distributed system configuration (if you're using one) in the CONFIGURATION tab, which provides the information shown in Table 10.4.

Detail	Description
HOST	Hostname.
ACTIVE	Shows if the host is running.
HOST STATUS	Shows if the host is running correctly.
FAILOVER STATUS	Displays if host is standby or active.
NAME SERVER ROLE (CONFIGURED)	The role of the name server as it has been configured, that is, master1, master2, or slave.
NAME SERVER ROLE (ACTUAL)	The role the server is currently running as.
INDEX SERVER ROLE (CONFIGURED)	The role of the index server as it has been configured, that is, worker, index server, or standby.
INDEX SERVER ROLE (ACTUAL)	The role the server is currently running as.
FAILOVER GROUP	In a failover, the server will attempt to hand over to a host in the group.
STORAGE PARTITION	Shows the number of the subdirectory *mnt000* used under the *DATA* and *LOG* directory.

Table 10.4 Components of the Configuration Tab

10.3.6 Exporting and Importing Table Data and Definitions

You can export and import table data between systems and hosts. For row-based data tables, you can export the data in comma-delimited format (CSV). For column-based data tables, you can also choose a binary format. Binary formats tend to be smaller in size and also faster, but this option should only be used if you're moving data tables between SAP HANA systems (e.g., from production to a development box).

To export tables, go to the Systems pane in SAP HANA Studio, navigate to the table(s) you want data from and select Export from the right-click context menu for the table. This will take you to an export wizard (Figure 10.24) that will guide you through the process of selecting tables and available formats. You can also choose to export only the table definitions (catalog) or include the data as well (catalog and data).

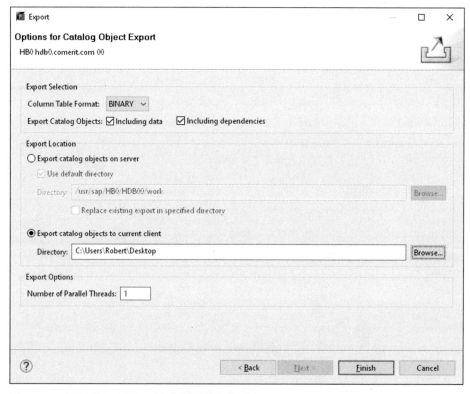

Figure 10.24 The Export Wizard in SAP HANA Studio

Select where you want to store the file and how many threads you want to use for the export. The more threads you select, the faster the export will execute. However, selecting too many threads may impact system performance for others, so keep it small (one to five) unless you do this on a large system, during off times, or on systems with little usage. The export wizard will save the file where you specified in the format selected.

To import table(s) into SAP HANA from the file, simply right-click on the catalog in the SYSTEMS pane in SAP HANA Studio and select IMPORT from the context menu. After entering the file path where the file is located, you can select the tables you want. You may have to type in the names of the tables if you're using a remote host. The last import steps tell the system the format of the file (CSV or binary) and enter the threads to be used. The table is now automatically imported into your system and can be seen in the SYSTEMS pane.

10.3.7 Monitoring Memory Usage

Memory in SAP HANA is used for a variety of purposes. First, the operating systems and support files are using memory. Second, SAP HANA has its own code and stack of program files that also consume memory. Third, memory is consumed by the column and row stores where data is stored. Finally, SAP HANA needs memory for its working space where computations occur, temporary results are stored, and shared user memory consumption occurs.

In short, physical memory is the maximum memory available, some of which is used by the operating systems and files. The allocated limit is what is "given" to SAP HANA, and the remaining memory is free space. These allocations are important because you're using preallocated memory pools, and you can't rely on Linux operating system information for memory management. However, you can get this information in many other ways.

In addition to the memory consumption and memory tracking information in the preceding sections, you can also obtain memory information using SQL statements. In the M_SERVICE_MEMORY view, you can execute a set of predefined SQL statements provided by SAP, including those shown in Listing 10.1, Listing 10.2, and Listing 10.3. To access these statements, open the SQL Console from the context menu of the VIEWS folder in the SYS schema.

```
Select round(sum(USED_FIXED_PART_SIZE +USED_VARIABLE_PART_SIZE)/1024/
1024) AS "Row Tables MB" FROM M_RS_TABLES;
```

Listing 10.1 Total Memory Used by All Row Tables

```
Select round(sum(MEMORY_SIZE_IN_TOTAL)/1024/1024) AS "Column Tables MB"
FROM M_CS_TABLES;
```
Listing 10.2 Total Memory Used by All Column Tables

```
Select SCHEMA_NAME AS "Schema", round(sum(MEMORY_SIZE_IN_TOTAL) /1024/
1024) AS "MB" FROM M_CS_TABLES GROUP BY SCHEMA_NAME ORDER BY "MB" DESC;
```
Listing 10.3 Total Memory Used by All Column Tables in a Schema

For column tables, SAP HANA sometimes unloads infrequently used columns from memory to free up space when the allocated memory threshold is near the used capacity. So, when memory consumption is estimated, it's important to look at all column tables, not just those currently loaded in memory. You can see all column table sizes in a schema by using the SAP-provided SQL statement in Listing 10.4.

```
Select TABLE_NAME AS "Table", round(MEMORY_SIZE_IN_TOTAL/1024/1024, 2)
as "MB" FROM M_CS_TABLES WHERE SCHEMA_NAME = 'SYSTEM' ORDER BY "MB"
DESC;
```
Listing 10.4 Total Memory by Column Tables in a Schema

By default, SAP HANA can preallocate up to 90% of the host's physical memory. You can also set the memory allocation limit, which is, however, normally set by the installation vendor. Changing the value can be useful if you've bought a license for less than your current hardware capacity.

10.3.8 Managing Large Tables with Partitioning

When monitoring the system, you can sometimes see tables that have grown so large in SAP HANA that it makes sense to split them "horizontally" into smaller partitions. By default, you can partition column tables in SAP HANA, which is ideal for managing high data volumes. The SQL statements—or any data manipulation language (DML) statements—do not need to know that the data is partitioned. Instead, SAP HANA automatically manages the partitions behind the scenes. Thus, SAP HANA simplifies access and frontend development and gives administrators a key tool to manage disks, memory, and large column stores.

In a distributed (scaled-out) SAP HANA system, you can also place the partitions on different nodes and thereby increase performance even more because more processors are available for your users. In fact, this may become the standard deployment method for extremely large systems with tens of thousands of users.

Currently, SAP HANA supports up to 2 billion rows in a single column table. In a partitioned schema, you can now have 2 billion rows per partition with virtually no limit on how many partitions you can add. You are limited, not by a database limitation, but by hardware and landscape architecture issues. You can create partitions in SAP HANA in three different ways from an administration standpoint: with a range, with a hash, and by the round-robin method. While more complex schemas are possible with multilevel partitioning, these three options cover the basics used in the higher-level options. Let's take a look at these fundamental partitioning choices.

Partitioning Column Tables Using a Range

If you know your data really well, you can partition the data by any range in your table. Although the most common is date, you can also partition by material numbers, postal codes, customer numbers, and so on.

Partitioning by date makes sense if you want to increase query speed and keep current data on a single node. Partitioning by customer number makes sense if you are trying to increase the speed of delta merges because multiple nodes can be used at the same time during data loads. You'll have to spend some time thinking of what benefits you want to achieve before undertaking any partitioning scheme. Note that the maintenance of range partitions is somewhat higher than the other options because you have to keep adding new partitions as data outside the existing partitions emerge (e.g., next year's data if you partition by year now).

Partitioning is done using SQL with the syntax seen in Listing 10.5.

```
CREATE COLUMN TABLE SALES (sales_order INT, customer_number INT,
quantity INT, PRIMARY KEY (sales_order))
PARTITION BY RANGE (sales_order)
(PARTITION 1 <= values < 100000000,
 PARTITION 100000000 <= values < 200000000,
 PARTITION OTHERS)
```

Listing 10.5 Partitioning in SQL

This syntax creates a table with three partitions. The first two have 100 million rows each, and the last partition has all the other records. However, you must follow some basic rules: First, the field you are partitioning on has to be part of the primary key (i.e., `sales_order`). Second, the field has to be defined as a string, a date, or an integer. Finally, you can only partition column stores, not row stores by ranges.

Partitioning Column Tables Using a Hash

Unlike partitioning by ranges, partitioning column stores by a hash doesn't require any in-depth knowledge of the data. Instead, partitions are created by an internal algorithm applied to one or more fields in the database by the system itself. This algorithm is known as a *hash*. Records are then assigned to the required partitions based on this internal hash number. The partitions are created in SQL with the following syntax:

```
CREATE COLUMN TABLE SALES (sales_order INT, customer_number INT,
quantity INT, PRIMARY KEY (sales_order, customer_number))
PARTITION BY HASH (sales_order, customer_number)
PARTITIONS 6
```

This example creates six partitions by sales orders and customer numbers. Some rules apply here as well: If the table has a primary key, the primary key must be included in the hash. If you add more than one column, and your table has a primary key, all fields used to partition must be part of the primary key also. If you leave off the number 6, the system will determine the optimal number of partitions itself based on your configuration. Therefore, using PARTITIONS without a number is the recommended setting for most hash partitions.

Partitioning Column Tables Using the Round-Robin Method

In a round-robin partition, the system assigns records to partitions on a rotating basis. The round-robin method makes efficient assignments and requires no knowledge of the data. However, removing partitions in the future will be more difficult because both new and old data will be in the same partitions.

The partitions are created in SQL with the following syntax:

```
CREATE COLUMN TABLE SALES (sales_order INT, customer_number INT,
quantity INT)
PARTITION BY ROUNDROBIN
PARTITIONS 6
```

This example creates six partitions and assigns records on a rotating basis. If you change the last statement to PARTITIONS GET_NUM_SERVERS(), the system will assign the optimal number of partitions based on your system landscape. The only requirement for the round-robin method is that the table cannot contain a primary key.

10.3.9 Moving Files and Partitions for Load Balancing

You can periodically move files and file partitions for column tables to achieve better load balancing across hosts. Redistributions are particularly useful if you are adding or removing a node from the system, creating new partitions, or load-balancing existing ones that have grown very large.

However, before you start, make sure you save your current distributions so that you can recover in case you make a mistake. If you have the system privilege RESOURCE ADMIN, you can open the ADMINISTRATION OVERVIEW in SAP HANA and choose LANDSCAPE • REDISTRIBUTION, followed by clicking SAVE. Then select NEXT and EXECUTE. You've now saved the current distribution and can recover it if anything goes wrong.

Now, go to the NAVIGATOR pane in SAP HANA Studio and select the TABLE DISTRIBUTION EDITOR. From this screen, you'll the catalog, schemas, and tables. Select the object you want to display and choose SHOW TABLE DISTRIBUTION. You can also filter to a single host as needed. The first 1,000 tables in the area you selected will be displayed. If more tables are available, you'll see a message box.

In the overview lists, you can now select any table you want to analyze, and the details will be displayed in the TABLE PARTITION DETAILS area. You can move the table to another host by right-clicking on the table and selecting MOVE TABLE. If you want to move a partition instead of a table, you can select the partition instead and do the same. This may be useful if you want to load-balance large tables across multiple hosts or want to consolidate your partitions to a single host. For detailed recommendations on load balancing, see SAP Note 1650394: For Large Table Management.

10.3.10 Fixing a Disk Full Event

If you run out of disk space, the "disk full" event is triggered. The event will appear on alerts and will also suspend the use of the database. You'll have to resolve this event before the system becomes available again.

To fix this, go to the ADMINISTRATION OVERVIEW and the VOLUMES tab. In this tab, you'll find information about the disk usage under the SHOW STORAGE option. If the disk is full due to other files being stored (i.e., temporary staging files for data movement), you can delete these and mark the event as handled in the OVERVIEW tab, in the DISK FULL EVENTS link. This will stop the suspension of the database.

If all the unneeded files are removed, and the disk is still full, you'll have to add additional disks before flagging the events as handled.

10.3.11 Support for Unresponsive Systems

If your system is unresponsive, and SQL statements can't be executed, you can gather system information for support using a Python script provided by SAP. You'll need system administration privileges to run this script.

To execute the script, navigate to the Python support directory *.../exe/<installation_type>/<server_version>/python_support fullSystemInfoDump.py*. Executing the script will create a ZIP file with system information that will be stored in the directory *DIR_TEMP/system_dump*. If you also want usage information, simply add the handle `-h` to the end of the command.

If you're unsure about where your temporary directory is, you can find this information in the *sapprofile.ini* file, or by entering `hdbsrvutil -z | grep DIR_TEMP=` in the command line on your SAP HANA server.

The ZIP file contains valuable system information and can help SAP support resolve issues related to your system. The content of the ZIP file will depend on whether the system can be reached by SQL or not. If SQL can't be executed, the file will have mostly system configuration data, topology, and trace files. However, if SQL can be executed, the file will also have information about the system tables and views as well as system statistics that can be useful for SAP support and diagnostics.

10.4 Updates

In this section, we'll briefly discuss the two types of updates for SAP HANA: updates for the appliance itself and updates for SAP HANA Studio.

10.4.1 Updating the SAP HANA Appliance

Systems that were installed with the SAP HANA Unified Installer can use the automated update procedure. During the update procedure, a backup is completed, data replication is suspended, and the business is made aware of the planned outage. You may want to do this on a quarterly basis when other systems are scheduled for maintenance at the same time (e.g., holidays).

The Software Update Manager (SUM) for SAP HANA support package stack (SPS) can execute automatic updates of the LIFECYCLE MANAGEMENT perspective as part of a self-update. So, unless your hardware partner installed SUM as part of the install, you'll have to install it from the SAP Marketplace before you can use it because it's not part of the typical base SAP HANA installation.

During the install, it's important to note that all archives, including *SUMFOR-HANA*, must be located in the same directory as the *stack.xml* file. Additional details on the release of SUM can be found in SAP Note 1545815. After the SUM is installed, you can choose to apply either SPSs that contain larger upgrades or individual support packages based on your needs or upgrade schedule.

You can also perform updates from the SAP HANA Lifecycle Manager. You can reach the SAP HANA Lifecycle Manager through the HANA APPLICATION LIFECYCLE MANAGEMENT tile in the SAP HANA LIFECYCLE MANAGEMENT tile catalog (Figure 10.25).

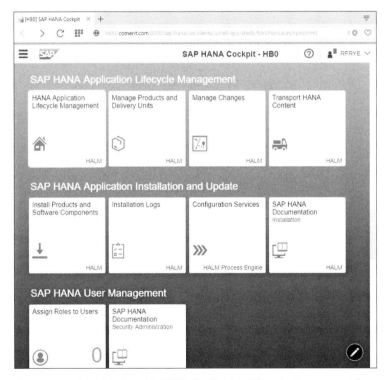

Figure 10.25 Opening the SAP HANA Application Lifecycle Management from the SAP HANA Cockpit

You can also navigate directly to the SAP HANA Lifecycle Manager in your web browser (Figure 10.26). Go to *http://<HANA_server>:80<instance>/sap/hana/xs/lm/* and login with your account. You'll need to have the `sap.hana.xs.lm.roles::Administrator` role in order to access the SAP HANA Lifecycle Manager. When you've logged in, select the INSTALLATION tile, and follow the prompts to locate and install your update.

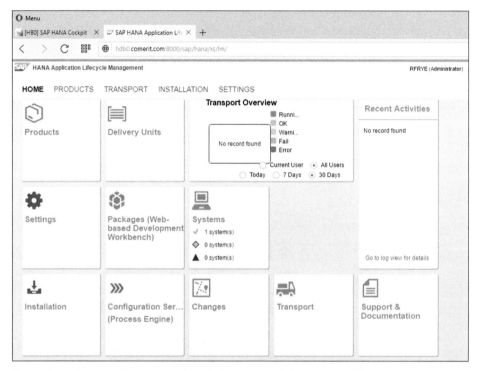

Figure 10.26 Using the SAP HANA Lifecycle Manager to Update SAP HANA

As of July 2016, you will need to download the update from the SAP Support Portal and save it on your system landscape in order to install the update. Then you just need to specify the folder location where you saved the update to install the update.

10.4.2 Updating SAP HANA Studio

You'll periodically need to update the SAP HANA Studio software. You can choose to update the software automatically based on periodic updates with SUM, or you can execute the software update manually.

However, in both cases, you'll first need to point your SAP HANA system to the site from which updates are downloaded. You can do this by going to the main menu and selecting WINDOW • PREFERENCES. In the PREFERENCES navigation pane, choose INSTALL/UPDATE • AVAILABLE SOFTWARE SITES. Click ADD to add the site, which should be entered one of the following formats: *http://<host_name>:<port_number>/tools/hdb.studio.update* or *file://update_server/hdbstudio/repository/*.

You'll be notified immediately if another update is available. The system will then take you through the upgrade process based on available components. After the site has been added, you can also set up automatic updates. To set up automatic updates, just go to the main menu and select WINDOW • PREFERENCES. In the PREFERENCES dialog box, choose INSTALL/UPDATE • AUTOMATIC UPDATES (Figure 10.27). You can now decide how frequently you want to apply automated updates.

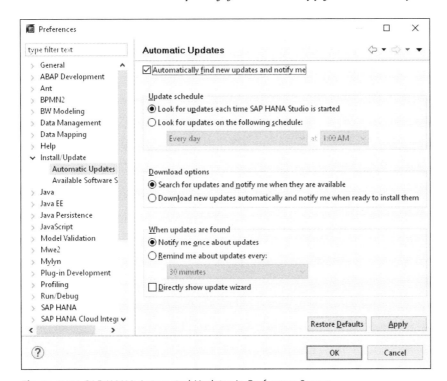

Figure 10.27 SAP HANA Automated Updates in Preference Screen

To perform a manual check for updates in SAP HANA Studio, you can go to the main menu and select HELP • CHECK FOR UPDATES (Figure 10.28).

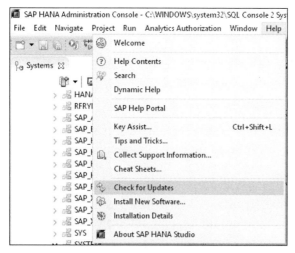

Figure 10.28 Checking for Updates Manually

10.5 Security

In this section, we'll discuss the basics of what you need to know about managing security in SAP HANA, including authentication, authorization, and password policies.

10.5.1 System Privileges

The right to execute services and to access data and software components in SAP HANA is determined by the privileges and roles of database users (Figure 10.29 and Figure 10.30).

The highest set of privileges is maintained in the system user called SYSTEM. This database user should only be granted to a very few individuals because these users would basically have access to do whatever they want. Internal system users such as _SYS_STATISTICS and SYS are used by the system itself. You can't logon using these database users.

An operating system administrator user was also created during the installation of SAP HANA. You can logon with this user to stop or start a database, to execute recovery processes, to add new system privileges to a role, and to grant that role to a user.

Figure 10.29 Granted Privileges in SAP HANA

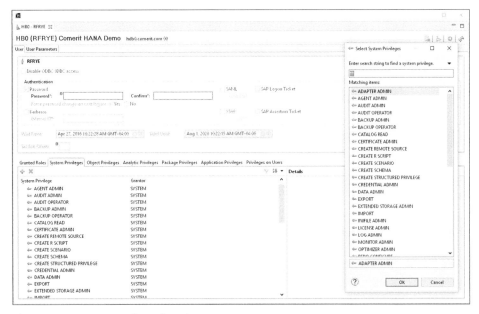

Figure 10.30 System Privileges for Administrators

10.5.2 Authentication Security

SAP HANA has two forms for authentication security: user authentication and external authentication. User authentication is referred to as an *internal authentication* and consists of validating a password with a user name.

You can also use external authentication with Kerberos or through the Security Assertion Markup Language (SAML). When using Kerberos, users in the key distribution center should be mapped to database users in SAP HANA by making the user's principal name the external ID when creating or modifying the database user.

To use SAML, you need to create a SAML identity provider first. For more information, see the Kerberos protocols on user principal name (UPN) mapping and the key distribution center or the *SAP HANA Database Security Guide*.

10.5.3 Authorization Security

After the user identity has been established (authentication), the user has to be granted privileges to do something through authorizations. Users can be assigned privileges through a direct assignment, or they can inherit privileges through roles.

Adding or Deactivating Users

To add a user, go to the SYSTEMS pane in SAP HANA Studio and select the system where you want to create the new user. Select the SECURITY folder and then right-click on the USERS folder (Figure 10.31). Select NEW USER from the context menu. Give the user a distinct name following your corporate naming standards. If you have no standards, we advise that you create some before adding users in the system. Allowing user names to be made up without any rules can lead to unnecessary complications later.

Select your authentication method (internal, Kerberos, or SAML) and assign roles, system, SQL, and/or analytical privileges. If you want the user to be able to also grant his privileges to other users, you can select the GRANTABLE TO OTHER USERS AND ROLES option. This option should only be used in rare cases where such authority to grant privileges is distributed (e.g., to different administrators in business units). If you allow this, the user can grant his role to others (Figure 10.32). For most organizations, granting privileges will be managed centrally instead.

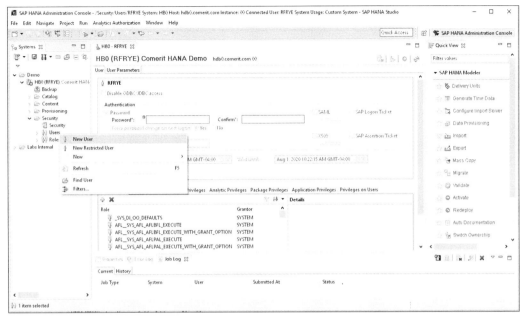

Figure 10.31 Adding a New User

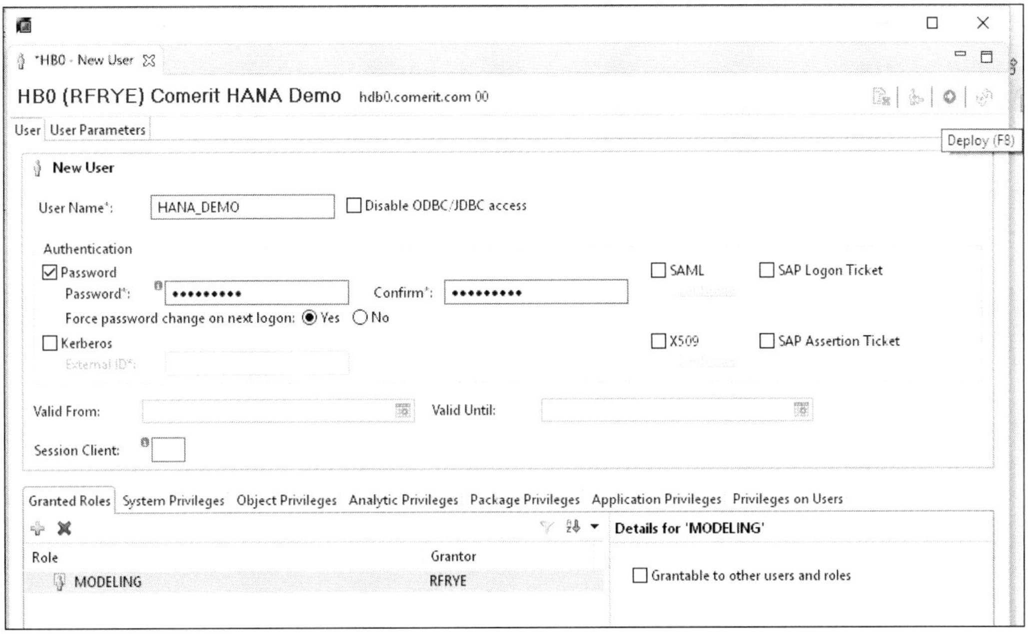

Figure 10.32 Granting Roles to Users

Select DEPLOY to save the user definitions. You must have the privilege ROLE ADMIN to create new users or modify existing users.

To deactivate users, go to the SYSTEMS pane in SAP HANA Studio and select the system with the user that needs to be deactivated. Select the SECURITY folder and then expand the USERS. Select the user to be deactivated. In the USER EDITOR, you can now click on DEACTIVATE USER on the toolbar, and the user will no longer have access to the system.

More options on SAP HANA security at the services and data level are maintained in the *SAP Security Guide* on the SAP Marketplace and in SAP Notes 1598623 and 1514967.

Adding and Modifying Roles

To add roles, go to the SYSTEMS pane in SAP HANA Studio and select the system where the new role needs to be created. Select the SECURITY folder and then right-click the ROLES icon. Select NEW ROLE from the context menu (Figure 10.33).

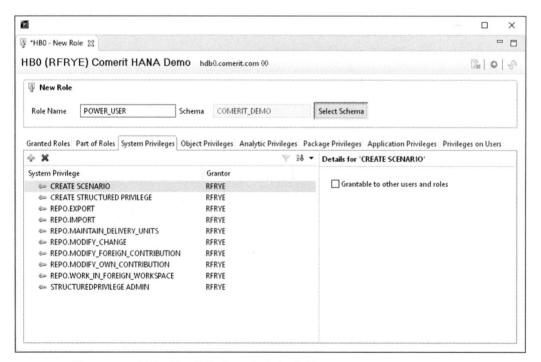

Figure 10.33 Adding New Roles from the Roles Folder

Give the role a distinct name following your corporate standards. If you have no standards, we advise that you create them before adding roles in the system. Allowing role names to be made up without any controls can be problematic.

After you've given the role a name, you can assign the SQL, analytical, package, or system privileges and save the role definitions. You must have the privilege ROLE ADMIN to create new roles or modify existing roles.

Assigning Administration Roles and Privileges

For administrators, certain privileges must be assigned so that they can do their jobs. Table 10.5 lists some of the critical privileges administrators may need.

Administration Privileges or Roles	Administration Task Enabled
MONITORING	This grants read-only access to the ADMINISTRATION EDITOR.
SERVICE ADMIN	Under PERFORMANCE • THREADS, you can grant users the ability to cancel operations. In the LANDSCAPE tab, the ability to start and stop database services is enabled.
MONITOR ADMIN	This grants the ability to mark as handled any "disk full" events.
TRACE ADMIN	This grants the ability to start and stop performance traces and delete trace files.
ROLE ADMIN	This grants the ability to add new roles or modify existing roles.
USER ADMIN	This grants the ability to add new users or modify existing users.
INIFILE ADMIN	This controls the ability to configure database and SQL traces, change any configuration settings on the CONFIGURATION tab, or modify check settings in the ALERTS tab.
SQL privilege SELECT for the SQL schema _SYS_STATISTICS	In the OVERVIEW and ALERTS tabs, this grants the ability to view alert information.
System privilege DATA ADMIN; or CATALOG READ and SQL privilege ALTER for the respective table(s)	This allows you to move tables or partitions to other hosts in a distributed system.

Table 10.5 Administrator Privileges

Administration Privileges or Roles	Administration Task Enabled
System privileges EXPORT and IMPORT as well as SQL privilege INSERT and SELECT	These allow you to import and export data tables.

Table 10.5 Administrator Privileges (Cont.)

To have access to manage resources in SAP HANA, you may need the RESOURCE ADMIN privileges added to your role, which can be found under the SYSTEM PRIVILEGES tab in the security settings for your user. You can also assign CONTENT ADMIN privileges to a role (Figure 10.34). CONTENT ADMIN privileges allow a user to administer and manage the content in SAP HANA but not the system settings.

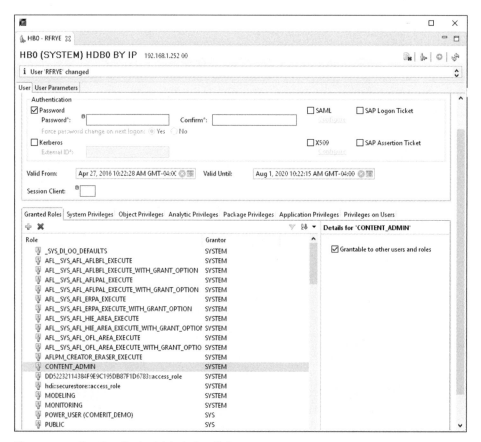

Figure 10.34 Granting Content Admin to a Role

Database administrators also may need to see all the schemas in a system. This functionality is turned off by default through schema filtering. To gain access to all schemas, you need to go to the SYSTEMS pane and select the respective system. Right-click the CATALOG folder and select FILTERS. The FILTER dialog box appears where you can select the option DISPLAY ALL SCHEMAS and click OK. This imparts the users with the privileges DATA ADMIN, CATALOG READ, and SYSTEM.

10.5.4   Setting a Password Policy

You can also set your own password policy for SAP HANA. This includes minimum password length, use of characters, maximum number of logon attempts, blacklisted passwords, password expiration rules, and notifications. To change a password policy, right-click on the SAP HANA system in the SYSTEMS pane and select SECURITY • OPEN SECURITY CONSOLE (Figure 10.35).

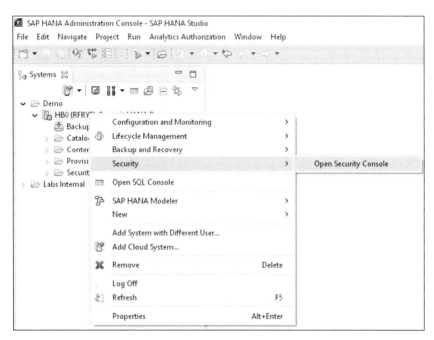

Figure 10.35 Accessing the SAP HANA Security Console

Under the PASSWORD POLICY tab, you can change all the settings to conform to your company's password rules (Figure 10.36). Unusually, the information security group manages this tab in SAP HANA.

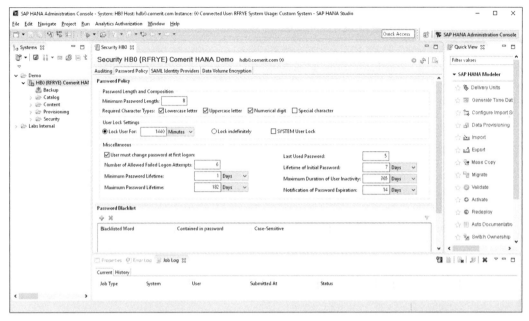

Figure 10.36 Setting a Password Policy in SAP HANA

10.6 License Keys

The two types of license keys for SAP HANA are temporary keys (typically 90 days) and permanent keys. To check your type of license keys and expiration dates, right-click on a system in the SYSTEMS pane in SAP HANA Studio, select PROPERTIES (Figure 10.37), and choose LICENSE.

Permanent keys identify how much memory you're licensed to use on the SAP HANA system. In addition, keys can be enforced or unenforced. If you have enforced keys, the SAP HANA system will shut down if you try to use the system for more memory than you're licensed for. (In reality, SAP grants a little extra memory consumption before shutting down.) If the system is shut down due to a license key violation, you can't access the system via queries nor can the system be backed up. To see if your keys are enforced or not, take a look inside the license file. If you see *SWPRODUCTNAME=SAP-HANA*, your keys are not enforced. If you see *SWPRODUCTNAME=SAP-HANA-ENF*, your license keys are enforced.

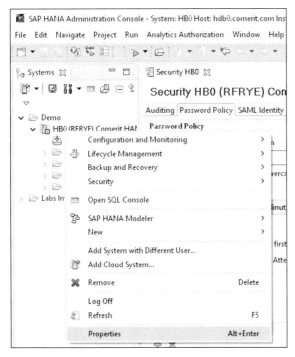

Figure 10.37 Checking License Keys

10.6.1 Temporary License Keys

Most SAP HANA systems come with temporary license keys installed from the vendor, so you have to make sure you install permanent keys before the temporary license keys expire. In our example (Figure 10.38), the permanent license has been installed. To install your permanent license, you'll need to go to the SAP Marketplace (*https://service.sap.com/support*), logon with your credentials from SAP, and select KEYS & REQUESTS. If a permanent key expires, you'll automatically be granted a 28-day extension to get new keys to avoid operational disruption to your organization.

Changes to license keys can only be made by administrators with the system privilege LICENSE ADMIN in their security role. More information on monitoring license keys is found in SAP Note 1704499.

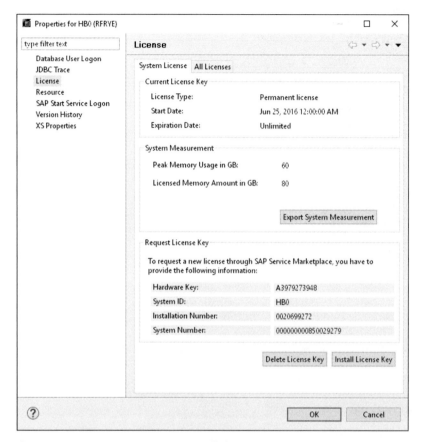

Figure 10.38 Permanent License Key Installed

10.6.2 Permanent License Keys

When you first bought SAP HANA, temporary license keys may have been included. To activate the license, go to the SAP HANA Studio SYSTEMS pane and right-click on the system you want to manage. Choose PROPERTIES and then select LICENSES. Administrators can also delete license keys in this area.

If you have a temporary license, you'll see the system ID and hardware key under the REQUEST LICENSE KEY area. You'll need this information when requesting the permanent keys on the SAP Marketplace website. SAP will send you the permanent license key file by email, and after you've downloaded it, you can go back to the REQUEST LICENSE KEY area and select INSTALL LICENSE KEY. After this, you select the file you downloaded from the email, and the key will automatically be installed.

10.7   Backup and High Availability

Today, SAP HANA is a system with backup, disaster recovery, and failover support in its architecture. In the system fails, you can restore from backups. You can have synchronous backups between your production system and your backup storage. You can even have a standby system that receives data continuously and then use this as a "warm" standby system that is ready to kick in if the primary system goes down for any reason. Finally, you can have standby hosts ready to take over if a host inside your system has issues. The latter is referred to as *fault-tolerance recovery*, which is built into your SAP HANA system together with the existing service autostart that automatically tries to restart any service that fails.

Next, let's take a quick look at some of the options included for backup and high availability in SAP HANA.

10.7.1   Backup

Two basic ways of backing up data in SAP HANA are available. The traditional file backup has been supported since version 1.0, and the newer BACKINT application programming interface (API) provides support for certified third-party vendors. Because this feature is available starting in SPS 5, for some older installations, you may be required to apply SPS 5 or higher to take advantage of the backup and restore features of other vendor solutions.

Many backup features are now automated, so you no longer need to run the ALTER SYSTEM RECLAIM LOG SQL script after every backup to check that log segments were removed. Instead, you set enable_auto_log_backup to yes and the log_mode to normal.

For those using the traditional file backup from SAP, four parameters are available in SAP HANA Studio under the CONFIGURATION tab (Figure 10.39). These parameters are known as *basepath* options.

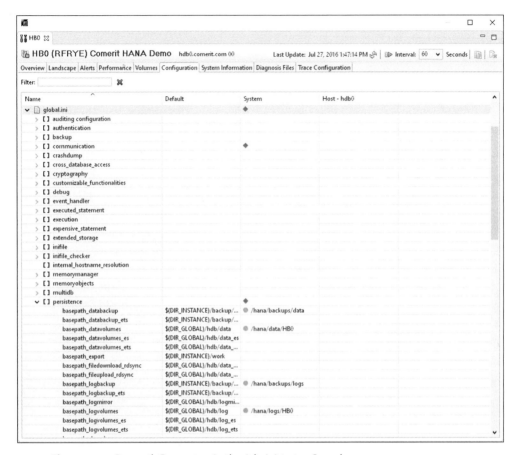

Figure 10.39 Basepath Parameters in the Administrator Console

The basepath options for a standard backup of SAP HANA settings and recommendations include the following:

▶ `basepath_databackup`
For setting up an external mount point, `basepath_databacku` points to where your standard backups will be saved. For faster backups, you can also back up your SAP HANA system to a disk and afterward move the backup to an external mount point.

▶ `basepath_datavolumes`
The permanent location for data volumes, you should never attempt to delete any data volume files on the operating system. Deleting data volume files may make your system unusable and cause the system to become unresponsive.

▶ basepath_logbackup

This points to an external mount point because log segments are copied automatically every 15 minutes in SAP HANA.

▶ basepath_logvolumes

The permanent location for log volumes, you can clean this directory using the ALTER SYSTEM RECLAIM LOG program, but you should never delete any log volumes files directly.

Your SAP HANA installation should have an alert for backups created by default, and you can adjust the settings to meet your needs. To do so, simply go to the ALERTS tab and click on the CONFIGURE CHECK SETTINGS button. Next, select the CONFIGURE CHECK THRESHOLDS tab (Figure 10.40) and enter "backup" in the search box to filter the existing alerts. Enter the alert severity thresholds that best reflect your company's backup strategy.

Other vendors have also started to create backup solutions for SAP HANA, and you can now use IBM's Tivoli Storage Manager to centrally manage your SAP HANA backups. In addition, SAP provides a script in SAP Note 1651055 to help clean up the log files in SAP HANA if they become too large and your backup times start to suffer.

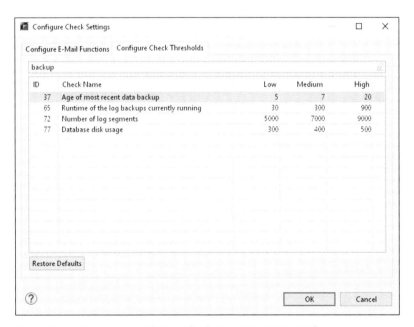

Figure 10.40 Monitoring Backups with Alerts in SAP HANA Studio

10.7.2   High Availability

When you buy SAP HANA, you can buy additional hardware to be in a standby mode for failover in case the system experiences issues. You can keep the server running and ready to take over at any time. However, in this cold standby mode, no SQL is executed on the system, and a system restore may take a few minutes if the primary system goes down.

Currently, you can assign up to three master servers as name servers and select one of these as the active server. The active server is assigned a master index server and a statistics server, while those in standby mode have none. If the active master name server fails, the system restores itself to any available standby master and uses this system instead.

The index server keeps tracks of the directories in a volume where the files are located. If the index server fails, the name server will automatically try to restart it, which can take 2 to 3 minutes. If that fails, the name server looks for any standby index servers. The restore occurs by having the name server assign the volume to the standby index server. After the process is complete, the system becomes available again.

Because the statistics server is stored on the name server, any failure of the statistics server triggers a name server failover. In response, the system will create a new statistics server on the new active name server, and the old statistics server is removed automatically.

Groups of failover systems can also be defined for each of the hosts to ensure that preferred standby servers on the same hardware are used first. Defining groups of failover systems helps to restore the servers more quickly because less data and fewer configurations need to physically be moved on the network.

Setting up high availability and failover systems should be done by SAP partners and hardware vendors to ensure the correct system sizing connectivity, provisioning, and future support.

10.8   Virtualization

Beginning with SAP HANA SPS 5, SAP-certified VMware Hypervisor was the first technology capable of virtualizing SAP HANA servers. Virtualization is the process of creating a virtual instance of a resource within a framework that can be used to run multiple logical instances of a resource in a single physical environment. This virtual resource may be an operating system, a storage device, a database, or even a network resource. See Figure 10.41 for a comparison of a standard and a virtualized deployment of SAP HANA.

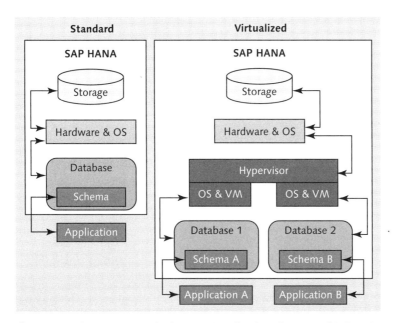

Figure 10.41 Comparing Standard versus Virtualized Deployment of SAP HANA

Virtualization offers many advantages when compared to the cost, effort, and risk involved in maintaining numerous physical servers. For example, in a virtualized environment, you can quickly reallocate CPUs and memory resources to your SAP HANA servers to meet the changing needs of your business. Figure 10.42 provides a closer look at a virtualized SAP HANA landscape.

You will generally also have a lower total cost of ownership (TCO) in virtualized environments. A lower TCO is possible because many vendors allow on-demand access for your SAP HANA appliances. For example, Amazon Web Services offers on-demand licensing, which only charges for the time that your cloud environment is on and available for use.

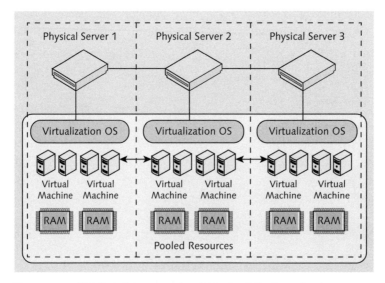

Figure 10.42 Distributed Resources in a Virtualized Hardware Landscape

On-demand licensing also offers a convenient and inexpensive path to creating and maintaining sandbox environments for proofs of concept (POCs). You can create a small SAP HANA instance with very moderate resource requirements and save a copy of this clean environment. When you need to test new ideas, you can simply bring a copy of the clean environment online, complete the POC work, and then delete the copy when you're finished. The clean copy will still be available for you to use in your next POC effort. Using on-demand licensing for these sandbox environments is both much more convenient and much less expensive than maintaining both the physical hardware and licensing required for a physical sandbox environment.

Virtualization through a vendor also serves as a convenient and relatively inexpensive gateway to deploy SAP HANA for small companies. As your business grows, and the need for more CPUs and more memory increases, you can scale your licensing and hardware requirements easily within a virtual landscape. As a result, you can select the size of system that you need right now and re-evaluate your needs periodically. If you need to move to a larger environment, adding processors and memory is simple, and you won't be left with older hardware that is inadequate to meet your needs.

Some of the benefits of virtualization include:

- Easy hardware replacement, as there is no need to recertify the operating system and SAP software installations
- IT ownership that can be separated into software and hardware layers
- Independent monitoring of the operating system
- Inexpensive high-availability capabilities

See Table 10.6 for a comprehensive list of approved virtualization vendors as well as the required SAP HANA SPS levels. Please be sure to check the SAP Community Network (SCN) for the latest guidance on supported virtualization vendors. As of this writing, SAP Note 1788665 is the most recent guidance about virtualization, but new vendors may be added frequently, and nonproduction vendors may be certified soon.

Vendor	Software version	Required SPS
VMware vSphere	5.1	SPS 5 or higher, nonproduction
	5.5	SPS 7 or higher, production
	6.0	SPS 9 nonproduction
		SPS 11 production
Hitachi LPAR	2.0	SPS 7 or higher, production
Huawei FusionSphere	3.1	SPS 9 or higher, production
	5.1	SPS 10 or higher, production
IBM PowerVM	LPAR	Production on IBM Power Systems
KVM	SUSE SLES 11 & 12, Redhat RHEL 7.x	SPS 11 or higher, nonproduction
XEN	SUSE SLES 11 & 12	SPS 11 or higher, nonproduction

Table 10.6 SAP HANA-Approved Virtualization Vendors

Virtualization is a rapidly growing field in the SAP landscape, so you may also want to examine the notes in Table 10.7 for more guidance before choosing your virtualization vendor and purchasing any hardware.

SAP Note	Description
1788665	SAP HANA Support for virtualized/partitioned (multitenant) environments
2020657	SAP Business One, version for SAP HANA on VMware vSphere
2232700	SAP HANA on Lenovo X6 FlexNode in production

Table 10.7 SAP Notes about Virtualization

SAP Note	Description
2024433	Multiple SAP HANA VMs on VMware vSphere in production
2103848	SAP HANA on HP nPartitions in production
2157587	SAP Business Warehouse, powered by SAP HANA on VMware vSphere in scaled-out and production systems
2096000	SAP HANA multitenant database containers—additional information

Table 10.7 SAP Notes about Virtualization (Cont.)

10.9 Multiple Databases and Components on the Same Hardware

SAP HANA both allows you to run multiple software applications on a single SAP HANA database and on a single system. We'll discuss both of these options in more detail next.

10.9.1 Multiple Components One Database

Running software applications on a single database is known as the Multiple Components in One Database (MCOD) configuration. Note that MCOD is not the same as having multiple databases on one hardware appliance. An MCOD system simply refers to having multiple software applications on one database. You can see Figure 10.43 for a comparison between the standard and MCOD SAP HANA deployments.

In MCOD mode, SAP supports any custom-developed data marts that work with other SAP HANA components. However, you can also run any of the following components together on a single database:

▸ SAP Business Warehouse (SAP BW) powered by SAP HANA
▸ SAP Finance and Controlling Accelerator for the SAP Material Ledger
▸ SAP ERP Operational Reporting with SAP HANA
▸ SAP Finance and Controlling Accelerator: Production Cost Planning
▸ SAP Rapid Marts
▸ SAP CO-PA Accelerator
▸ SAP Operational Process Intelligence

▸ SAP Cash Forecasting

▸ SAP HANA Application Accelerator/Suite Accelerator

▸ Smart Meter Analytics

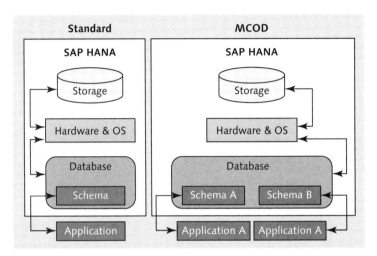

Figure 10.43 Standard versus MCOD SAP HANA Deployment

If you're running your SAP HANA system as MCOD, you have to consider that all backup, recovery, and failover measures now pertain to all applications. You can't back up a single application. Therefore, any restarts, failovers, and restores now impact all components on the database. You're also sharing the system resources and will have to size your SAP HANA system accordingly.

From an administration standpoint, the software applications are managed individually in their respective interfaces, while the database is managed as a central unit through standard SAP HANA database administration functions. Finally, if you're planning to use MCOD with SAP BW as one of the software components, you should also study the special considerations for this MCOD scenario in SAP Note 1666670.

10.9.2 Multiple Components One System

You can also install multiple SAP HANA databases on a single SAP HANA hardware appliance, which is known as Multiple Components in One System (MCOS), sometimes referred to as a *multi-SID (system ID) configuration*. Take a look at Figure 10.44 for a comparison between standard and MCOS SAP HANA deployments.

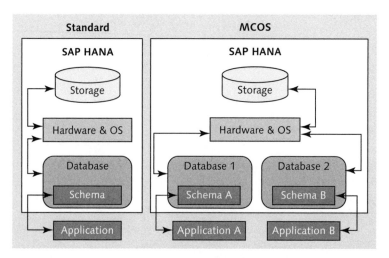

Figure 10.44 Standard versus MCOS SAP HANA Deployment

MCOS is an evolving capability, and there are some limitations in what SAP supports from a nontechnical standpoint. For example, if you buy a single-node SAP HANA box, you'll have a single install of the SAP HANA database on the system. However, you can also install an additional database on this node, and SAP will provide support as long as it is in a nonproduction system.

SAP will not currently support MCOS if you move this configuration to a production system. However, as long as you keep it in development (DEV), sandbox, testing, and training environments, you'll have support. While this limitation is likely to change in the future, consult with SAP before attempting to use MCOS on a production system.

If you choose to run MCOS on a single-node, nonproduction box, each database is managed individually in SAP HANA Studio, while the hardware is shared. This structure may be a cost-effective solution for smaller organizations who simply want a small sandbox or training environment without having to buy another SAP HANA appliance. Just make sure you have the system sized accordingly because the databases will be competing for the same system resources.

10.10 Multitenancy and Multitenant Database Containers

With multitenancy, a server runs a single instance of some required software and serves multiple tenants with that single instance. Here, a tenant is a group of users who share a common view of the system, with access only to their own logical partition of the software, data, and services within that system. With SAP HANA SPS 9, SAP introduced support for multitenant databases in SAP HANA.

Multitenant database containers (also referred to as *tenant databases*) are intended for deployment in either on-premise or cloud scenarios. In the cloud, multitenant database containers can be implemented in both the SAP HANA Cloud Platform (SAP HCP) and the SAP HANA Enterprise Cloud (SAP HEC).

For on-premise scenarios, multitenant database containers are intended to replace most MCOS deployments (Figure 10.45), as well as replace many MCOD scenarios, such as quality assurance or development environments; supplemental data marts; and deployments that combine SAP ERP, SAP CRM, and SAP BW.

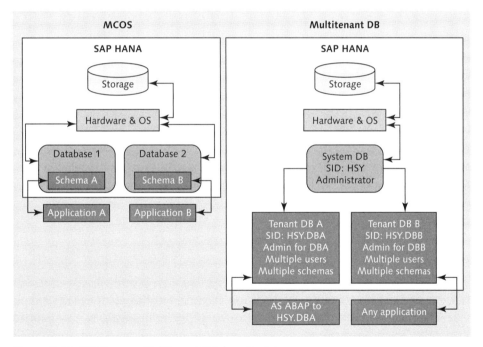

Figure 10.45 MCOS versus Multitenant Database Containers

When you move to multitenancy, you need to be aware that the administration of the database containers is highly segmented. The overall system configuration, administration, and monitoring can be done from the system database. Separate administrator accounts will be created for each tenant database, and the creation and configuration of users, roles, authorizations, and schemas authorizations will be handled through the tenant databases.

Using multitenant database containers in SAP HANA is a fairly new area, so be sure to download the latest *SAP HANA Administration Guide* for a more complete explanation of the installation, configuration, and administration of multitenant database containers in SAP HANA. If you're considering migrating your single container system to a multitenant system, please be aware that such a migration is a one-way process. You cannot migrate to multitenancy and then revert to a single container system.

> **Note**
>
> Please be aware that simply upgrading to SPS 9 or higher will not automatically migrate your system from a single container to a multitenant system. If you want to move to a multicontainer system, you'll have to trigger the migration.

In the following sections, we'll compare multitenancy to virtualization. We'll also explain the possibilities for consuming data from multiple platforms, and we'll discuss some possible scenarios for scaling-out a multitenant system.

10.10.1 Multitenancy versus Virtualization

Let's take a look at how multitenant database containers compare to virtualized SAP HANA deployments. Multitenant database containers generally have a lower TCO because of the licensing advantages in a single software stack. Configuration and administration are also centralized through the primary system database, and many of your data sources (if not all of them) will already be federated with a multitenant database deployment.

You may also see improved performance if you compare a virtualized system to a multitenant system, as there will be no performance lost to the hypervisor management of the virtual environment. Finally, third-party licensing is not required in a multitenant database.

On the other hand, a virtualized environment allows you to install separate SAP HANA revisions, which allows for testing new revisions in a separate, isolated environment. You can also make use of SAP HANA smart data access (SDA) to federate your data, so you'll still have the capacity to provide a centralized virtual data source to your users. All things considered, the major disadvantage to virtualization is the need to license third-party virtualization software.

As you can see, the choice between virtualization and multitenancy is not a simple one, so you should work closely with your chosen SAP HANA implementation partner to choose the solution that best meets your needs.

> **Note**
>
> It's important to note that you can combine virtualization and multitenancy in one SAP HANA environment. For example, your entire SAP HANA system landscape may be virtualized, and multitenancy can also be configured on a virtualized SAP HANA system within your landscape.

10.10.2 Cross-Platform Data Consumption

Beginning with SAP HANA SPS 9, revision 90, users were given the ability to create cross-database queries between tenant database containers. These cross-database queries are supported in both the SQL engine and the in-memory computing engine (IMCE), but the queries between containers are read-only. As a result, you can create views using tables and views from other database containers or even script SQL queries, such as:

```
SELECT *
FROM schema1.table1 AS Table1, db2.schema2.table2 AS Table2
WHERE Table2.column2 = 'North Carolina'
```

For cross-platform queries and views, you can access the following data types from the remote database:

- Row and column store tables
- SQL views
- Graphical calculation views (as long as no virtual tables, functions, or script-based calculation views are used as a data source within the graphical view)
- Schemas
- Synonyms

Remote data types can be used in the following objects within the local tenant database:

- Procedures
- Scripted and graphical calculation views
- Synonyms
- SQL views

To enable cross-platform data consumption, the system administrator must enable the feature and configure which tenant containers are allowed to consume data from each other.

10.10.3 Scaling-Out with Multitenancy

With multitenant database containers in SAP HANA, you still have the ability to scale out to multiple nodes. In a scale-out scenario, each host in the multinode landscape will have a system database, although only one of these system databases will be active at any given time, and the rest of the system databases will be on standby. If the node with the active system database fails, the system database in the next node of the multinode system will become active. In the event of a failed node, the tenant database containers on the failed host will also become active on the standby node, so in effect, the failover process in a multitenant system functions very much like the failover on a single container system.

See Figure 10.46 for an example of a possible system landscape in a multinode, multitenant SAP HANA deployment.

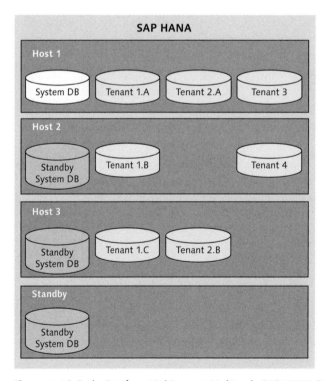

Figure 10.46 Scale-Out for a Multitenant, Multinode SAP HANA Deployment

10.11 Multi-tier Data Management

Next, we'll take a look at multi-tier data management, which allows us to keep our most frequently used data in our fastest storage and retrieval medium, while staging less frequently accessed data in a less expensive, but slower, storage medium. In this section, we'll discuss dynamic tiering in SAP HANA and look at some of the tools SAP has provided to enable us to take advantage of multi-tiered data storage. We'll discuss the Data Lifecycle Manager, an XS-based tool for relocating data to dynamic tiering, SAP IQ, and Hadoop. Finally, we'll discuss SAP HANA Vora, the in-memory query engine that integrates with the Apache Spark framework to enable interactive analytics in Hadoop.

10.11.1 Dynamic Tiering

Dynamic tiering addresses the fact that not all data is created equally. Consider the number of reports that your analytics teams have developed that were used only for a few months and then abandoned. Or consider your year-end reports, which are only used at the close of a given fiscal year. While that data may not be used very frequently, it's critical to the accounting processes required in running a business.

We must ask ourselves: Is it really necessary to store all of that data in memory? Could we not, instead, store data that is used in daily or real-time reporting scenarios (hot data) in memory and store the data that is rarely needed on a traditional hard drive? By using this approach, SAP lowers the TCO for SAP HANA implementations. With dynamic tiering, we can acquire the right mix of hardware to take advantage of the in-memory database for our real-time tasks and move our less frequently used data to less expensive storage media, both in terms of hardware and licensing costs.

Support for dynamic tiering was introduced with SAP HANA SPS 9 and divides data into two basic categories:

▶ **Hot data**
Hot data is always stored in memory and consists of data that is used for daily reporting or high-priority reporting scenarios. Data required for daily sales reports in a retail environment is an excellent example of hot data. The hot data store consists of classic SAP HANA tables, and the database algorithms used for the hot data store are optimized for in-memory data.

519

▶ **Warm data**

Warm data is any data that is used less often in your application and reporting landscape. Tax reporting data that is only needed at the end of the fiscal year is one possible example of warm data. With dynamic tiering, this warm data is stored as a primary image on a traditional hard disk (or a solid-state drive) in columnar database format.

The warm data store is composed of *extended tables*, a new type of table introduced in SPS 9. The extended table is a disk-based columnar data table. In an extended table, the table definition is stored in memory, while the actual data physically resides on disk.

In the following sections, we'll discuss the architecture of dynamic tiering as well as options for establishing dynamic tiering in your SAP HANA landscape. We'll discuss how to install, administer, and monitor a system with dynamic tiering, and we'll also explain how to make use of extended store tables in your dynamic tiering deployment.

Architecture

Let's take a closer look at the system architecture for dynamic tiering (Figure 10.47).

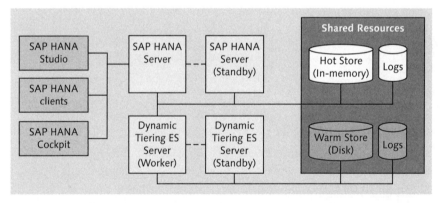

Figure 10.47 System Landscape with SAP HANA and Dynamic Tiering

In our example, we have two dynamic tiering hosts (the worker and the standby) as well as two SAP HANA servers. The standby host is available as a failover from the worker host. Please note that the standby host for dynamic tiering does not require a separate license. The SAP HANA host and the dynamic tiering worker host will work together through an encrypted internal communication channel.

In dynamic tiering, query optimizations for data access may be pushed to either the hot or warm stores. In order to minimize the workload for the SAP HANA server, queries that require access to data in the warm store are pushed to the dynamic tiering worker.

Dynamic tiering is also possible in a multitenant deployment. The relationship between tenant databases and dynamic tiering workers is one-to-one. In this scenario, each tenant database can only be associated with one dynamic tiering worker (or a worker/standby pair, if you've configured a failover host), and each worker (or worker/standby pair) can only manage one tenant database.

Deployment Options

You can install dynamic tiering in your system landscape in two ways: a dedicated host deployment and a same host deployment. In a production environment, dynamic tiering and SAP HANA must each be installed on different, standalone servers, which is known as *dedicated host deployment*.

> **Note**
>
> Dedicated host deployment is required for production because the same host deployment method offers no way to control the sharing of resources between the SAP HANA server and the dynamic tiering server. If both are trying to use the same CPU resources or the same memory, your overall performance for both systems may be degraded; thus, same host deployment should only be used in nonproduction environments.

In same host deployment, both SAP HANA and dynamic tiering are installed on the same server. You can select how many CPUs may be used by dynamic tiering in the `max_concurrent_queries` parameter in the *esserver.ini* file; however, you cannot specify conditions regarding which CPUs may be used or when they may be used. On the other hand, you can limit the memory usage for an SAP HANA system, but you cannot limit memory usage in dynamic tiering. If both systems allowed specific control of CPUs and memory resource allocation, then it would be possible to deploy a same host implementation of dynamic tiering in production. However, as of SPS 12, same host deployment is not approved for production.

Installation

When you have decided which deployment scenario is right for you, you will need to follow the installation path that matches your requirements. You'll need to:

1. Select either the same host or dedicated deployment.

2. Use your SAP Marketplace ID to download the installation package from *http://launchpad.support.sap.com*. Search the Downloads section for DYNAMIC TIERING.

3. Extract the installation package.

4. Start the installer.

5. Install dynamic tiering (dedicated host or same host).

6. Add a dynamic tiering worker host.

7. Add a dynamic tiering standby host (optional).

The dynamic tiering installation may be completed through either the graphical interface or the console interface. For complete instructions on how to install dynamic tiering as either a dedicated host or same host deployment, download the *SAP HANA Dynamic Tiering: Installation and Update Guide* from the SAP Marketplace.

Administration and Monitoring

Administering and monitoring your dynamic tiering deployment is generally handled through SAP HANA Studio and the SAP HANA Cockpit. You will monitor the overall health of the SAP HANA system and the dynamic tiering host through the cockpit, where you can examine the table usage and resource utilization within both systems.

In SAP HANA Studio, you can manage the extended storage disks and the extended store tables. You can also check the status of the dynamic tiering service and operating system processes. The dynamic tiering service is the `esserver`, whereas the host is the `hdbesserver`. See Sections 10.1 through 10.3 for more information about monitoring and administration of your SAP HANA landscape with SAP HANA Studio and the SAP HANA Cockpit.

Using Extended Store Tables

Once you have installed and configured dynamic tiering, the process for creating a table in hot or warm storage is nearly identical. The SQL script in Listing 10.6 can be used to create a simple table for sales order items in hot storage.

```
CREATE TABLE "RFRYE"."SALES_ORDER_ITEM_HOT" (
   "ORDER_ID"              INTEGER NOT NULL
   ,"SHIP_DT"              DATE NOT NULL
   ,"LINE_ITEM_ID"         SMALLINT NOT NULL
   ,"PRODUCT_ID"           INTEGER NOT NULL
   ,"QUANTITY"             INTEGER NOT NULL
   ,PRIMARY KEY ("ORDER_ID","LINE_ITEM_ID"));
```

Listing 10.6 Creating a Table in Hot Storage (In-Memory) in SAP HANA

To create the same table in warm storage, we simply add the following line of code to the end of the table declaration (before the semicolon):

```
USING EXTENDED STORAGE
```

Our new extended table declaration should then look like Listing 10.7.

```
CREATE TABLE "RFRYE"."SALES_ORDER_ITEM_WARM" (
   "ORDER_ID"              INTEGER NOT NULL
   ,"SHIP_DT"              DATE NOT NULL
   ,"LINE_ITEM_ID"         SMALLINT NOT NULL
   ,"PRODUCT_ID"           INTEGER NOT NULL
   ,"QUANTITY"             INTEGER NOT NULL
   ,PRIMARY KEY ("ORDER_ID","LINE_ITEM_ID")
) USING EXTENDED STORAGE;
```

Listing 10.7 Creating a Table in Warm Storage Using Dynamic Tiering

Tables that have been created in extended storage are then identified with the word "EXTENDED" after the table name when viewed in the target schema.

Once you've created the extended tables, creating a stored procedure to take care of the next step in the process is relatively simple. For example, if we wanted to create a stored procedure to move orders (and their line items) that were more than 1 year old from hot to warm storage, first you'll want to declare a variable to calculate the cutoff date (today minus 1 year). Then, you'll use an insert statement to select orders older than the variable date and insert them into the extended table in warm storage. Next, you'll complete the move by deleting the older orders from the table in hot storage (in memory). To run the procedure, simply call it from the SQL command editor. For more information on creating and calling stored procedures, see Chapter 8.

One more thing to consider is that there will likely be times when you need to see all the data together, combining the hot and warm storage tables. To do so, you can simply create a view that unions the tables together. Listing 10.8 shows an example of creating a view that simply selects from both tables and unions the results.

```
CREATE VIEW "SALES_ORDERS_ALL" AS
    SELECT * FROM "RFRYE"."SALES_ORDERS_WARM"
    UNION
    SELECT * FROM "RFRYE"."SALES_ORDERS_HOT";
```
Listing 10.8 Joining Data from Hot and Warm Storage through a View

> **Note**
>
> You can create views through an SQL script, the SAP HANA development perspective in SAP HANA Studio, or even using the SAP Web IDE. Chapter 8 contains in-depth information about the various modeling tools available for use with SAP HANA.

10.11.2 Data Lifecycle Manager

The Data Lifecycle Manager (DLM) is part of the SAP HANA data warehousing foundation (DWF). DLM provides SAP HANA administrators with the tools required to create aging rules for SAP HANA tables. In other words, DLM takes the processes that we described in Listing 10.6, Listing 10.7, and Listing 10.8 and allows you to create models that accomplish the same tasks, without the need to model and execute SQL script from the SQL console in SAP HANA Studio.

DLM is intended for close integration with dynamic tiering, as it allows you to move data that is old or infrequently used into warm storage. You may also use SAP IQ by integrating SDA with your system landscape and using SDA to connect to SAP IQ. In the following sections, we'll take a brief look at using DLM for installation, monitoring, and administration.

Installation

The version of DLM that is appropriate for your environment will depend on which version of SAP HANA is installed. DWF delivery units must be matched to the correct SAP HANA version, or you'll receive errors during the installation. The current dependencies are listed in Table 10.8, but be sure to consult the *SAP HANA DWF Installation Guide* for a complete list of dependencies before beginning the installation.

SAP HANA DWF Version	SAP HANA Version
SAP HANA DWF 1.0 SPS 0	SAP HANA SPS 8
SAP HANA DWF 1.0 SPS 1	SAP HANA SPS 9
SAP HANA DWF 1.0 SPS 2	SAP HANA SPS 10
SAP HANA DWF 1.0 SPS 3	SAP HANA SPS 11
SAP HANA DWF 1.0 SPS 4	SAP HANA SPS 12

Table 10.8 SAP HANA DWF Dependencies by SAP HANA Version

To install DLM, download the delivery unit for DWF from the SAP marketplace. Search the DOWNLOADS section for DATA WAREHOUSING FOUNDATION and download the installation product.

To install the delivery unit, first go to the SAP HANA Cockpit, either by navigating to the page in your web browser or through the context menu in SAP HANA Studio (Figure 10.48). From the SAP HANA Cockpit, select the SAP HANA APPLICATION LIFECYCLE MANAGEMENT tile.

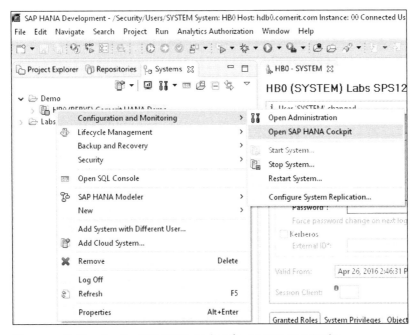

Figure 10.48 Opening the SAP HANA Cockpit from SAP HANA Studio

> **Note**
>
> To open the SAP HANA Application Lifecycle Manager, you will need to be logged into the SAP HANA Cockpit with a user account with the `sap.hana.xs.lm.roles::Administrator` role assigned.

The SAP HANA Application Lifecycle Management cockpit will open (Figure 10.49), where you can select INSTALLATION to navigate to the INSTALL AND UPDATE SAP HANA PRODUCTS AND SOFTWARE COMPONENTS screen. From this screen, click the BROWSE button and navigate through your folders to find the location where you downloaded the DLM delivery unit.

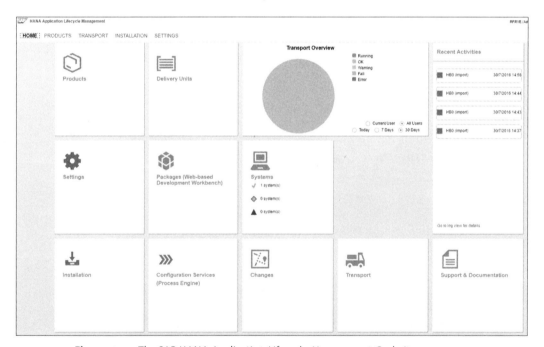

Figure 10.49 The SAP HANA Application Lifecycle Management Cockpit

You'll receive a message that the system is validating and uploading the delivery unit. Next, you should select the DW CONTENT checkbox and click INSTALL in the bottom right of the window to install the delivery unit (Figure 10.50).

Figure 10.50 Installing the SAP Data Warehousing Content for DLM

When the installation has completed successfully, you can reach the DLM by browser at *http://<server_address>:8000/sap/hdm/dlm*.

Monitoring

From the DLM home screen, you can access tiles with important key performance indicators (KPIs), including:

▶ RUNS IN SYSTEM
This KPI includes information about the latest data relocation runs, with the status and completion rate of the three most recent runs as well as all runs completed in the last week.

▶ NODE UTILIZATION FORECAST
For multihost SAP HANA systems, you can see a projection of the utilization for the nodes in the SAP HANA landscape, including the percentage of utilization and the size of the row and column store tables.

Administration

You also have access to several administrative tiles, including:

- ▸ EXPLORE
  Explore source persistence objects.

- ▸ MANAGE STORAGE DESTINATIONS
  Define relocation destinations.

- ▸ MANAGE MODELED PERSISTENCE OBJECTS
  Define groups of persistence objects.

- ▸ MANAGE LIFECYCLE PROFILES
  Create parameters for data relocation within a lifecycle profile; schedule and execute data relocation.

- ▸ LOGS
  Examine the logs for the system.

To manage the users in your DLM environment, you'll need to use one of several locations. To create users, you'll need to use SAP HANA Studio. Roles may be granted to users through SAP HANA Studio or through the SAP HANA Web-Based Development Workbench. You can also use HDBSQL scripts for processing user deletions, deactivations, and reactivations.

For a complete explanation of the administration tasks in DLM, you can download the *SAP HANA Data Warehousing Foundation—Data Lifecycle Manager Administration Guide* from the SAP Support Portal.

10.11.3 SAP HANA Vora

SAP HANA Vora is a plug-in for the Apache Spark execution framework that provides an in-memory query engine for interactive analytics on Hadoop. SAP HANA Vora allows you to integrate and analyze Hadoop and corporate data using familiar online analytical processing (OLAP) and standard programming languages.

SAP HANA Vora was designed to address several challenges in the realm of big data. First, Hadoop data lakes and enterprise SAP systems are often separated within the same corporate data landscape. Despite Hadoop's ability to manage unstructured data, enriching corporate data from SAP using the data lake can be challenging. The lack of semantics required to integrate the data from the data lake can make this task quite difficult.

The implementation of Hadoop also results in numerous data platforms within the same enterprise, adding to the complexity and risk involved in many information management tasks. Finally, Hadoop's batch-mode data processing tools are not ideally suited to the fast-paced, highly granular analysis of data required in the modern corporate landscape.

SAP HANA Vora provides data hierarchy enhancements and compiled queries using Spark SQL, which accelerates the processing of data from Hadoop. The compiled queries allow for faster data processing across the Hadoop Distributed File System (HDFS) nodes. Using SAP HANA Vora, detailed drilldown analysis combining corporate data and Hadoop is possible. SAP HANA Vora also simplifies the process of combining data access and processing across the combined Hadoop and SAP HANA landscapes.

> **Note**
>
> SAP HANA and SAP HANA Vora are licensed independently of each other, so the SAP HANA platform is not required for SAP HANA Vora.

In the following sections, let's look at installing and using SAP HANA Vora.

Installation

With the introduction of SAP HANA Vora 1.2, the previously complex installation process for SAP HANA Vora was simplified significantly. In previous versions of SAP HANA Vora, a complex series of downloads were required from numerous sites in order to install and use SAP HANA Vora. However, the latest release now presents a unified installation package for either Ambari or Cloudera.

The SAP HANA Vora 1.2 installation package contains the components shown in Table 10.9, each of which must be installed and deployed from the Ambari or Cloudera cluster provisioning tool.

SAP HANA Vora Component	Description
SAP HANA Vora V2Server	SAP HANA Vora engine
SAP HANA Vora Base	Required libraries and binaries
SAP HANA Vora Catalog	Distributed metadata store
SAP HANA Vora Discovery	Hashicorp's Discovery Service for managing service registration
SAP HANA Vora Distributed Log	Distributed log manager for persistence of the SAP HANA Vora catalog

Table 10.9 Components of SAP HANA Vora Installed Through Ambari or Cloudera

SAP HANA Vora Component	Description
SAP HANA Vora Thriftserver	Gateway compatible with Hive JDBC driver
SAP HANA Vora Tools	Web-based user interface with OLAP modeler and SQL editor

Table 10.9 Components of SAP HANA Vora Installed Through Ambari or Cloudera (Cont.)

You can download the MapR distribution of Apache Hadoop from the SAP Support Portal. The installation package is *VORA_MR<version>.TGZ*. For MapR installation information, download the *SAP HANA Vora for MapR Guide*.

Although SAP HANA Vora installation process has been streamlined considerably in version 1.2, the process is still fairly lengthy. The following general steps are required to install SAP HANA Vora:

1. Install the SAP HANA Vora engine (with Ambari or Cloudera).
2. Install the SAP HANA Vora Spark Extension Library.
3. Install the SAP HANA Vora Zeppelin Interpreter.
4. Connect the SAP HANA Spark Controller to SAP HANA Vora.
5. Connect SAP BusinessObjects Lumira to SAP HANA Vora (for reporting).
6. Update SAP HANA Vora, including:
   ▶ Update the SAP HANA Vora engine (with Ambari or Cloudera).
   ▶ Update the SAP HANA Vora Spark Extension Library.

> **Note**
>
> SAP HANA Vora is a new technology and is being updated frequently (three new versions were released between November 2015 and July 2016), so make sure you download the latest version of the *SAP HANA Vora Installation and Administration Guide* from the SAP Support Portal before you begin your installation. You can also see Table 10.10 for the most recent notes about SAP HANA Vora.

SAP Note	Subject
2203837	SAP HANA Vora: Central Release Note
2220859	SAP HANA Vora Documentation Corrections
2213226	Prerequisites for Installing SAP HANA Vora: Operating Systems and Hadoop Components

Table 10.10 SAP Notes for SAP HANA Vora

Using SAP HANA Vora

Beginning with SAP HANA Vora 1.2, SAP HANA Vora Tools is provided as a convenient, web-based user interface for using SAP HANA Vora. The browser interface includes an SQL editor to run and create SQL scripts and a data browser for exporting and viewing data from tables and views. A data browser also allows you to view and export data from tables and views. To access the SAP HANA Vora Tools, go to *http://<Vora_server>:9225/datatools/web*.

From the tools screen, you can access the DATA BROWSER, SQL EDITOR, and MODELER from their tiles (Figure 10.51).

Figure 10.51 SAP HANA Vora Tools

The SQL EDITOR is very straightforward and is similar in function to the SQL Console in SAP HANA Studio. Simply enter the SQL that you want to execute and click a button to execute the SQL script. You can create tables, views, and hierarchies; load data; and delete tables from the SQL Editor.

The DATA BROWSER tile allows you to select and view tables that are loaded in Hadoop (Figure 10.52). Simply click the table to display the table contents.

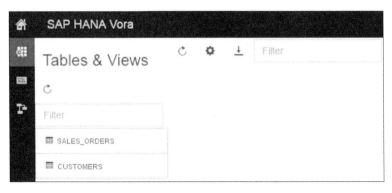

Figure 10.52 The Data Browser in the SAP HANA Vora Tools

From the MODELER (Figure 10.53), you can use the graphical editor to add tables, create joins, and select the output for the view. You can also create aggregations (sum, count, average, minimum, and maximum); add a WHERE CLAUSE to filter your data; GROUP BY a selected column; ORDER BY a selected column; and even create complex join conditions.

Figure 10.53 The Graphical Modeler in SAP HANA Vora

Note

For a complete explanation of developing with the SAP HANA Vora Tools, download the *SAP HANA Vora Developer Guide* from the SAP Support Portal.

10.12 SAP Solution Manager and SAP HANA

SAP Solution Manager can be connected to SAP HANA and be used for many of the same tasks you use SAP Solution Manager for today. As part of your installation, you should work with your hardware partner to make sure that SAP HANA is connected to SAP Solution Manager. The reason for this connection is due to SAP's central agent infrastructure and requires the setup of connectivity, roles, and assignments of rich agents that are used in the SAP HANA system and that communicate with SAP Solution Manager. Thankfully, SAP has created a wizard that will help you connect the SAP HANA system with SAP Solution Manager (Figure 10.54). You can find detailed information in the *SAP Solution Manager System Landscape Setup Guide* on the SAP Marketplace.

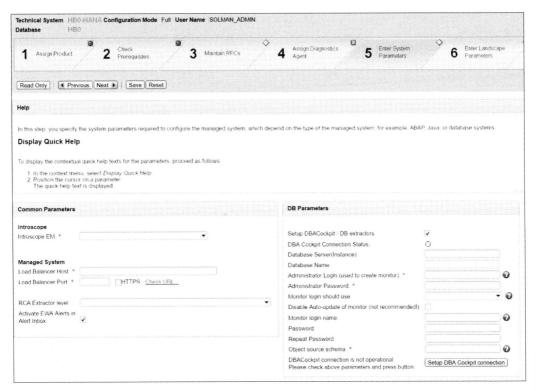

Figure 10.54 Step-by-Step Wizard to Connect SAP Solution Manager to SAP HANA

The connection will provide monitoring from the DBA Cockpit as well as all database alerts in SAP HANA. You'll also get access to SAP HANA information in SAP EarlyWatch Alert reports. These should be reviewed by the SAP HANA system administrators on a weekly or monthly basis, much the same way as you are monitoring SAP ERP and traditional SAP BW systems today.

An additional feature of SAP Solution Manager is the ability to use the central Change and Transport System (CTS+) for managing changes and configurations between your SAP HANA environments in way similar to change management in the SAP ERP system.

10.13 DBA Cockpit for SAP HANA

Most of the information in this chapter is applicable regardless of which implementation of SAP HANA you are using. However, in this section, we want to spend a bit of time on the Database Administrator (DBA) Cockpit, which is relevant for implementations of SAP BW on SAP HANA.

Inside the data warehouse solution SAP Business Warehouse (BW), you'll find the DBA Cockpit as shown in Figure 10.55. You can use the DBA Cockpit to manage and monitor the underlying relational or SAP HANA-based database and is available for organizations with SAP BW 7.3 SP 5 and higher.

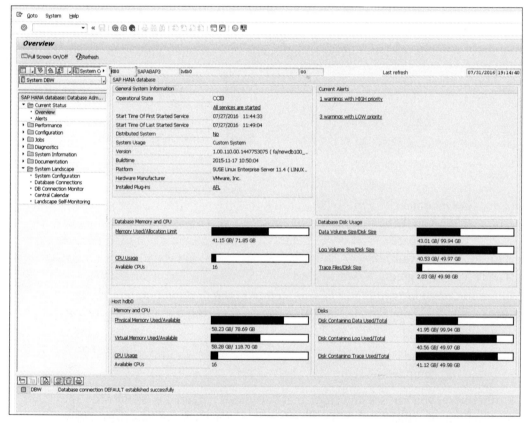

Figure 10.55 DBA Cockpit for SAP HANA

The cockpit is available under Transaction DBACOCKPIT, which requires that your role has been assigned the security authorizations S_TCODE and S_RZL_ADM. In the DBA interface, you can pass basic transaction calls to the SAP HANA system and get an overview of how it is performing without going to the SAP HANA Studio interface. Table 10.11 lists some of the transactions supported in the DBA Cockpit.

Area	Transaction Code	SAP BW Action	SAP HANA Action in DBA Cockpit
Diagnostics	DB01	Analyze Exclusive Lockwaits	Locks: Blocked Transactions
	DB02	Tables and Indexes Monitor	Missing Tables and Indexes
	DB12	DBA Backup Logs	Backup Catalog
Current Status	DB50	SAP DB Assistant	Current Status Overview
	ST04	DB Performance Monitor	Current Status Overview
Jobs	DB13	DBA Planning Calendar	DBA Planning Calendar
	DB13C	Central DBA Planning Calendar	Central Calendar
Configuration	DB26	DB Profile: Monitor and Configuration	Configuration INI Files
	DB03	Parameter Changes in Database	Configuration INI Files

Table 10.11 Supported Transactions

In the DB Performance Monitor (Transaction DB13) and SAP DB Assistant (Transaction DB50), you'll find information about the current status of the system, such as available disk space and physical memory. The bar is colored black if the usage is up to 97% of available disk, and red, if usage is over 98%. If the operational state is flagged as green, all services are running, whereas yellow means that one or more services have not started or are not currently running.

These transactions also include other information, such as the start time of the first and last started service. If you have a distributed system, you'll see the start time of the first and last server here. You'll also see when the SAP HANA database software was compiled under the BUILD TIME tab.

Furthermore, you can see any alerts that have been triggered in SAP HANA and notifications of critical events if a disk is full. If you click the FULL DISK EVENT message and select the event, you can also handle selected events. In addition, you can display the CPU consumption, memory allocations, and the number of CPUs available, as well as data volume, log, and trace files sizes, compared to the size of the disk(s). Finally, you can monitor the host physical memory, CPU, and virtual memory and see the disks containing data, log, and trace files on a specific host. All of these features make the DBA Cockpit in SAP BW a very valuable tool for SAP BW administrators who are using SAP HANA as their database.

You can also use the performance warehouse features in the DBA Cockpit to see how your system is performing overall. To access it, select PERFORMANCE • PERFORMANCE WAREHOUSE in the DBA Cockpit. To use this, you must have the Solution Manager Diagnostics (SMD) enabled. If you don't have it enabled, you can use the SMD Setup Wizard to install it.

SAP HANA and Nearline Storage (NLS) Management

If you want to reduce the size of your active data in SAP BW, SAP HANA still supports nearline storage (NLS).

NLS is simply a method to offload data that is infrequently used to a smaller database system (not an in-memory database). For example, an organization with 10 years of data in its data warehouse may want to move the oldest data to a small database system. Because this NLS system is accessed infrequently by few users, the hardware is much smaller and there may be little reasons to spend thousands of dollars to keep this in memory inside SAP HANA. In short, the old data is available but not in memory.

The business intelligence (BI) analytical engine in SAP BW knows if the data is on NLS or if it's in memory, so there's no need for query developers or users to direct their queries to one side or the other. SAP BW on SAP HANA automatically directs queries to the relevant data. Several partner solutions for NLS on SAP HANA are available, including Dynamic Near Line Access, PBS, IBM DB2 Viper, DataVard, and SAP's own NLS solution based on SAP IQ.

10.14 Summary

Although the SAP HANA administration tasks are numerous and may be executed by system administrators, security administrators, developers, and hardware vendors, it's important to have a basic understanding of the major functions you'll need to know to successfully manage an SAP HANA system. In this chapter, we provided an introduction to some of these functions. Additional version-specific administration tasks are outlined in SAP Notes, which are updated when new releases and service packs are made available. You should periodically review the relevant SAP Notes before embarking on system changes to your SAP HANA installation.

The Authors

Penny Silvia is a managing director and SAP HANA leader for Deloitte Consulting with a focus on SAP analytics. Penny brings more than 20 years of SAP experience to this role and has been helping SAP customers determine their analytics strategies since 1998. During her more than 20 year career working with SAP products, Penny has held leadership and executive positions at Cap Gemini, IBM, as well as small boutique firms. This range of experiences has allowed Penny to work with clients large and small, across many industries and geographies, and has helped to forge her global perspective that she uses to help her clients navigate the sometimes murky and confusing waters of maximizing their investments with SAP analytics tools and solutions.

Rob Frye served in the NC Army National Guard for nearly two decades, and is a combat veteran of Operation Iraqi Freedom. After retiring from military service, he received a bachelor's degree in computer science from Lenoir-Rhyne University, where he was the First Honor Graduate with a 4.0 GPA. He is the manager of ComeritLabs, in Huntersville, NC, which provides infrastructure, remote development, and training services for COMERIT, Inc. He is an experienced SAP HANA and SAP BusinessObjects developer, and has created content, training material, and processes for SAP HANA and SAP BW InfoObjects on SAP HANA for Fortune 500 companies.

He was the lead author for The SAP BW to HANA Migration Handbook, one of the first books to provide comprehensive, step-by-step instructions for completing the DMO (database migration option) process. He has provided live training on SAP HANA and the SAP BusinessObjects toolset in the United States, Canada, Mexico, and South Africa. He is also a PhD student at the University of North Carolina in Charlotte, where he is conducting research into natural language processing for authorship attribution in web content.

 **Dr. Berg** is an internationally recognized expert in business intelligence and a frequent speaker at major BI and SAP conferences world-wide. He regularly publishes articles in international BI journals and has written five books on business intelligence, analytics, and SAP HANA. Currently, he is a partner at PwC, where he is leading an analytics and business intelligence practice. He has over 25 years experience in business intelligence development and data warehousing from several banks and consulting firms.

He holds a bachelor of science in finance from Appalachian State University, an MBA in finance from East Carolina University, a doctorate in information systems from the University of Sarasota, and a Ph.D. in information technology from the University of North Carolina. Dr. Berg also attended the Norwegian Military Academy, and served as an officer in the Armed Forces.

Index

▶ Implement SAP HANA as a data warehouse for analytics

▶ Integrate SAP HANA with SAP Data Services and SAP BusinessObjects BI

▶ Keep your system and your data safe by setting up authorizations, analytic privileges, and more

Haun, Hickman, Loden, Wells

Implementing SAP HANA

If you're ready to implement SAP HANA as a data warehouse for analytics, you'll want this book along for the ride. Explore the steps in a complete SAP HANA implementation, and then play with downloadable sample data that you can use to test your skills. Become an expert in data provisioning with SAP Data Services, data modeling, and connecting to the BOBJ platform. Take your SAP HANA knowledge to the next level!

860 pages, 2nd edition, pub. 12/2014
E-Book: $69.99 | **Print:** $79.95 | **Bundle:** $89.99

www.sap-press.com/3703

Interested in reading more?

Please visit our website for all new
book and e-book releases from SAP PRESS.

www.sap-press.com